D0379972

ATTACK ON TITAN 18

HAJIME ISAYAMA

"Attack on Titan" Character Introductions

104th Corps

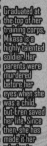

Graduated at the top of her training corps, Mikasa is a highly talented soldier. Her parents were murdered before her eyes when she was a child, but Eren saved her life. Since then, she has made it her mission to protect him.

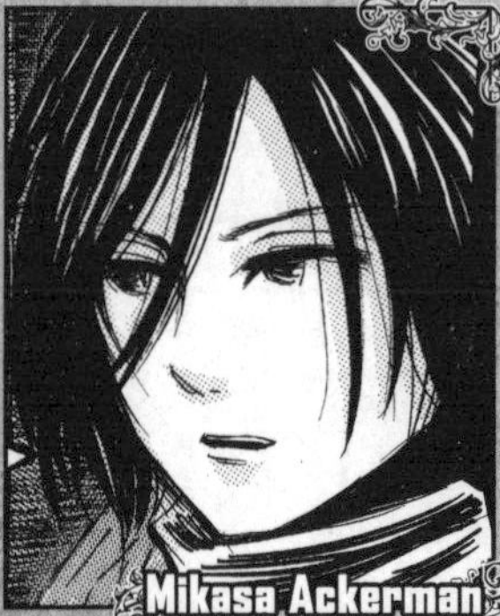
Mikasa Ackerman

Eren joined the Survey Corps out of his longing for the outside world and his hatred of the Titans. He has the power to turn himself into a Titan, but its origins are unknown.

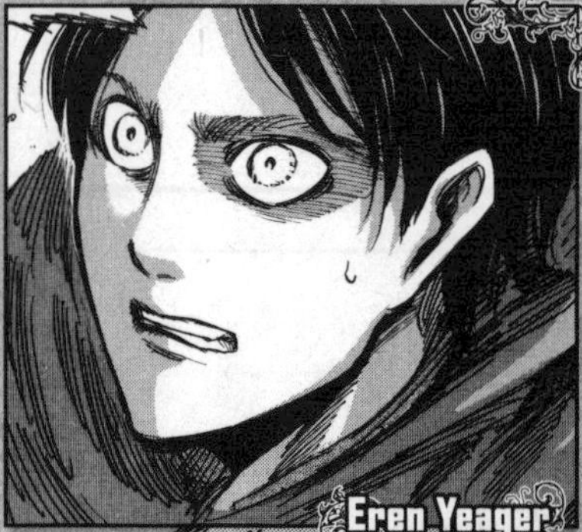
Eren Yeager

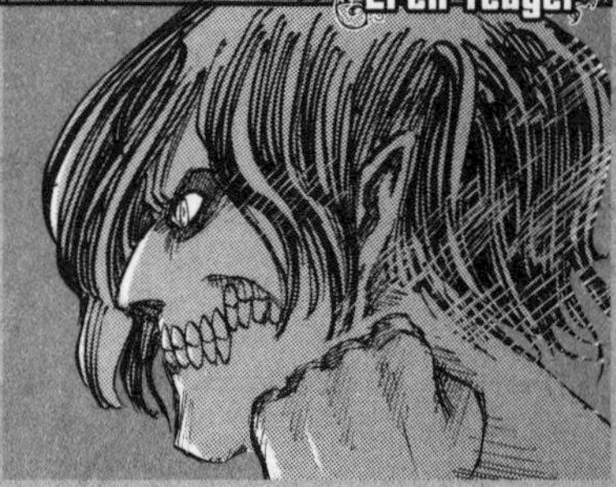

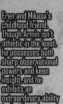

Eren and Mikasa's childhood friend. Though Armin isn't athletic in the least, he possesses both sharp observational powers and keen insight, and he exhibits an extraordinary ability to develop strategies.

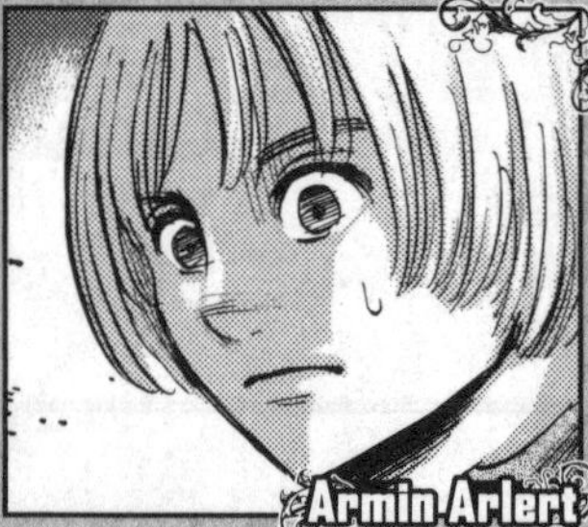
Armin Arlert

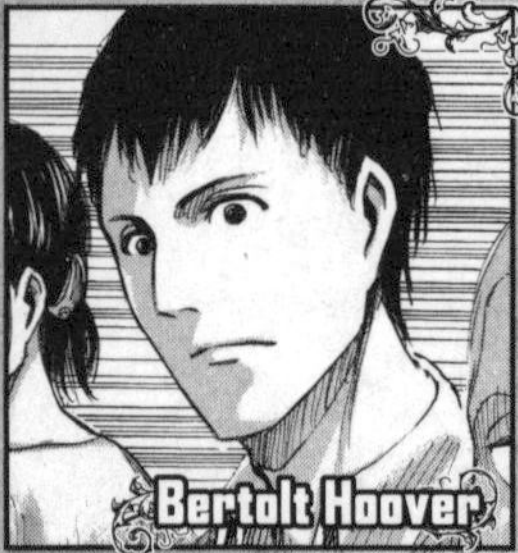
Bertolt Hoover

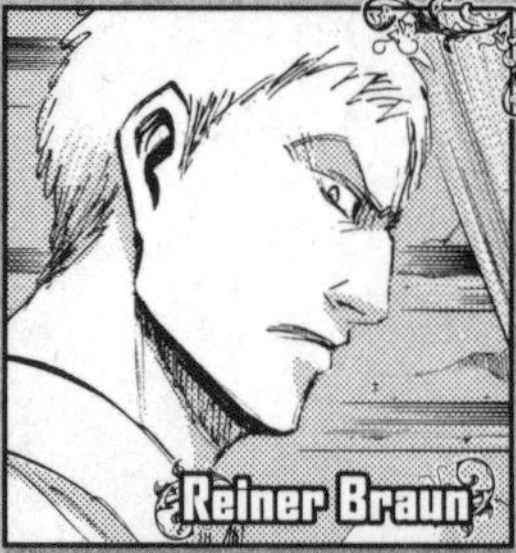
Reiner Braun

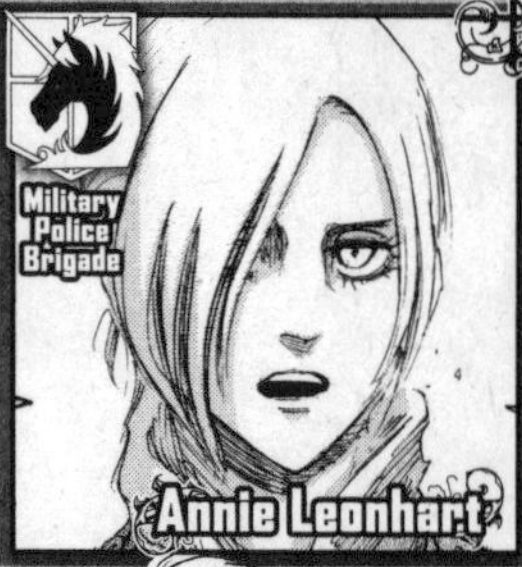
Military Police Brigade
Annie Leonhart

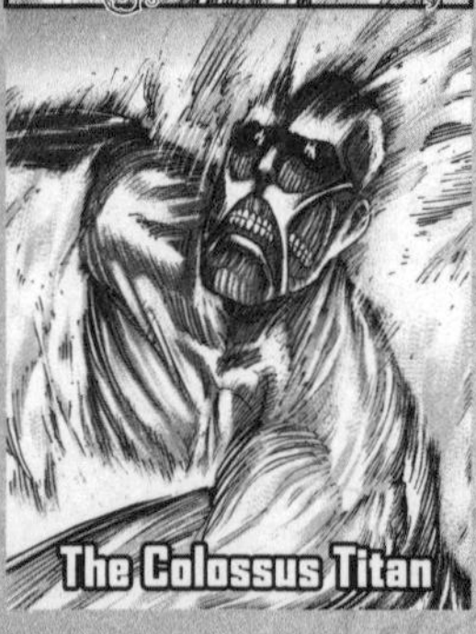
The Colossus Titan

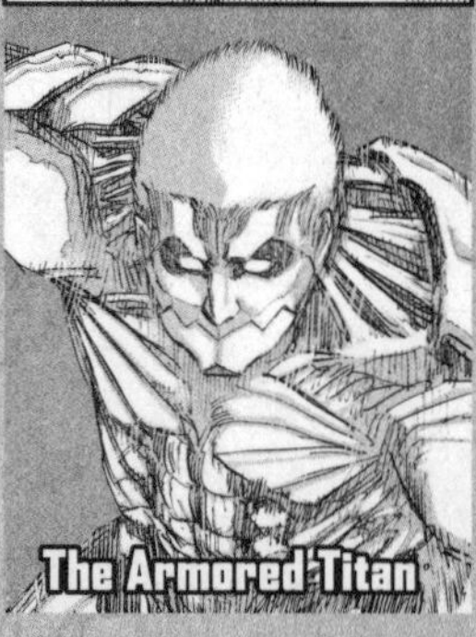
The Armored Titan

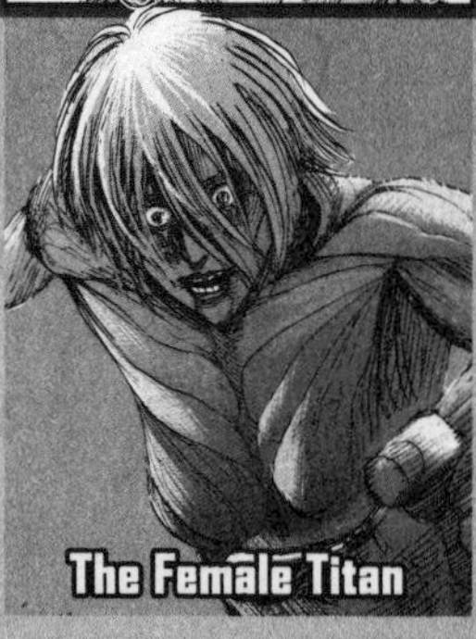
The Female Titan

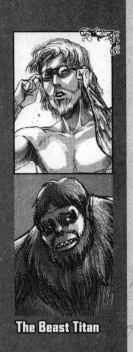

Survey Corps

Soldiers who are prepared to sacrifice themselves as they brave the Titan territory outside the walls.

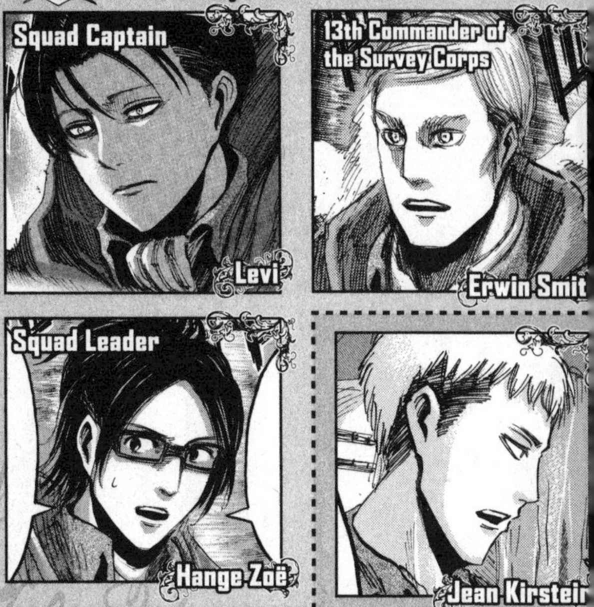
13th Commander of the Survey Corps
Erwin Smit
Squad Captain
Levi
Jean Kirstein
Squad Leader
Hange Zoë

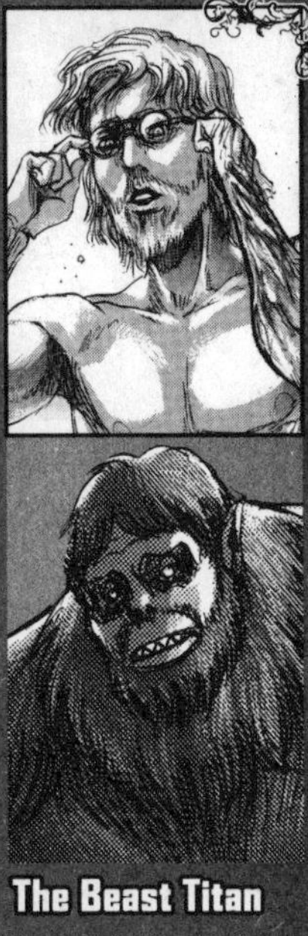
The Beast Titan

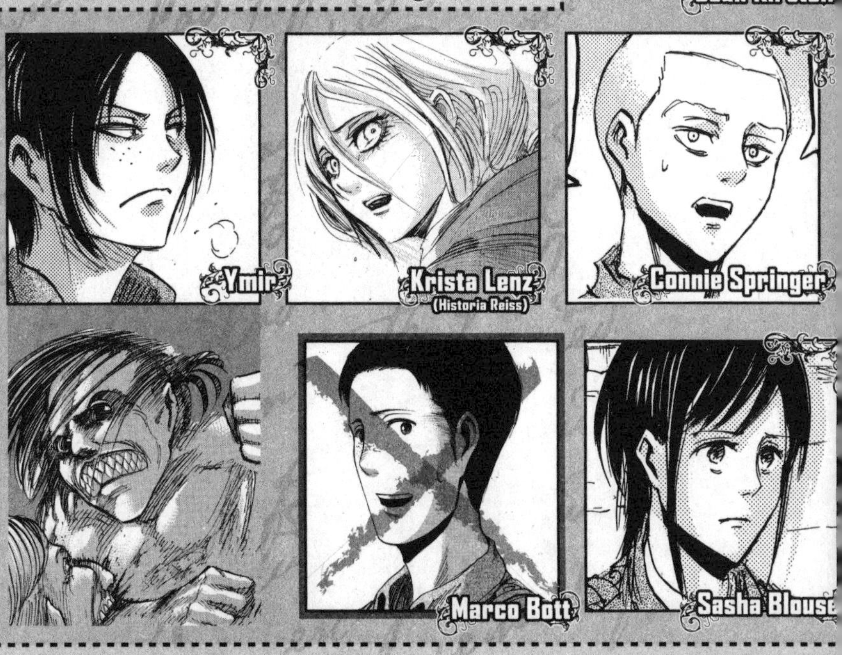
Connie Springer
Krista Lenz
(Historia Reiss)
Ymir
Sasha Blouse
Marco Bott

ATTACK on TITAN

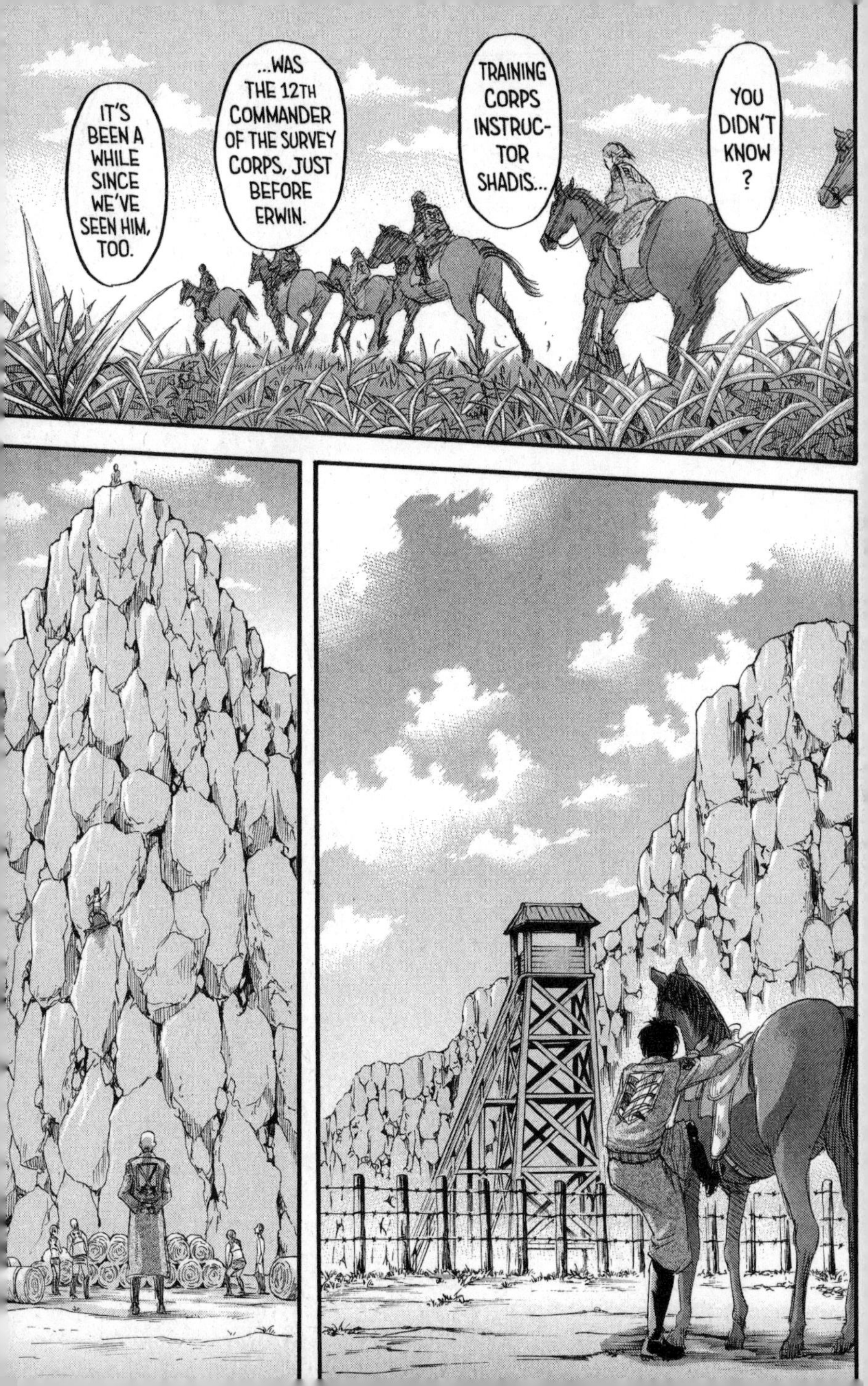
YOU DIDN'T KNOW?
TRAINING CORPS INSTRUCTOR SHADIS...
...WAS THE 12TH COMMANDER OF THE SURVEY CORPS, JUST BEFORE ERWIN.
IT'S BEEN A WHILE SINCE WE'VE SEEN HIM, TOO.

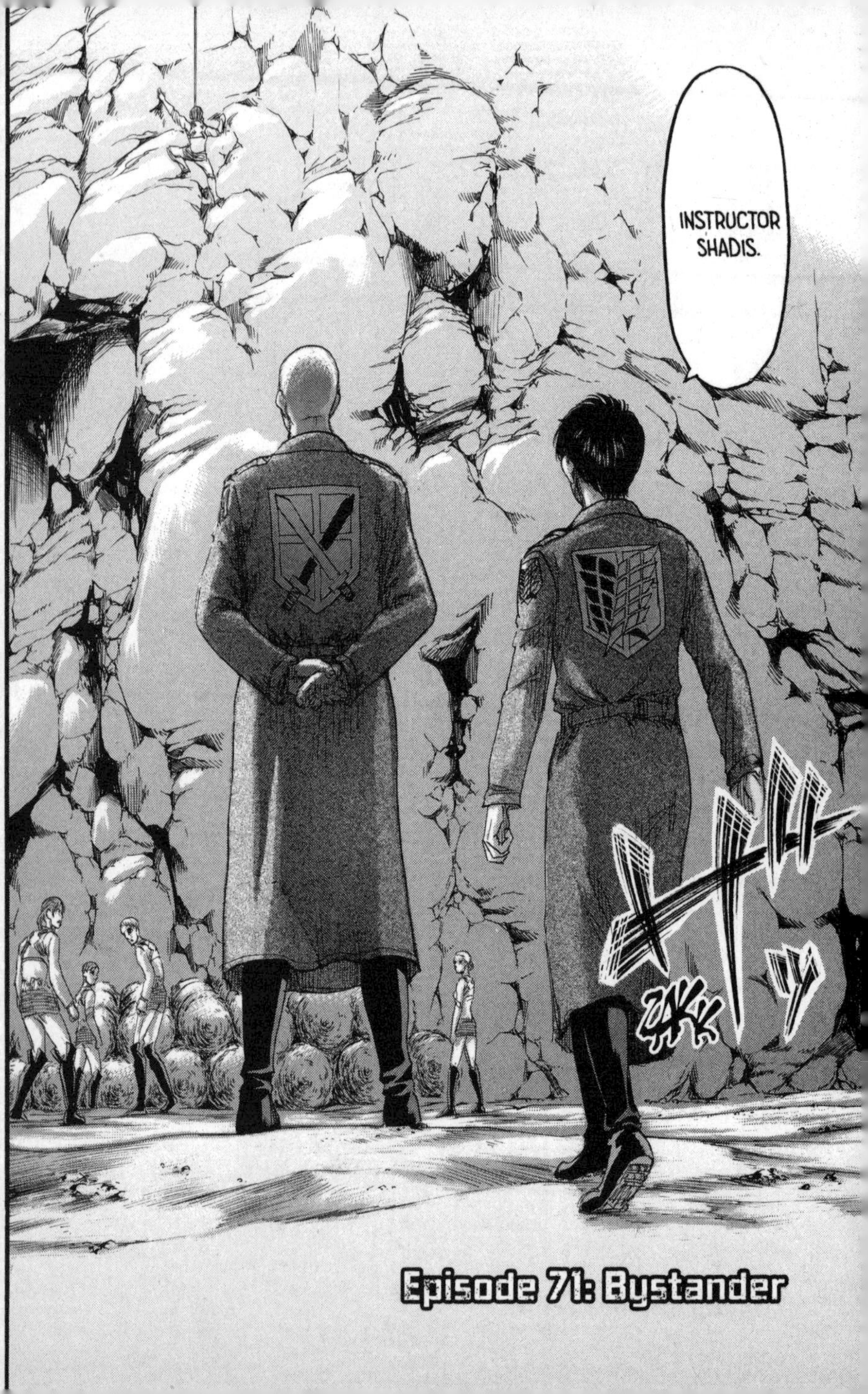
INSTRUCTOR SHADIS.
ZAK
Episode 71: Bystander

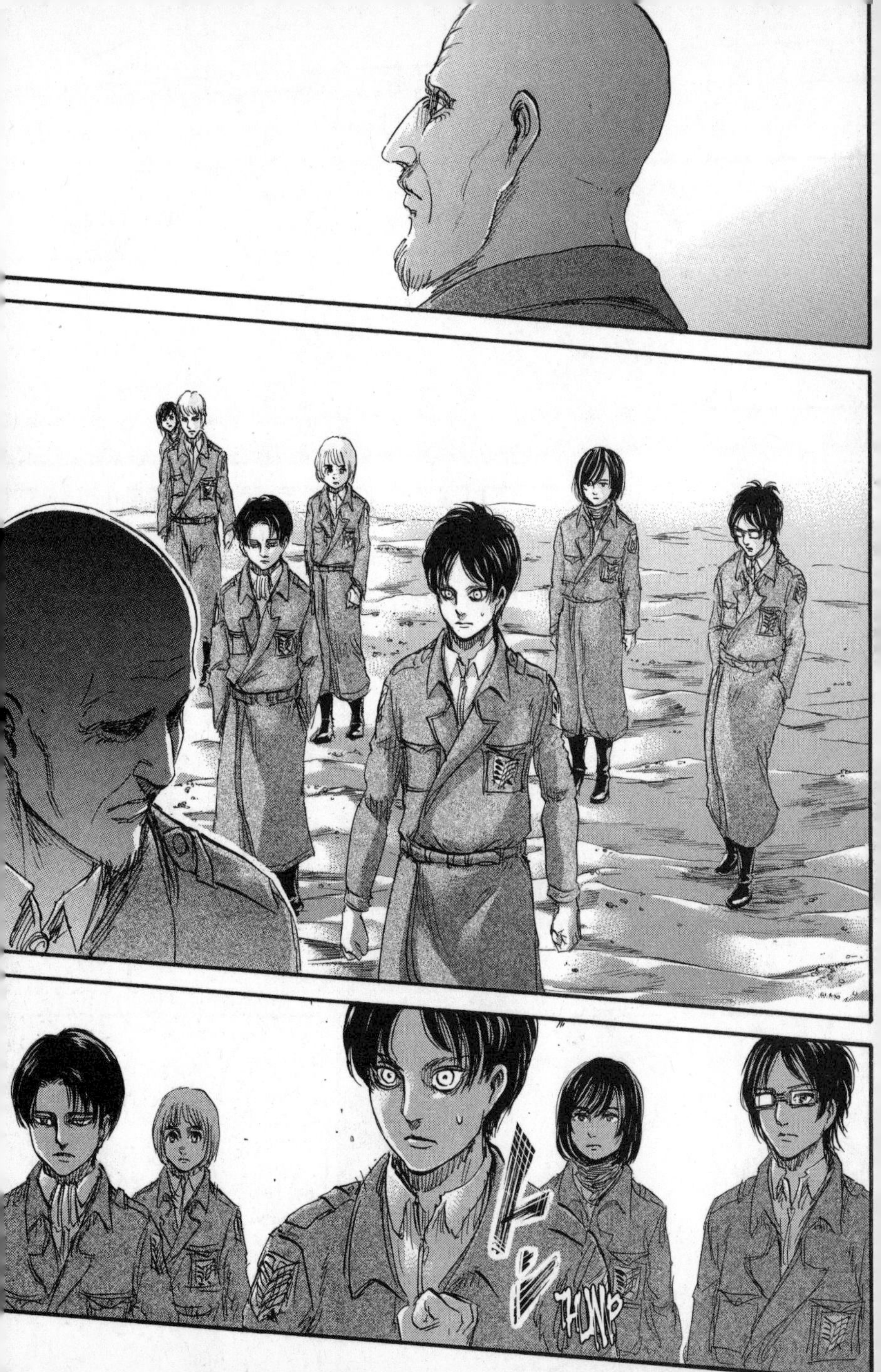
ドン
THUMP

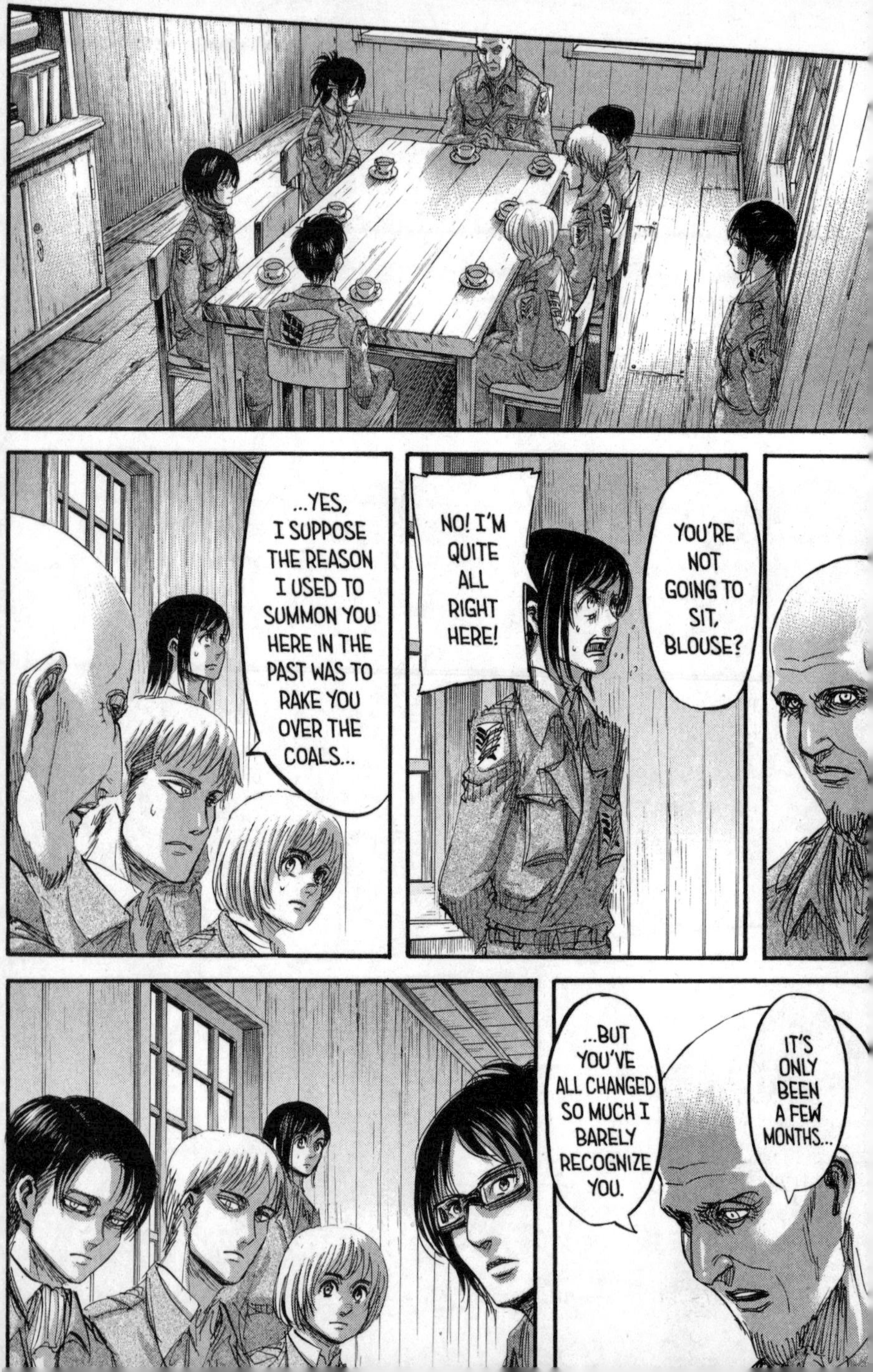
YOU'RE NOT GOING TO SIT, BLOUSE?
NO! I'M QUITE ALL RIGHT HERE!
...YES, I SUPPOSE THE REASON I USED TO SUMMON YOU HERE IN THE PAST WAS TO RAKE YOU OVER THE COALS...
IT'S ONLY BEEN A FEW MONTHS...
...BUT YOU'VE ALL CHANGED SO MUCH I BARELY RECOGNIZE YOU.

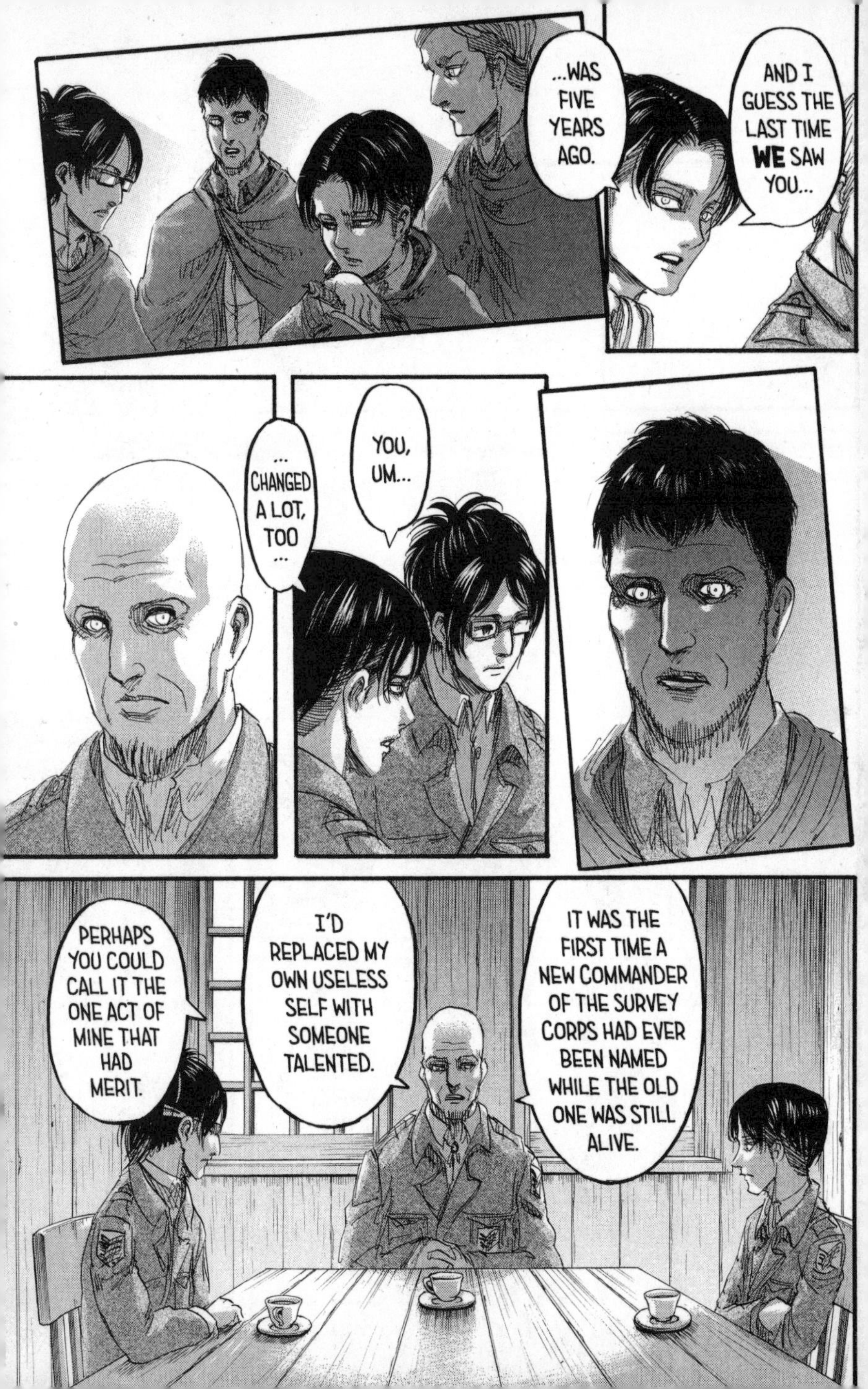
AND I GUESS THE LAST TIME **WE** SAW YOU...
...WAS FIVE YEARS AGO.
YOU, UM...
...CHANGED A LOT, TOO...
IT WAS THE FIRST TIME A NEW COMMANDER OF THE SURVEY CORPS HAD EVER BEEN NAMED WHILE THE OLD ONE WAS STILL ALIVE.
I'D REPLACED MY OWN USELESS SELF WITH SOMEONE TALENTED.
PERHAPS YOU COULD CALL IT THE ONE ACT OF MINE THAT HAD MERIT.

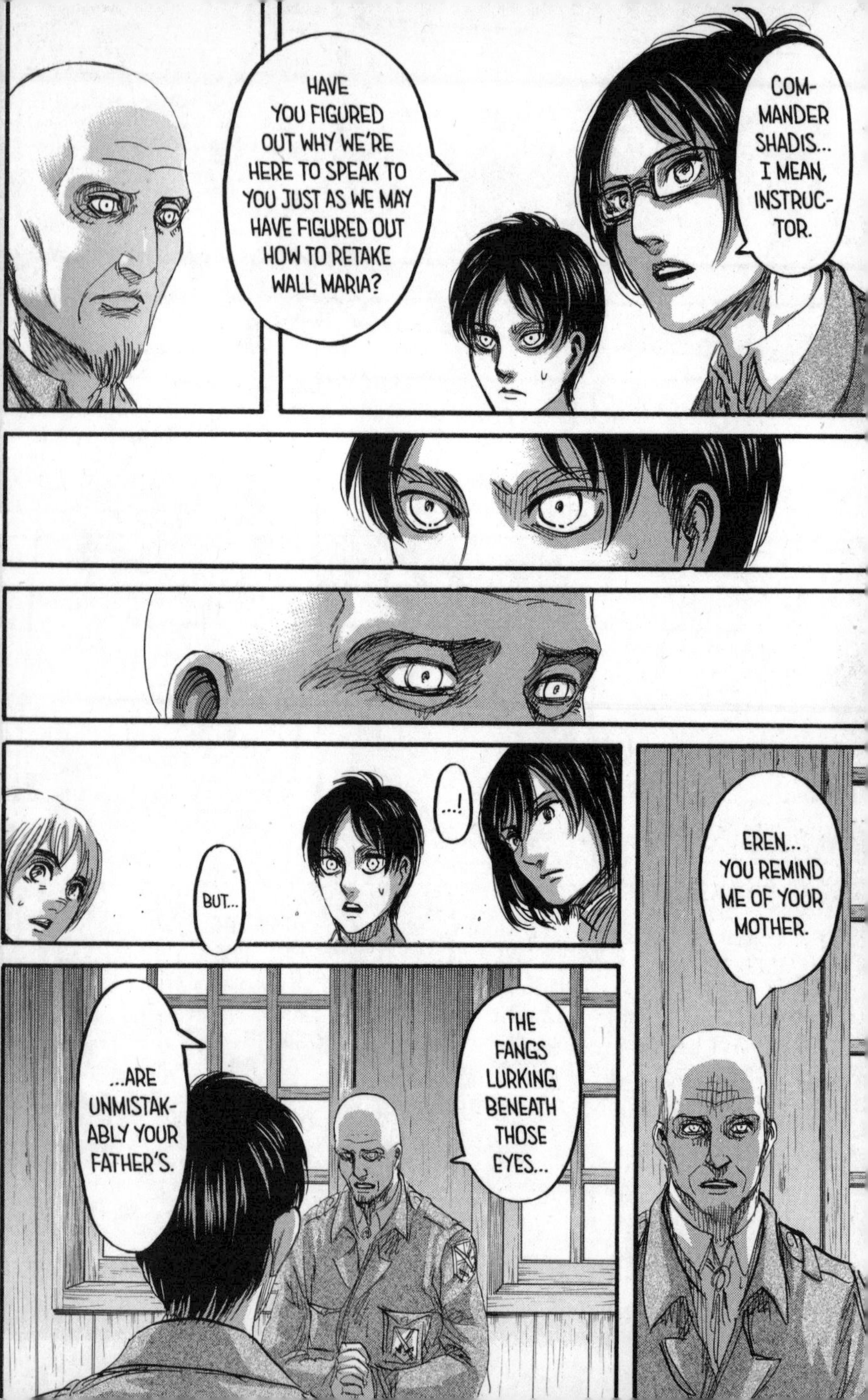
COM-MANDER SHADIS... I MEAN, INSTRUC-TOR.
HAVE YOU FIGURED OUT WHY WE'RE HERE TO SPEAK TO YOU JUST AS WE MAY HAVE FIGURED OUT HOW TO RETAKE WALL MARIA?
EREN... YOU REMIND ME OF YOUR MOTHER.
...!
BUT...
THE FANGS LURKING BENEATH THOSE EYES...
...ARE UNMISTAK-ABLY YOUR FATHER'S.

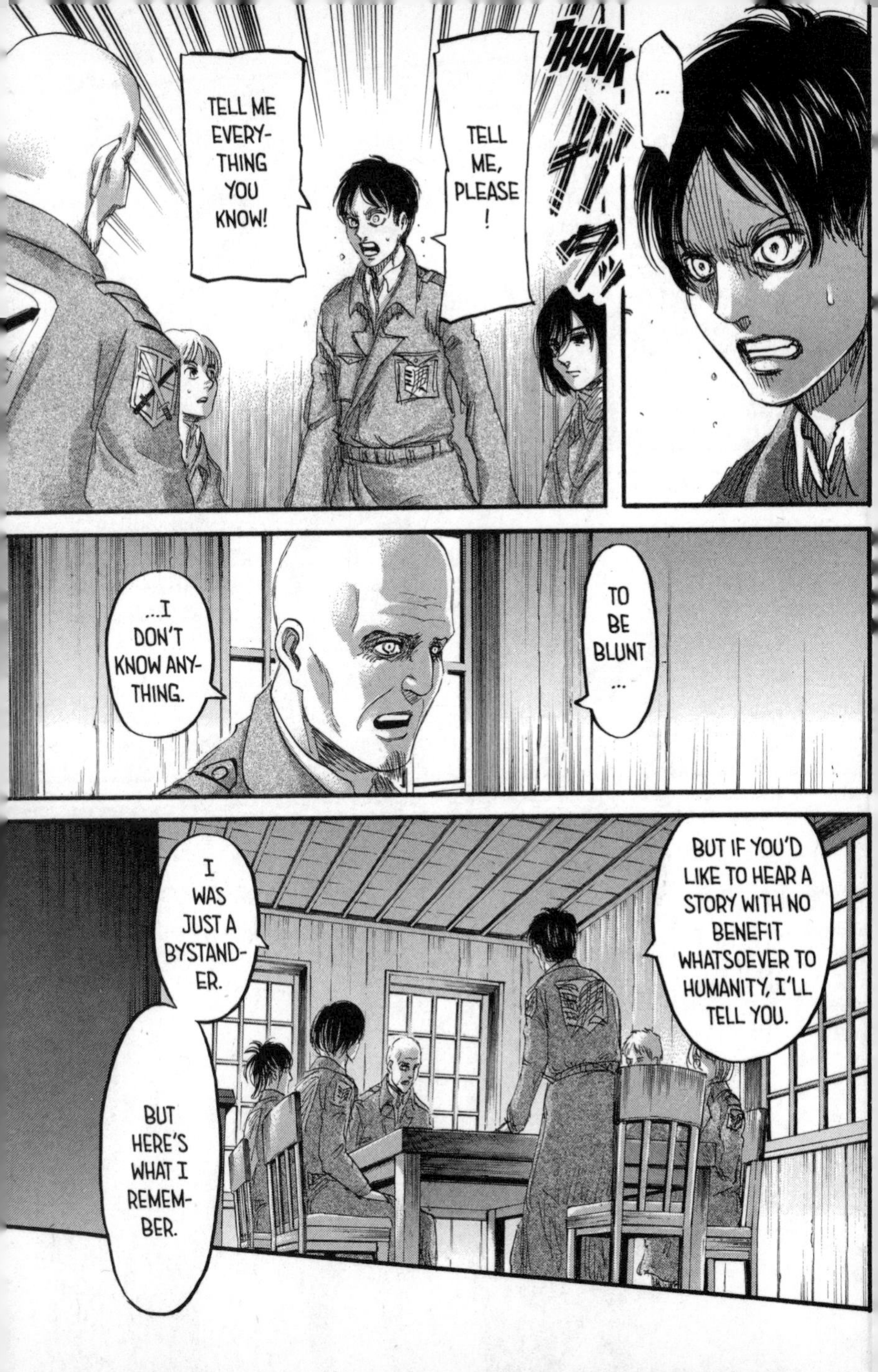
THUNK
...
TELL ME, PLEASE!
TELL ME EVERYTHING YOU KNOW!
TO BE BLUNT...
...I DON'T KNOW ANYTHING.
BUT IF YOU'D LIKE TO HEAR A STORY WITH NO BENEFIT WHATSOEVER TO HUMANITY, I'LL TELL YOU.
I WAS JUST A BYSTANDER.
BUT HERE'S WHAT I REMEMBER.

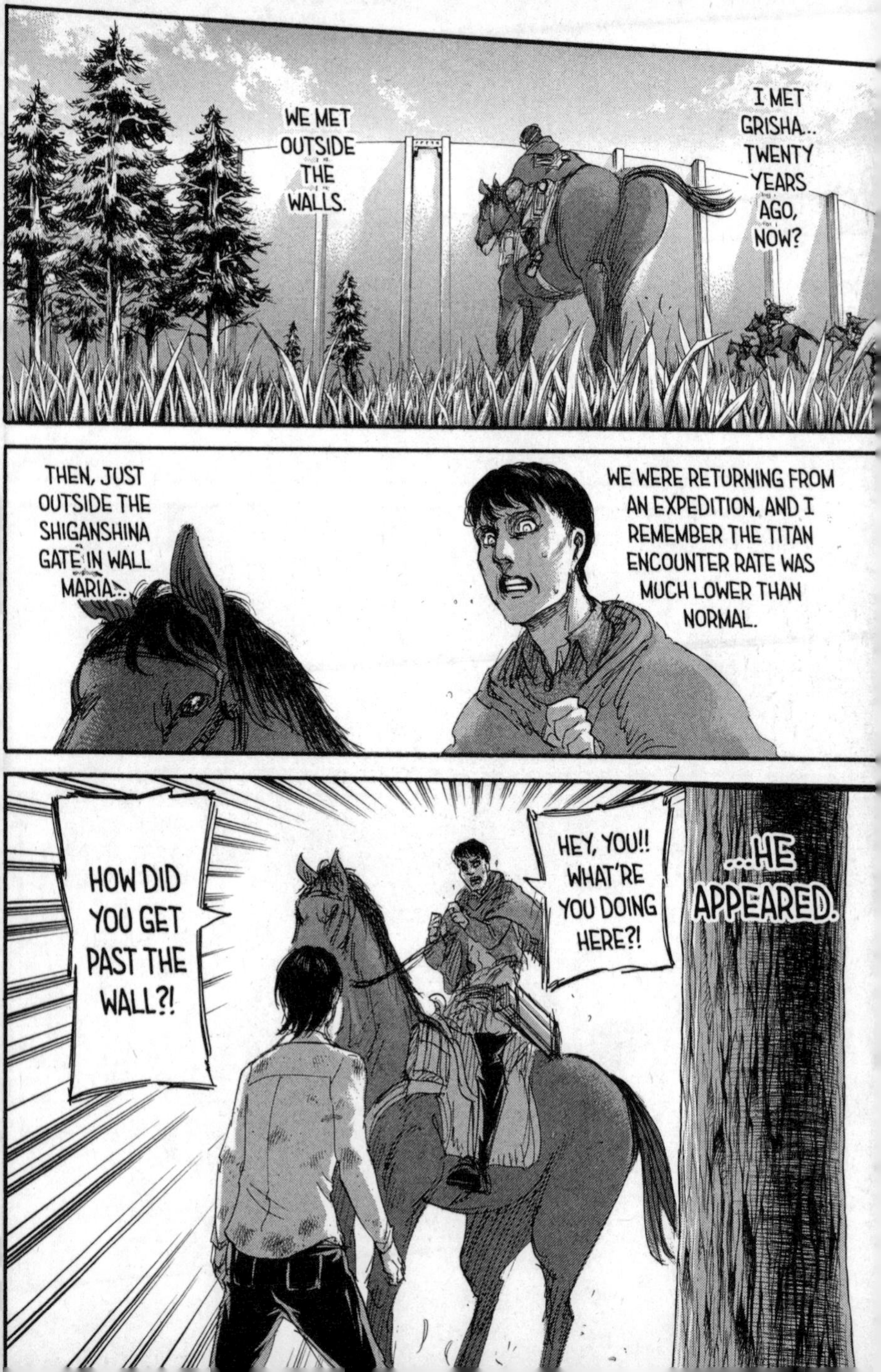
I MET GRISHA... TWENTY YEARS AGO, NOW?
WE MET OUTSIDE THE WALLS.
WE WERE RETURNING FROM AN EXPEDITION, AND I REMEMBER THE TITAN ENCOUNTER RATE WAS MUCH LOWER THAN NORMAL.
THEN, JUST OUTSIDE THE SHIGANSHINA GATE IN WALL MARIA...
...HE APPEARED.
HEY, YOU!! WHAT'RE YOU DOING HERE?!
HOW DID YOU GET PAST THE WALL?!

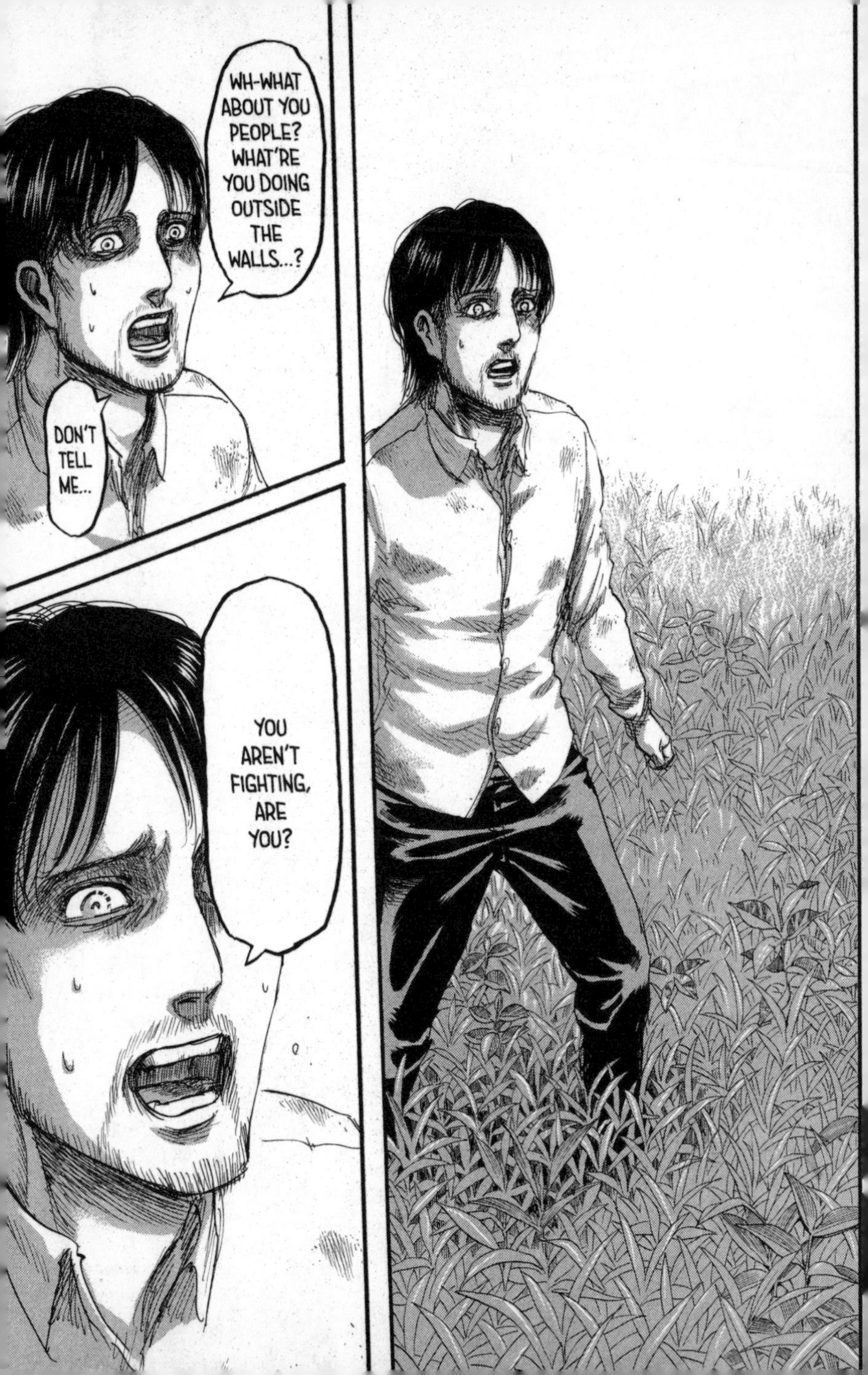
WH-WHAT ABOUT YOU PEOPLE? WHAT'RE YOU DOING OUTSIDE THE WALLS...?
DON'T TELL ME...
YOU AREN'T FIGHTING, ARE YOU?

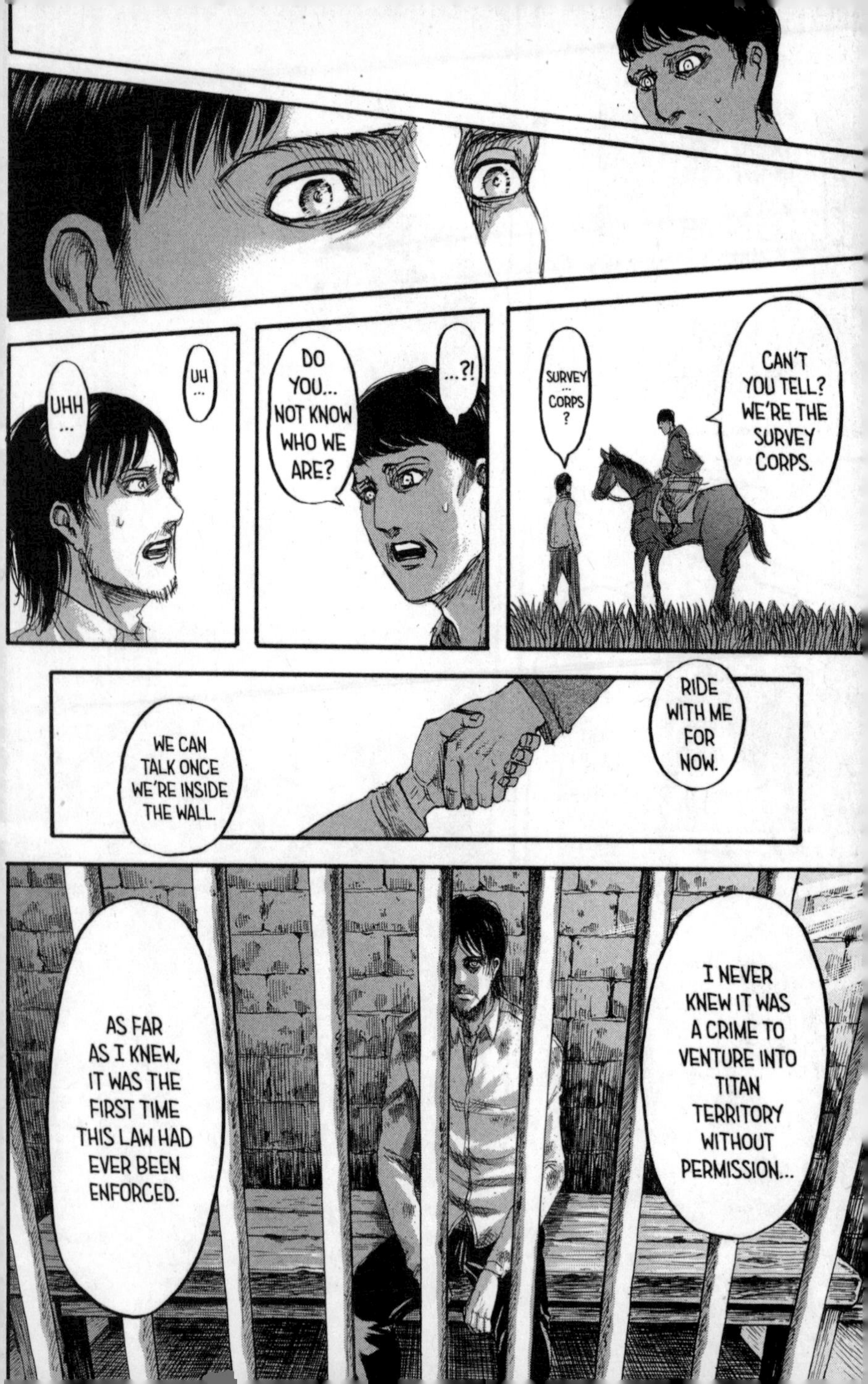
CAN'T YOU TELL? WE'RE THE SURVEY CORPS.
SURVEY... CORPS?
...?!
DO YOU... NOT KNOW WHO WE ARE?
UH...
UHH...
RIDE WITH ME FOR NOW.
WE CAN TALK ONCE WE'RE INSIDE THE WALL.
I NEVER KNEW IT WAS A CRIME TO VENTURE INTO TITAN TERRITORY WITHOUT PERMISSION...
AS FAR AS I KNEW, IT WAS THE FIRST TIME THIS LAW HAD EVER BEEN ENFORCED.

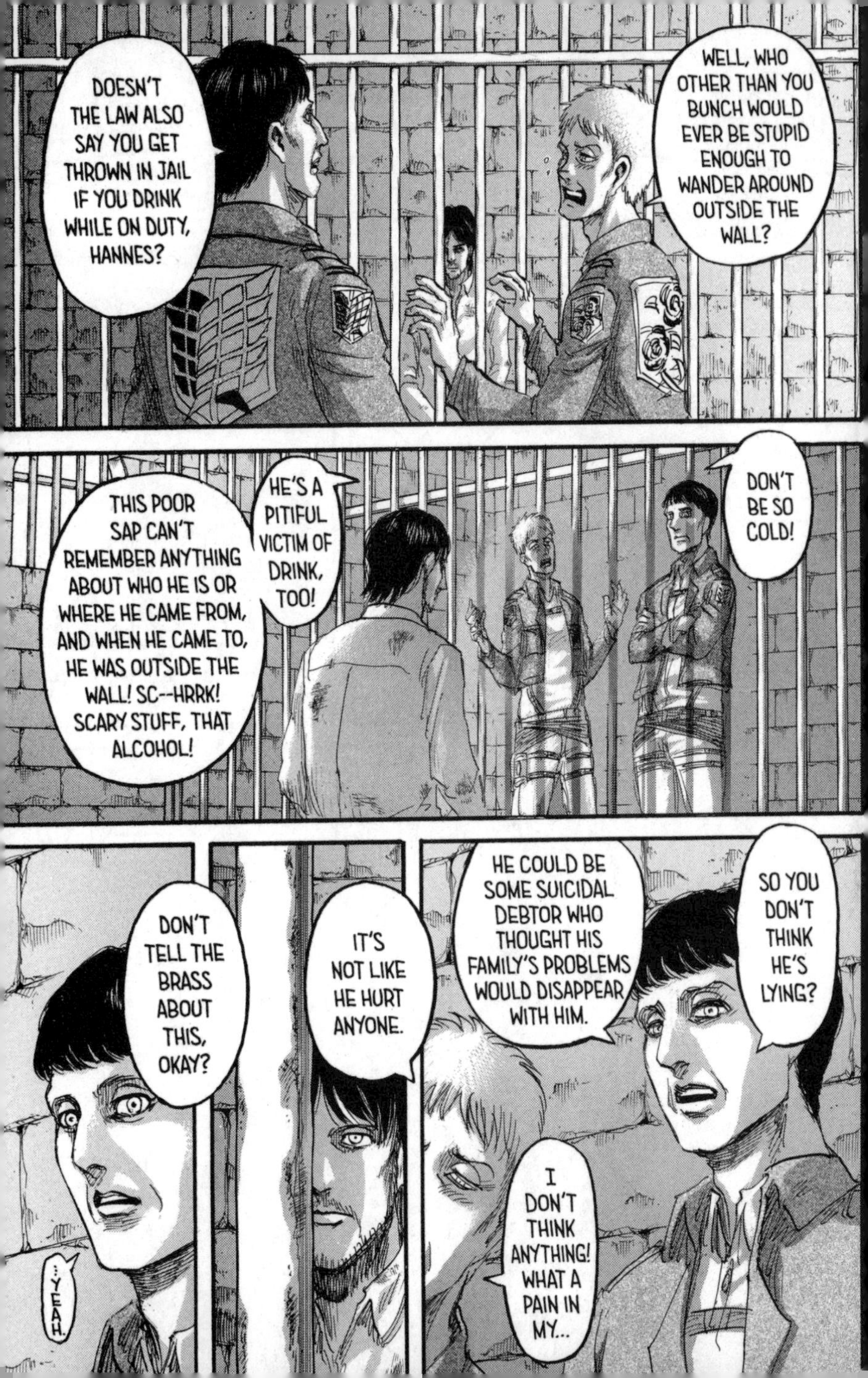
WELL, WHO OTHER THAN YOU BUNCH WOULD EVER BE STUPID ENOUGH TO WANDER AROUND OUTSIDE THE WALL?
DOESN'T THE LAW ALSO SAY YOU GET THROWN IN JAIL IF YOU DRINK WHILE ON DUTY, HANNES?
DON'T BE SO COLD!
HE'S A PITIFUL VICTIM OF DRINK, TOO!
THIS POOR SAP CAN'T REMEMBER ANYTHING ABOUT WHO HE IS OR WHERE HE CAME FROM, AND WHEN HE CAME TO, HE WAS OUTSIDE THE WALL! SC--HRRK! SCARY STUFF, THAT ALCOHOL!
SO YOU DON'T THINK HE'S LYING?
HE COULD BE SOME SUICIDAL DEBTOR WHO THOUGHT HIS FAMILY'S PROBLEMS WOULD DISAPPEAR WITH HIM.
I DON'T THINK ANYTHING! WHAT A PAIN IN MY...
IT'S NOT LIKE HE HURT ANYONE.
DON'T TELL THE BRASS ABOUT THIS, OKAY?
...YEAH.

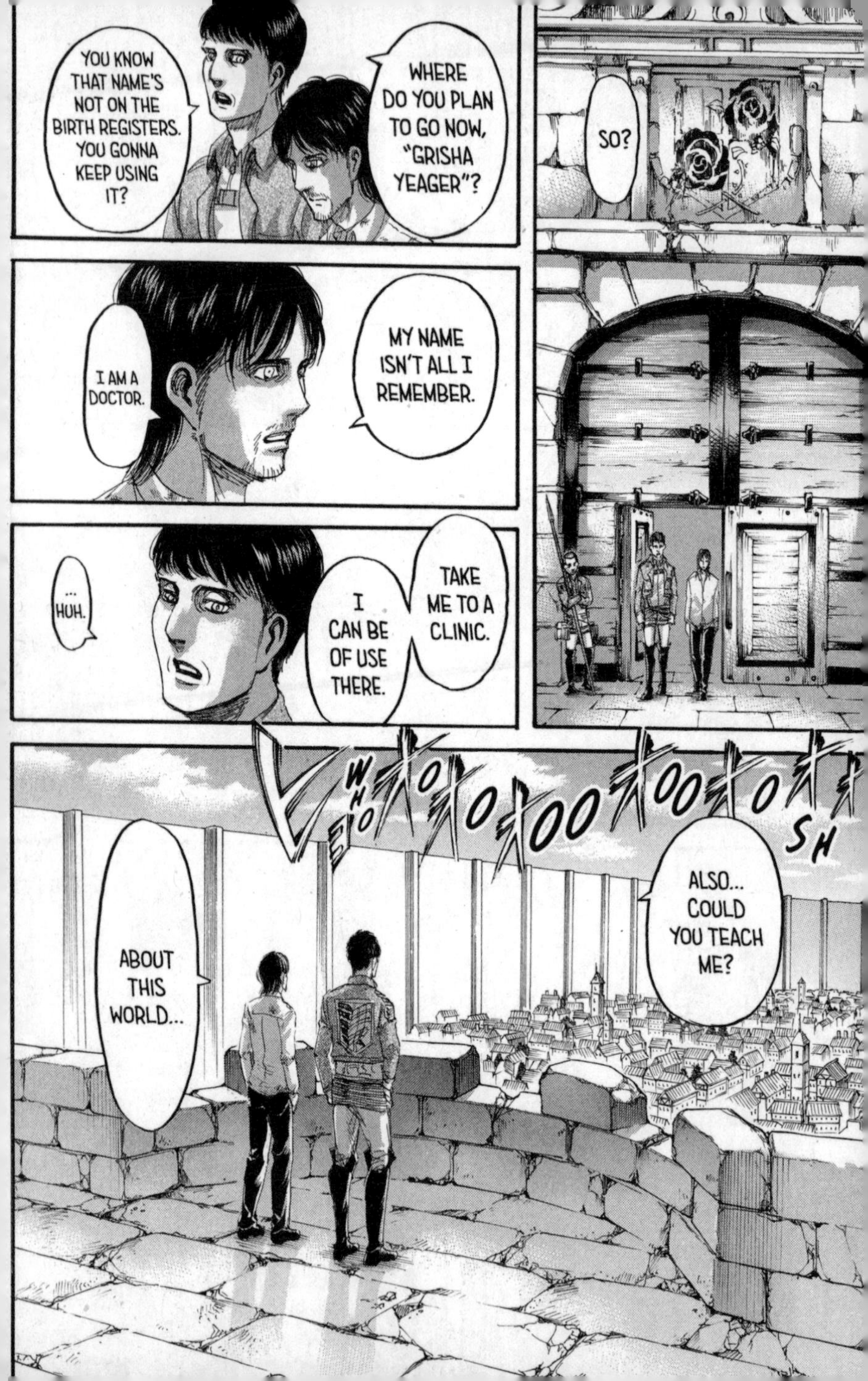

SO?
WHERE DO YOU PLAN TO GO NOW, "GRISHA YEAGER"?
YOU KNOW THAT NAME'S NOT ON THE BIRTH REGISTERS. YOU GONNA KEEP USING IT?
MY NAME ISN'T ALL I REMEMBER.
I AM A DOCTOR.
TAKE ME TO A CLINIC.
I CAN BE OF USE THERE.
... HUH.
WHOOOOOOOSH
ALSO... COULD YOU TEACH ME?
ABOUT THIS WORLD...

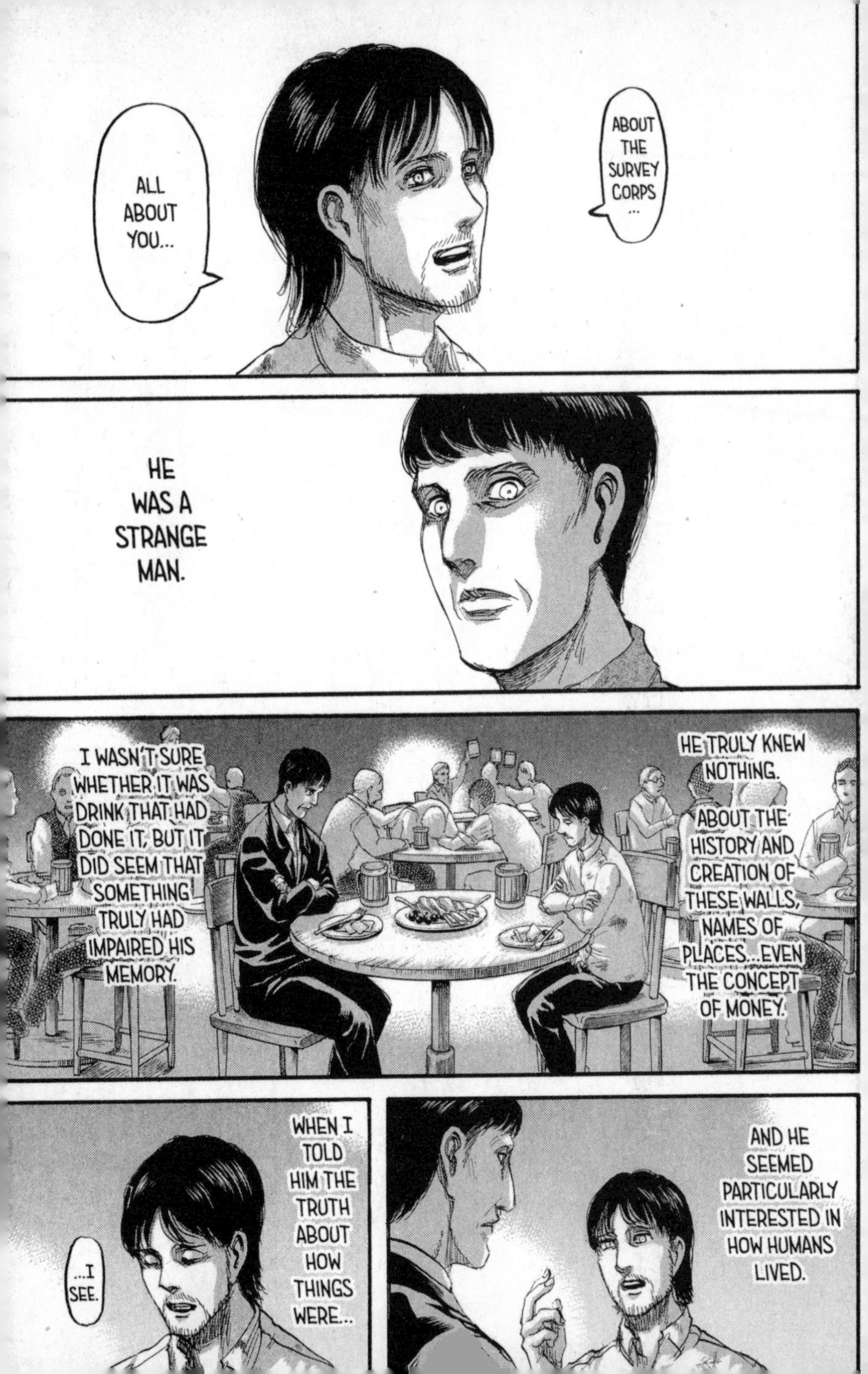
ABOUT THE SURVEY CORPS ...
ALL ABOUT YOU...
HE WAS A STRANGE MAN.
HE TRULY KNEW NOTHING.
ABOUT THE HISTORY AND CREATION OF THESE WALLS, NAMES OF PLACES...EVEN THE CONCEPT OF MONEY.
I WASN'T SURE WHETHER IT WAS DRINK THAT HAD DONE IT, BUT IT DID SEEM THAT SOMETHING TRULY HAD IMPAIRED HIS MEMORY.
AND HE SEEMED PARTICULARLY INTERESTED IN HOW HUMANS LIVED.
WHEN I TOLD HIM THE TRUTH ABOUT HOW THINGS WERE...
...I SEE.

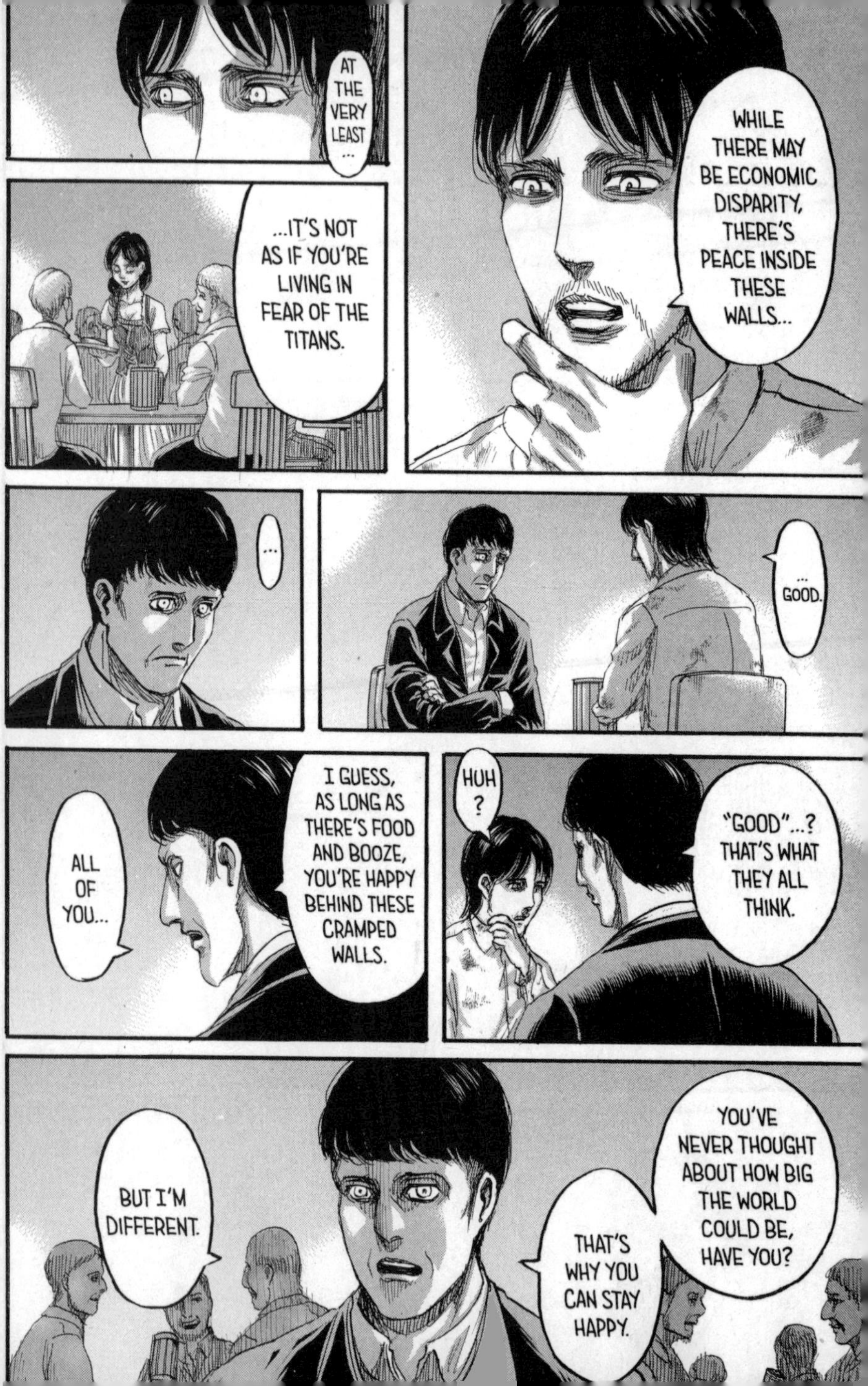
WHILE THERE MAY BE ECONOMIC DISPARITY, THERE'S PEACE INSIDE THESE WALLS...
AT THE VERY LEAST ...
...IT'S NOT AS IF YOU'RE LIVING IN FEAR OF THE TITANS.
... GOOD.
...
"GOOD"...? THAT'S WHAT THEY ALL THINK.
HUH ?
I GUESS, AS LONG AS THERE'S FOOD AND BOOZE, YOU'RE HAPPY BEHIND THESE CRAMPED WALLS.
ALL OF YOU...
YOU'VE NEVER THOUGHT ABOUT HOW BIG THE WORLD COULD BE, HAVE YOU?
THAT'S WHY YOU CAN STAY HAPPY.
BUT I'M DIFFERENT.

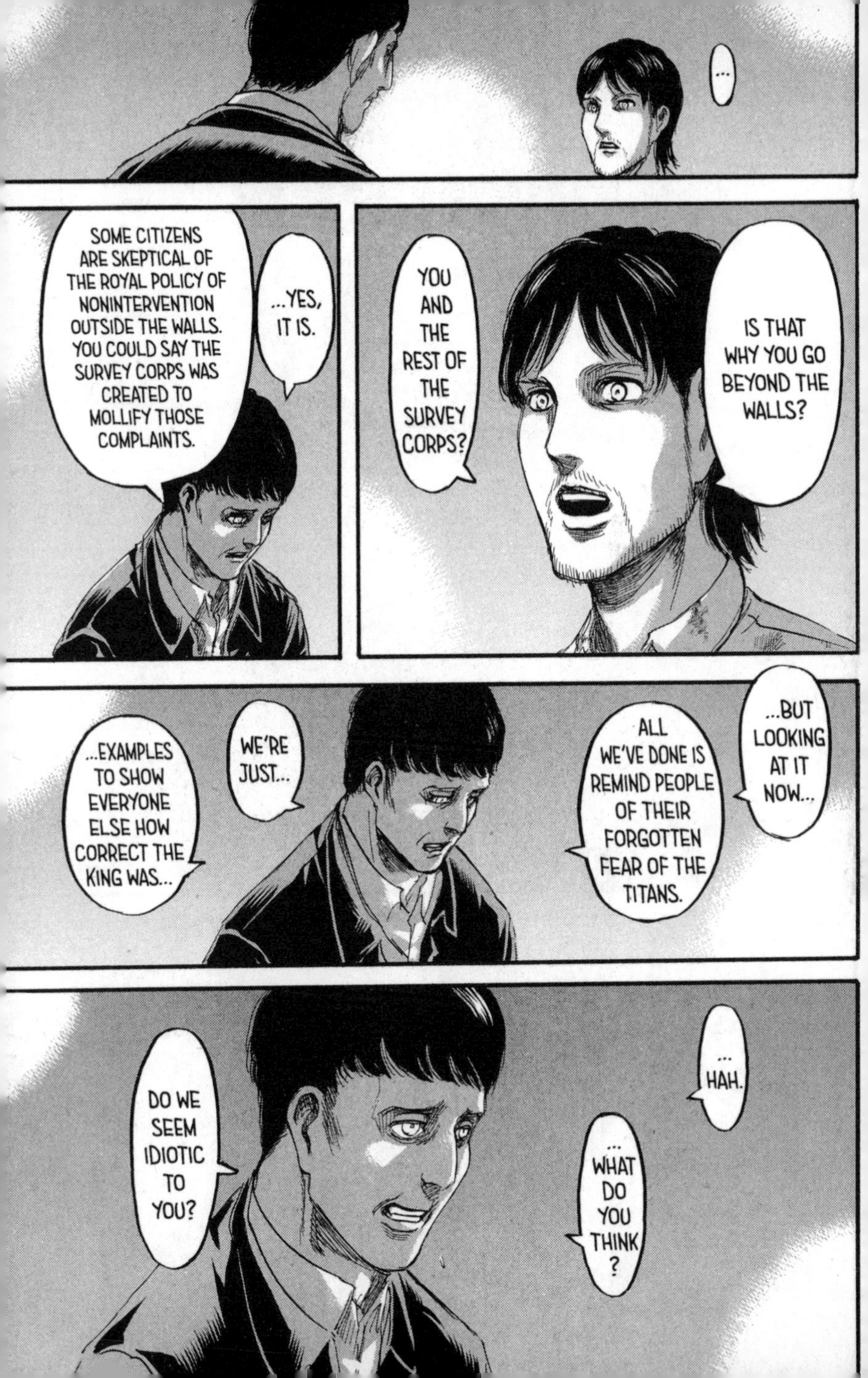
...
IS THAT WHY YOU GO BEYOND THE WALLS?
YOU AND THE REST OF THE SURVEY CORPS?
...YES, IT IS.
SOME CITIZENS ARE SKEPTICAL OF THE ROYAL POLICY OF NONINTERVENTION OUTSIDE THE WALLS. YOU COULD SAY THE SURVEY CORPS WAS CREATED TO MOLLIFY THOSE COMPLAINTS.
...BUT LOOKING AT IT NOW...
ALL WE'VE DONE IS REMIND PEOPLE OF THEIR FORGOTTEN FEAR OF THE TITANS.
WE'RE JUST...
...EXAMPLES TO SHOW EVERYONE ELSE HOW CORRECT THE KING WAS...
... HAH.
... WHAT DO YOU THINK?
DO WE SEEM IDIOTIC TO YOU?

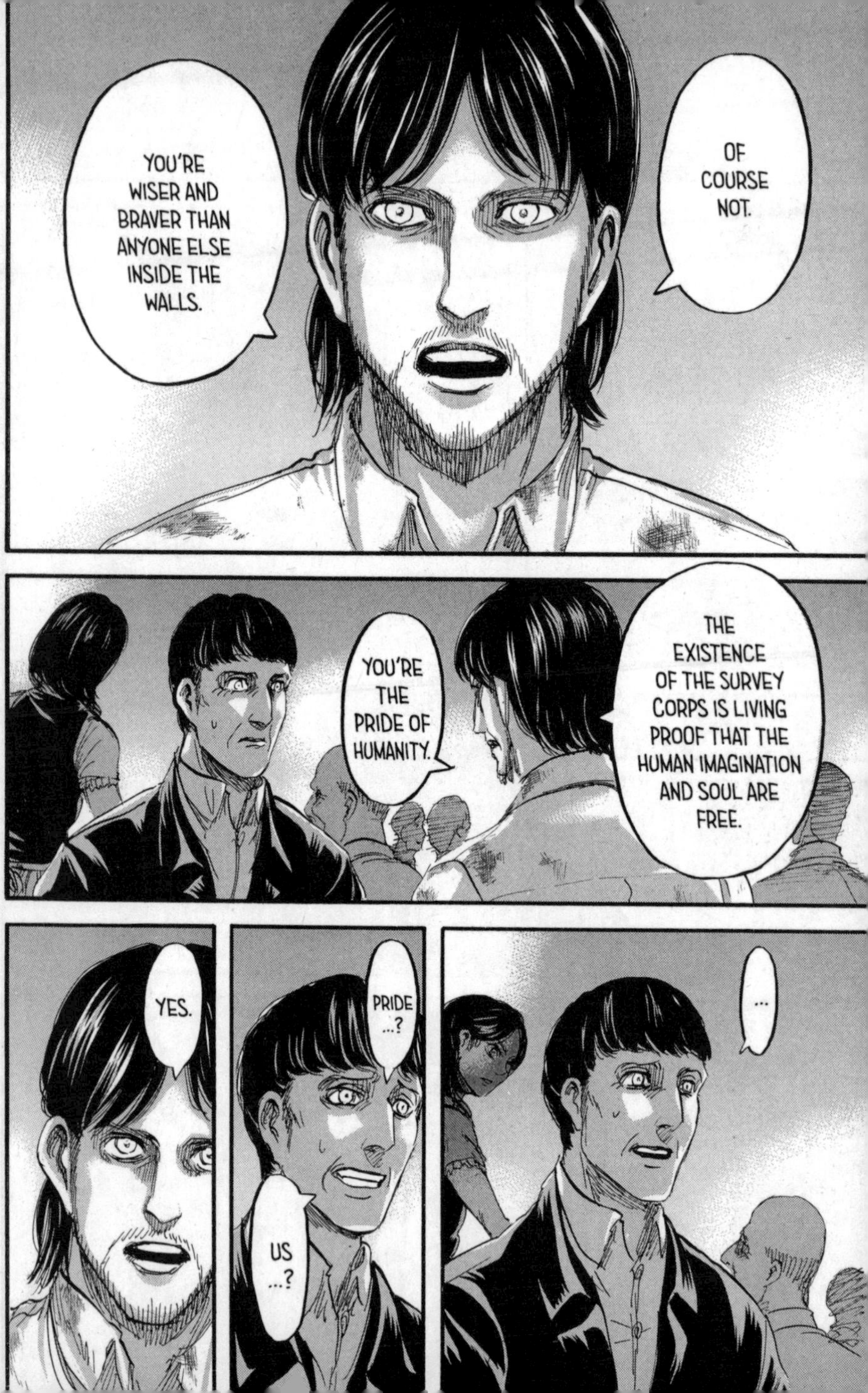
OF COURSE NOT.
YOU'RE WISER AND BRAVER THAN ANYONE ELSE INSIDE THE WALLS.
THE EXISTENCE OF THE SURVEY CORPS IS LIVING PROOF THAT THE HUMAN IMAGINATION AND SOUL ARE FREE.
YOU'RE THE PRIDE OF HUMANITY.
...
PRIDE ...?
US ...?
YES.

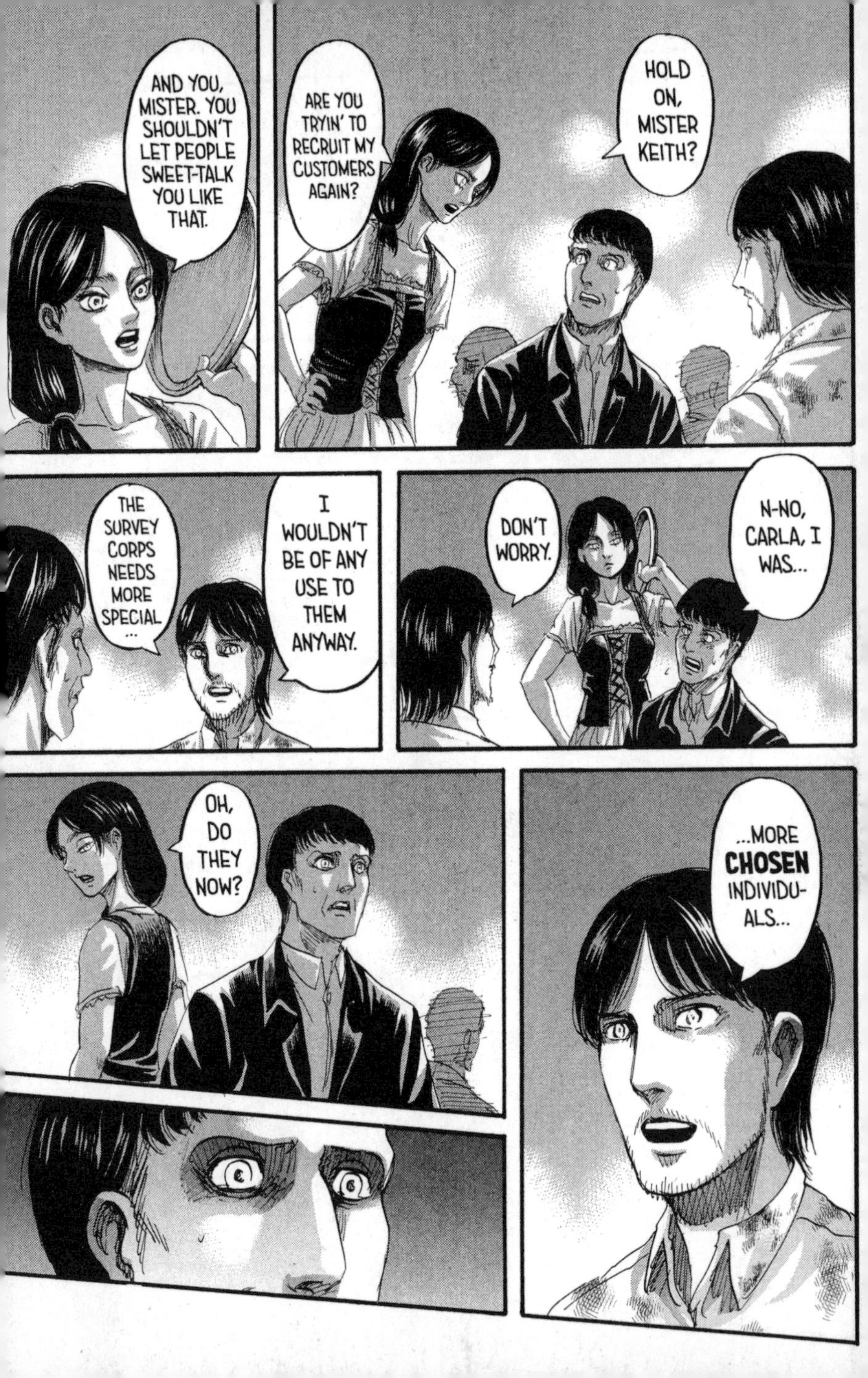
HOLD ON, MISTER KEITH?
ARE YOU TRYIN' TO RECRUIT MY CUSTOMERS AGAIN?
AND YOU, MISTER. YOU SHOULDN'T LET PEOPLE SWEET-TALK YOU LIKE THAT.
N-NO, CARLA, I WAS...
DON'T WORRY.
I WOULDN'T BE OF ANY USE TO THEM ANYWAY.
THE SURVEY CORPS NEEDS MORE SPECIAL ...
...MORE **CHOSEN** INDIVIDU-ALS...
OH, DO THEY NOW?

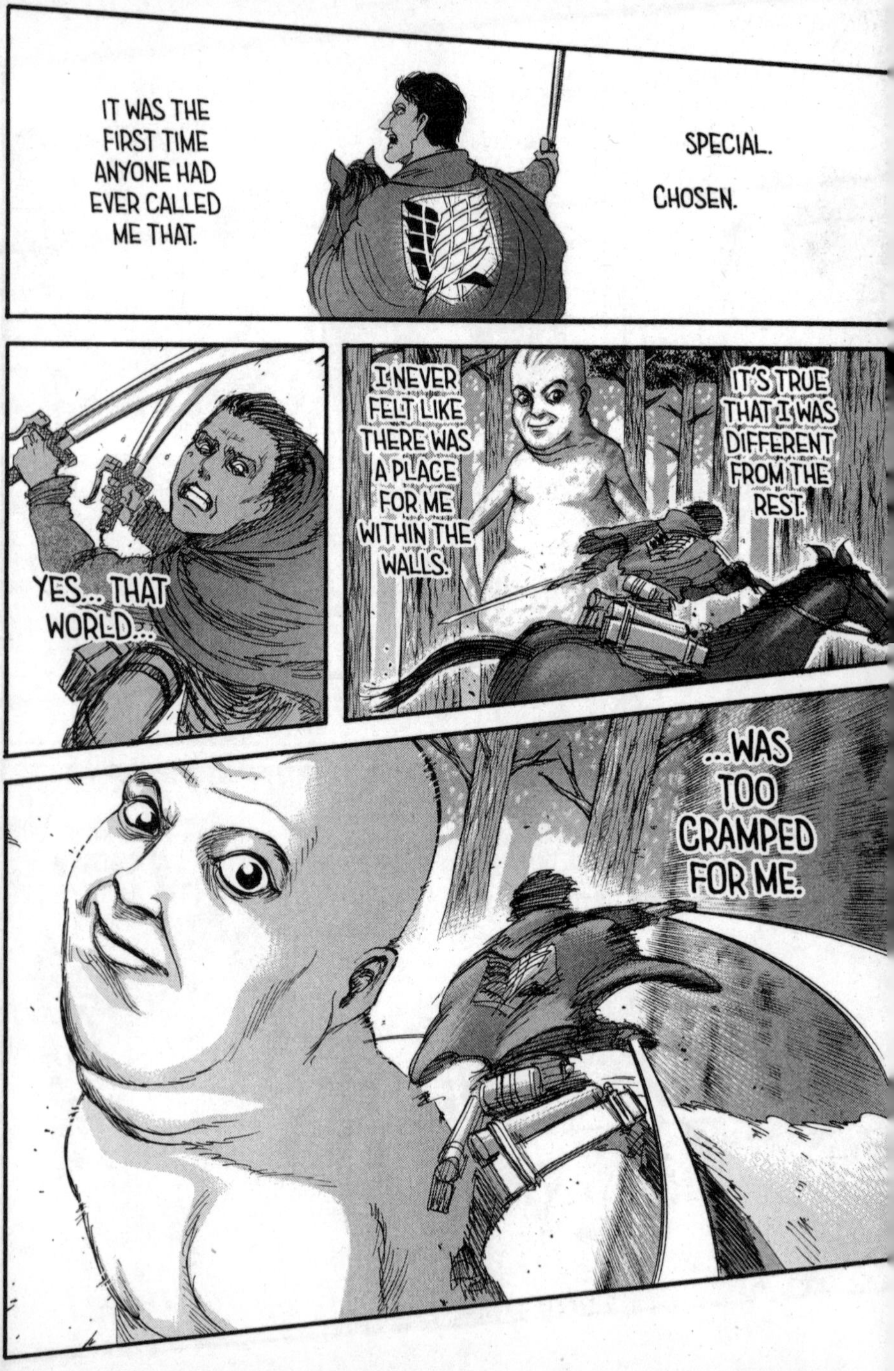
SPECIAL.
CHOSEN.
IT WAS THE FIRST TIME ANYONE HAD EVER CALLED ME THAT.
IT'S TRUE THAT I WAS DIFFERENT FROM THE REST.
I NEVER FELT LIKE THERE WAS A PLACE FOR ME WITHIN THE WALLS.
YES... THAT WORLD...
...WAS TOO CRAMPED FOR ME.

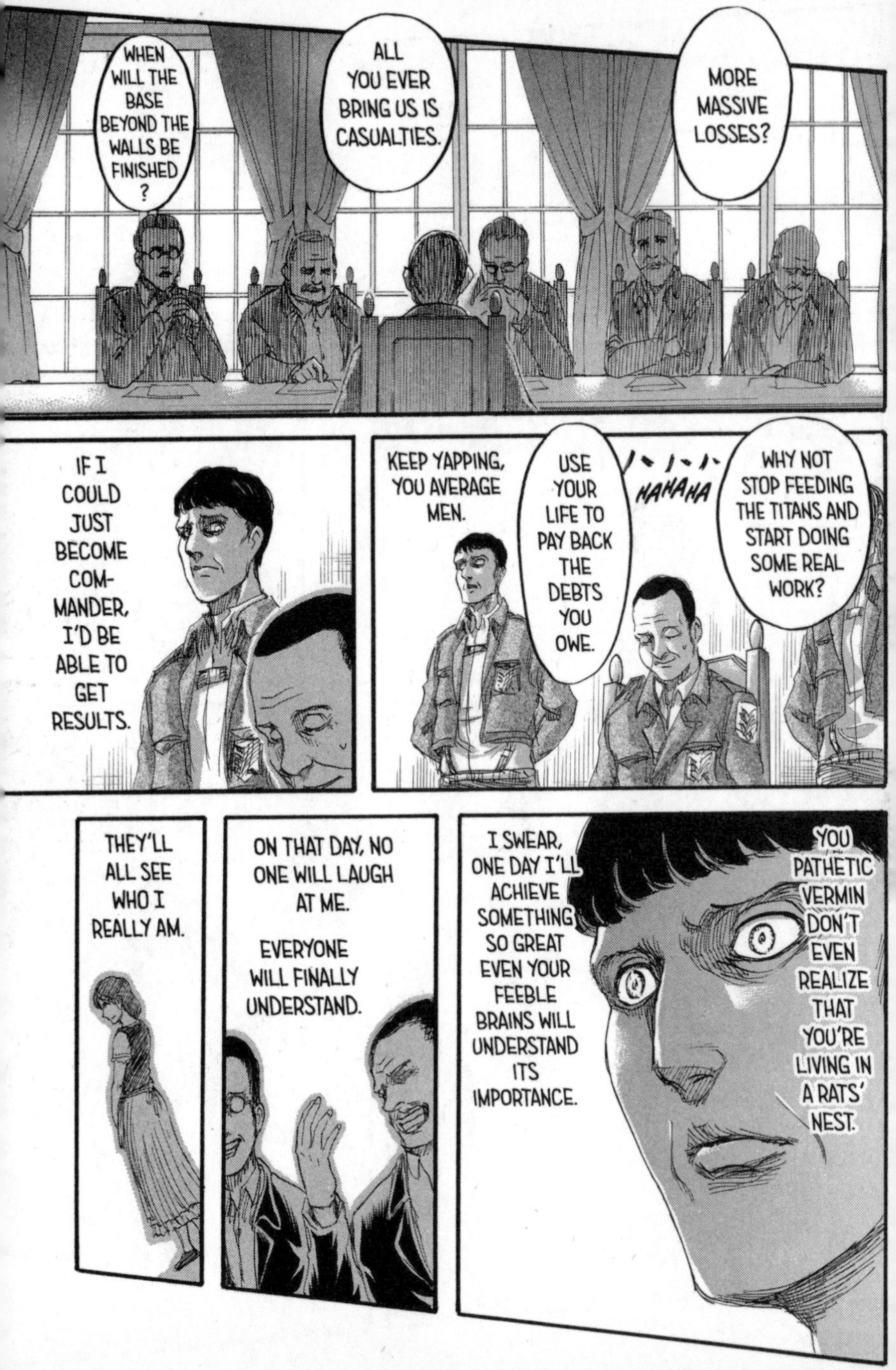
MORE MASSIVE LOSSES?
ALL YOU EVER BRING US IS CASUALTIES.
WHEN WILL THE BASE BEYOND THE WALLS BE FINISHED?
WHY NOT STOP FEEDING THE TITANS AND START DOING SOME REAL WORK?
HAHAHA
USE YOUR LIFE TO PAY BACK THE DEBTS YOU OWE.
KEEP YAPPING, YOU AVERAGE MEN.
IF I COULD JUST BECOME COM-MANDER, I'D BE ABLE TO GET RESULTS.
YOU PATHETIC VERMIN DON'T EVEN REALIZE THAT YOU'RE LIVING IN A RATS' NEST.
I SWEAR, ONE DAY I'LL ACHIEVE SOMETHING SO GREAT EVEN YOUR FEEBLE BRAINS WILL UNDERSTAND ITS IMPORTANCE.
ON THAT DAY, NO ONE WILL LAUGH AT ME.
EVERYONE WILL FINALLY UNDERSTAND.
THEY'LL ALL SEE WHO I REALLY AM.

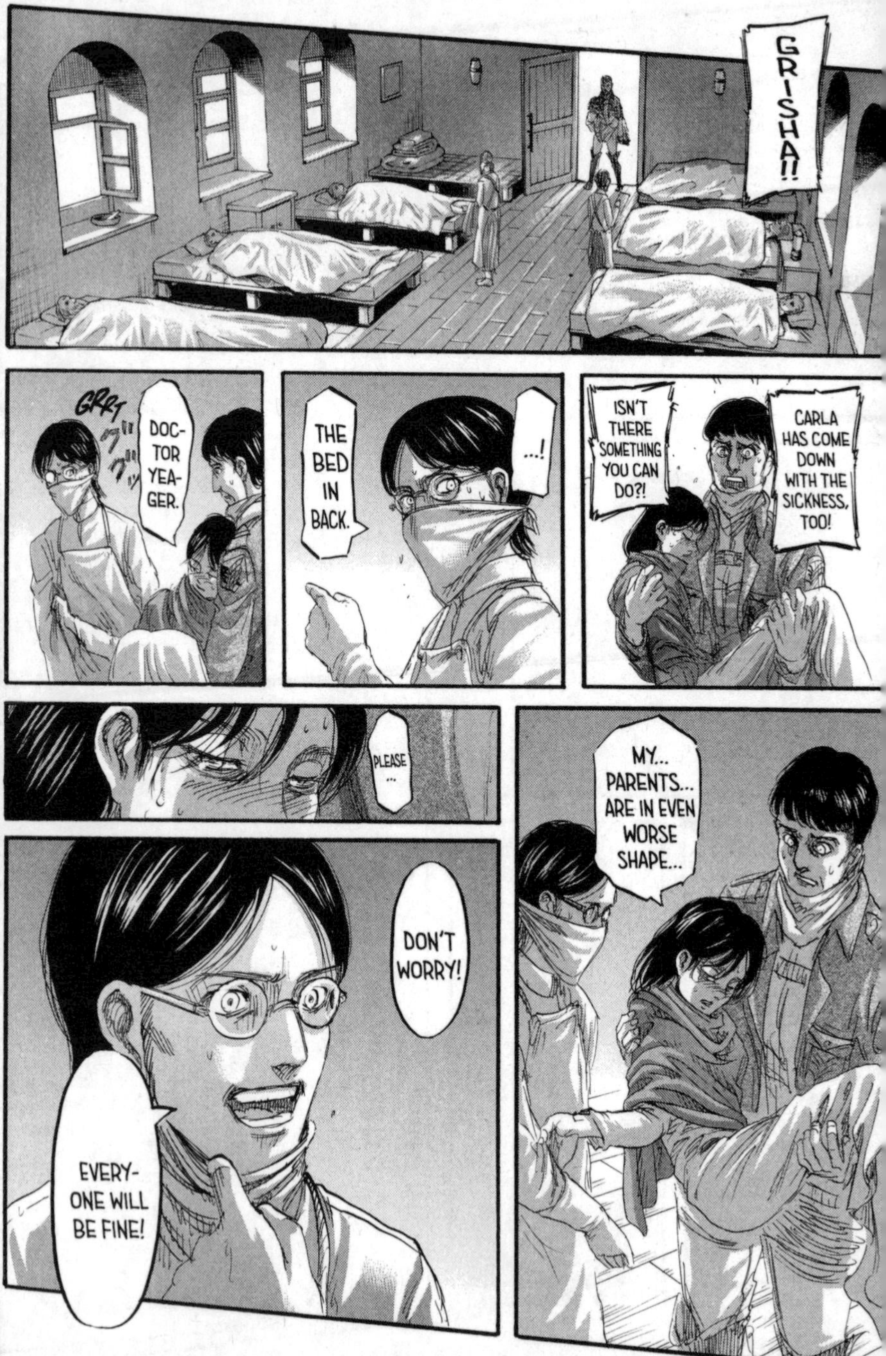
GRISHA!!
CARLA HAS COME DOWN WITH THE SICKNESS, TOO!
ISN'T THERE SOMETHING YOU CAN DO?!
...!
THE BED IN BACK.
GRRT
DOC-TOR YEA-GER.
MY... PARENTS... ARE IN EVEN WORSE SHAPE...
PLEASE...
DON'T WORRY!
EVERY-ONE WILL BE FINE!

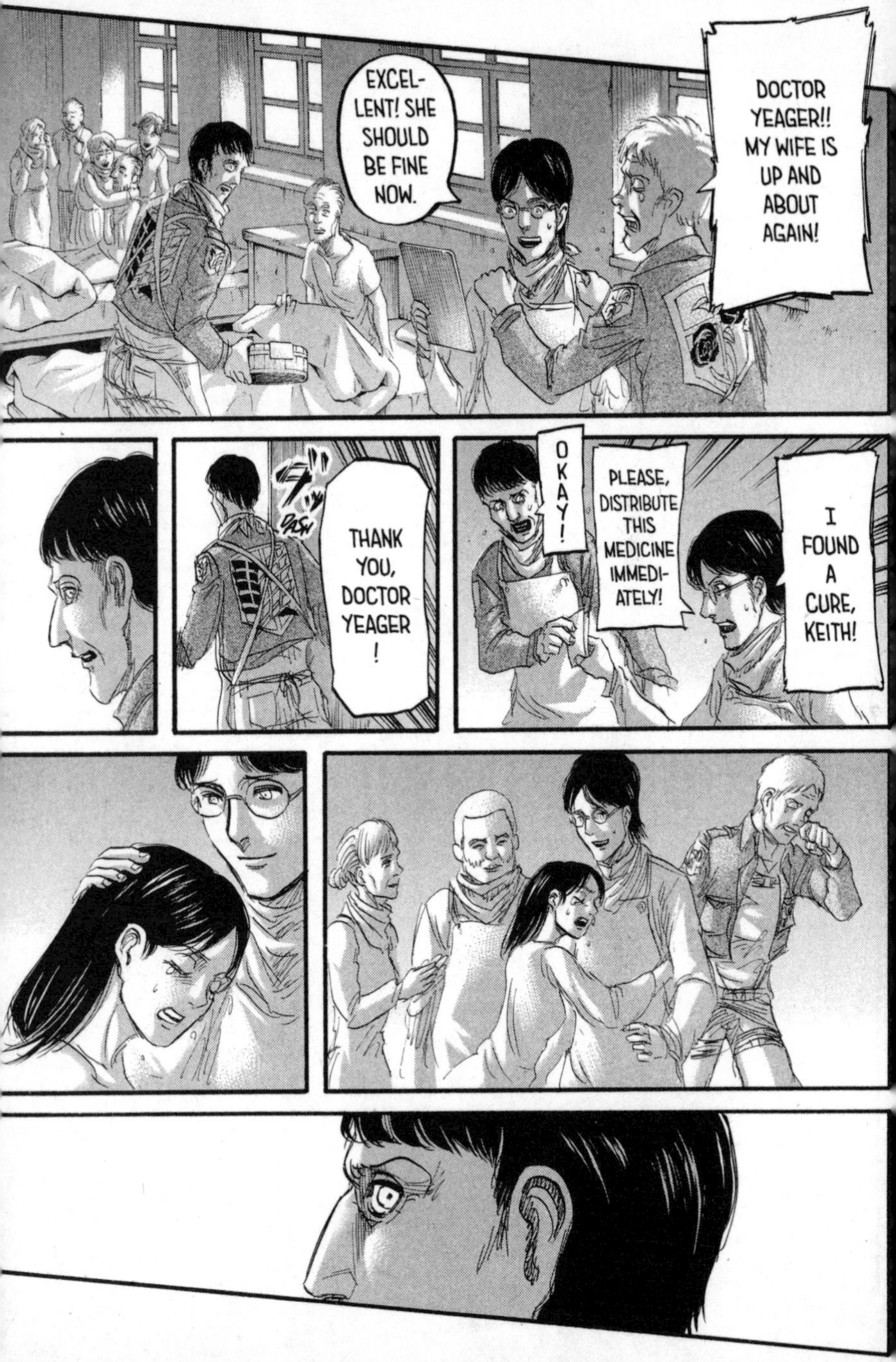
DOCTOR YEAGER!! MY WIFE IS UP AND ABOUT AGAIN!
EXCELLENT! SHE SHOULD BE FINE NOW.
I FOUND A CURE, KEITH!
PLEASE, DISTRIBUTE THIS MEDICINE IMMEDIATELY!
OKAY!
DASH
THANK YOU, DOCTOR YEAGER!

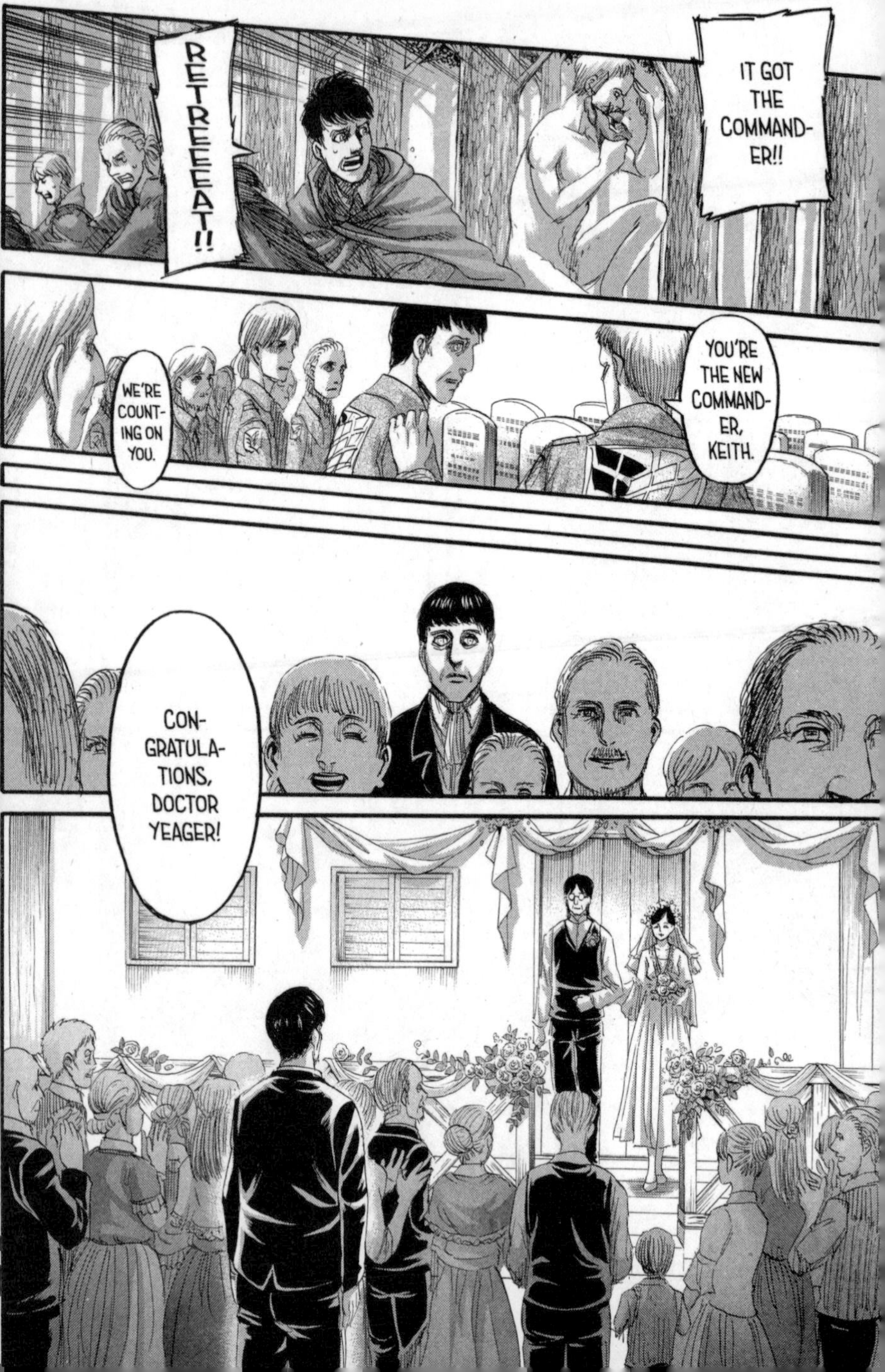
IT GOT THE COMMANDER!!
RETREEEAT!!
YOU'RE THE NEW COMMANDER, KEITH.
WE'RE COUNTING ON YOU.
CONGRATULATIONS, DOCTOR YEAGER!

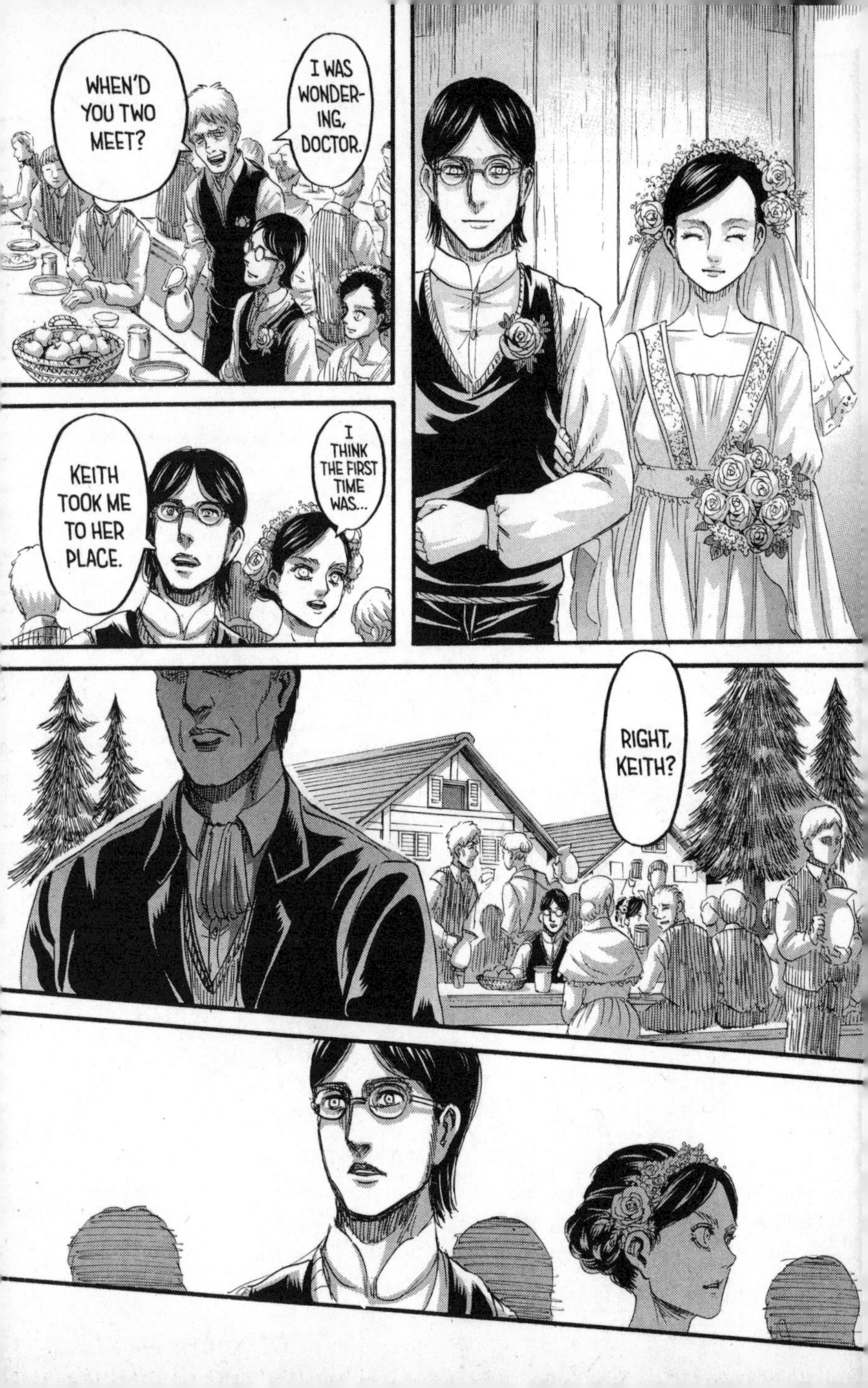
I WAS WONDER-ING, DOCTOR.
WHEN'D YOU TWO MEET?
I THINK THE FIRST TIME WAS...
KEITH TOOK ME TO HER PLACE.
RIGHT, KEITH?

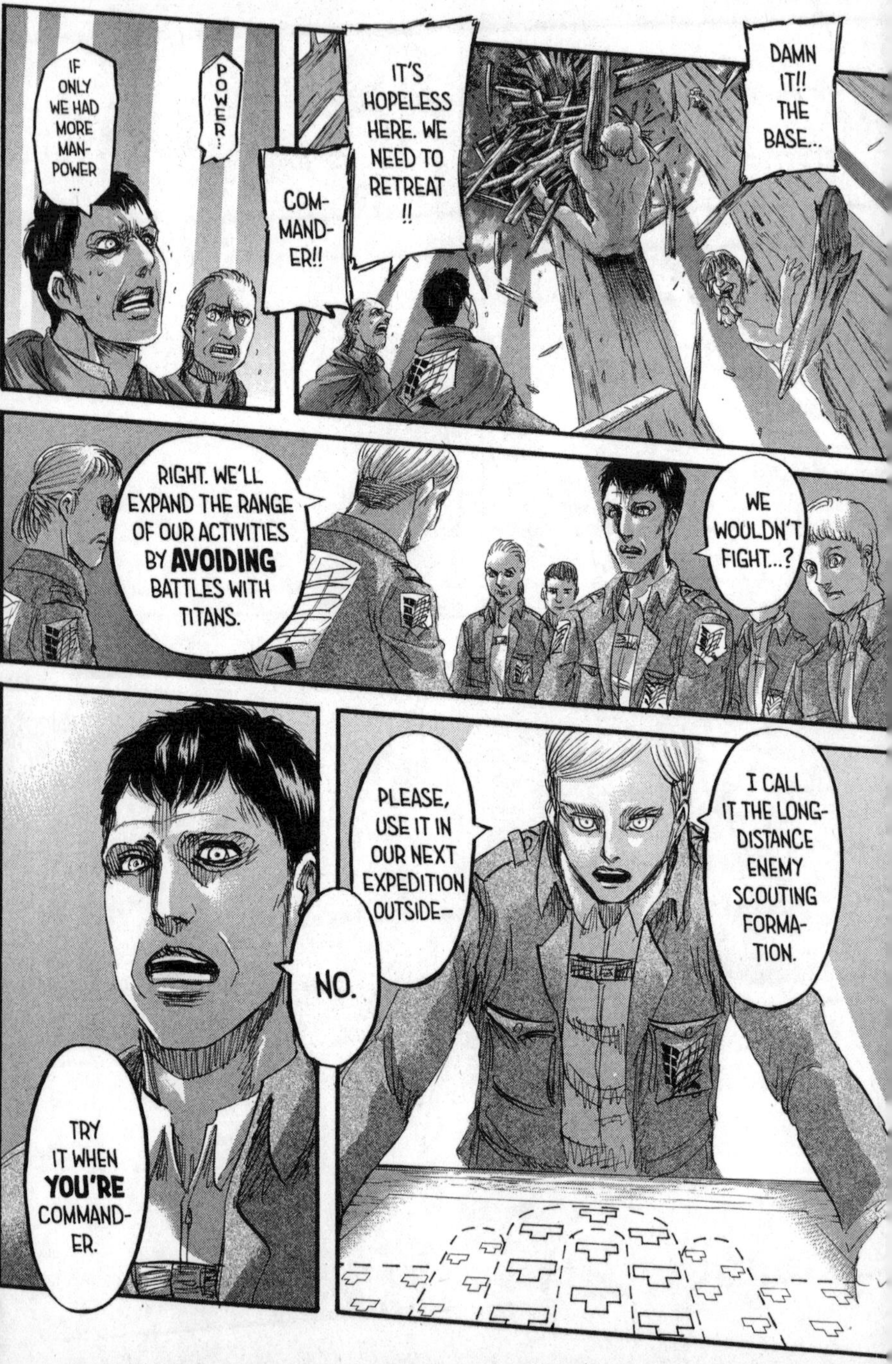
DAMN IT!! THE BASE...
IT'S HOPELESS HERE. WE NEED TO RETREAT !!
COMMANDER!!
IF ONLY WE HAD MORE MANPOWER...
POWER...
WE WOULDN'T FIGHT...?
RIGHT. WE'LL EXPAND THE RANGE OF OUR ACTIVITIES BY **AVOIDING** BATTLES WITH TITANS.
I CALL IT THE LONG-DISTANCE ENEMY SCOUTING FORMATION.
PLEASE, USE IT IN OUR NEXT EXPEDITION OUTSIDE—
NO.
TRY IT WHEN **YOU'RE** COMMANDER.

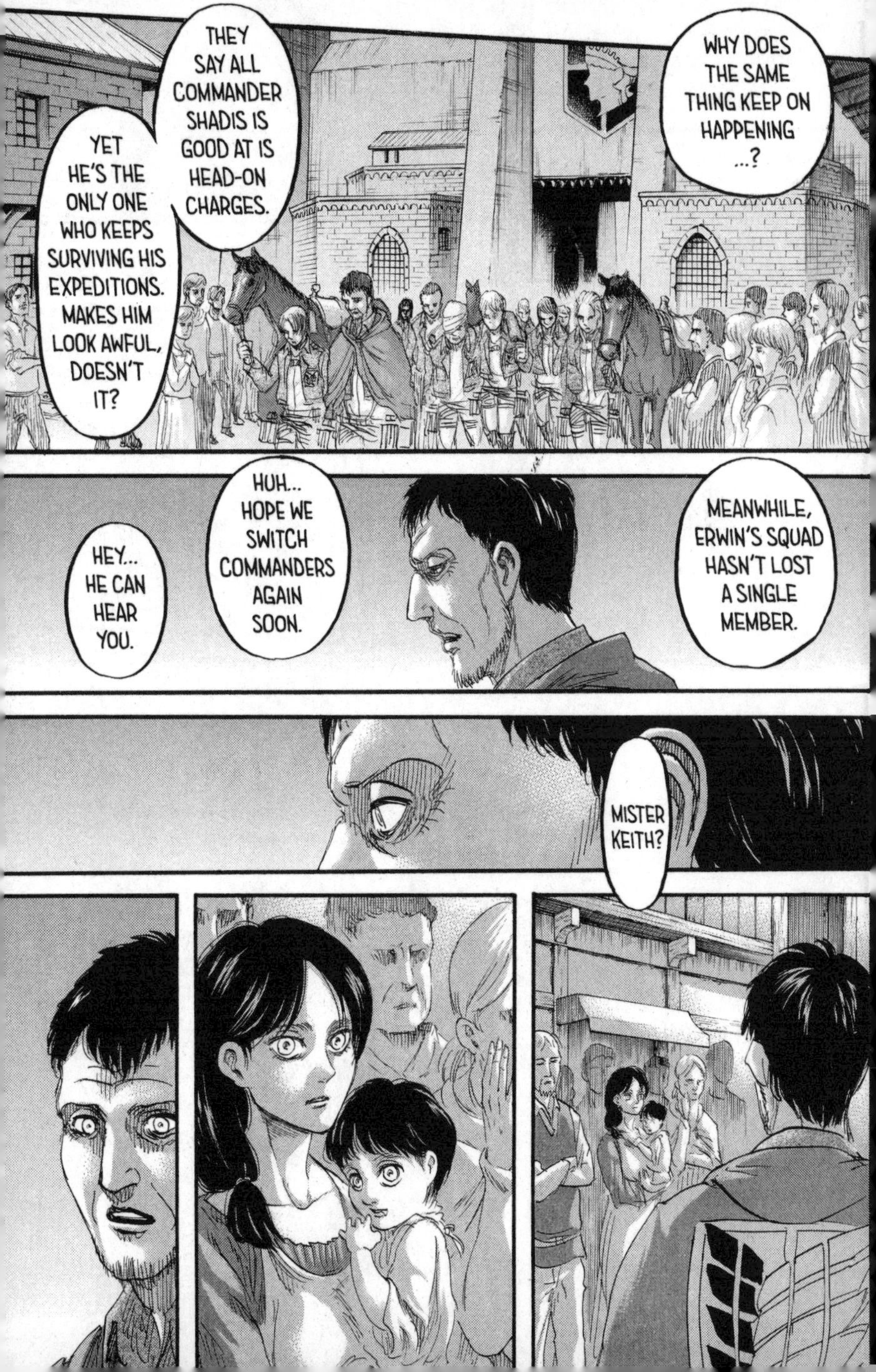
WHY DOES THE SAME THING KEEP ON HAPPENING ...?
THEY SAY ALL COMMANDER SHADIS IS GOOD AT IS HEAD-ON CHARGES.
YET HE'S THE ONLY ONE WHO KEEPS SURVIVING HIS EXPEDITIONS. MAKES HIM LOOK AWFUL, DOESN'T IT?
MEANWHILE, ERWIN'S SQUAD HASN'T LOST A SINGLE MEMBER.
HUH... HOPE WE SWITCH COMMANDERS AGAIN SOON.
HEY... HE CAN HEAR YOU.
MISTER KEITH?

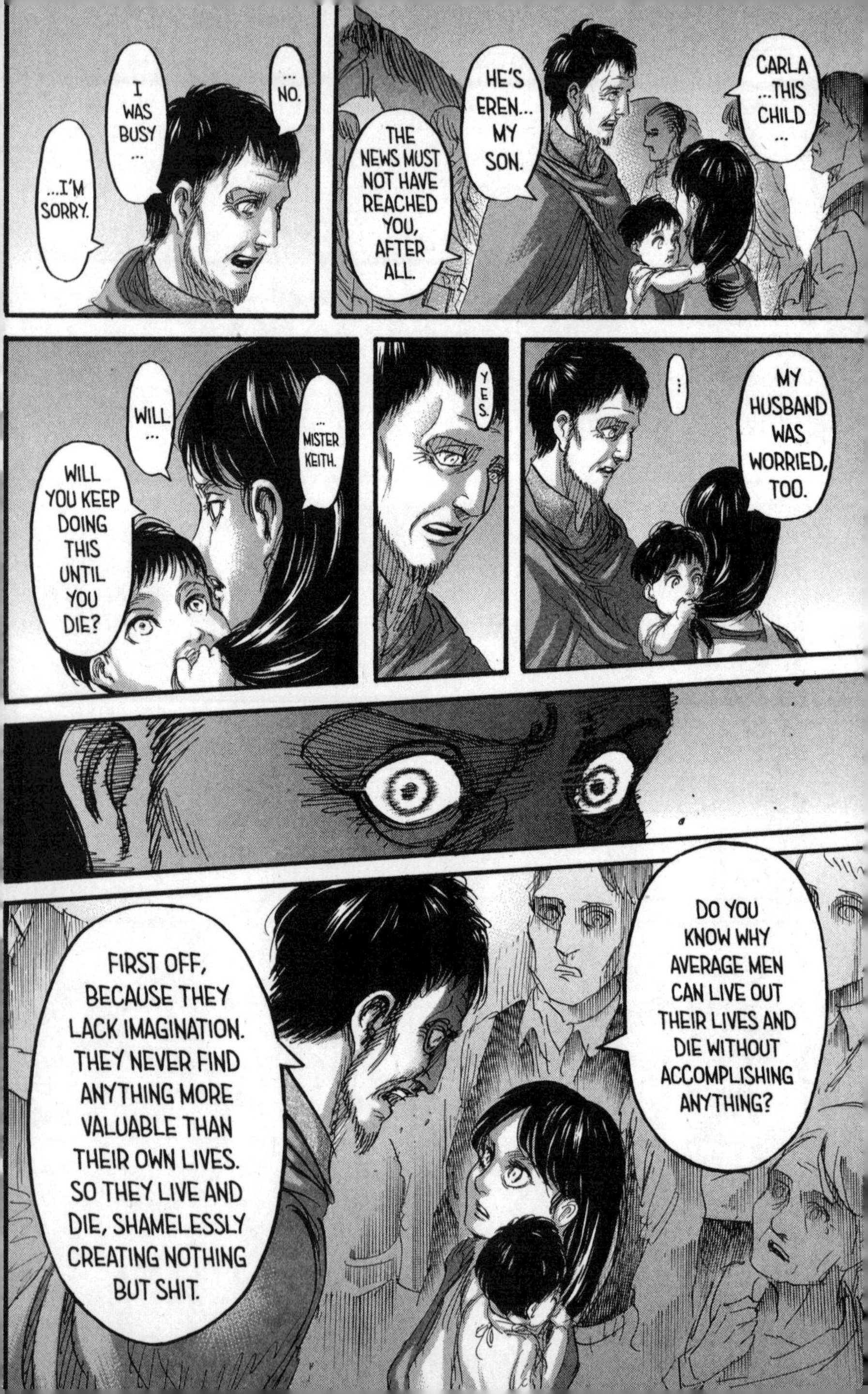
CARLA ...THIS CHILD ...
HE'S EREN... MY SON.
THE NEWS MUST NOT HAVE REACHED YOU, AFTER ALL.
... NO.
I WAS BUSY ...
...I'M SORRY.
MY HUSBAND WAS WORRIED, TOO.
...
YES.
... MISTER KEITH.
WILL ...
WILL YOU KEEP DOING THIS UNTIL YOU DIE?
DO YOU KNOW WHY AVERAGE MEN CAN LIVE OUT THEIR LIVES AND DIE WITHOUT ACCOMPLISHING ANYTHING?
FIRST OFF, BECAUSE THEY LACK IMAGINATION. THEY NEVER FIND ANYTHING MORE VALUABLE THAN THEIR OWN LIVES. SO THEY LIVE AND DIE, SHAMELESSLY CREATING NOTHING BUT SHIT.

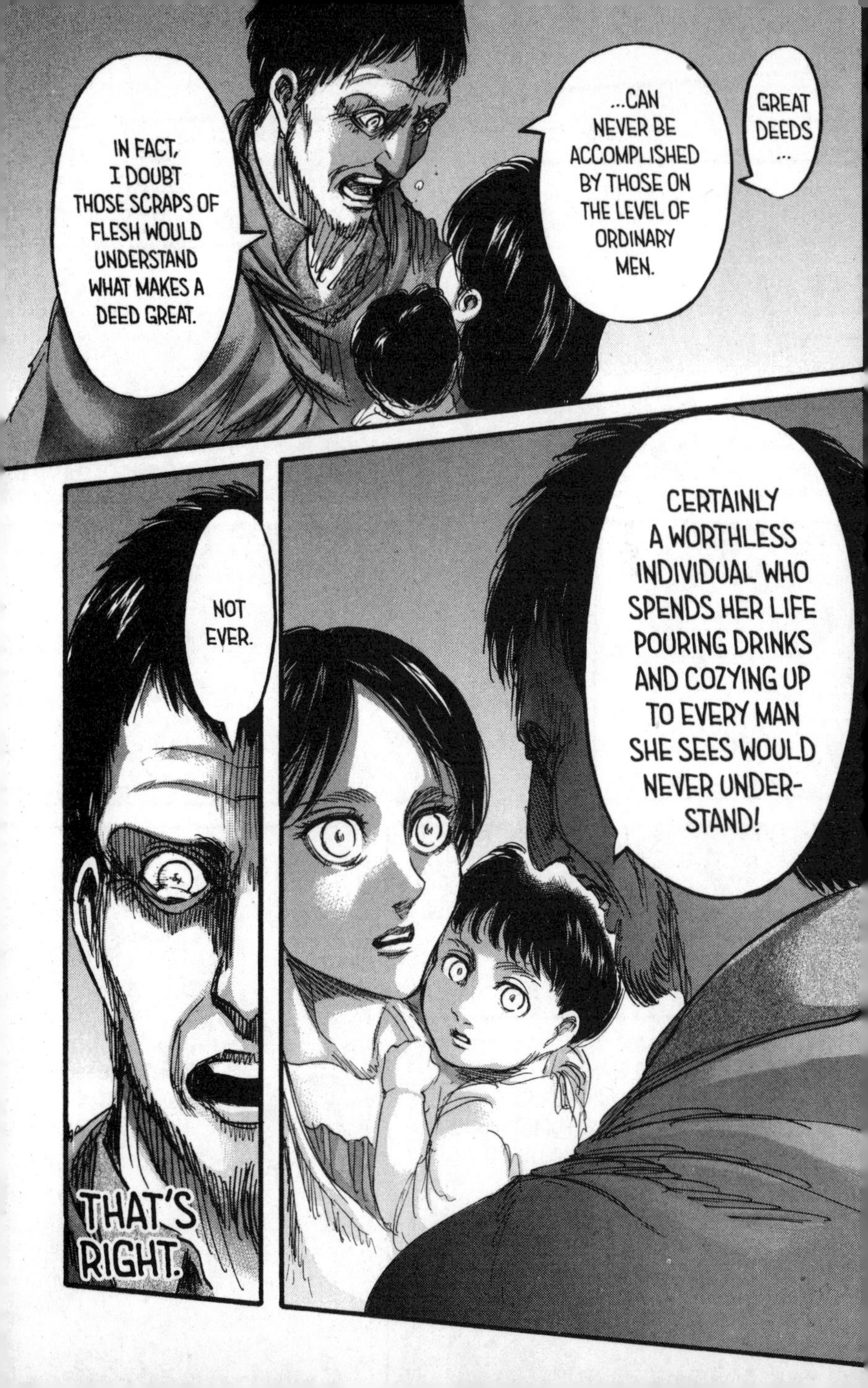
GREAT DEEDS ...
...CAN NEVER BE ACCOMPLISHED BY THOSE ON THE LEVEL OF ORDINARY MEN.
IN FACT, I DOUBT THOSE SCRAPS OF FLESH WOULD UNDERSTAND WHAT MAKES A DEED GREAT.
CERTAINLY A WORTHLESS INDIVIDUAL WHO SPENDS HER LIFE POURING DRINKS AND COZYING UP TO EVERY MAN SHE SEES WOULD NEVER UNDER-STAND!
NOT EVER.
THAT'S RIGHT.

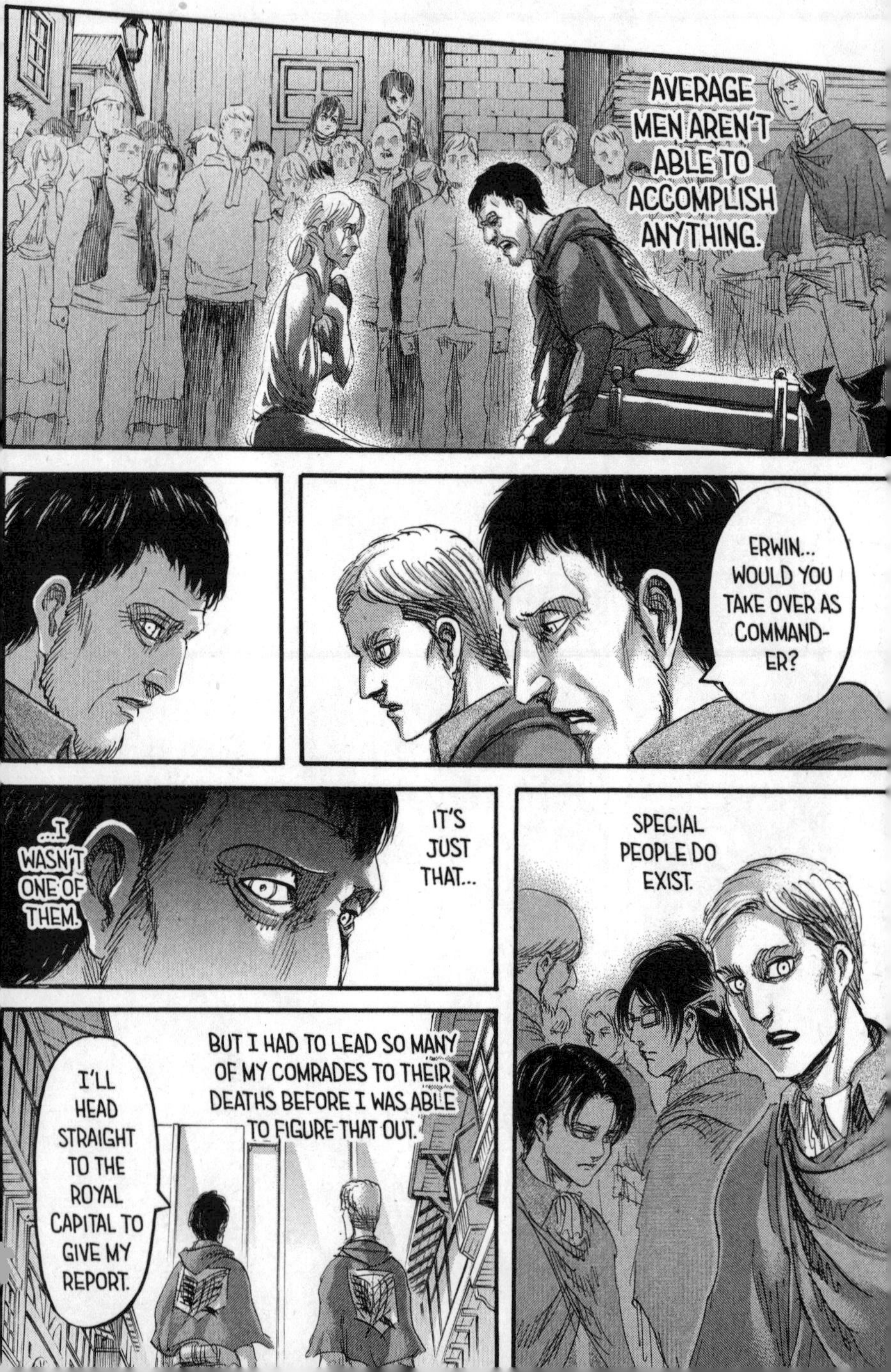
AVERAGE MEN AREN'T ABLE TO ACCOMPLISH ANYTHING.
ERWIN... WOULD YOU TAKE OVER AS COMMANDER?
SPECIAL PEOPLE DO EXIST.
IT'S JUST THAT...
...I WASN'T ONE OF THEM.
BUT I HAD TO LEAD SO MANY OF MY COMRADES TO THEIR DEATHS BEFORE I WAS ABLE TO FIGURE THAT OUT.
I'LL HEAD STRAIGHT TO THE ROYAL CAPITAL TO GIVE MY REPORT.

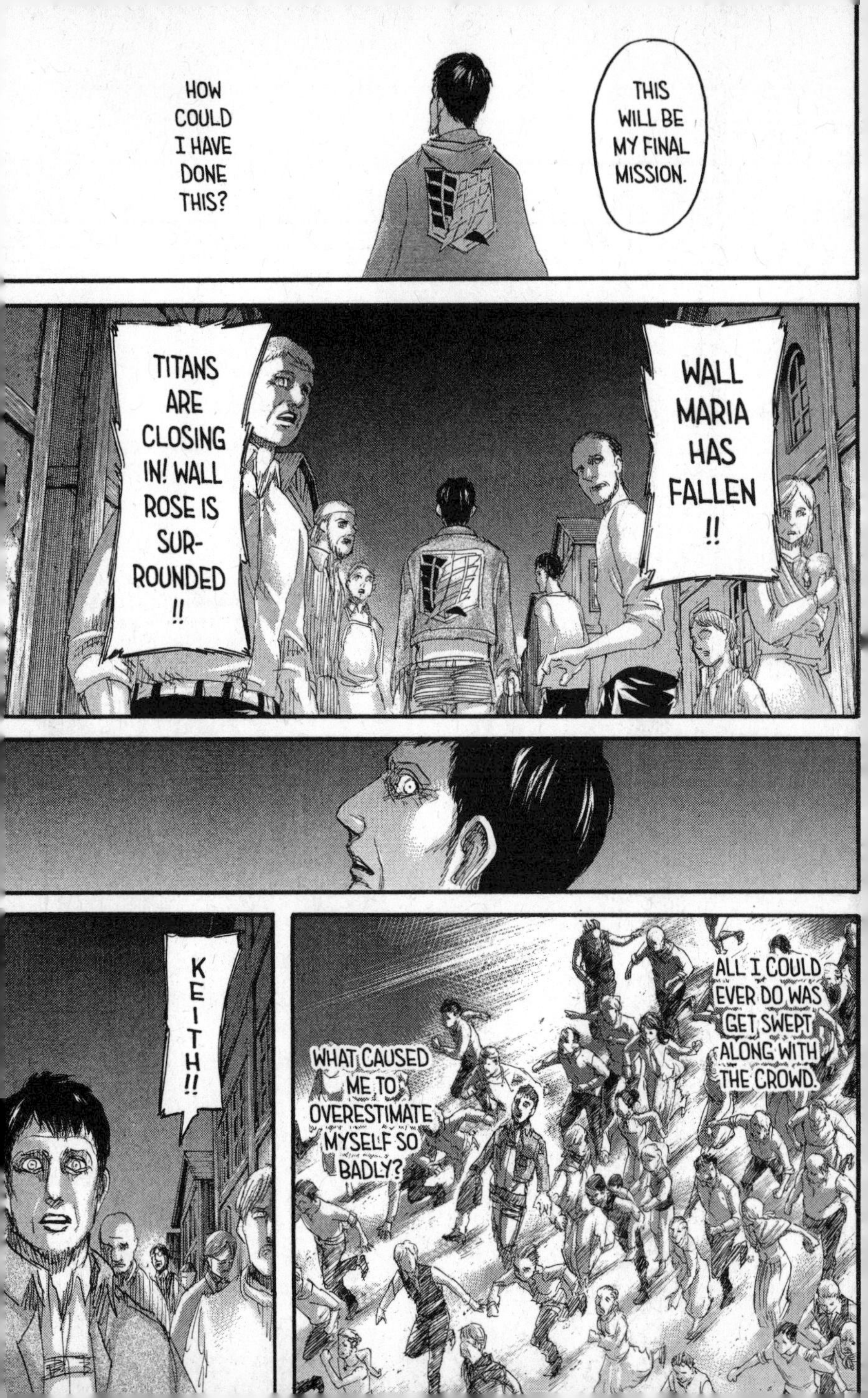
THIS WILL BE MY FINAL MISSION.
HOW COULD I HAVE DONE THIS?
WALL MARIA HAS FALLEN!!
TITANS ARE CLOSING IN! WALL ROSE IS SUR-ROUNDED!!
ALL I COULD EVER DO WAS GET SWEPT ALONG WITH THE CROWD.
WHAT CAUSED ME TO OVERESTIMATE MYSELF SO BADLY?
KEITH!!

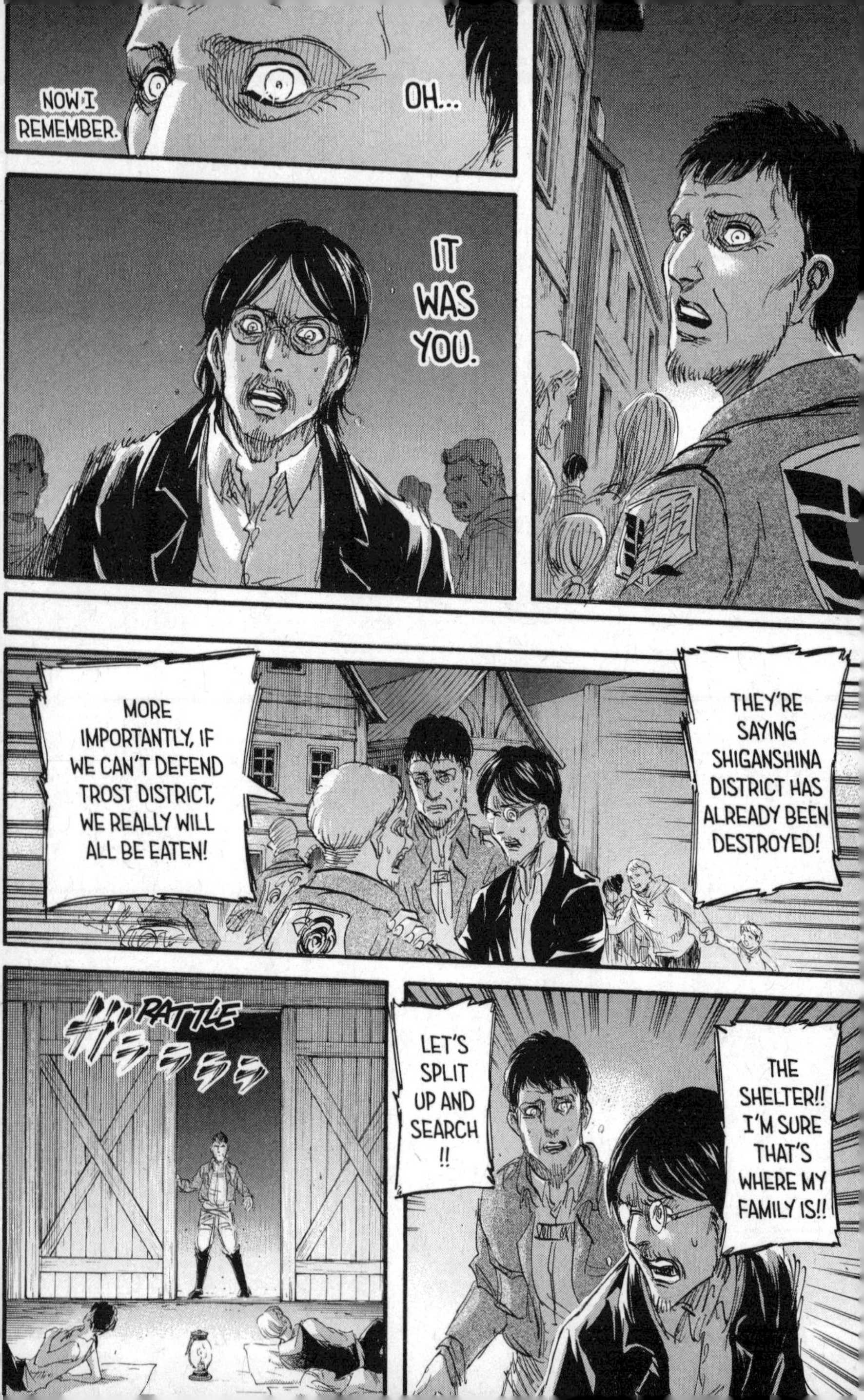
OH...
NOW I REMEMBER.
IT WAS YOU.
THEY'RE SAYING SHIGANSHINA DISTRICT HAS ALREADY BEEN DESTROYED!
MORE IMPORTANTLY, IF WE CAN'T DEFEND TROST DISTRICT, WE REALLY WILL ALL BE EATEN!
THE SHELTER!! I'M SURE THAT'S WHERE MY FAMILY IS!!
LET'S SPLIT UP AND SEARCH!!
RATTLE

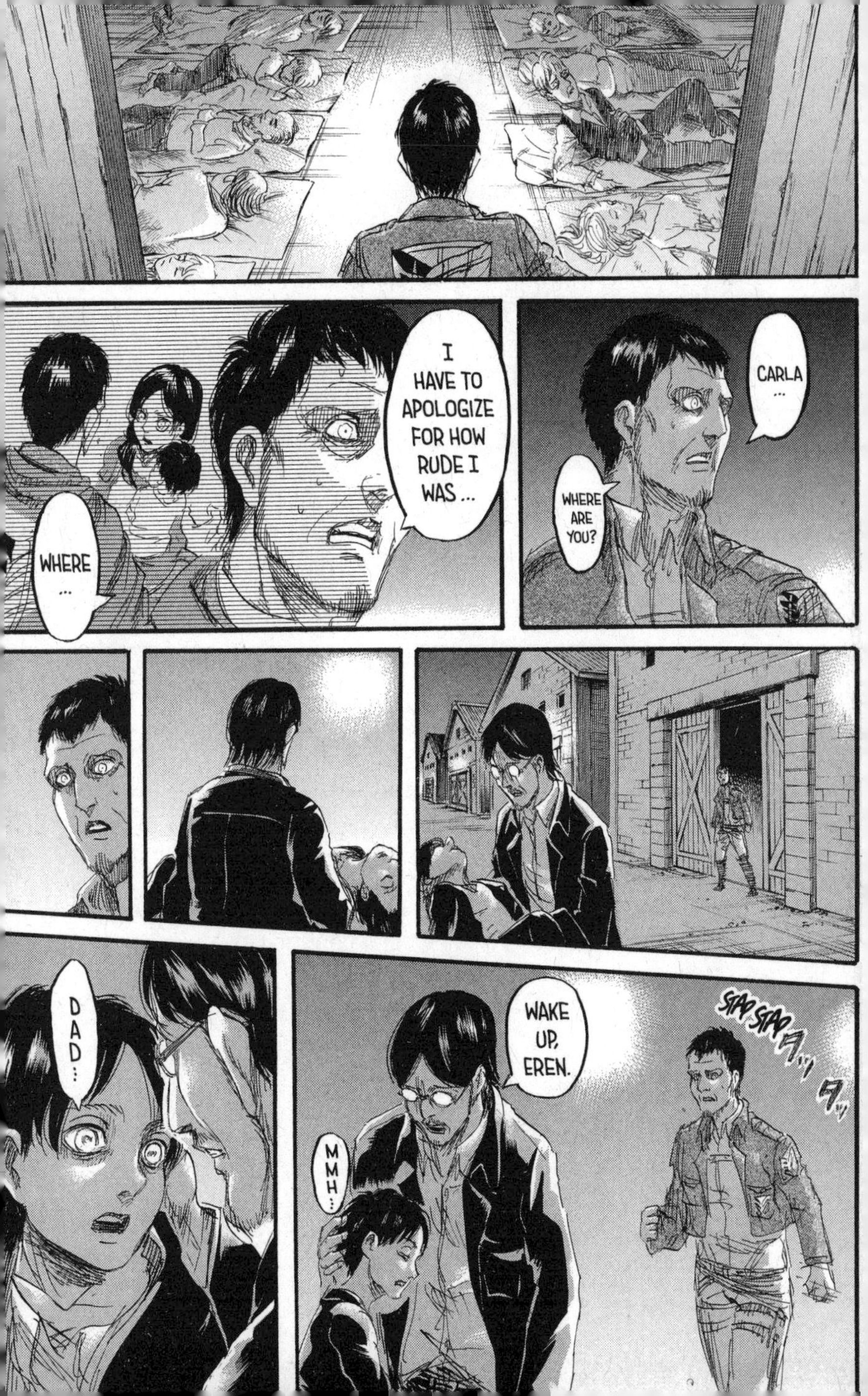
CARLA ...
WHERE ARE YOU?
I HAVE TO APOLOGIZE FOR HOW RUDE I WAS ...
WHERE ...
STAP STAP
WAKE UP, EREN.
MMH...
DAD...

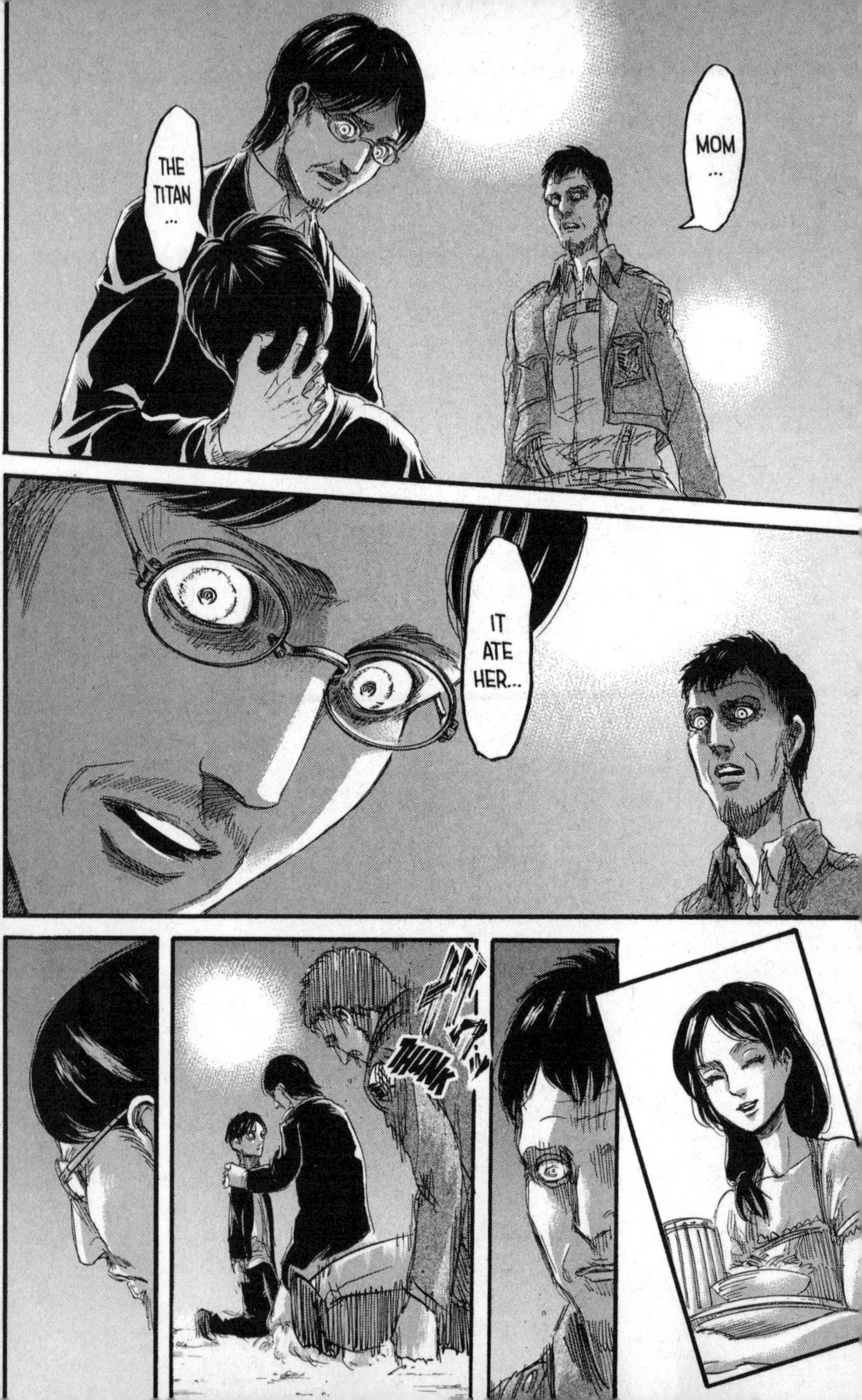
MOM ...
THE TITAN ...
IT ATE HER...
THUNK

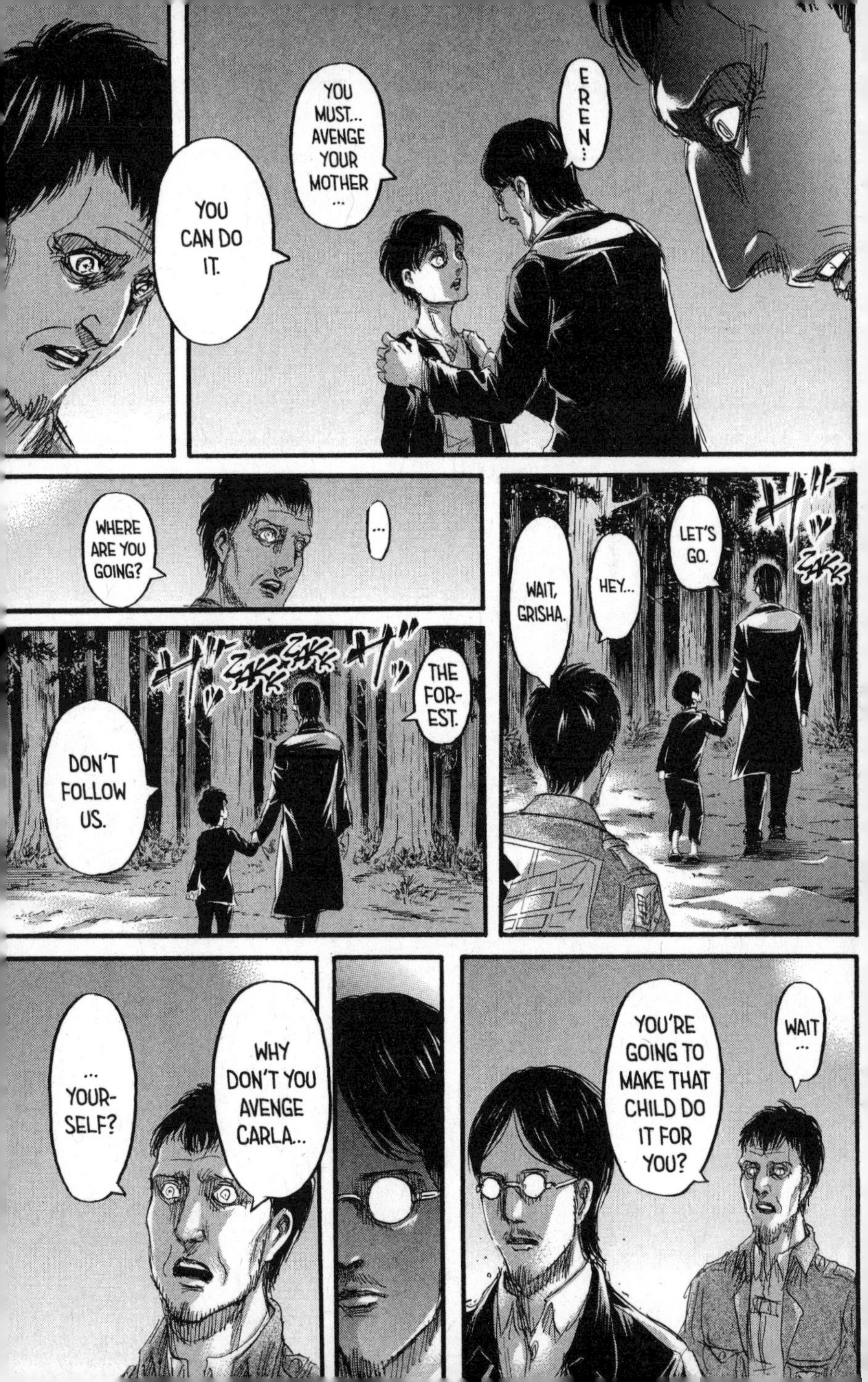
EREN...
YOU MUST... AVENGE YOUR MOTHER...
YOU CAN DO IT.
LET'S GO.
HEY...
WAIT, GRISHA.
ZAK
...
WHERE ARE YOU GOING?
ZAK ZAK
THE FOREST.
DON'T FOLLOW US.
WAIT...
YOU'RE GOING TO MAKE THAT CHILD DO IT FOR YOU?
WHY DON'T YOU AVENGE CARLA...
... YOURSELF?

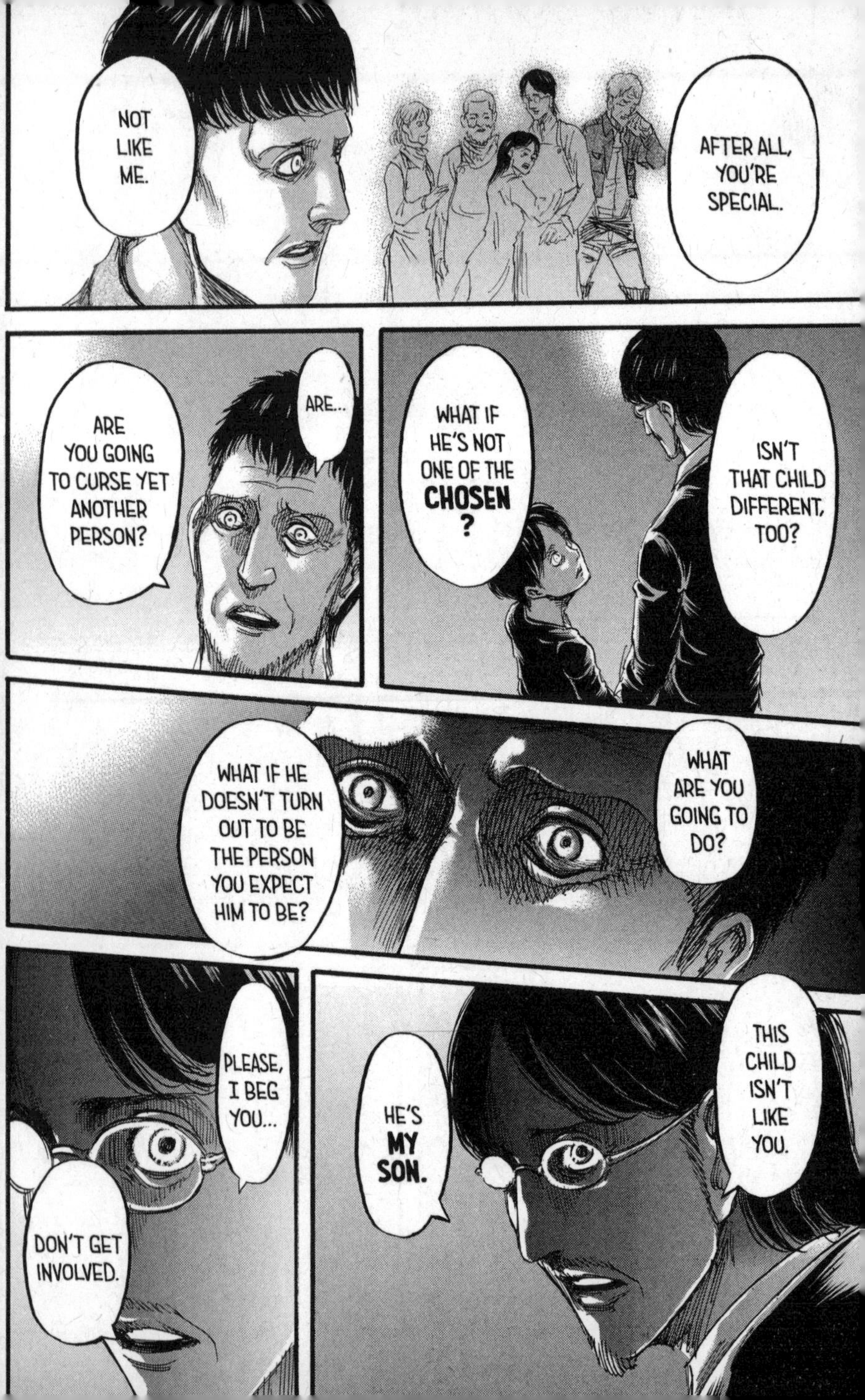
AFTER ALL, YOU'RE SPECIAL.
NOT LIKE ME.
ISN'T THAT CHILD DIFFERENT, TOO?
WHAT IF HE'S NOT ONE OF THE CHOSEN?
ARE...
ARE YOU GOING TO CURSE YET ANOTHER PERSON?
WHAT ARE YOU GOING TO DO?
WHAT IF HE DOESN'T TURN OUT TO BE THE PERSON YOU EXPECT HIM TO BE?
THIS CHILD ISN'T LIKE YOU.
HE'S MY SON.
PLEASE, I BEG YOU...
DON'T GET INVOLVED.

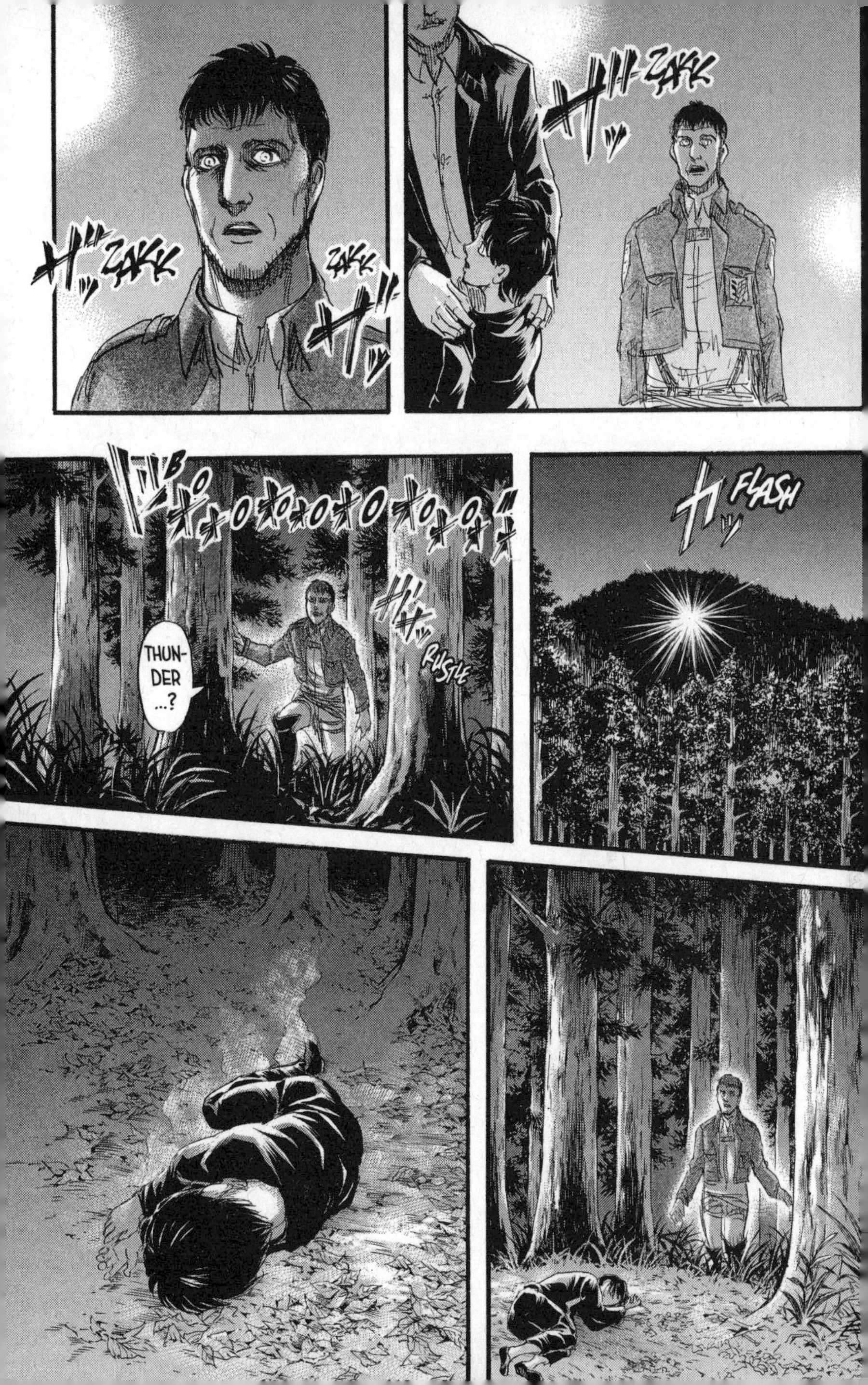
ZAKK
ZAKK
ZAKK
FLASH
THUNDER ...?
RUSTLE

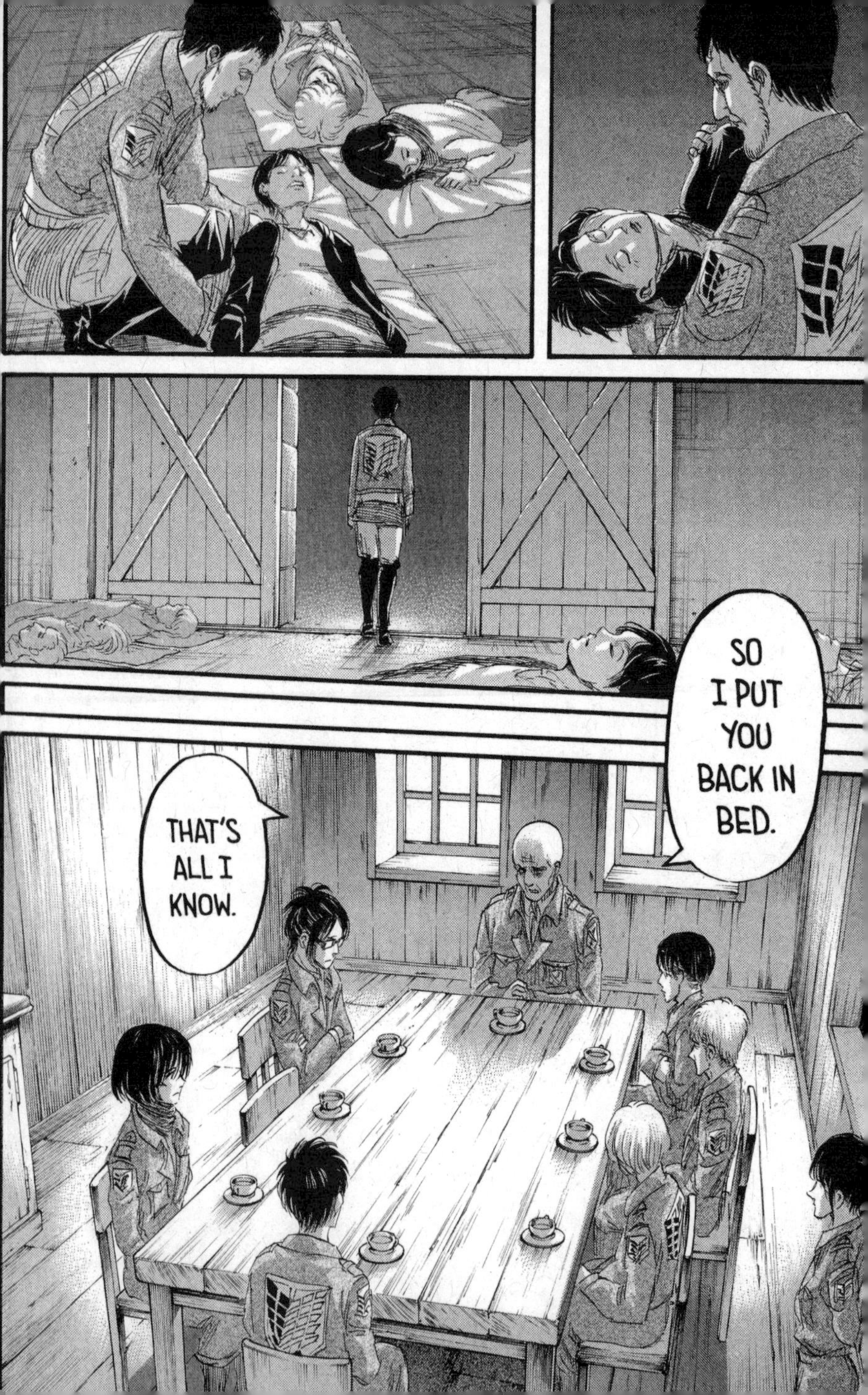
SO I PUT YOU BACK IN BED.
THAT'S ALL I KNOW.

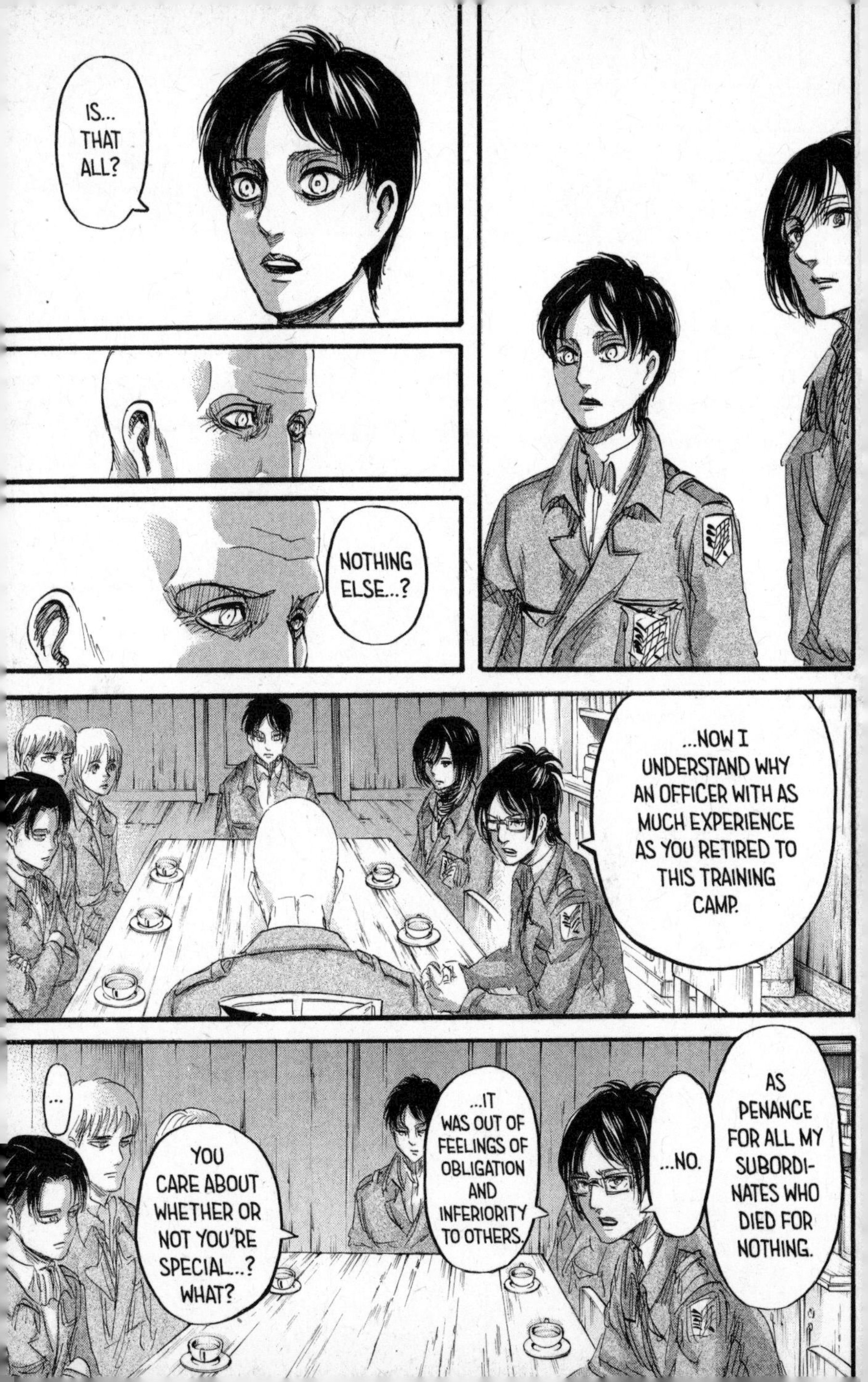
IS... THAT ALL?
NOTHING ELSE...?
...NOW I UNDERSTAND WHY AN OFFICER WITH AS MUCH EXPERIENCE AS YOU RETIRED TO THIS TRAINING CAMP.
AS PENANCE FOR ALL MY SUBORDI-NATES WHO DIED FOR NOTHING.
...NO.
...IT WAS OUT OF FEELINGS OF OBLIGATION AND INFERIORITY TO OTHERS.
YOU CARE ABOUT WHETHER OR NOT YOU'RE SPECIAL...? WHAT?
...

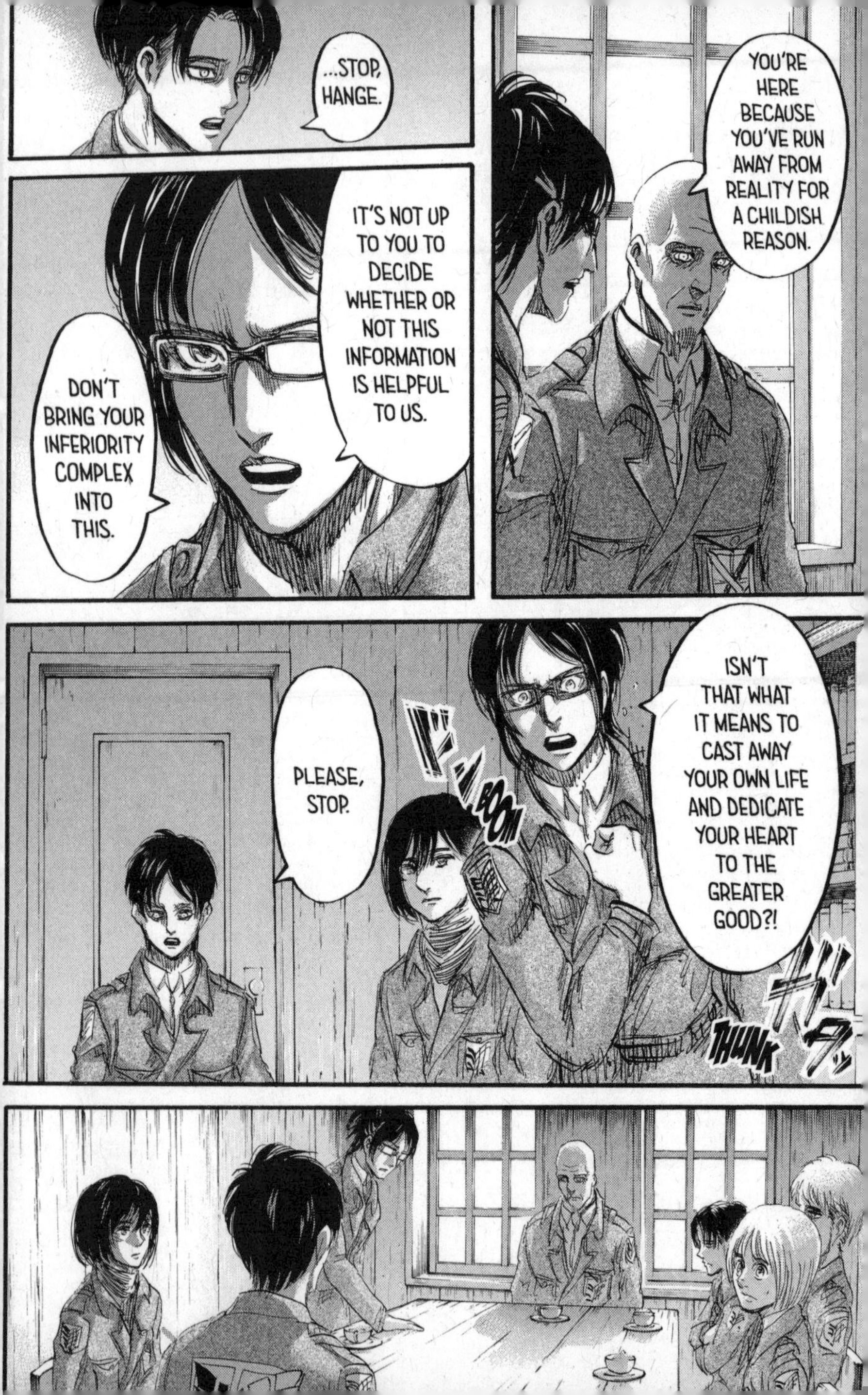
YOU'RE HERE BECAUSE YOU'VE RUN AWAY FROM REALITY FOR A CHILDISH REASON.
...STOP, HANGE.
IT'S NOT UP TO YOU TO DECIDE WHETHER OR NOT THIS INFORMATION IS HELPFUL TO US.
DON'T BRING YOUR INFERIORITY COMPLEX INTO THIS.
ISN'T THAT WHAT IT MEANS TO CAST AWAY YOUR OWN LIFE AND DEDICATE YOUR HEART TO THE GREATER GOOD?!
THUNK
BOOM
PLEASE, STOP.

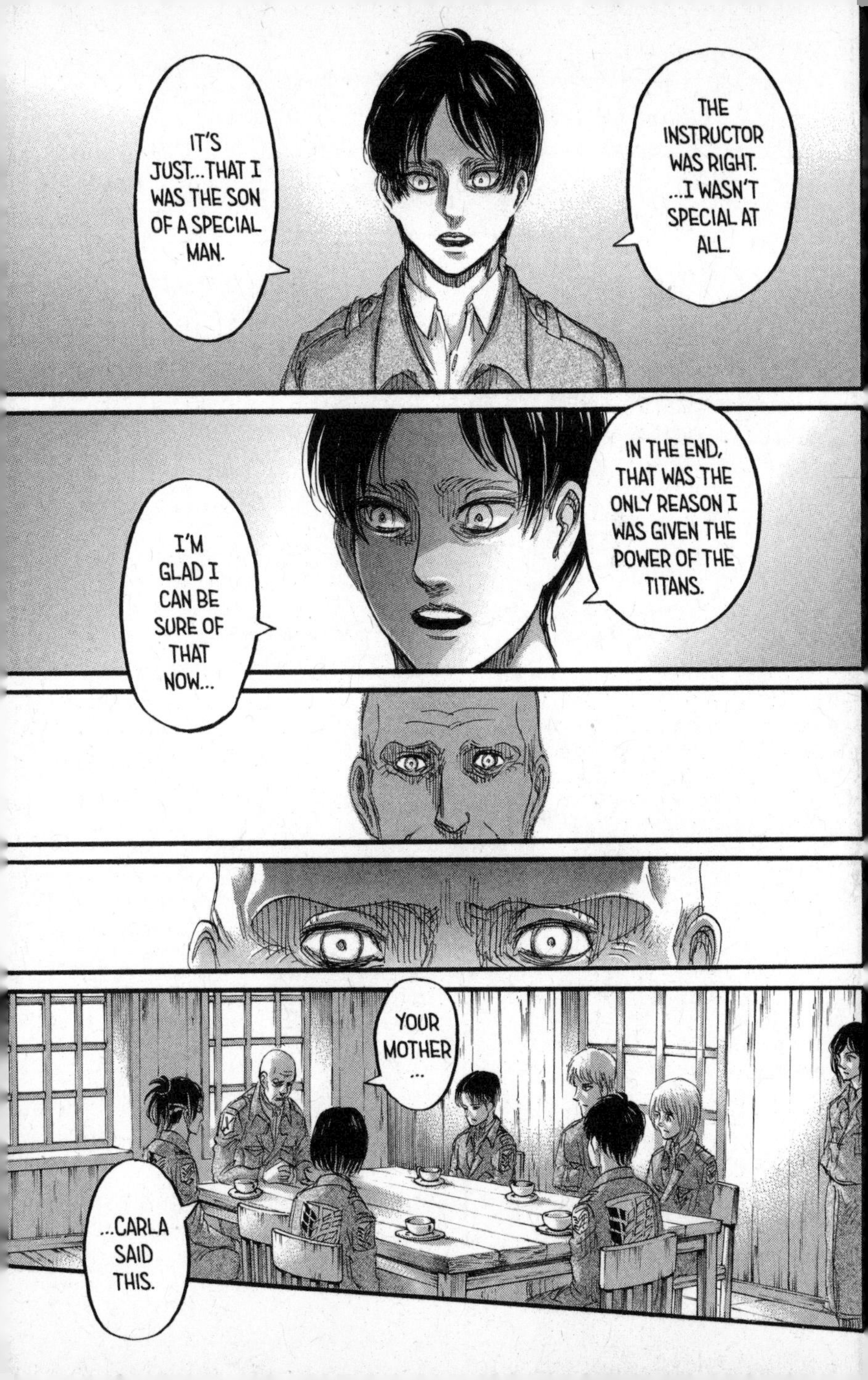
THE INSTRUCTOR WAS RIGHT. ...I WASN'T SPECIAL AT ALL.
IT'S JUST...THAT I WAS THE SON OF A SPECIAL MAN.
IN THE END, THAT WAS THE ONLY REASON I WAS GIVEN THE POWER OF THE TITANS.
I'M GLAD I CAN BE SURE OF THAT NOW...
YOUR MOTHER ...
...CARLA SAID THIS.

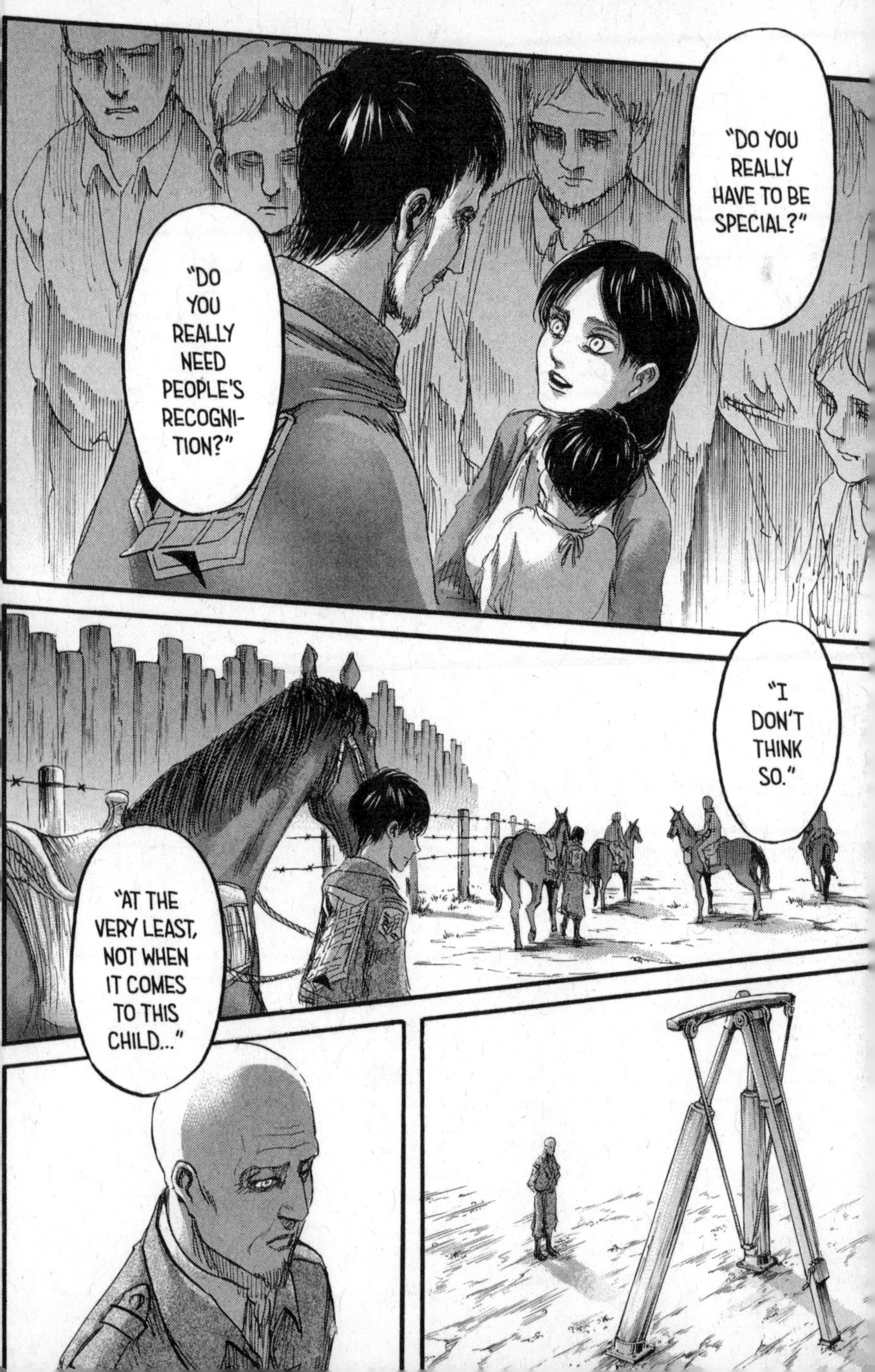
"DO YOU REALLY HAVE TO BE SPECIAL?"
"DO YOU REALLY NEED PEOPLE'S RECOGNI-TION?"
"I DON'T THINK SO."
"AT THE VERY LEAST, NOT WHEN IT COMES TO THIS CHILD..."

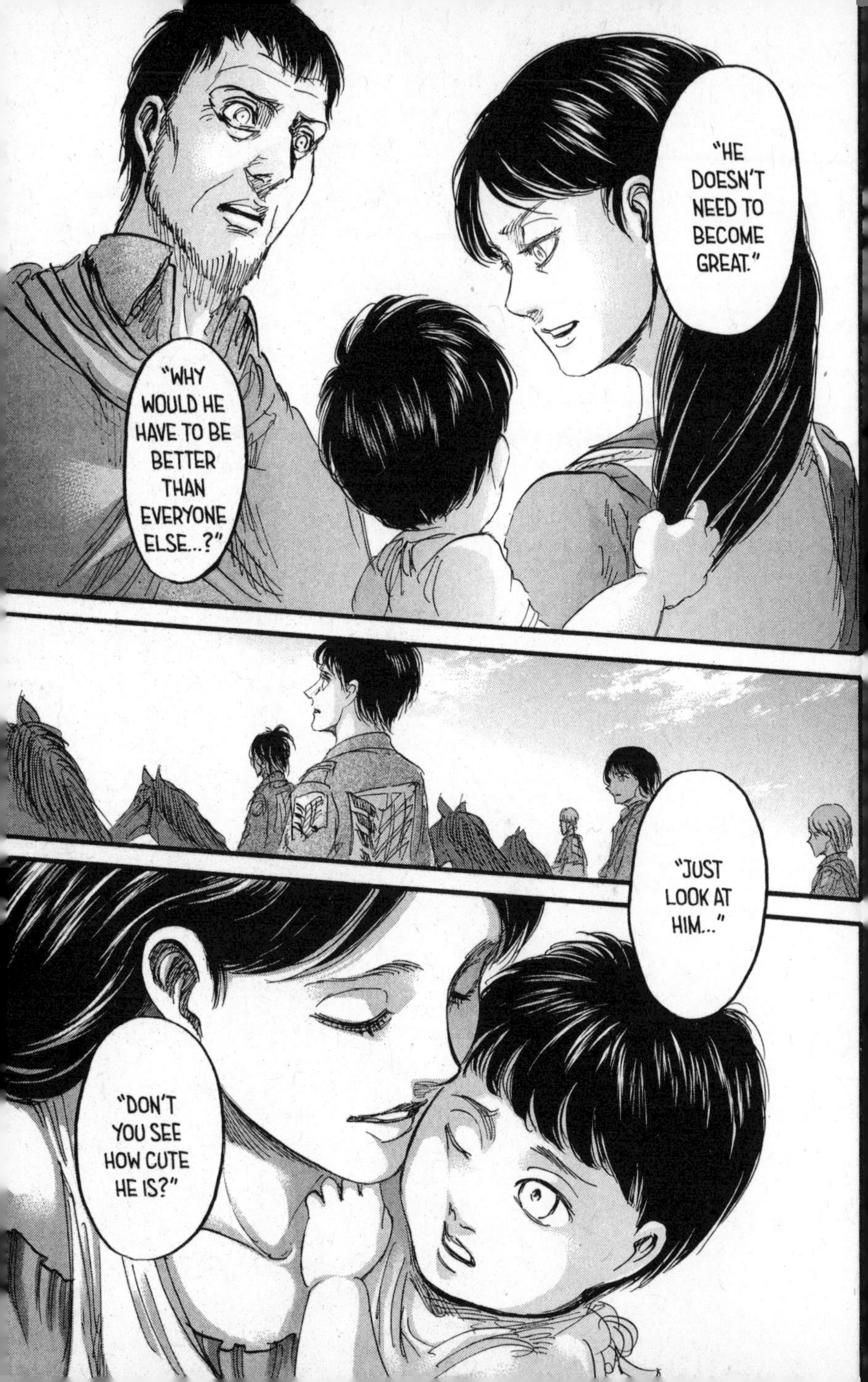
"HE DOESN'T NEED TO BECOME GREAT."
"WHY WOULD HE HAVE TO BE BETTER THAN EVERYONE ELSE...?"
"JUST LOOK AT HIM..."
"DON'T YOU SEE HOW CUTE HE IS?"

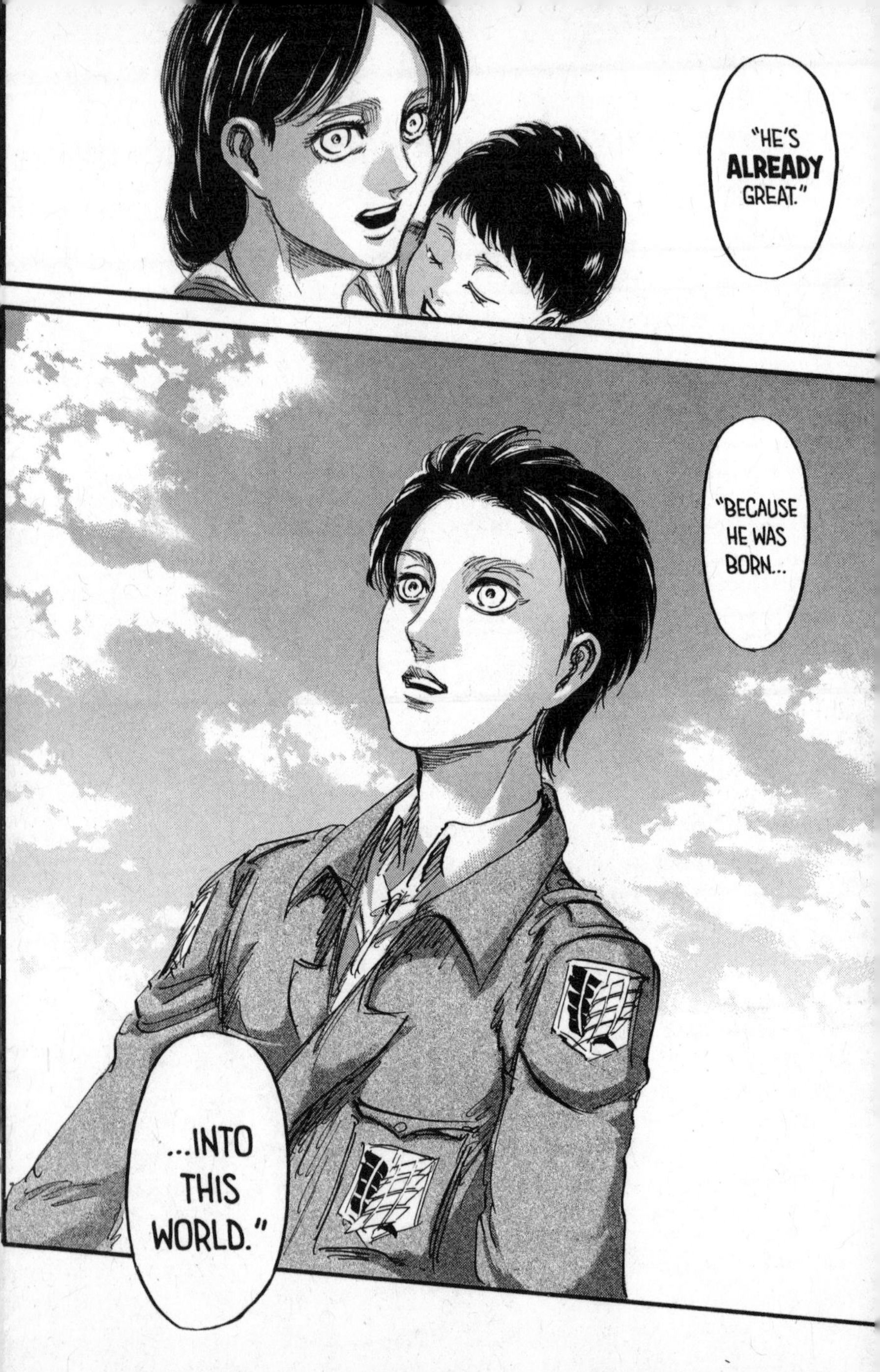
"HE'S **ALREADY** GREAT."
"BECAUSE HE WAS BORN...
...INTO THIS WORLD."

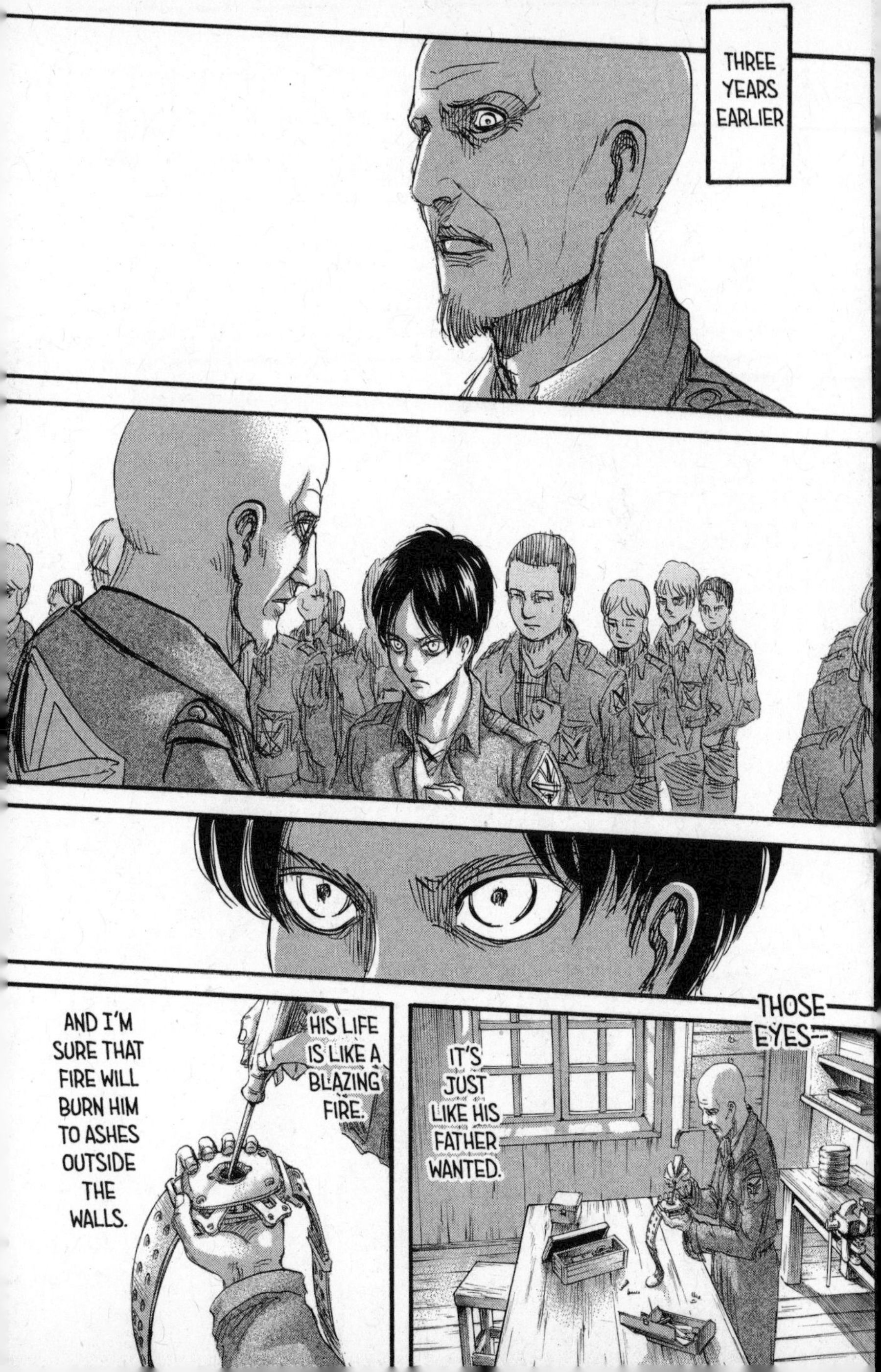
THREE YEARS EARLIER
THOSE EYES--
IT'S JUST LIKE HIS FATHER WANTED.
HIS LIFE IS LIKE A BLAZING FIRE.
AND I'M SURE THAT FIRE WILL BURN HIM TO ASHES OUTSIDE THE WALLS.

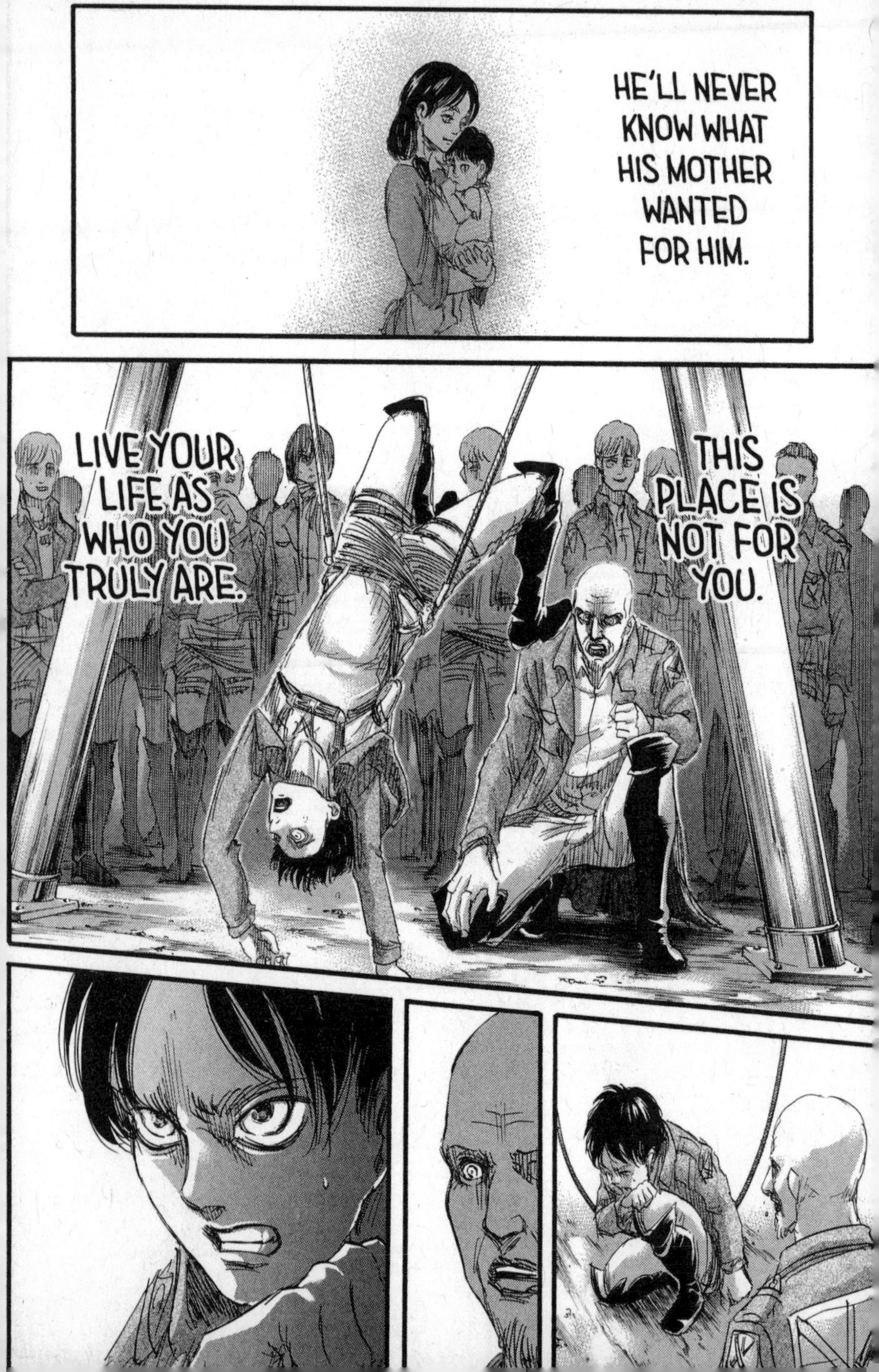
HE'LL NEVER KNOW WHAT HIS MOTHER WANTED FOR HIM.
THIS PLACE IS NOT FOR YOU.
LIVE YOUR LIFE AS WHO YOU TRULY ARE.

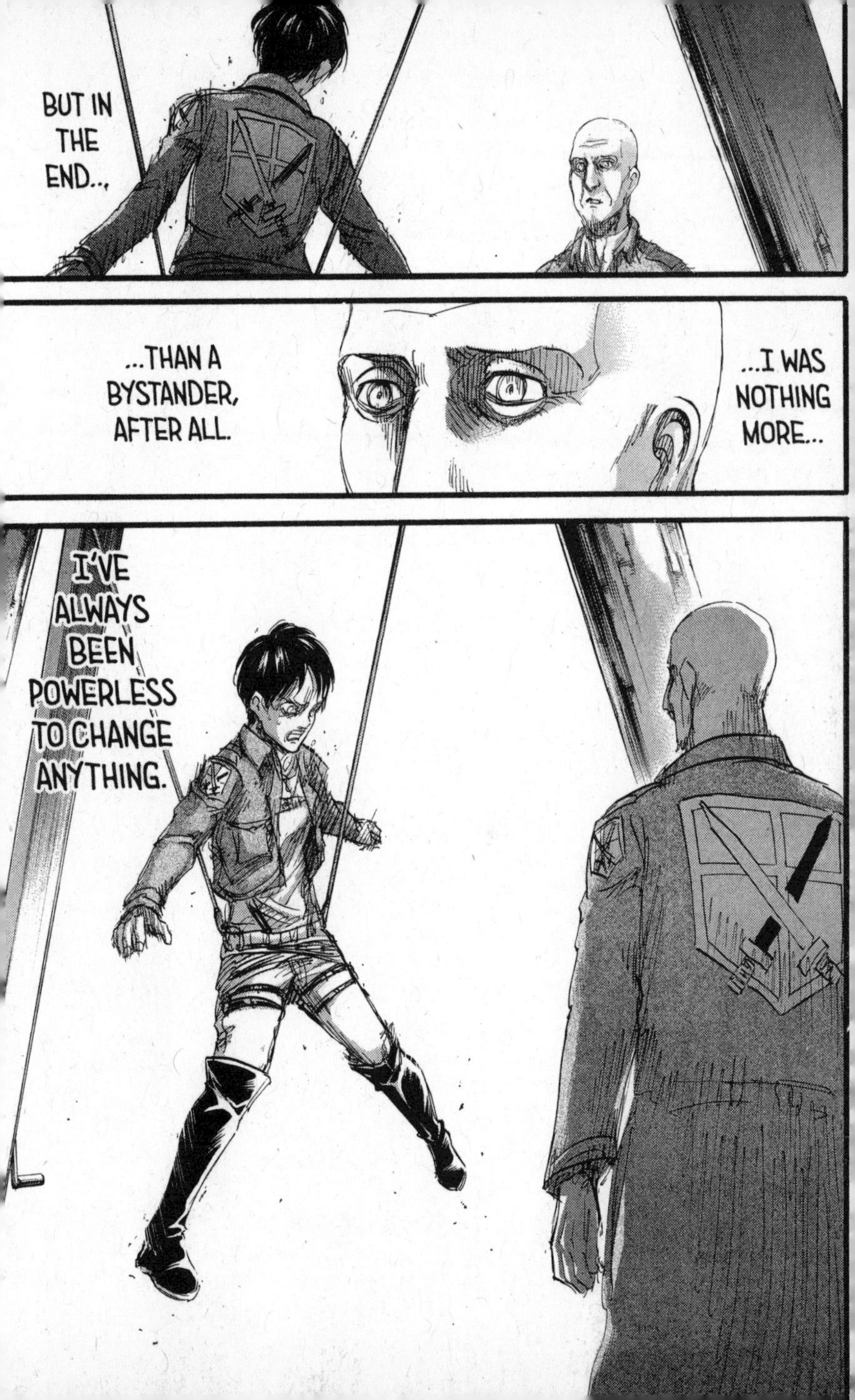
BUT IN THE END...
...I WAS NOTHING MORE...
...THAN A BYSTANDER, AFTER ALL.
I'VE ALWAYS BEEN POWERLESS TO CHANGE ANYTHING.

ATTACK on TITAN

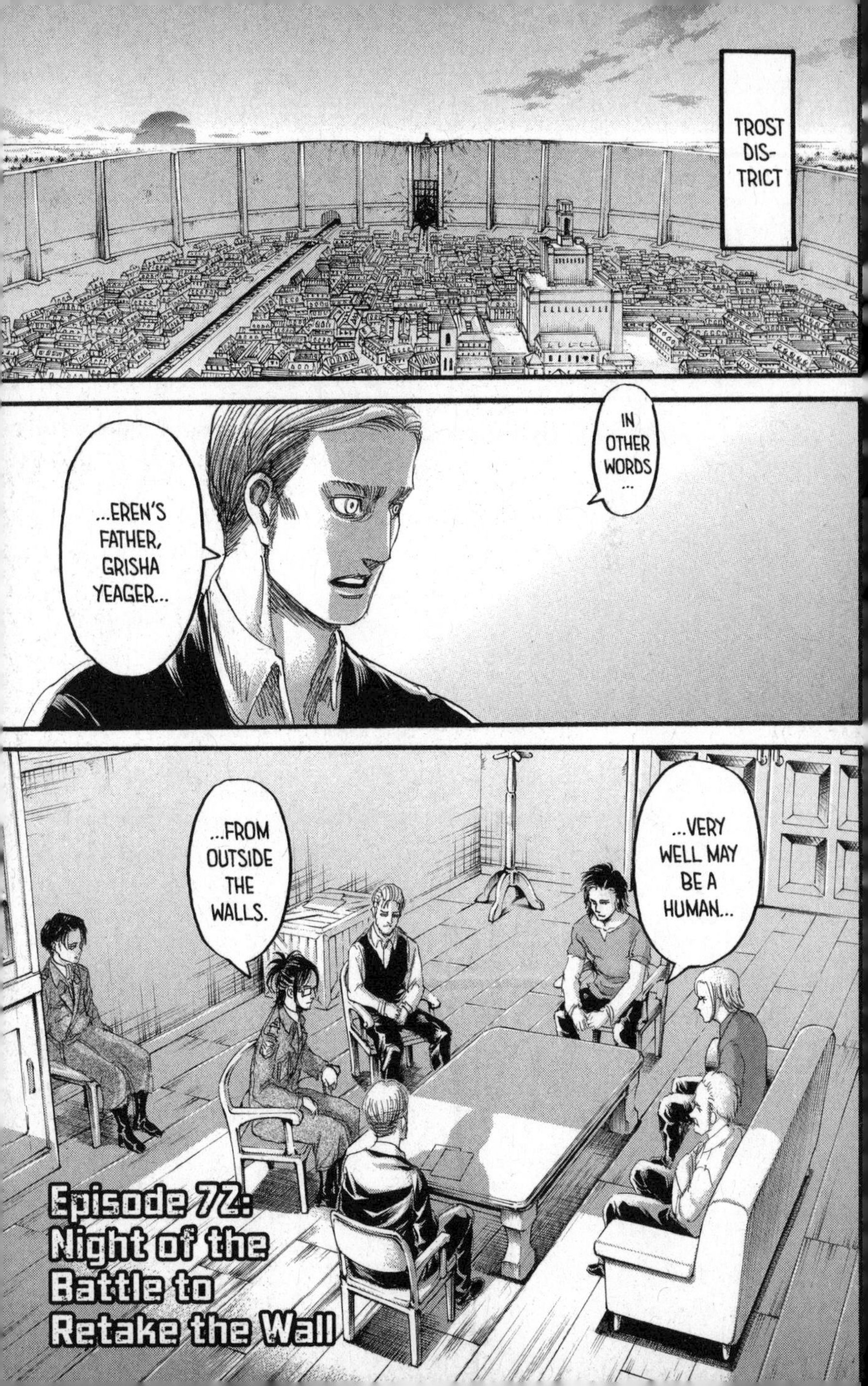
TROST DISTRICT
IN OTHER WORDS...
...EREN'S FATHER, GRISHA YEAGER...
...VERY WELL MAY BE A HUMAN...
...FROM OUTSIDE THE WALLS.
Episode 72: Night of the Battle to Retake the Wall

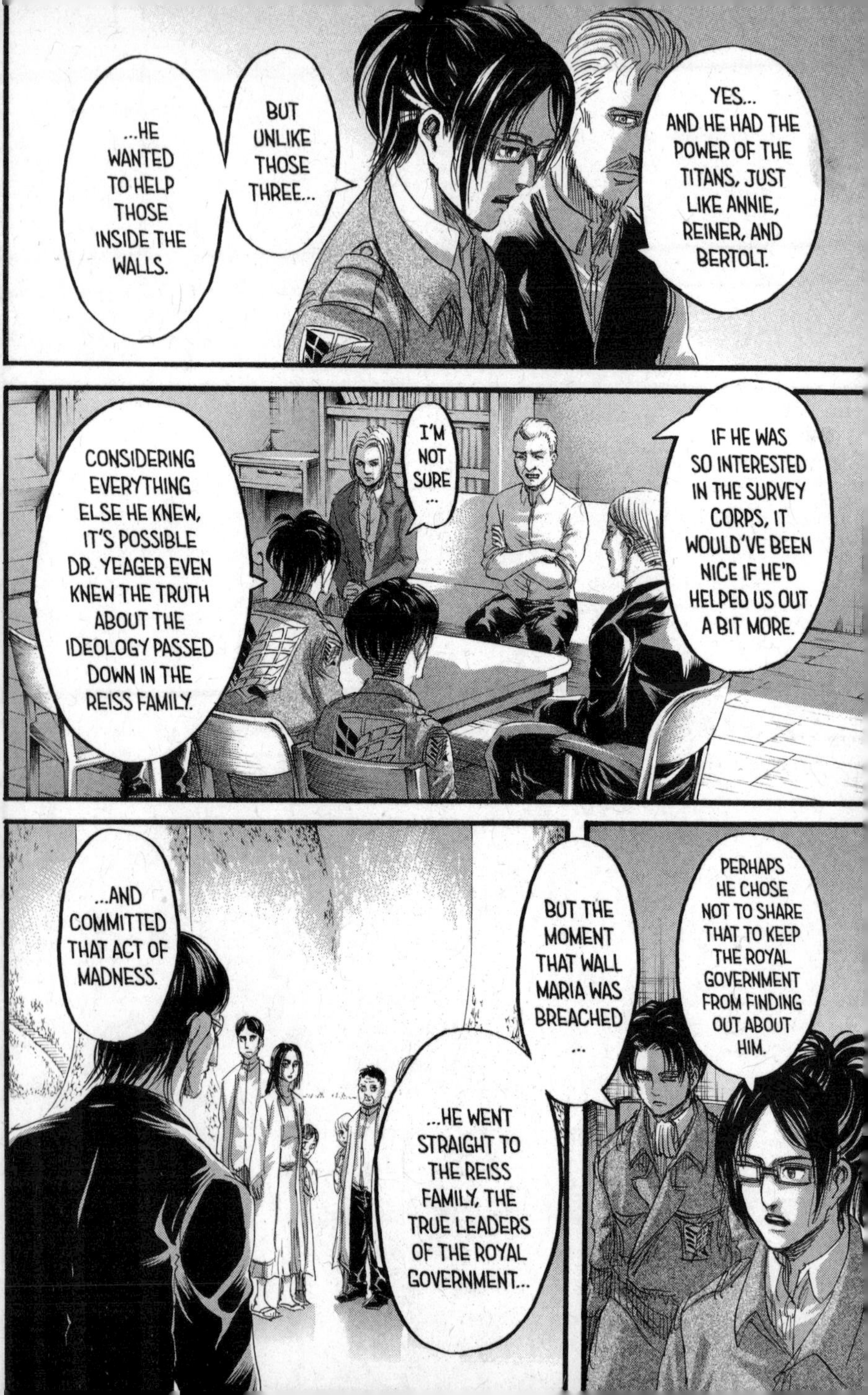
YES... AND HE HAD THE POWER OF THE TITANS, JUST LIKE ANNIE, REINER, AND BERTOLT.
BUT UNLIKE THOSE THREE...
...HE WANTED TO HELP THOSE INSIDE THE WALLS.
IF HE WAS SO INTERESTED IN THE SURVEY CORPS, IT WOULD'VE BEEN NICE IF HE'D HELPED US OUT A BIT MORE.
I'M NOT SURE ...
CONSIDERING EVERYTHING ELSE HE KNEW, IT'S POSSIBLE DR. YEAGER EVEN KNEW THE TRUTH ABOUT THE IDEOLOGY PASSED DOWN IN THE REISS FAMILY.
PERHAPS HE CHOSE NOT TO SHARE THAT TO KEEP THE ROYAL GOVERNMENT FROM FINDING OUT ABOUT HIM.
BUT THE MOMENT THAT WALL MARIA WAS BREACHED ...
...HE WENT STRAIGHT TO THE REISS FAMILY, THE TRUE LEADERS OF THE ROYAL GOVERNMENT...
...AND COMMITTED THAT ACT OF MADNESS.

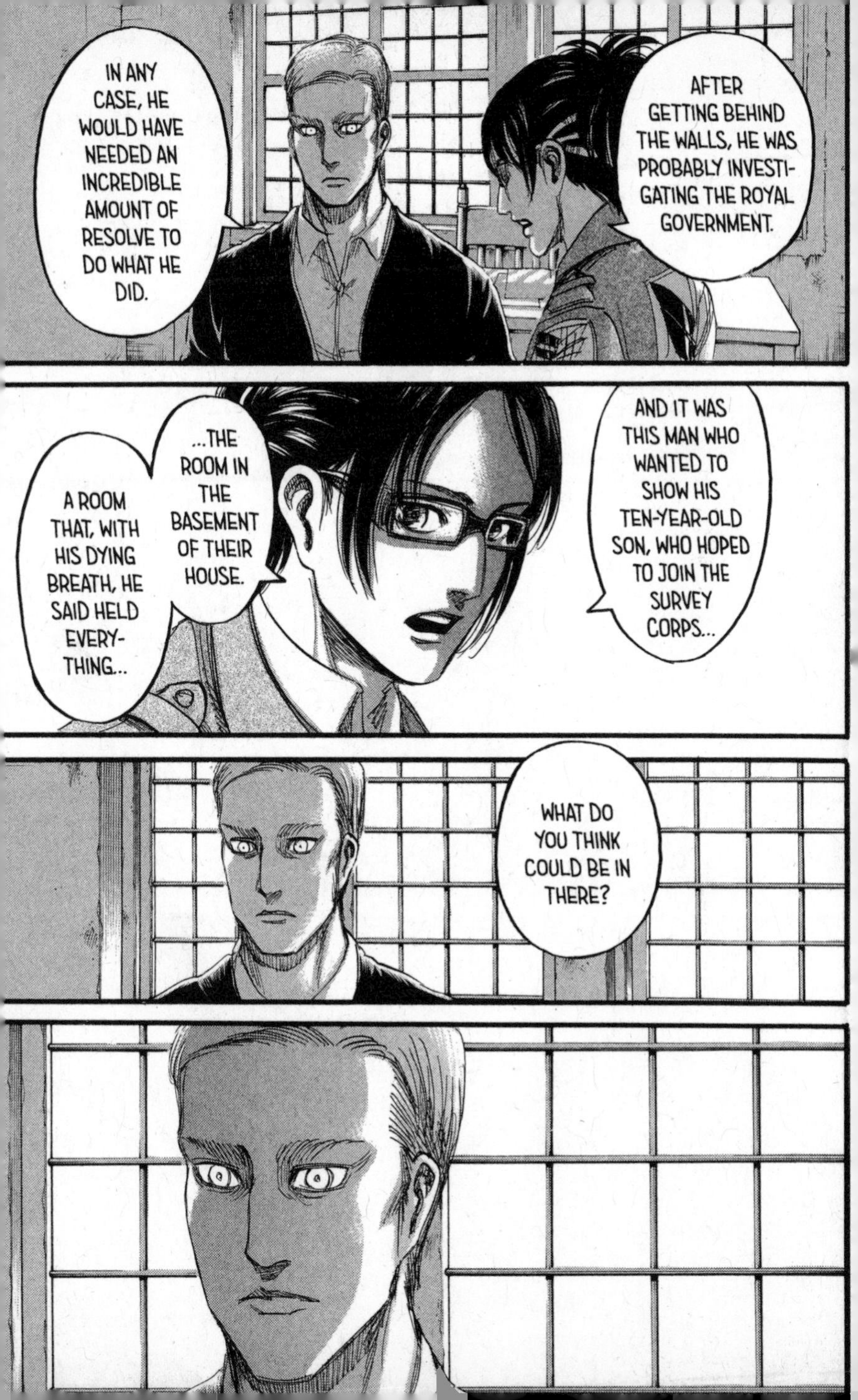
AFTER GETTING BEHIND THE WALLS, HE WAS PROBABLY INVESTI-GATING THE ROYAL GOVERNMENT.
IN ANY CASE, HE WOULD HAVE NEEDED AN INCREDIBLE AMOUNT OF RESOLVE TO DO WHAT HE DID.
AND IT WAS THIS MAN WHO WANTED TO SHOW HIS TEN-YEAR-OLD SON, WHO HOPED TO JOIN THE SURVEY CORPS...
...THE ROOM IN THE BASEMENT OF THEIR HOUSE.
A ROOM THAT, WITH HIS DYING BREATH, HE SAID HELD EVERY-THING...
WHAT DO YOU THINK COULD BE IN THERE?

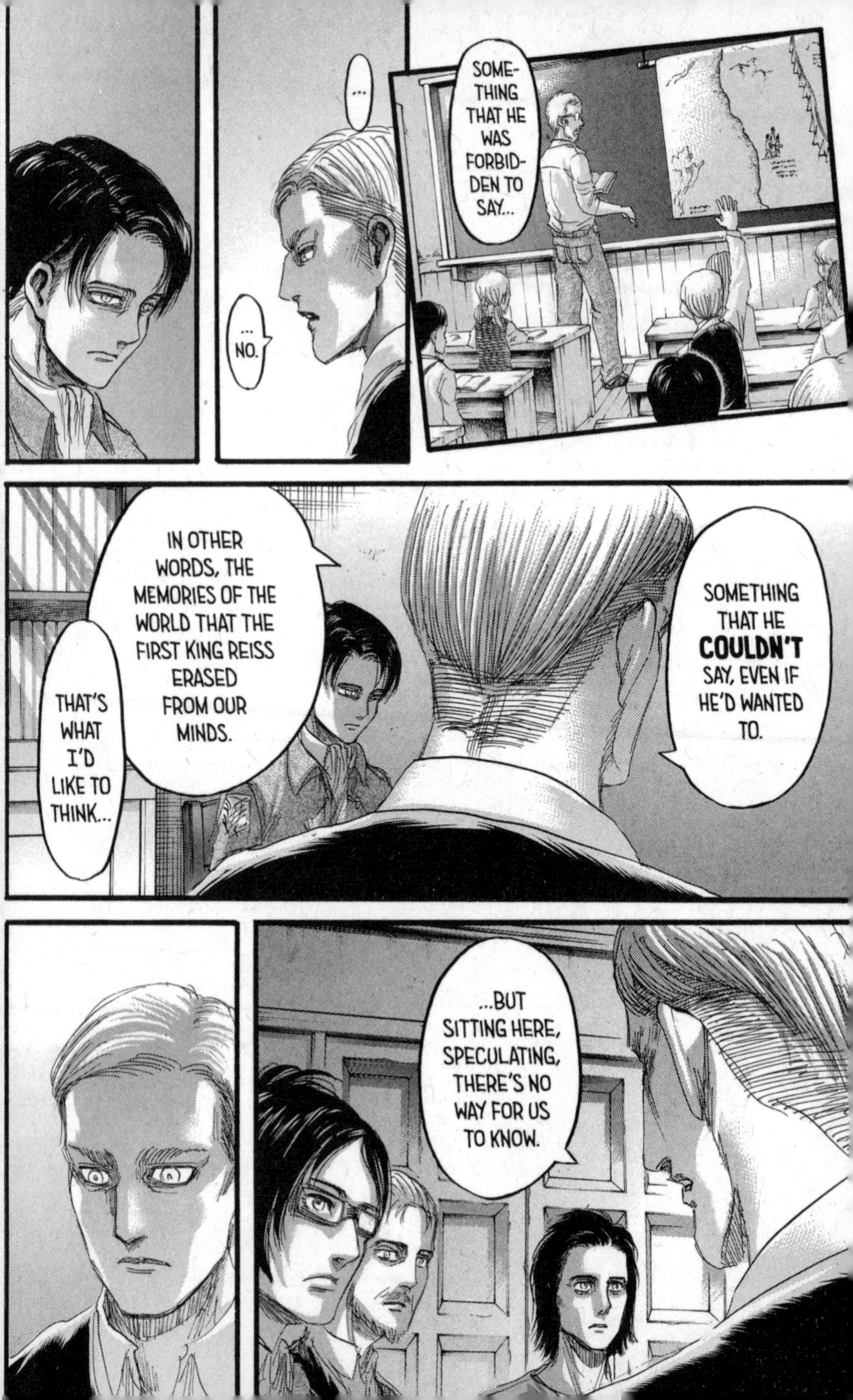
SOME-THING THAT HE WAS FORBID-DEN TO SAY...
...
... NO.
SOMETHING THAT HE **COULDN'T** SAY, EVEN IF HE'D WANTED TO.
IN OTHER WORDS, THE MEMORIES OF THE WORLD THAT THE FIRST KING REISS ERASED FROM OUR MINDS.
THAT'S WHAT I'D LIKE TO THINK...
...BUT SITTING HERE, SPECULATING, THERE'S NO WAY FOR US TO KNOW.

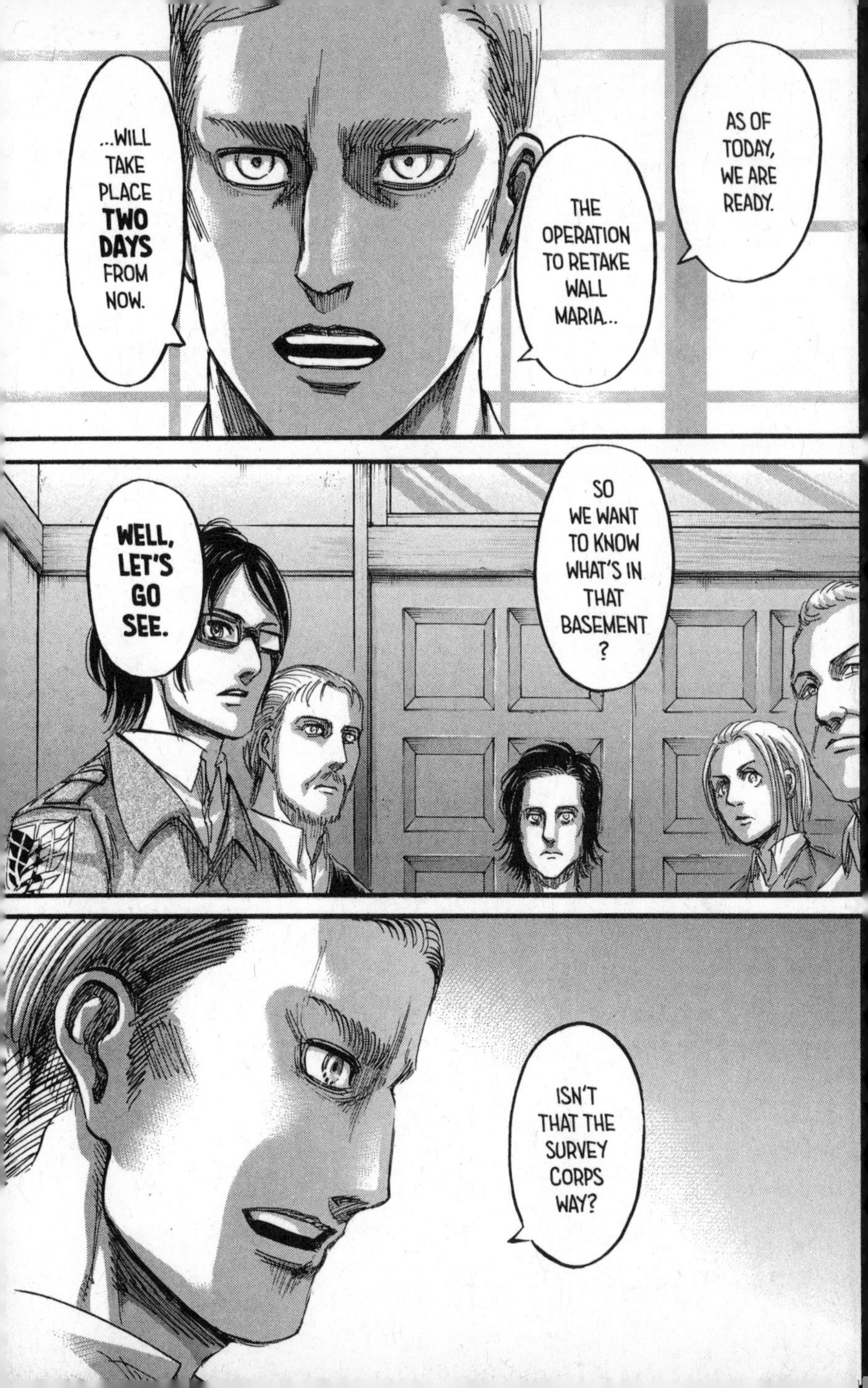
AS OF TODAY, WE ARE READY.
THE OPERATION TO RETAKE WALL MARIA...
...WILL TAKE PLACE **TWO DAYS** FROM NOW.
SO WE WANT TO KNOW WHAT'S IN THAT BASEMENT?
WELL, LET'S GO SEE.
ISN'T THAT THE SURVEY CORPS WAY?

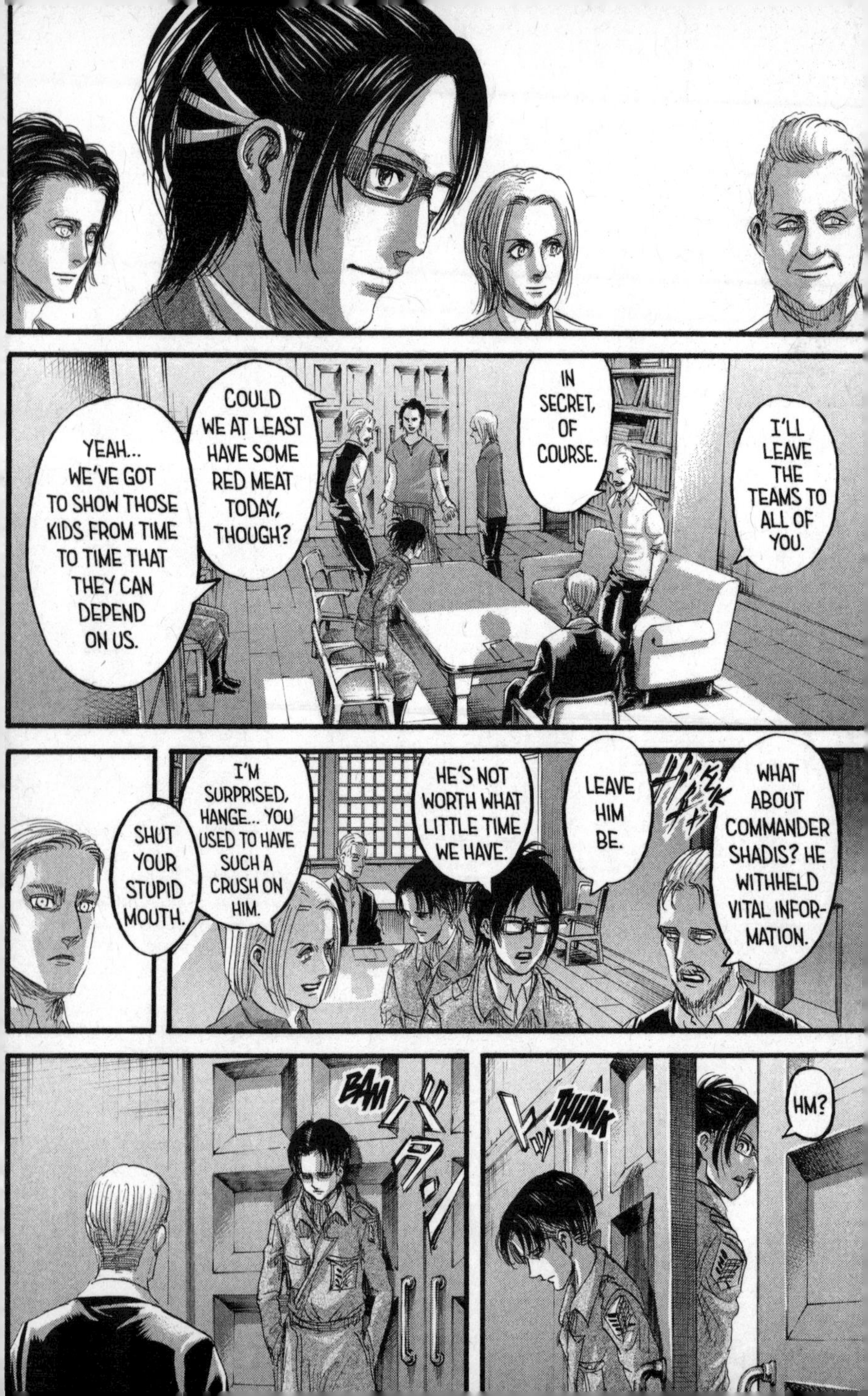
I'LL LEAVE THE TEAMS TO ALL OF YOU.
IN SECRET, OF COURSE.
COULD WE AT LEAST HAVE SOME RED MEAT TODAY, THOUGH?
YEAH... WE'VE GOT TO SHOW THOSE KIDS FROM TIME TO TIME THAT THEY CAN DEPEND ON US.
WHAT ABOUT COMMANDER SHADIS? HE WITHHELD VITAL INFOR-MATION.
LEAVE HIM BE.
HE'S NOT WORTH WHAT LITTLE TIME WE HAVE.
I'M SURPRISED, HANGE... YOU USED TO HAVE SUCH A CRUSH ON HIM.
SHUT YOUR STUPID MOUTH.
HM?
THUNK
BAM

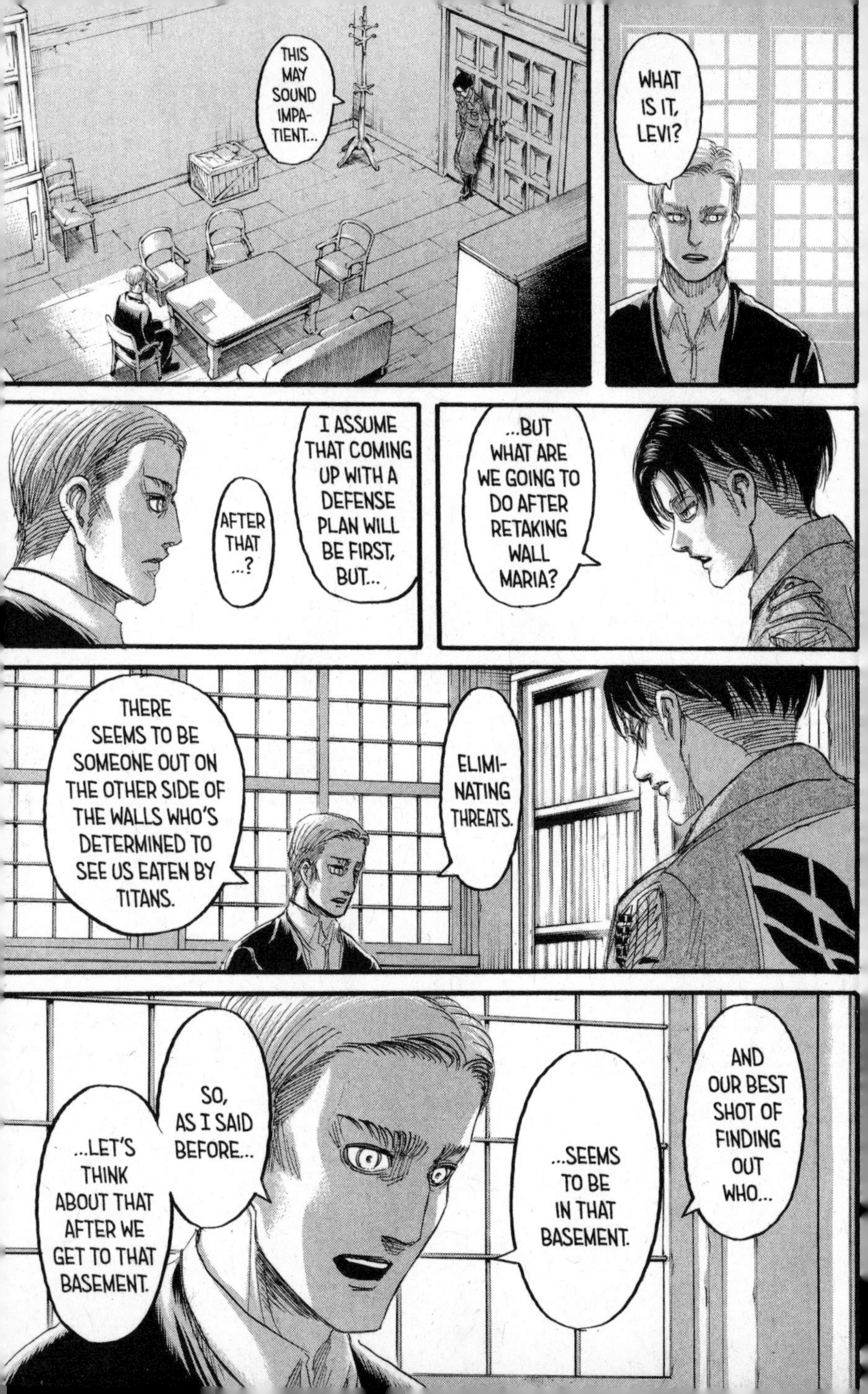
WHAT IS IT, LEVI?
THIS MAY SOUND IMPATIENT...
...BUT WHAT ARE WE GOING TO DO AFTER RETAKING WALL MARIA?
I ASSUME THAT COMING UP WITH A DEFENSE PLAN WILL BE FIRST, BUT...
AFTER THAT ...?
ELIMINATING THREATS.
THERE SEEMS TO BE SOMEONE OUT ON THE OTHER SIDE OF THE WALLS WHO'S DETERMINED TO SEE US EATEN BY TITANS.
AND OUR BEST SHOT OF FINDING OUT WHO...
...SEEMS TO BE IN THAT BASEMENT.
SO, AS I SAID BEFORE...
...LET'S THINK ABOUT THAT AFTER WE GET TO THAT BASEMENT.

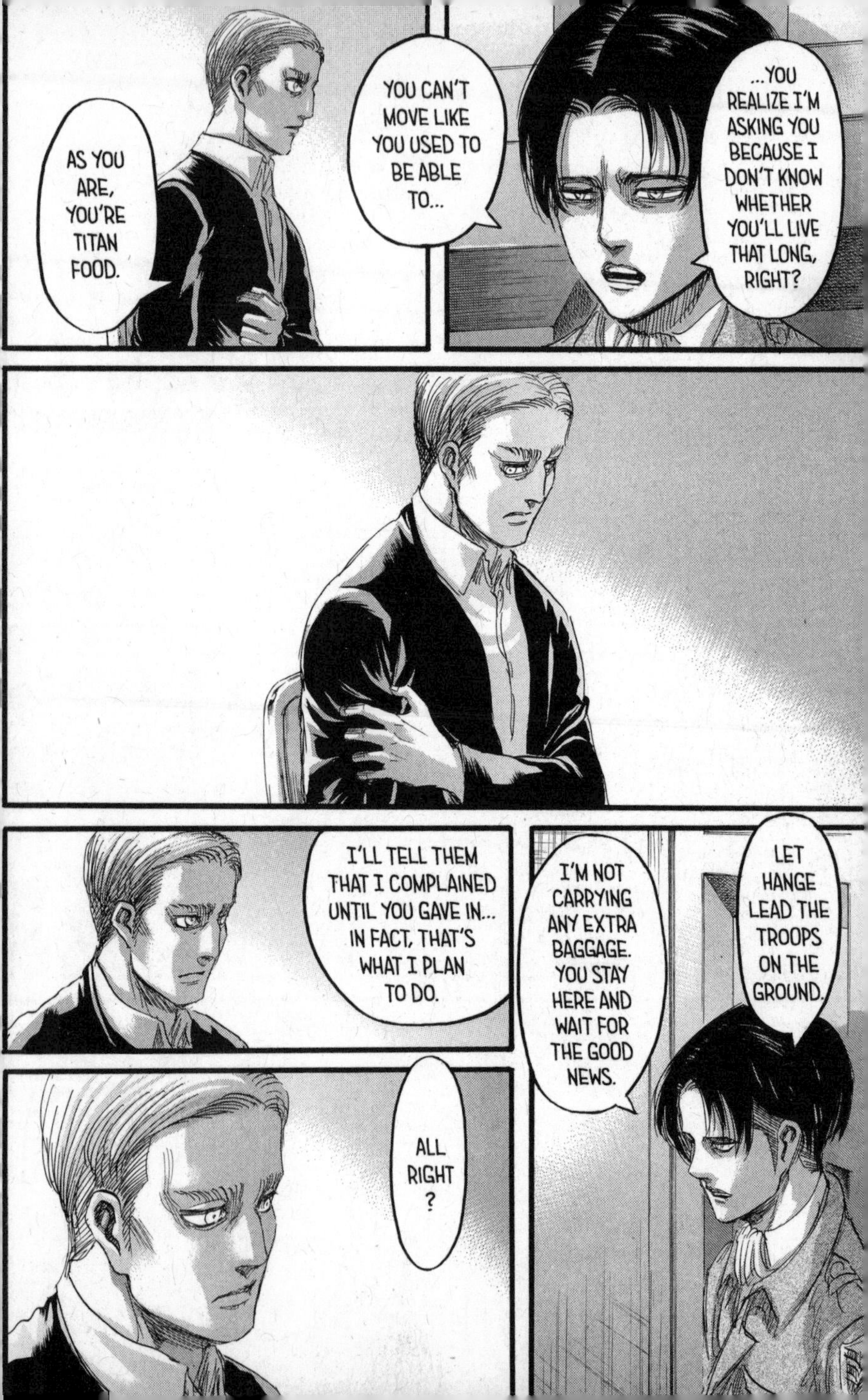
...YOU REALIZE I'M ASKING YOU BECAUSE I DON'T KNOW WHETHER YOU'LL LIVE THAT LONG, RIGHT?
YOU CAN'T MOVE LIKE YOU USED TO BE ABLE TO...
AS YOU ARE, YOU'RE TITAN FOOD.
LET HANGE LEAD THE TROOPS ON THE GROUND.
I'M NOT CARRYING ANY EXTRA BAGGAGE. YOU STAY HERE AND WAIT FOR THE GOOD NEWS.
I'LL TELL THEM THAT I COMPLAINED UNTIL YOU GAVE IN... IN FACT, THAT'S WHAT I PLAN TO DO.
ALL RIGHT?

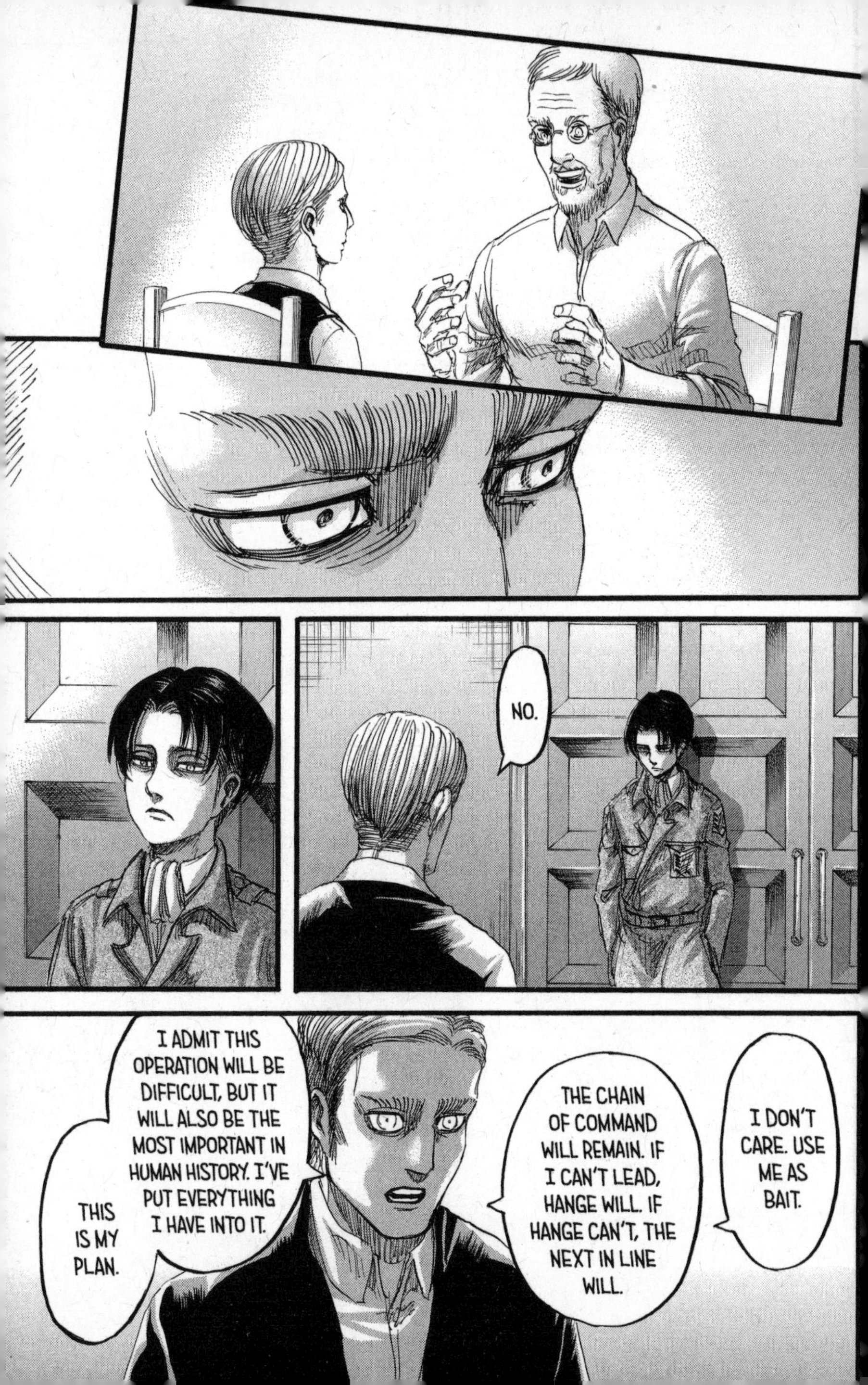
NO.
I DON'T CARE. USE ME AS BAIT.
THE CHAIN OF COMMAND WILL REMAIN. IF I CAN'T LEAD, HANGE WILL. IF HANGE CAN'T, THE NEXT IN LINE WILL.
I ADMIT THIS OPERATION WILL BE DIFFICULT, BUT IT WILL ALSO BE THE MOST IMPORTANT IN HUMAN HISTORY. I'VE PUT EVERYTHING I HAVE INTO IT.
THIS IS MY PLAN.

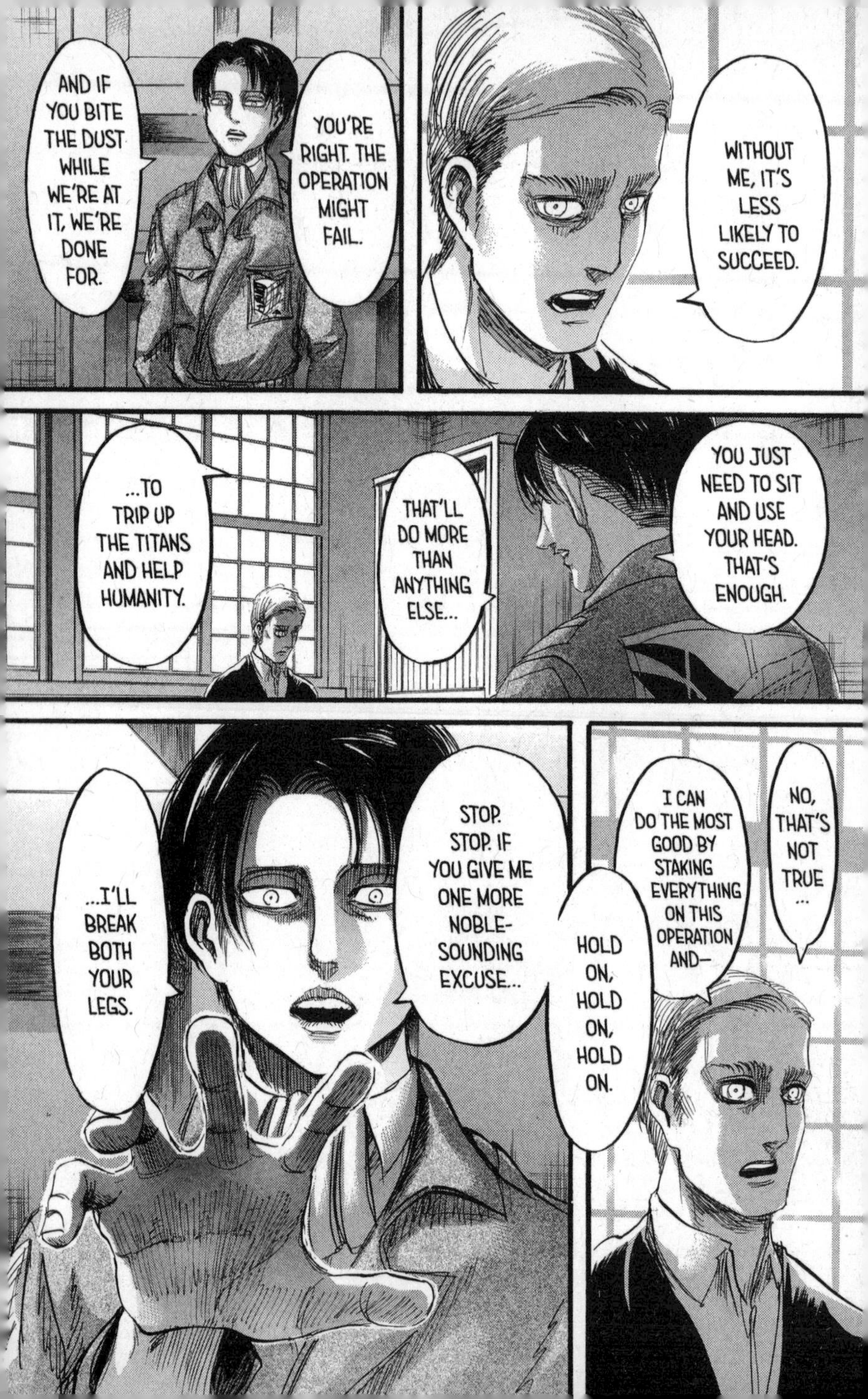
WITHOUT ME, IT'S LESS LIKELY TO SUCCEED.
YOU'RE RIGHT. THE OPERATION MIGHT FAIL.
AND IF YOU BITE THE DUST WHILE WE'RE AT IT, WE'RE DONE FOR.
YOU JUST NEED TO SIT AND USE YOUR HEAD. THAT'S ENOUGH.
THAT'LL DO MORE THAN ANYTHING ELSE...
...TO TRIP UP THE TITANS AND HELP HUMANITY.
NO, THAT'S NOT TRUE...
I CAN DO THE MOST GOOD BY STAKING EVERYTHING ON THIS OPERATION AND—
HOLD ON, HOLD ON, HOLD ON.
STOP. STOP. IF YOU GIVE ME ONE MORE NOBLE-SOUNDING EXCUSE...
...I'LL BREAK BOTH YOUR LEGS.

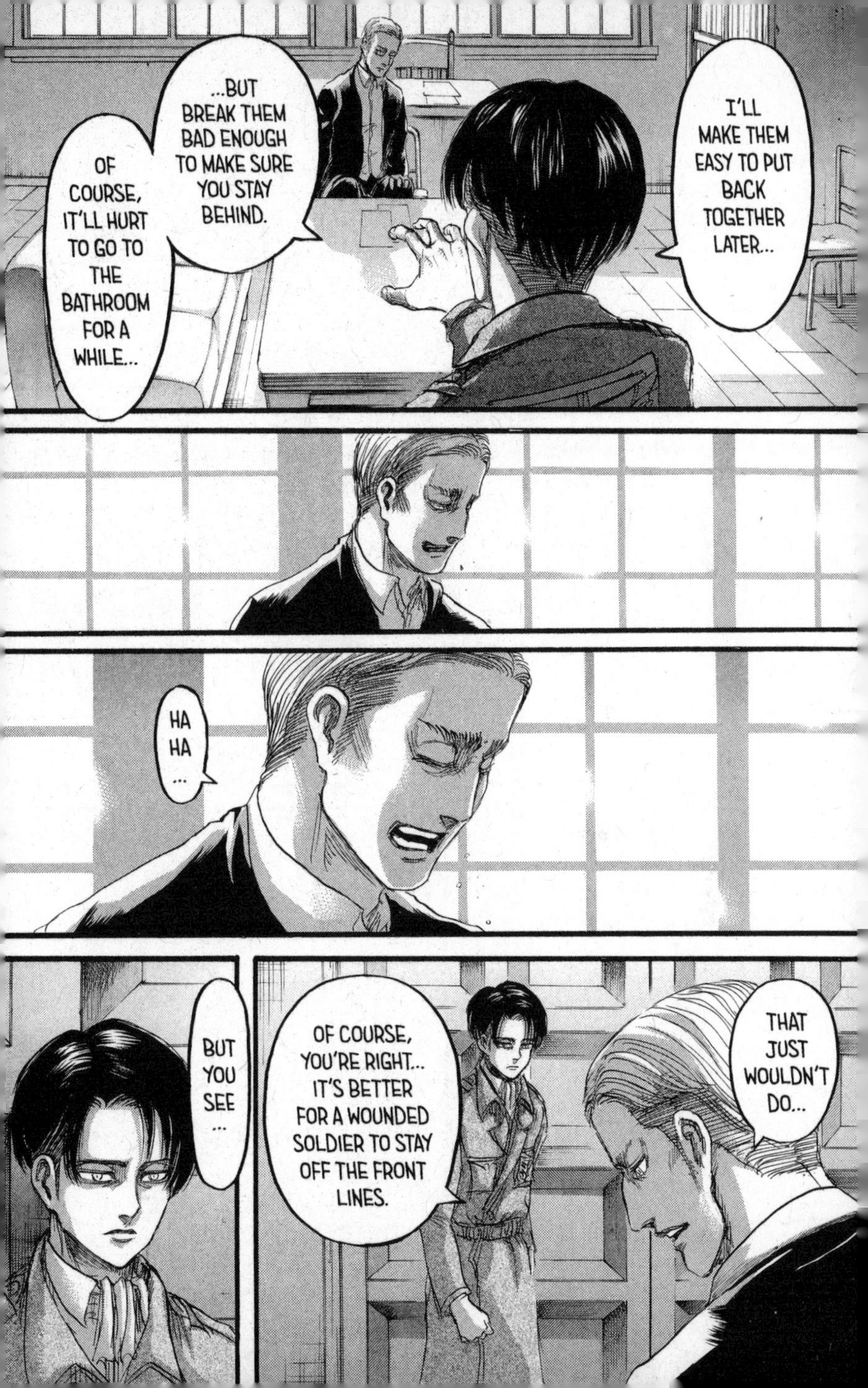
I'LL MAKE THEM EASY TO PUT BACK TOGETHER LATER...
...BUT BREAK THEM BAD ENOUGH TO MAKE SURE YOU STAY BEHIND.
OF COURSE, IT'LL HURT TO GO TO THE BATHROOM FOR A WHILE...
HA HA ...
THAT JUST WOULDN'T DO...
OF COURSE, YOU'RE RIGHT... IT'S BETTER FOR A WOUNDED SOLDIER TO STAY OFF THE FRONT LINES.
BUT YOU SEE ...

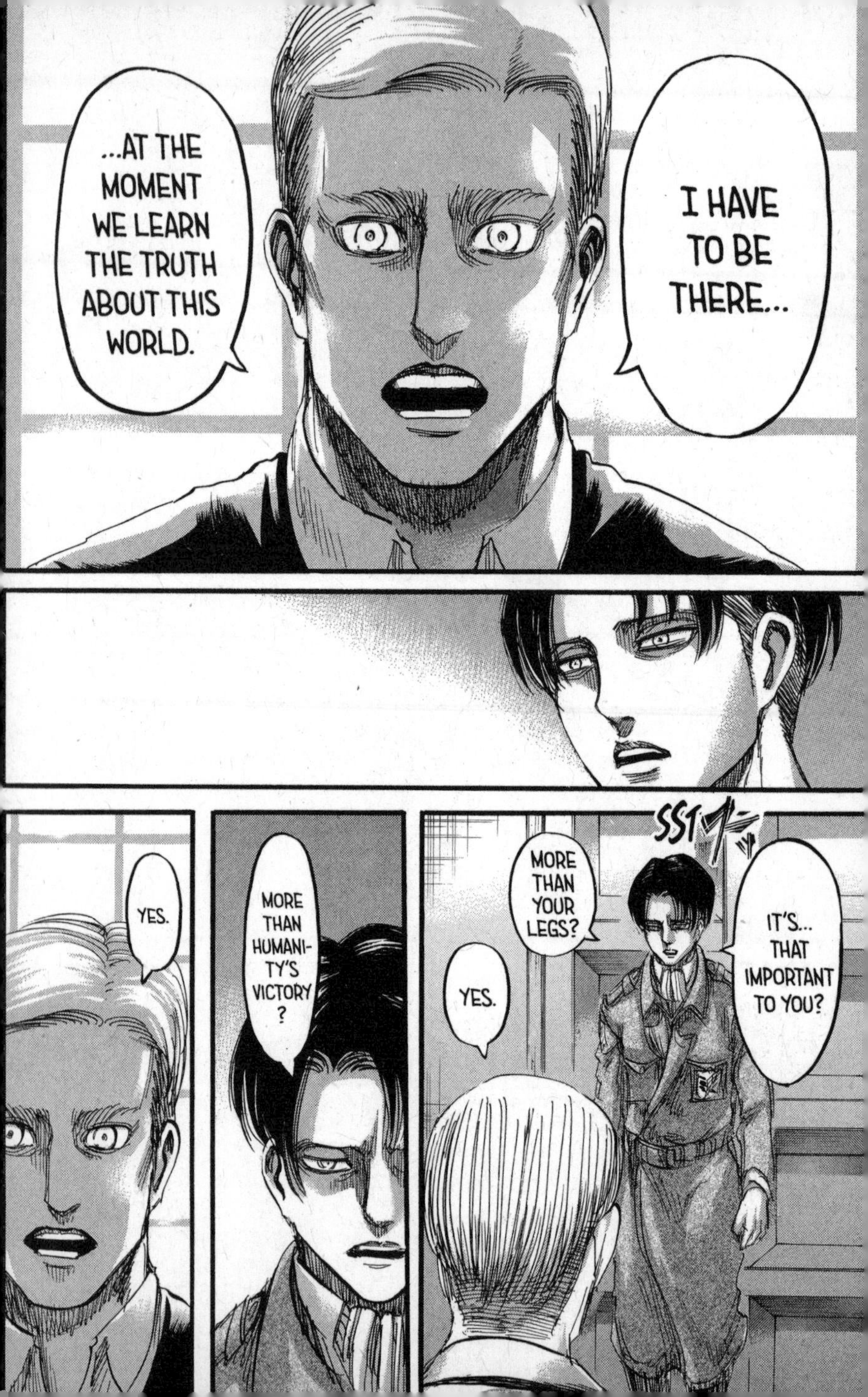
I HAVE TO BE THERE...
...AT THE MOMENT WE LEARN THE TRUTH ABOUT THIS WORLD.
SST
IT'S... THAT IMPORTANT TO YOU?
MORE THAN YOUR LEGS?
YES.
MORE THAN HUMANI-TY'S VICTORY ?
YES.

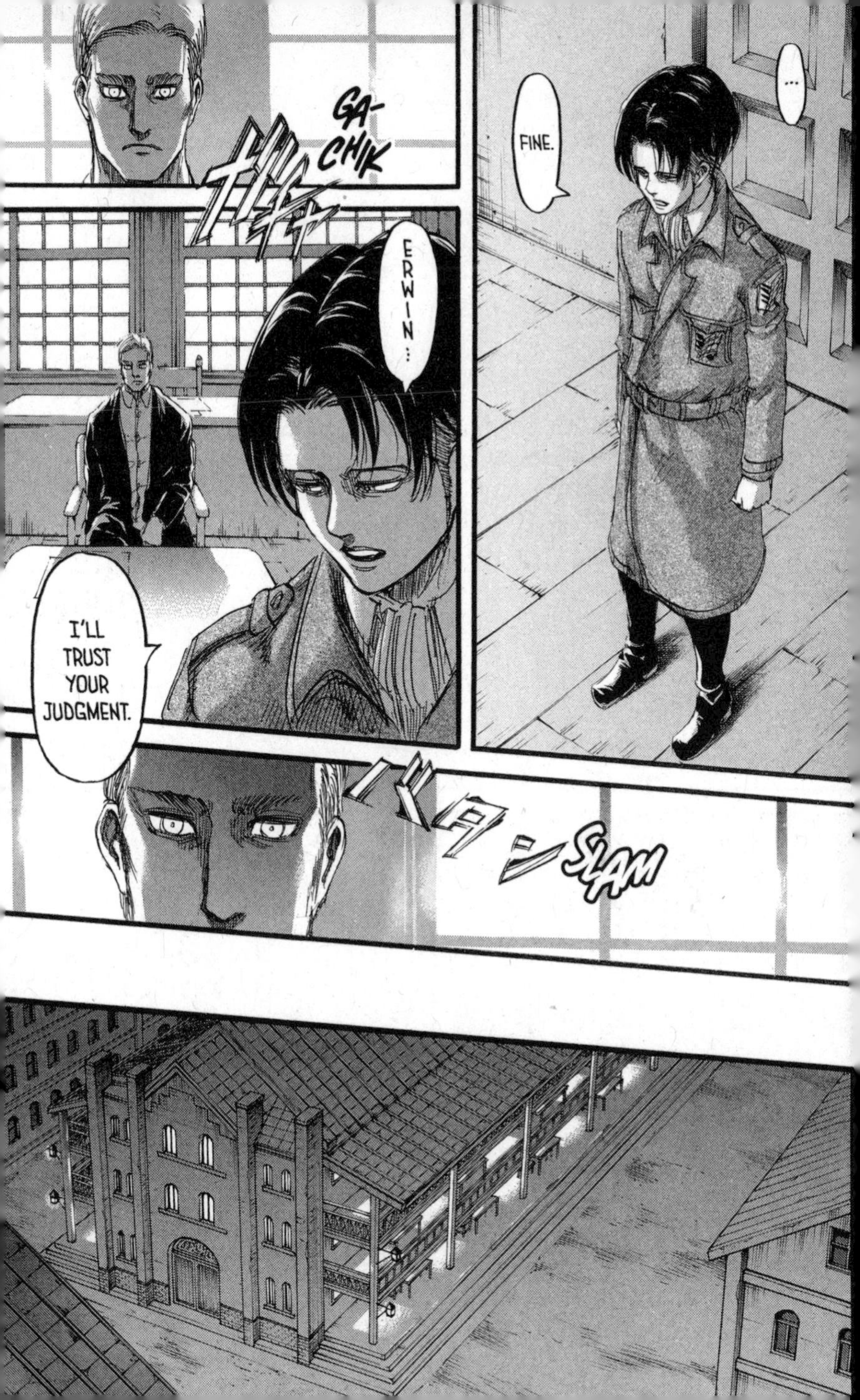
...
FINE.
GA-CHIK
ERWIN...
I'LL TRUST YOUR JUDGMENT.
SLAM

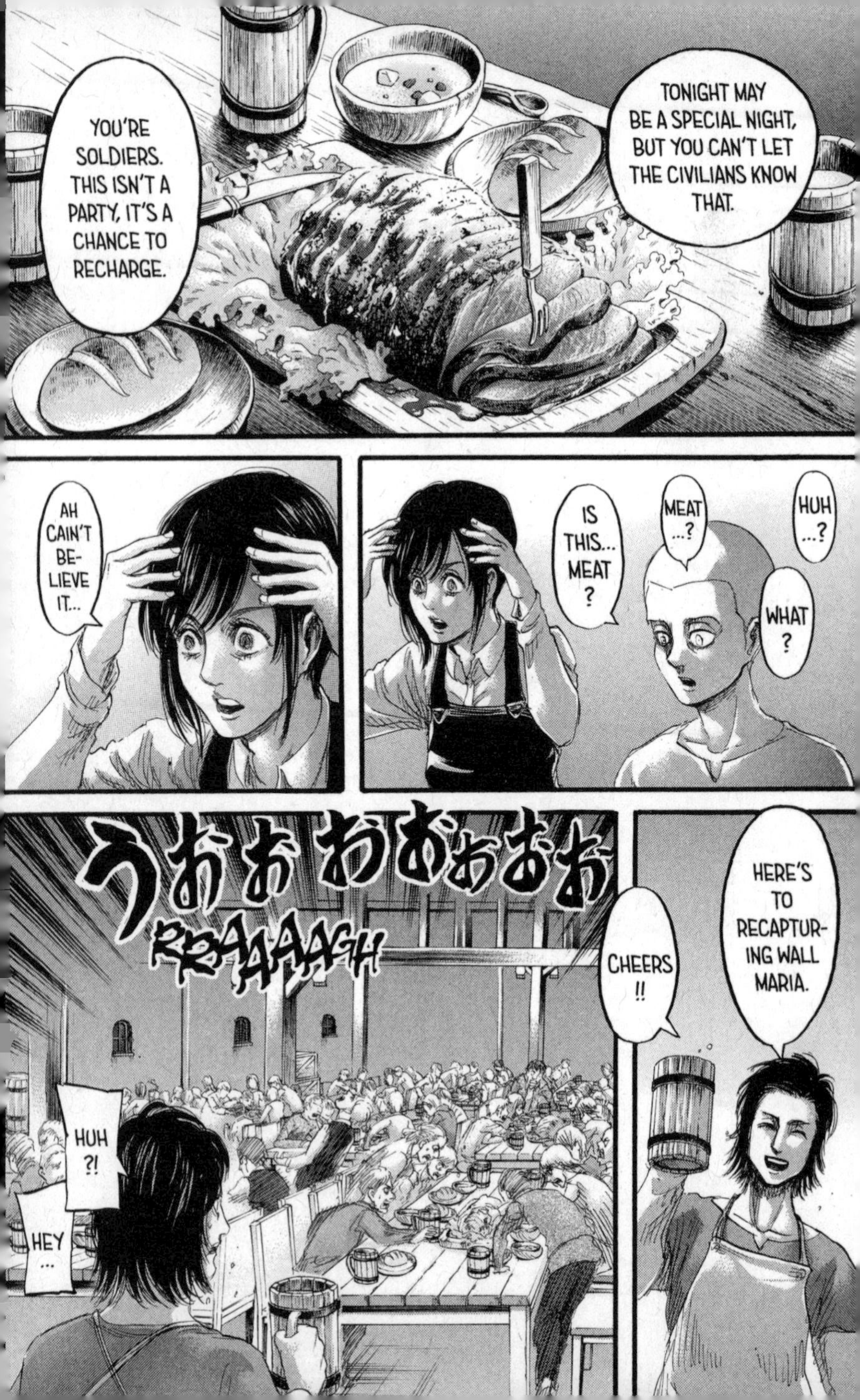
TONIGHT MAY BE A SPECIAL NIGHT, BUT YOU CAN'T LET THE CIVILIANS KNOW THAT.
YOU'RE SOLDIERS. THIS ISN'T A PARTY, IT'S A CHANCE TO RECHARGE.
HUH...?
MEAT...?
WHAT?
IS THIS... MEAT?
AH CAIN'T BE-LIEVE IT...
HERE'S TO RECAPTUR-ING WALL MARIA.
CHEERS!!
うおぉおおぉおお
RRAAAAGH
HUH?!
HEY...

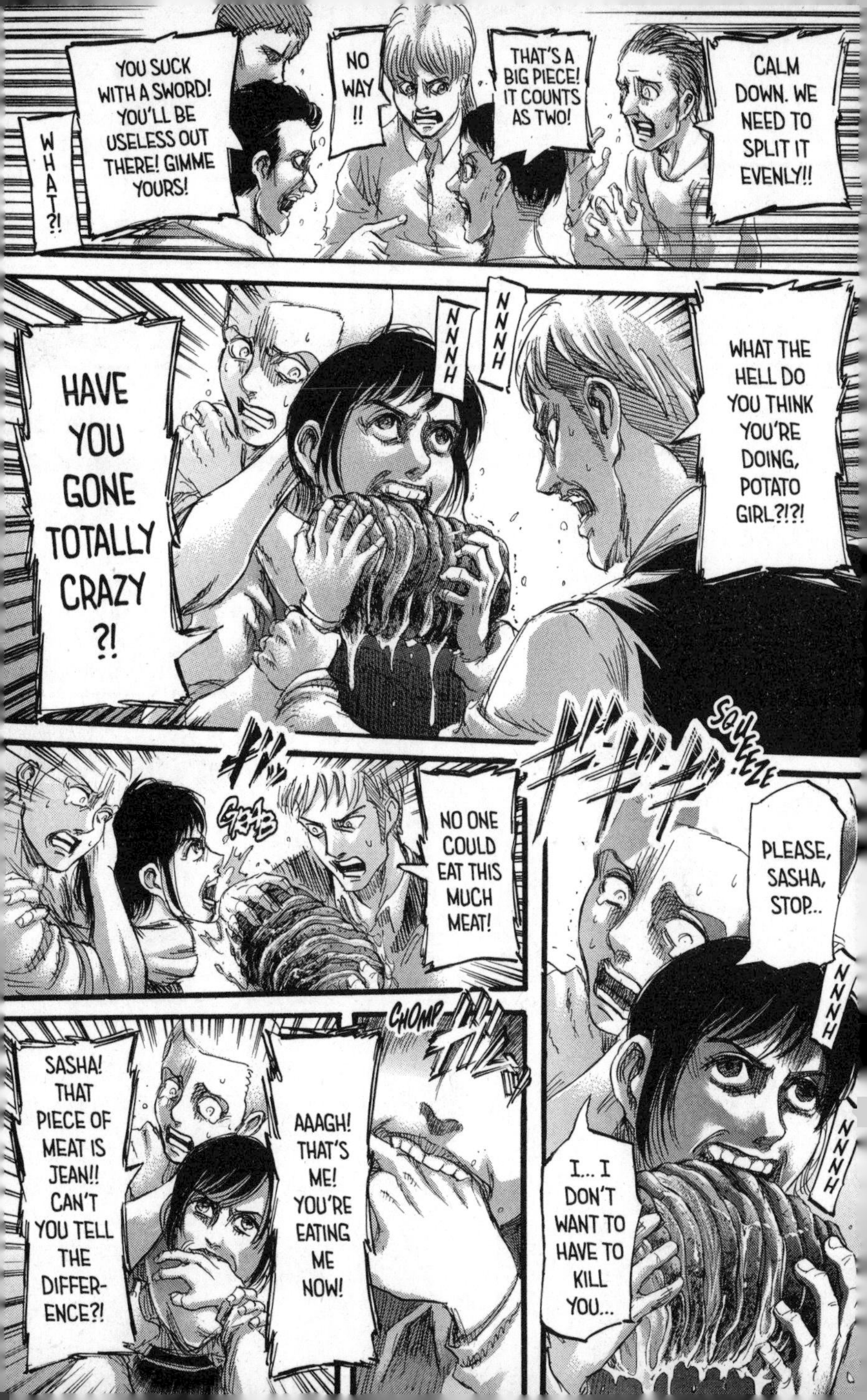
CALM DOWN. WE NEED TO SPLIT IT EVENLY!!
THAT'S A BIG PIECE! IT COUNTS AS TWO!
NO WAY !!
YOU SUCK WITH A SWORD! YOU'LL BE USELESS OUT THERE! GIMME YOURS!
WHAT?!
WHAT THE HELL DO YOU THINK YOU'RE DOING, POTATO GIRL?!?!
NNNH
NNNH
HAVE YOU GONE TOTALLY CRAZY ?!
SQUEEZE
PLEASE, SASHA, STOP...
NNNH
NNNH
I... I DON'T WANT TO HAVE TO KILL YOU...
NO ONE COULD EAT THIS MUCH MEAT!
GRAB
CHOMP
AAAGH! THAT'S ME! YOU'RE EATING ME NOW!
SASHA! THAT PIECE OF MEAT IS JEAN!! CAN'T YOU TELL THE DIFFERENCE?!

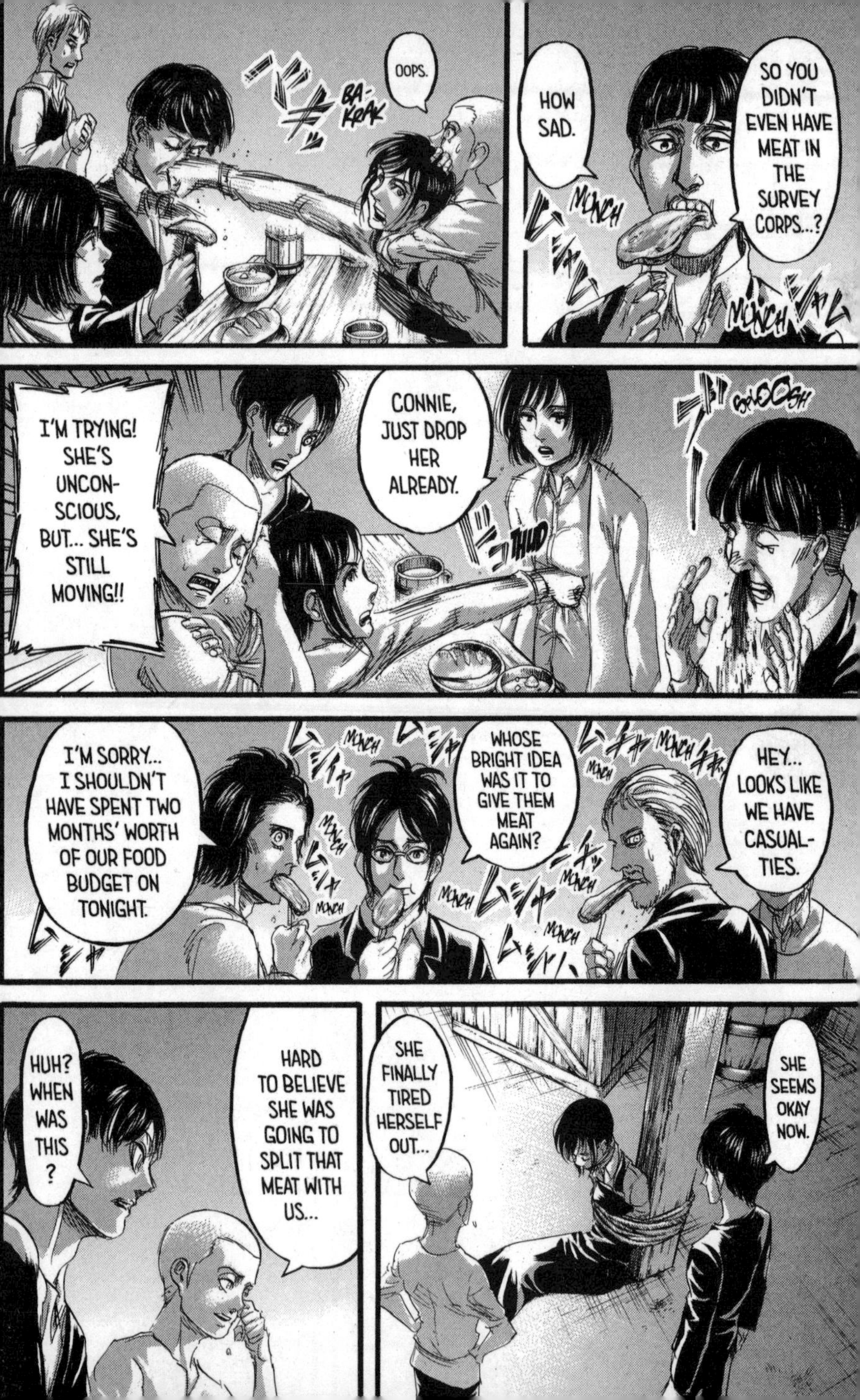
SO YOU DIDN'T EVEN HAVE MEAT IN THE SURVEY CORPS...?
HOW SAD.
MONCH
MONCH
OOPS.
BA-KRAK
CONNIE, JUST DROP HER ALREADY.
THUD
I'M TRYING! SHE'S UNCON-SCIOUS, BUT... SHE'S STILL MOVING!!
HEY... LOOKS LIKE WE HAVE CASUAL-TIES.
MONCH
WHOSE BRIGHT IDEA WAS IT TO GIVE THEM MEAT AGAIN?
MONCH
I'M SORRY... I SHOULDN'T HAVE SPENT TWO MONTHS' WORTH OF OUR FOOD BUDGET ON TONIGHT.
SHE SEEMS OKAY NOW.
SHE FINALLY TIRED HERSELF OUT...
HARD TO BELIEVE SHE WAS GOING TO SPLIT THAT MEAT WITH US...
HUH? WHEN WAS THIS ?

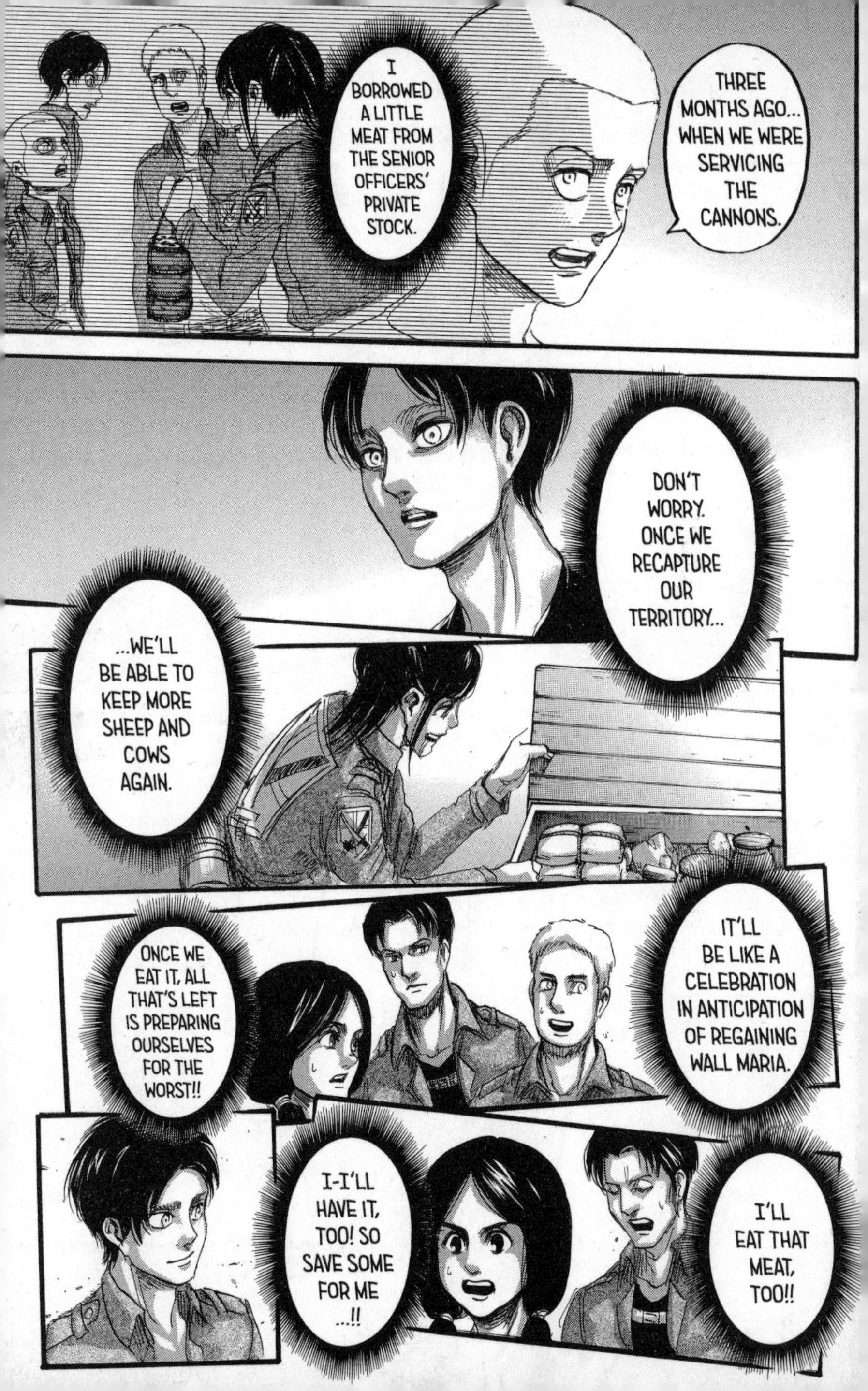
THREE MONTHS AGO... WHEN WE WERE SERVICING THE CANNONS.
I BORROWED A LITTLE MEAT FROM THE SENIOR OFFICERS' PRIVATE STOCK.
DON'T WORRY. ONCE WE RECAPTURE OUR TERRITORY...
...WE'LL BE ABLE TO KEEP MORE SHEEP AND COWS AGAIN.
IT'LL BE LIKE A CELEBRATION IN ANTICIPATION OF REGAINING WALL MARIA.
ONCE WE EAT IT, ALL THAT'S LEFT IS PREPARING OURSELVES FOR THE WORST!!
I'LL EAT THAT MEAT, TOO!!
I-I'LL HAVE IT, TOO! SO SAVE SOME FOR ME ...!!

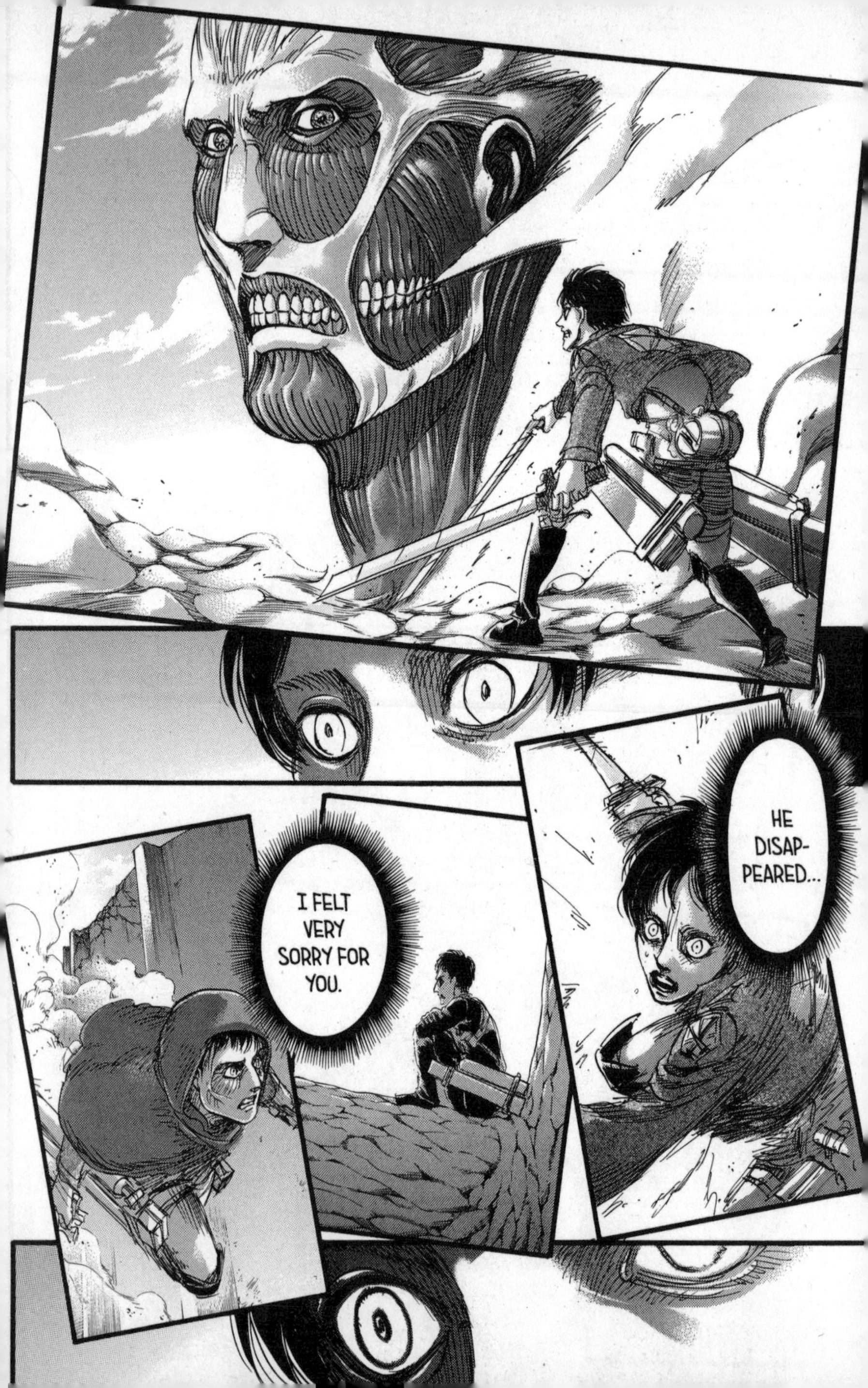
HE DISAP-PEARED...
I FELT VERY SORRY FOR YOU.

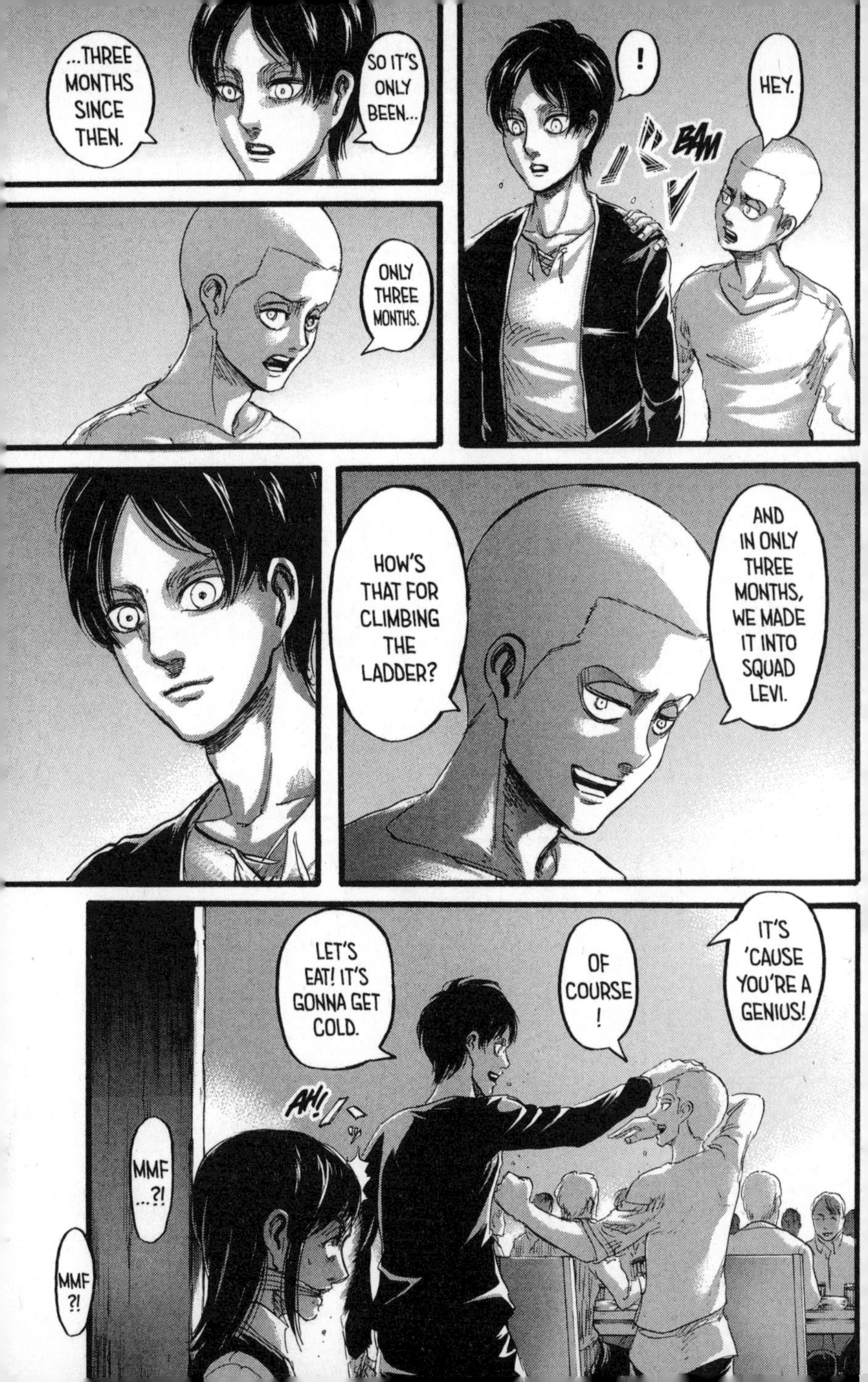
HEY.
!
BAM
SO IT'S ONLY BEEN...
...THREE MONTHS SINCE THEN.
ONLY THREE MONTHS.
AND IN ONLY THREE MONTHS, WE MADE IT INTO SQUAD LEVI.
HOW'S THAT FOR CLIMBING THE LADDER?
IT'S 'CAUSE YOU'RE A GENIUS!
OF COURSE!
LET'S EAT! IT'S GONNA GET COLD.
AH!
MMF...?!
MMF?!

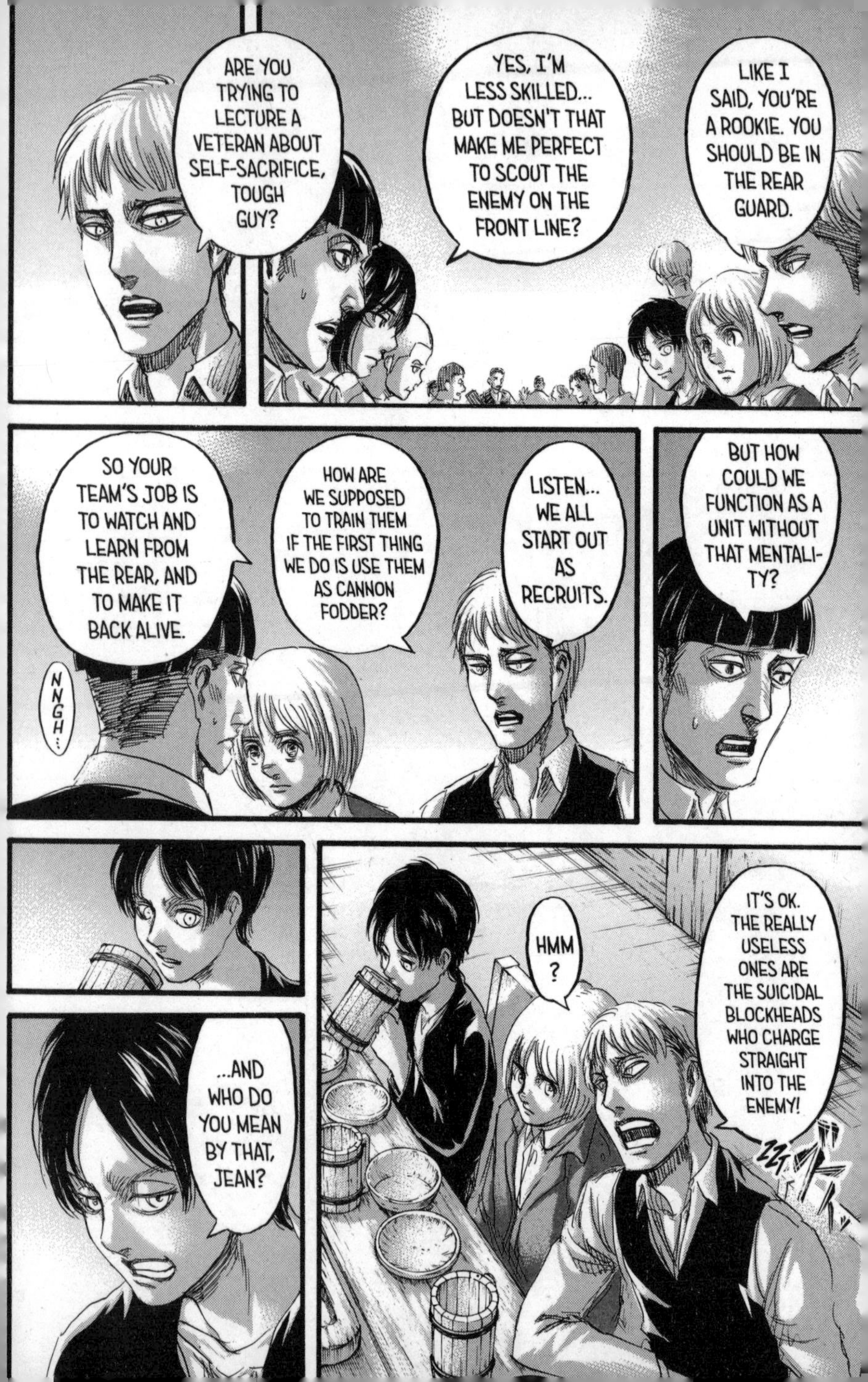
LIKE I SAID, YOU'RE A ROOKIE. YOU SHOULD BE IN THE REAR GUARD.
YES, I'M LESS SKILLED... BUT DOESN'T THAT MAKE ME PERFECT TO SCOUT THE ENEMY ON THE FRONT LINE?
ARE YOU TRYING TO LECTURE A VETERAN ABOUT SELF-SACRIFICE, TOUGH GUY?
BUT HOW COULD WE FUNCTION AS A UNIT WITHOUT THAT MENTALI-TY?
LISTEN... WE ALL START OUT AS RECRUITS.
HOW ARE WE SUPPOSED TO TRAIN THEM IF THE FIRST THING WE DO IS USE THEM AS CANNON FODDER?
SO YOUR TEAM'S JOB IS TO WATCH AND LEARN FROM THE REAR, AND TO MAKE IT BACK ALIVE.
NNGH...
IT'S OK. THE REALLY USELESS ONES ARE THE SUICIDAL BLOCKHEADS WHO CHARGE STRAIGHT INTO THE ENEMY!
HMM?
...AND WHO DO YOU MEAN BY THAT, JEAN?

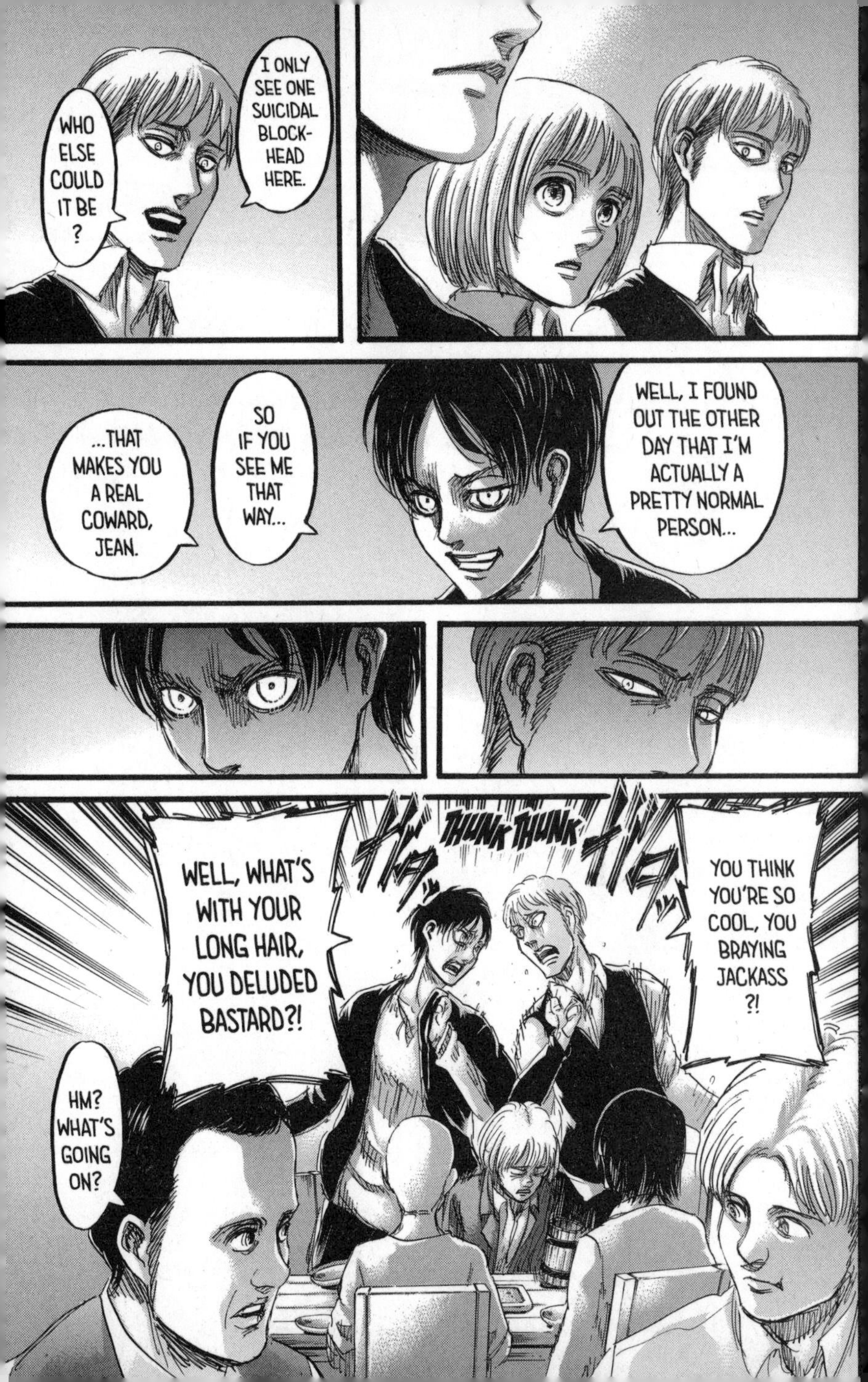
I ONLY SEE ONE SUICIDAL BLOCKHEAD HERE.
WHO ELSE COULD IT BE?
WELL, I FOUND OUT THE OTHER DAY THAT I'M ACTUALLY A PRETTY NORMAL PERSON...
SO IF YOU SEE ME THAT WAY...
...THAT MAKES YOU A REAL COWARD, JEAN.
THUNK THUNK
YOU THINK YOU'RE SO COOL, YOU BRAYING JACKASS?!
WELL, WHAT'S WITH YOUR LONG HAIR, YOU DELUDED BASTARD?!
HM? WHAT'S GOING ON?

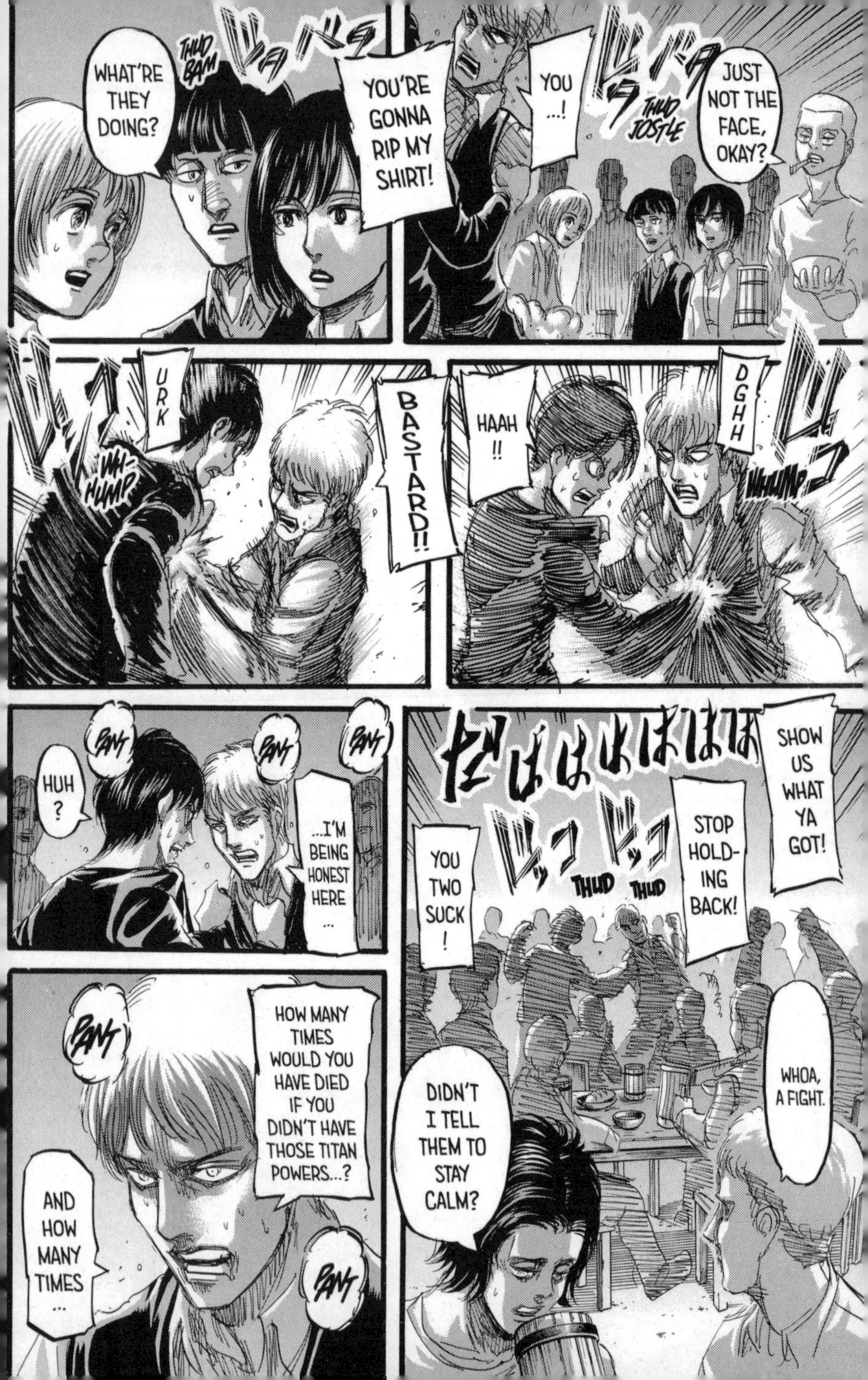
JUST NOT THE FACE, OKAY?
THUD JOSTLE
YOU ...!
YOU'RE GONNA RIP MY SHIRT!
THUD BAM
WHAT'RE THEY DOING?
DGHH
WHUMP
HAAH!!
BASTARD!!
URK
WH-HUMP
SHOW US WHAT YA GOT!
STOP HOLDING BACK!
THUD THUD
YOU TWO SUCK!
WHOA, A FIGHT.
DIDN'T I TELL THEM TO STAY CALM?
PANT PANT PANT
...I'M BEING HONEST HERE ...
HUH?
PANT
HOW MANY TIMES WOULD YOU HAVE DIED IF YOU DIDN'T HAVE THOSE TITAN POWERS...?
AND HOW MANY TIMES ...
PANT

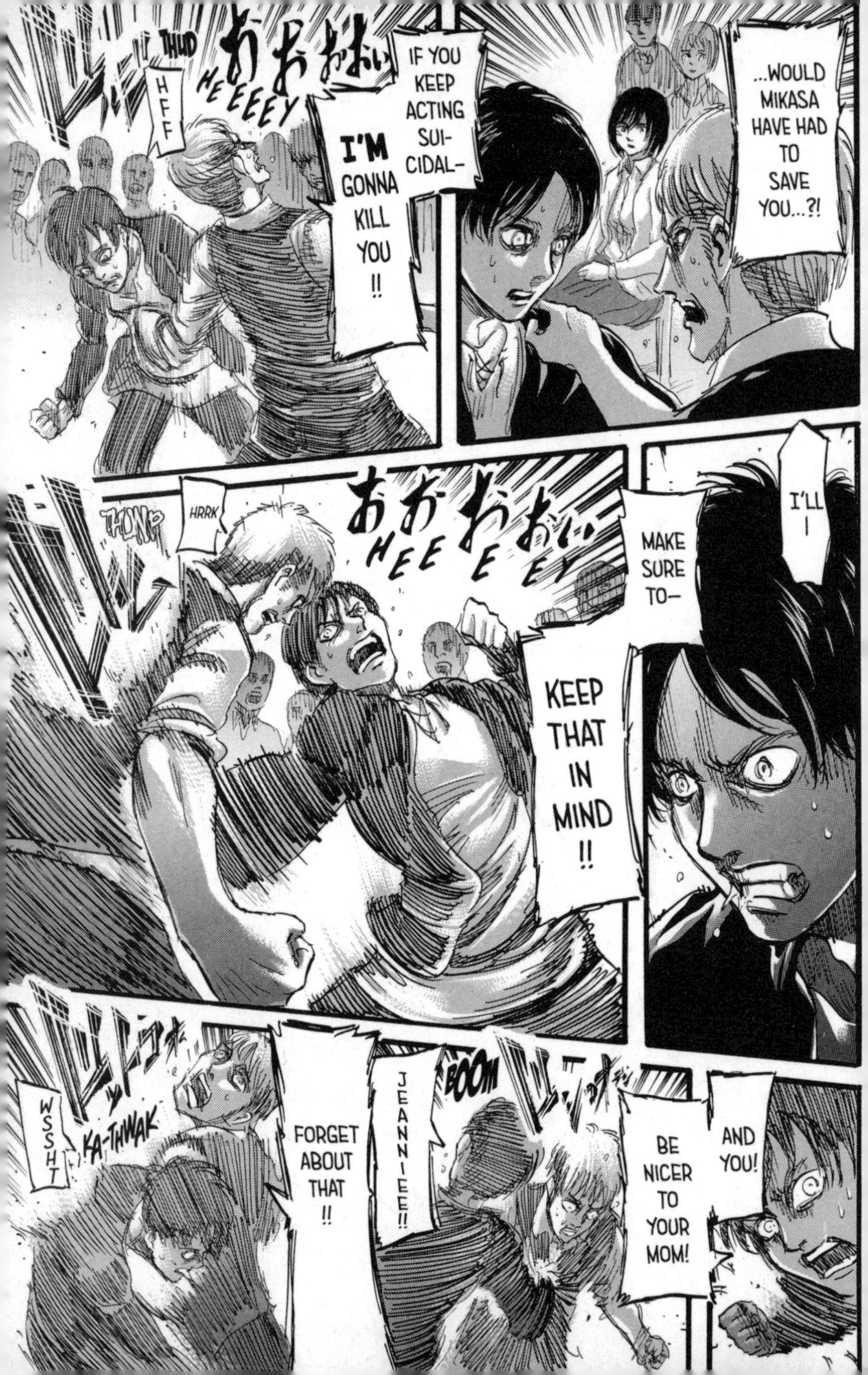

...WOULD MIKASA HAVE HAD TO SAVE YOU...?!
IF YOU KEEP ACTING SUI-CIDAL-
おおおおい
HEEEEEY
THUD
HFF
I'M GONNA KILL YOU !!
I'LL
MAKE SURE TO—
KEEP THAT IN MIND !!
おおおおい
HEEEEEY
HRRK
THONK
AND YOU!
BE NICER TO YOUR MOM!
BOOM
JEANNIEE!!
FORGET ABOUT THAT !!
KA-THWAK
WSSHT

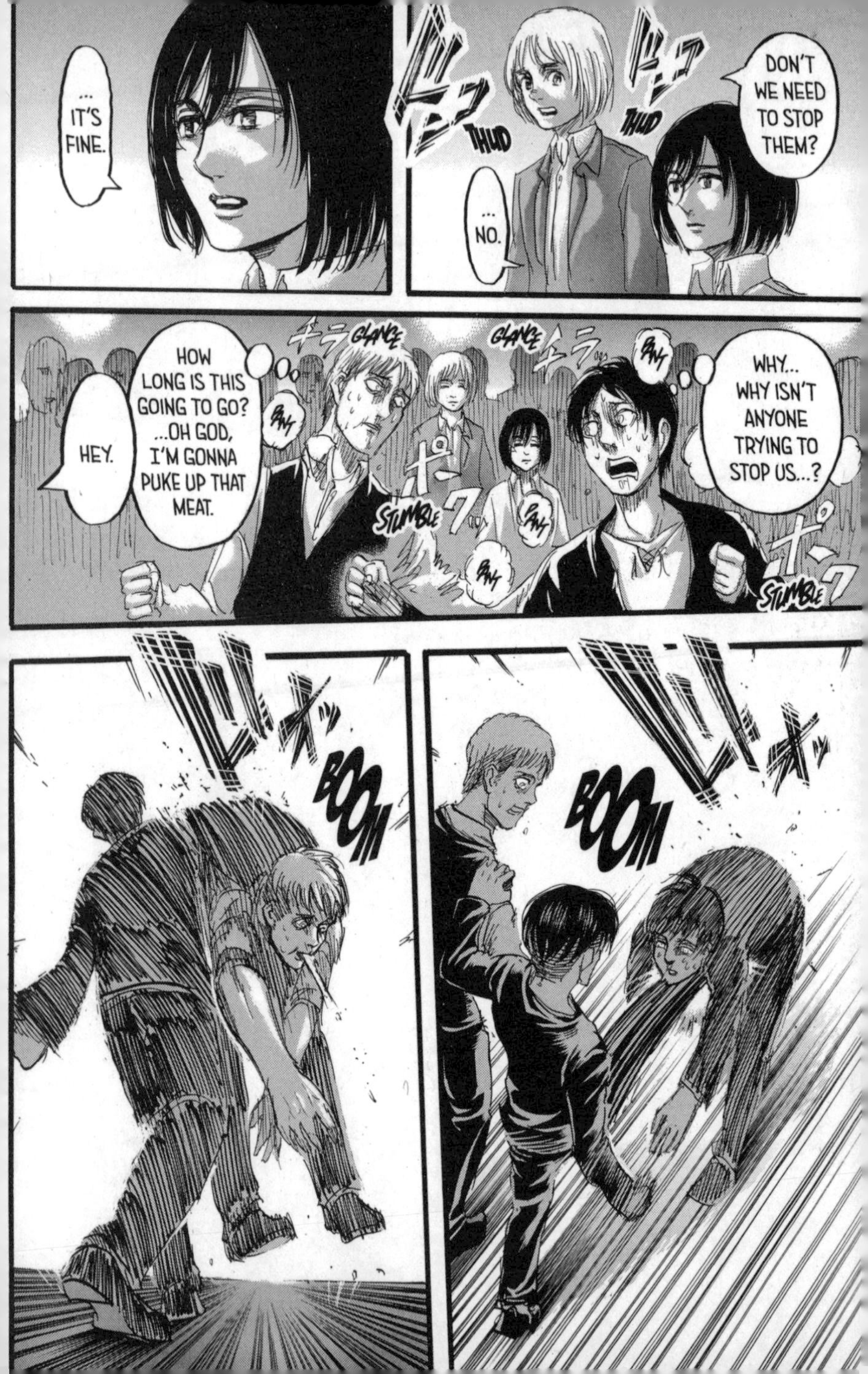
THUD
DON'T WE NEED TO STOP THEM?
... NO.
THUD
... IT'S FINE.
WHY... WHY ISN'T ANYONE TRYING TO STOP US...?
BAM
GLANCE
STUMBLE
BAM
BAM
GLANCE
HOW LONG IS THIS GOING TO GO? ...OH GOD, I'M GONNA PUKE UP THAT MEAT.
BAM
STUMBLE
HEY.
BOOM
BOOM

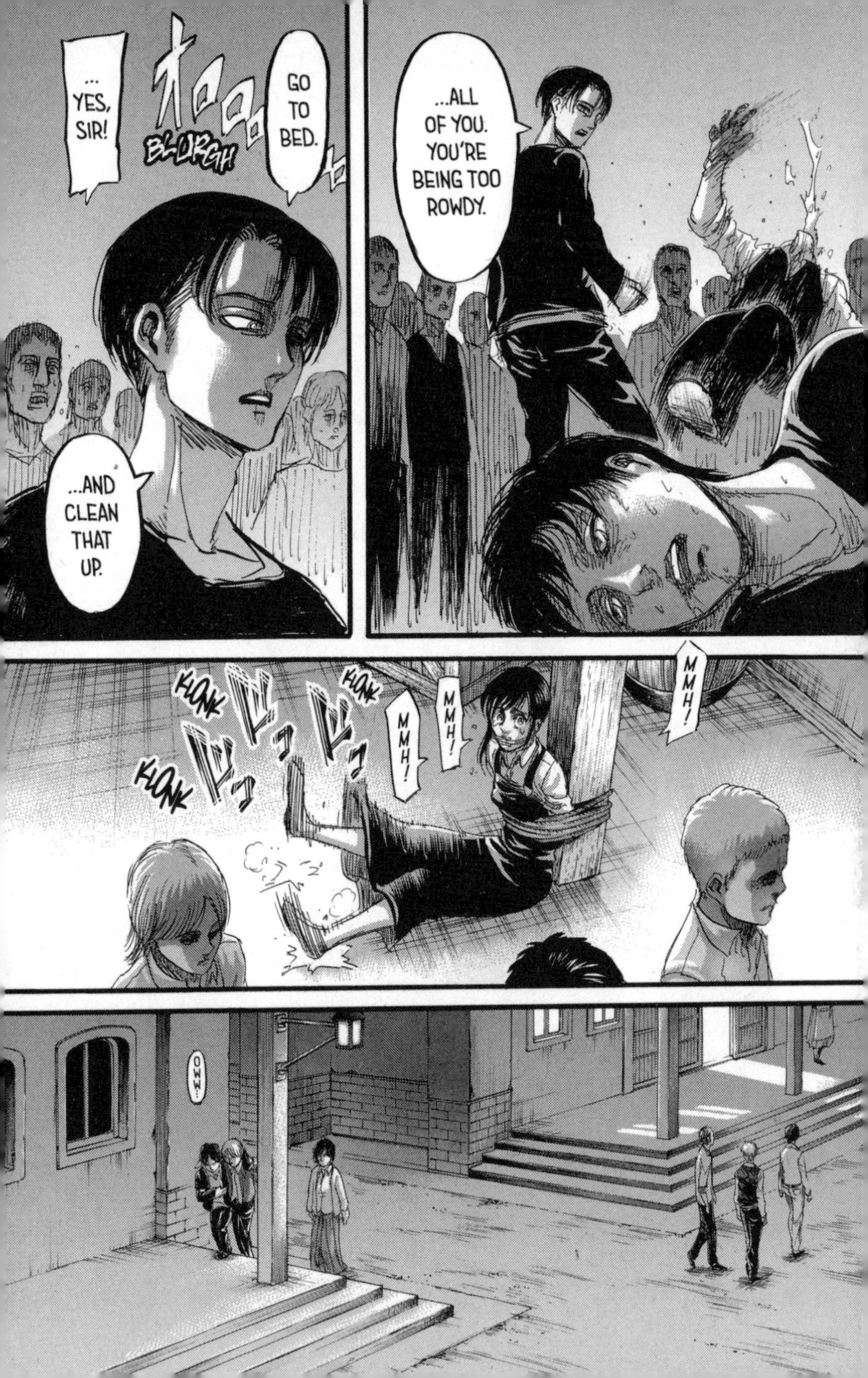
...ALL OF YOU. YOU'RE BEING TOO ROWDY.
GO TO BED.
BLORGH
... YES, SIR!
...AND CLEAN THAT UP.
MMH!
MMH!
MMH!
KLONK
KLONK
KLONK
OWW...

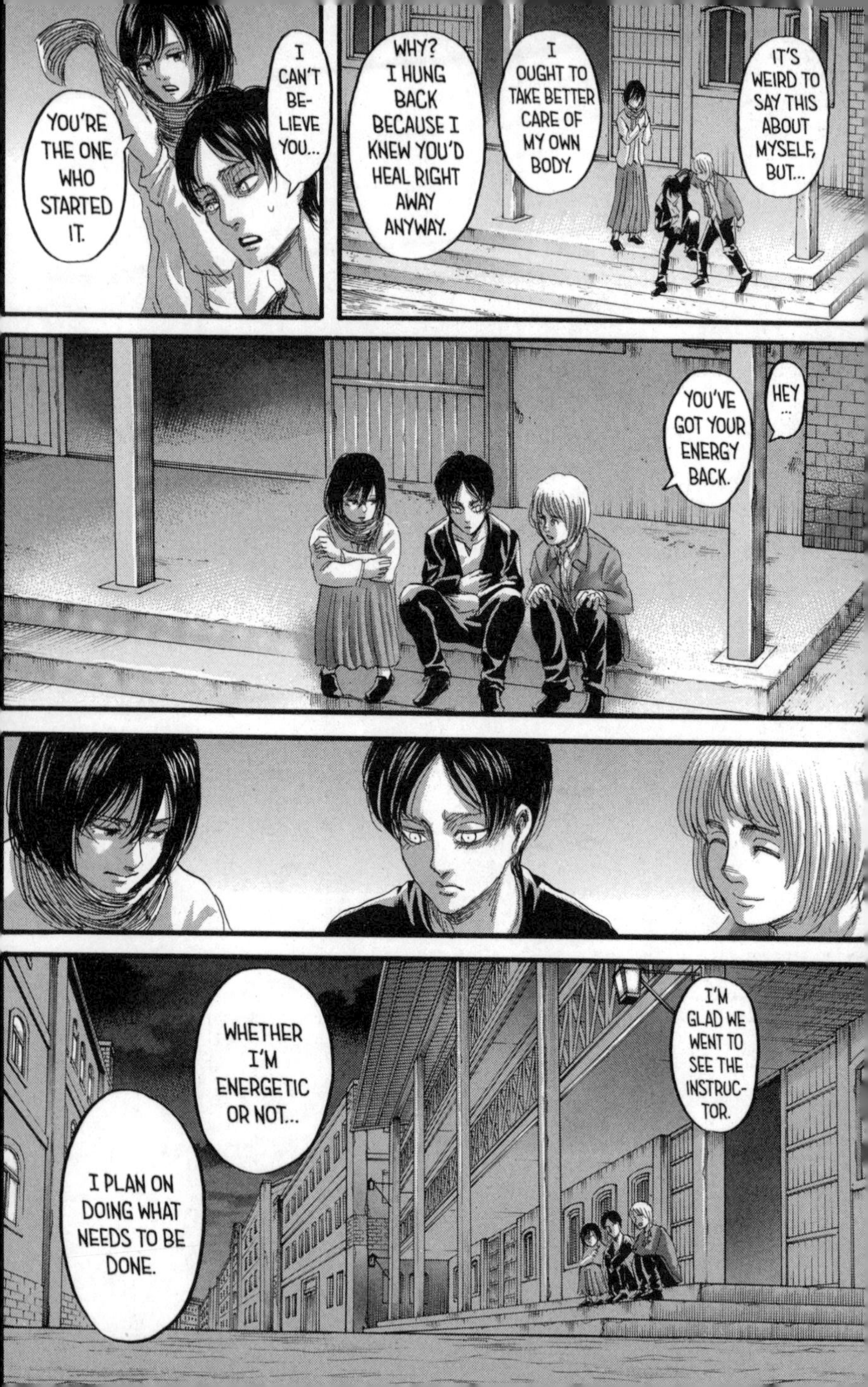
IT'S WEIRD TO SAY THIS ABOUT MYSELF, BUT...
I OUGHT TO TAKE BETTER CARE OF MY OWN BODY.
WHY? I HUNG BACK BECAUSE I KNEW YOU'D HEAL RIGHT AWAY ANYWAY.
I CAN'T BE-LIEVE YOU...
YOU'RE THE ONE WHO STARTED IT.
HEY...
YOU'VE GOT YOUR ENERGY BACK.
I'M GLAD WE WENT TO SEE THE INSTRUC-TOR.
WHETHER I'M ENERGETIC OR NOT...
I PLAN ON DOING WHAT NEEDS TO BE DONE.

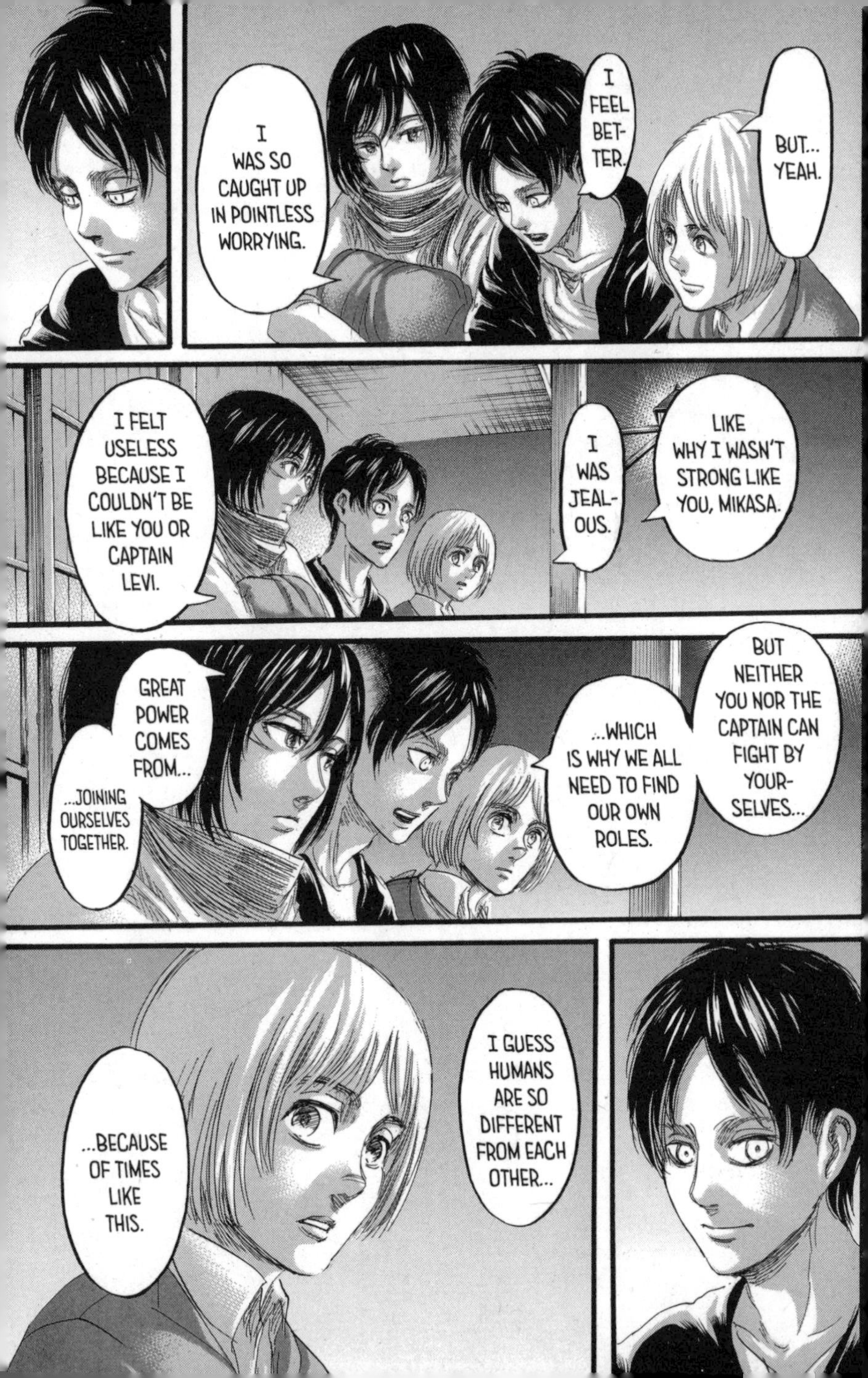
BUT... YEAH.
I FEEL BETTER.
I WAS SO CAUGHT UP IN POINTLESS WORRYING.
LIKE WHY I WASN'T STRONG LIKE YOU, MIKASA.
I WAS JEALOUS.
I FELT USELESS BECAUSE I COULDN'T BE LIKE YOU OR CAPTAIN LEVI.
BUT NEITHER YOU NOR THE CAPTAIN CAN FIGHT BY YOURSELVES...
...WHICH IS WHY WE ALL NEED TO FIND OUR OWN ROLES.
GREAT POWER COMES FROM...
...JOINING OURSELVES TOGETHER.
I GUESS HUMANS ARE SO DIFFERENT FROM EACH OTHER...
...BECAUSE OF TIMES LIKE THIS.

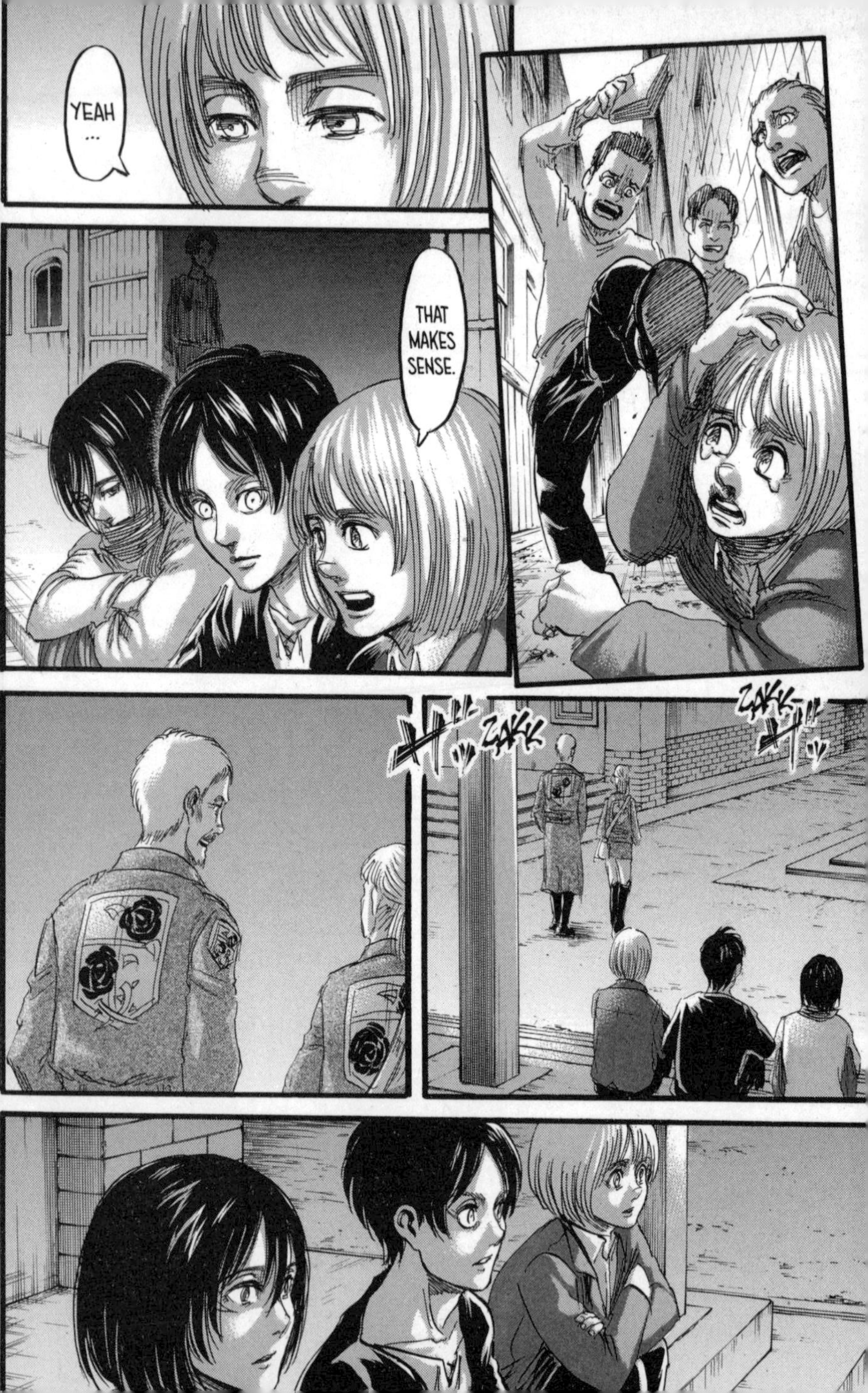
YEAH ...
THAT MAKES SENSE.
ZAKK
ZAKK

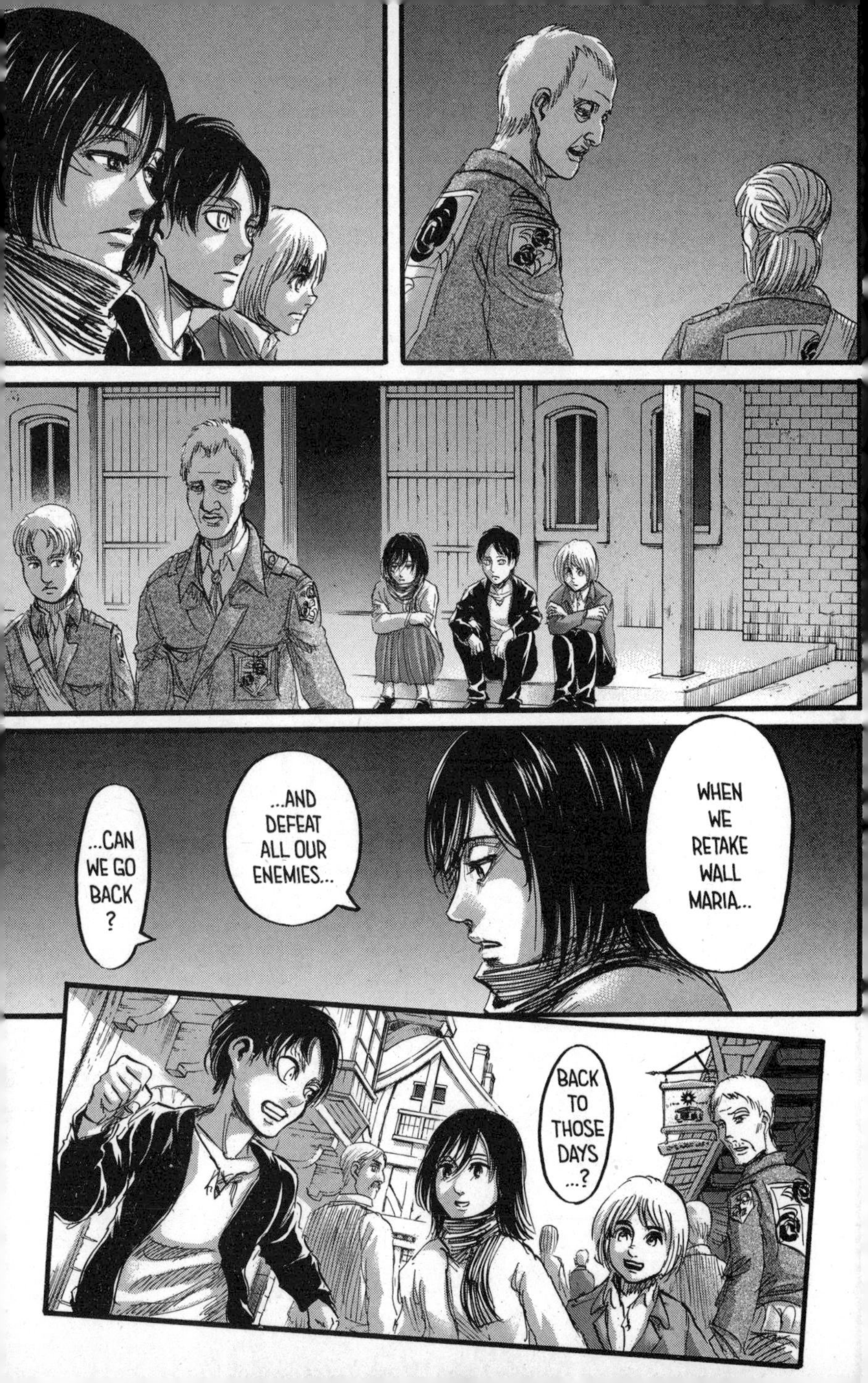
WHEN WE RETAKE WALL MARIA...
...AND DEFEAT ALL OUR ENEMIES...
...CAN WE GO BACK ?
BACK TO THOSE DAYS ...?

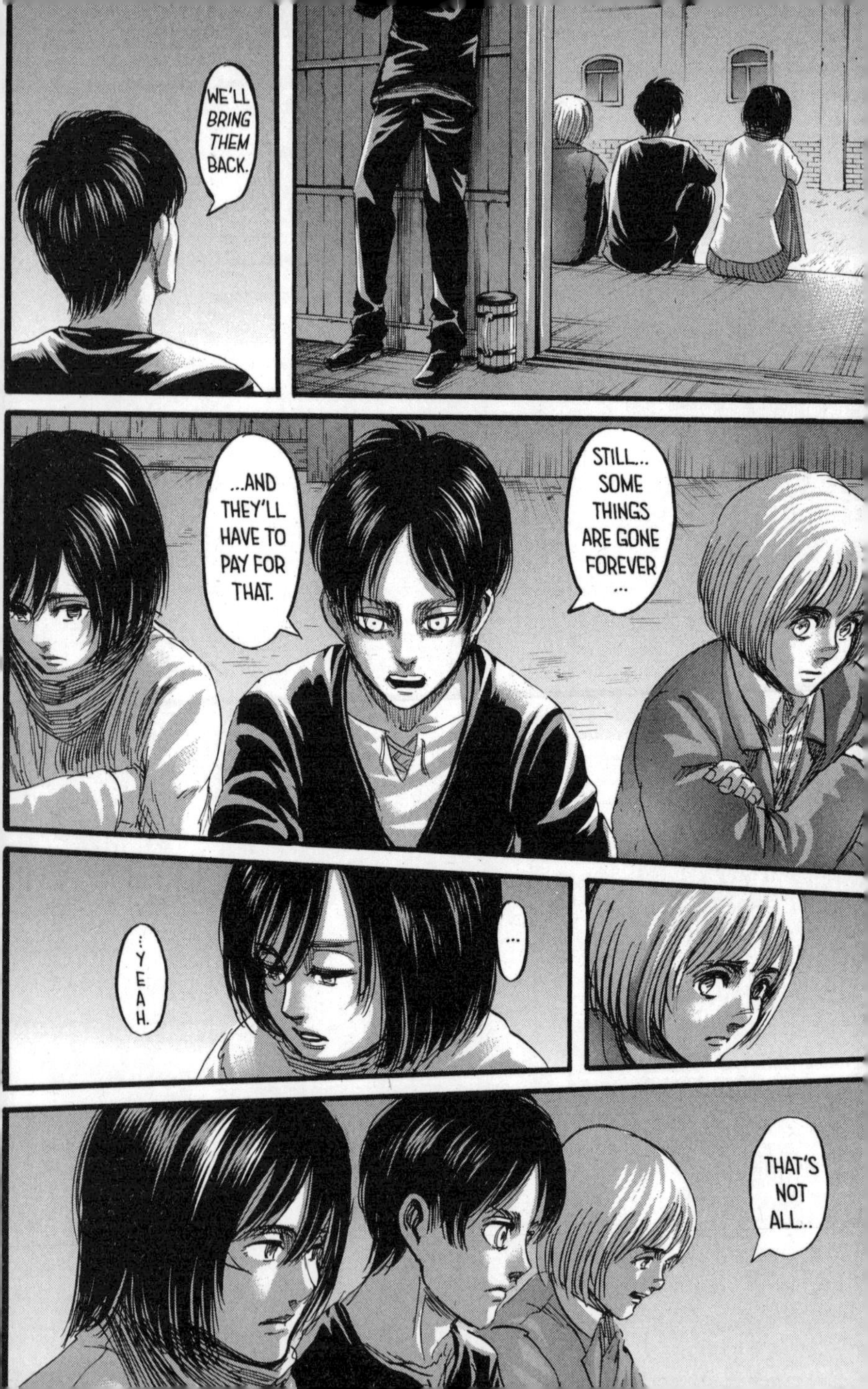
WE'LL BRING THEM BACK.
STILL... SOME THINGS ARE GONE FOREVER ...
...AND THEY'LL HAVE TO PAY FOR THAT.
...
...YEAH.
THAT'S NOT ALL...

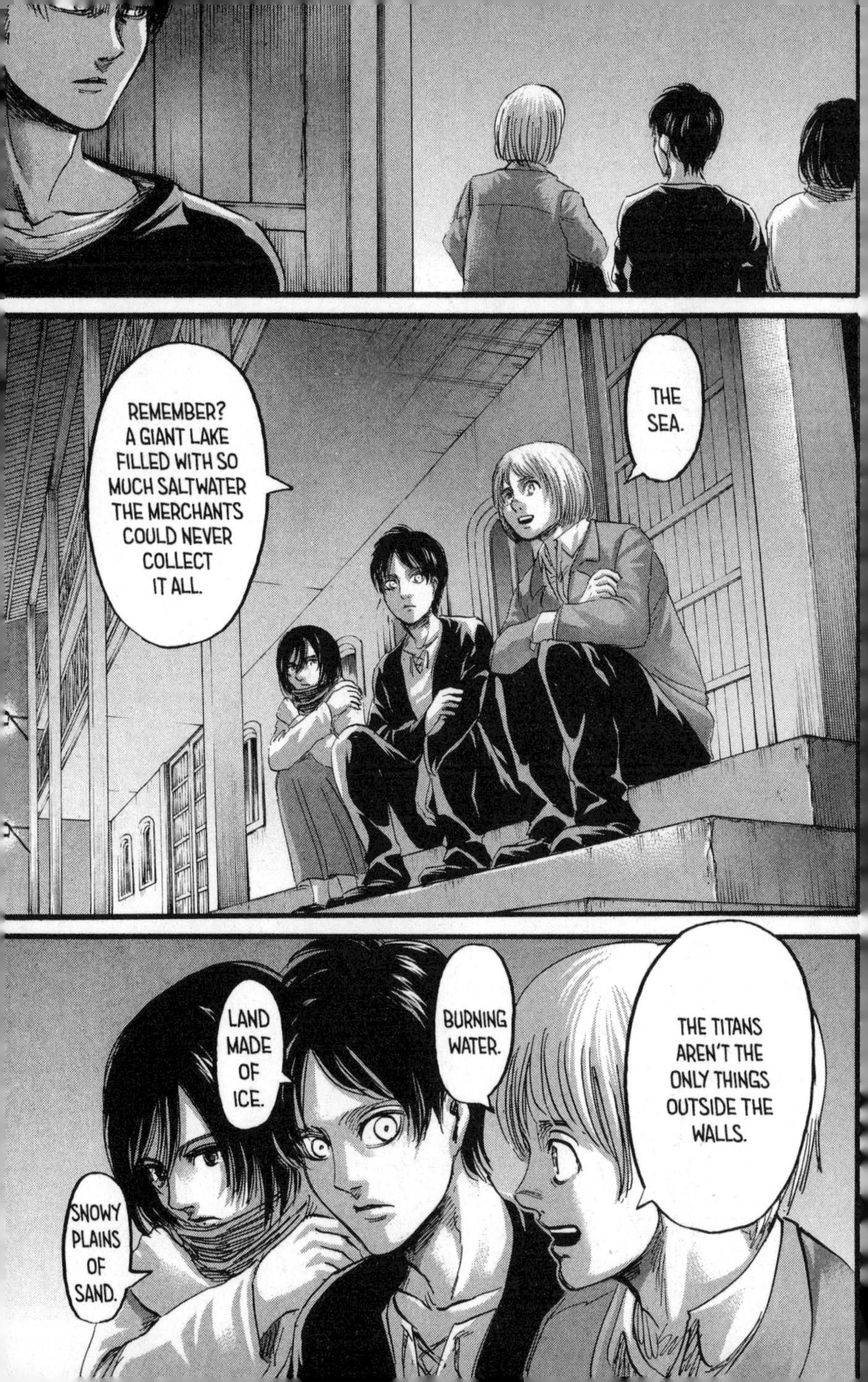
THE SEA.
REMEMBER? A GIANT LAKE FILLED WITH SO MUCH SALTWATER THE MERCHANTS COULD NEVER COLLECT IT ALL.
THE TITANS AREN'T THE ONLY THINGS OUTSIDE THE WALLS.
BURNING WATER.
LAND MADE OF ICE.
SNOWY PLAINS OF SAND.

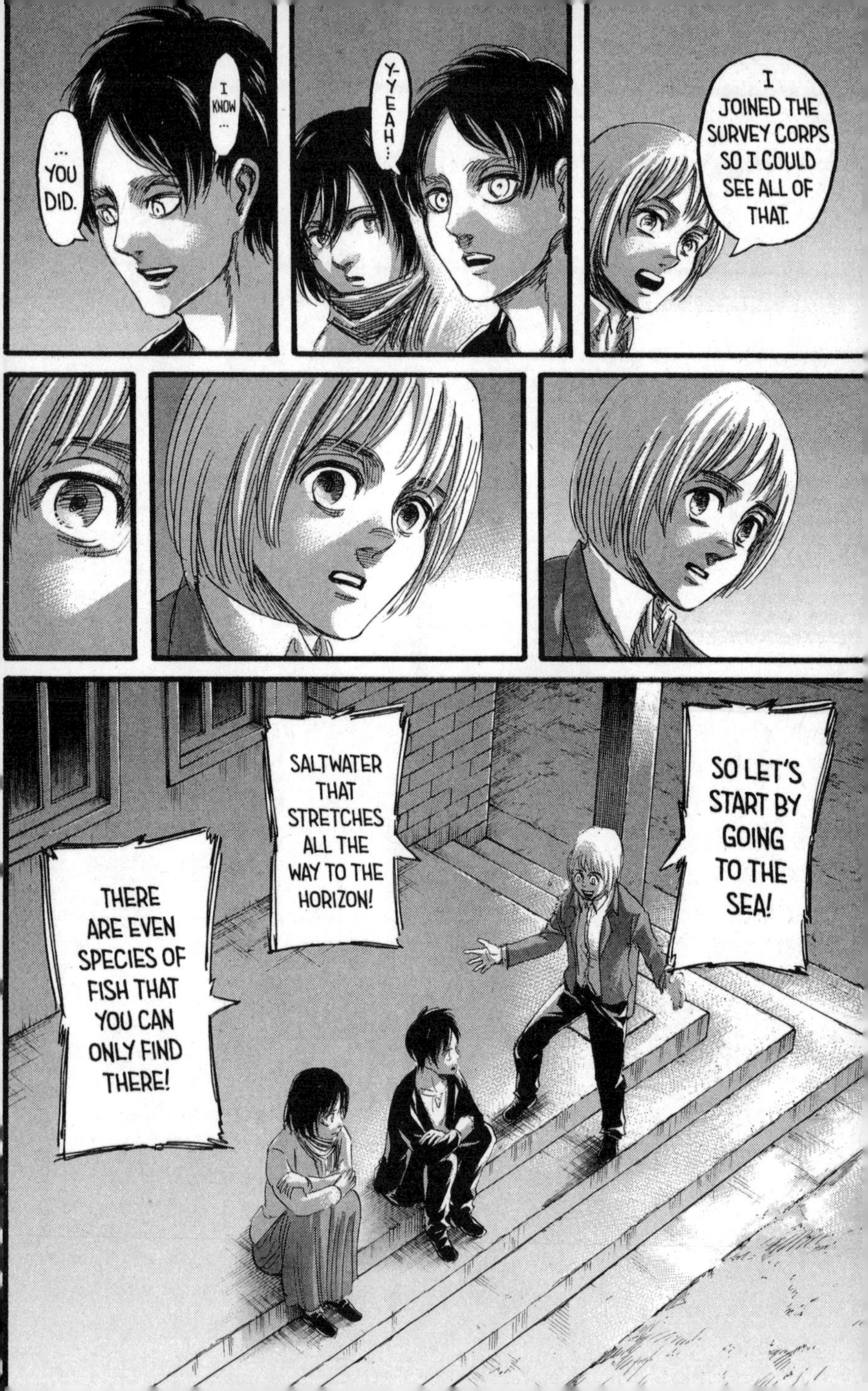
I JOINED THE SURVEY CORPS SO I COULD SEE ALL OF THAT.
Y-YEAH...
I KNOW...
...YOU DID.
SO LET'S START BY GOING TO THE SEA!
SALTWATER THAT STRETCHES ALL THE WAY TO THE HORIZON!
THERE ARE EVEN SPECIES OF FISH THAT YOU CAN ONLY FIND THERE!

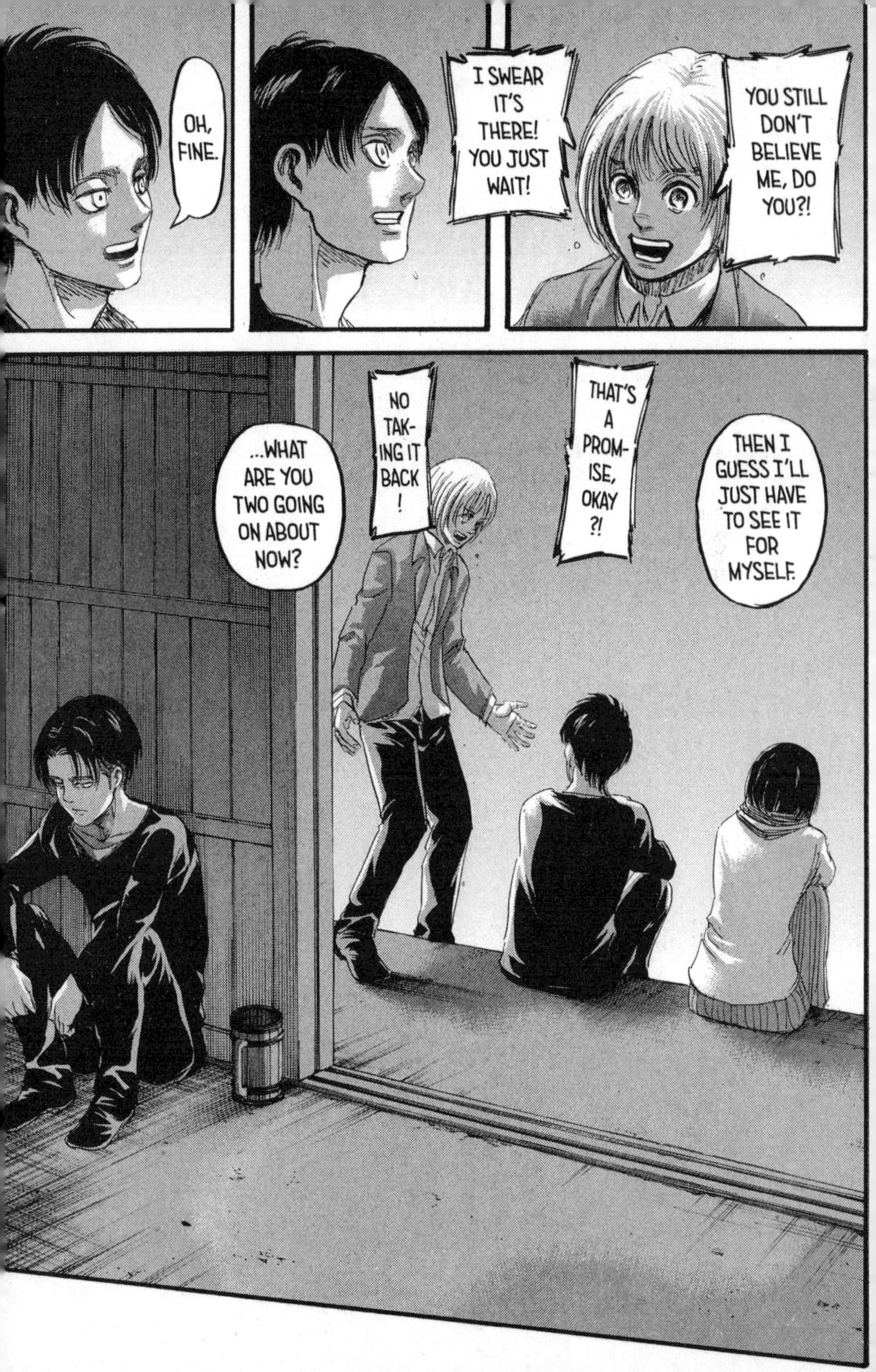
YOU STILL DON'T BELIEVE ME, DO YOU?!
I SWEAR IT'S THERE! YOU JUST WAIT!
OH, FINE.
THEN I GUESS I'LL JUST HAVE TO SEE IT FOR MYSELF.
THAT'S A PROM-ISE, OKAY?!
NO TAK-ING IT BACK!
...WHAT ARE YOU TWO GOING ON ABOUT NOW?

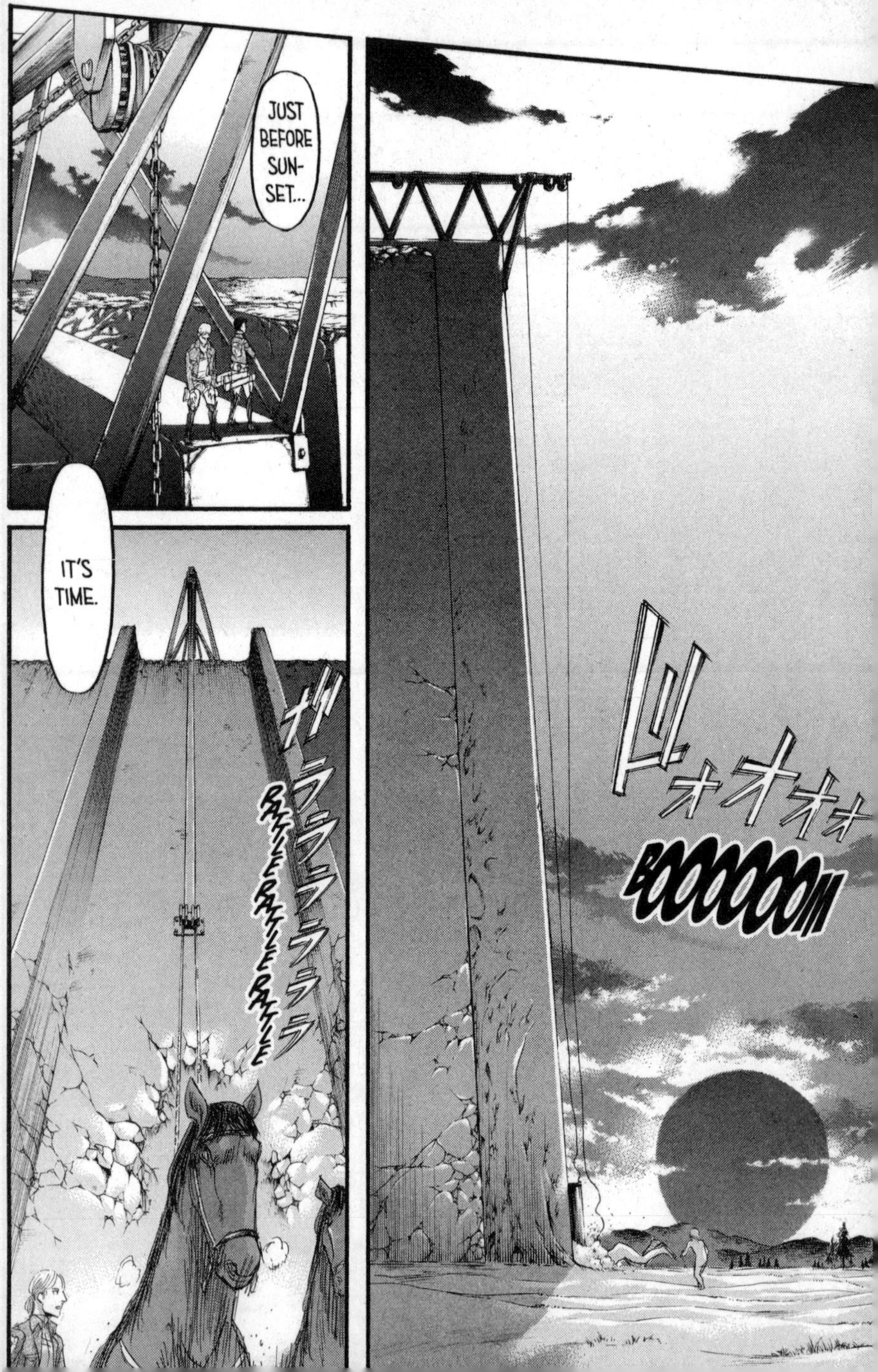
BOOOOOOM
JUST BEFORE SUN-SET...
IT'S TIME.
RATTLE RATTLE RATTLE

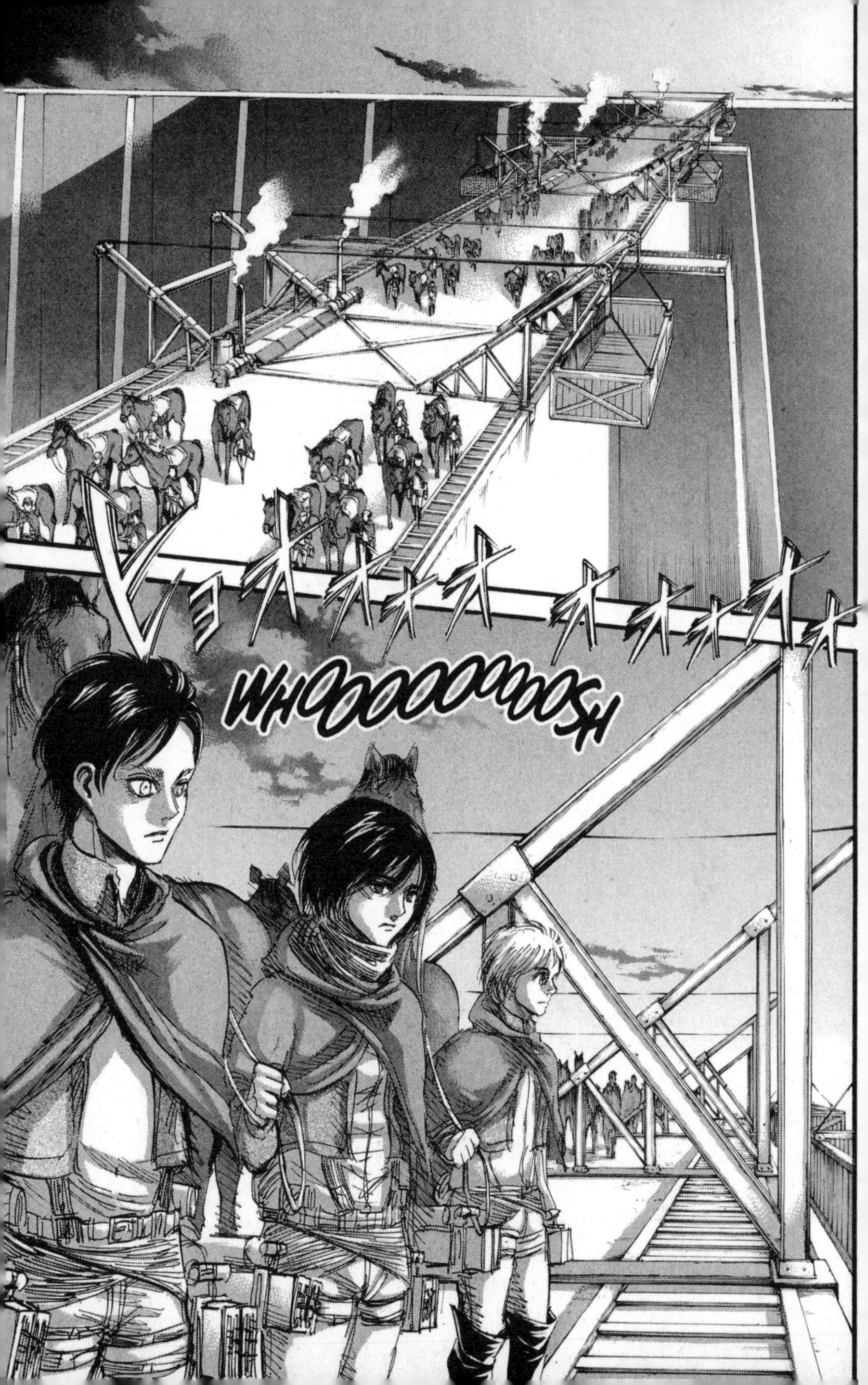
ビョオオオオ　オォォオォ
WHOOOOOOOOOSH

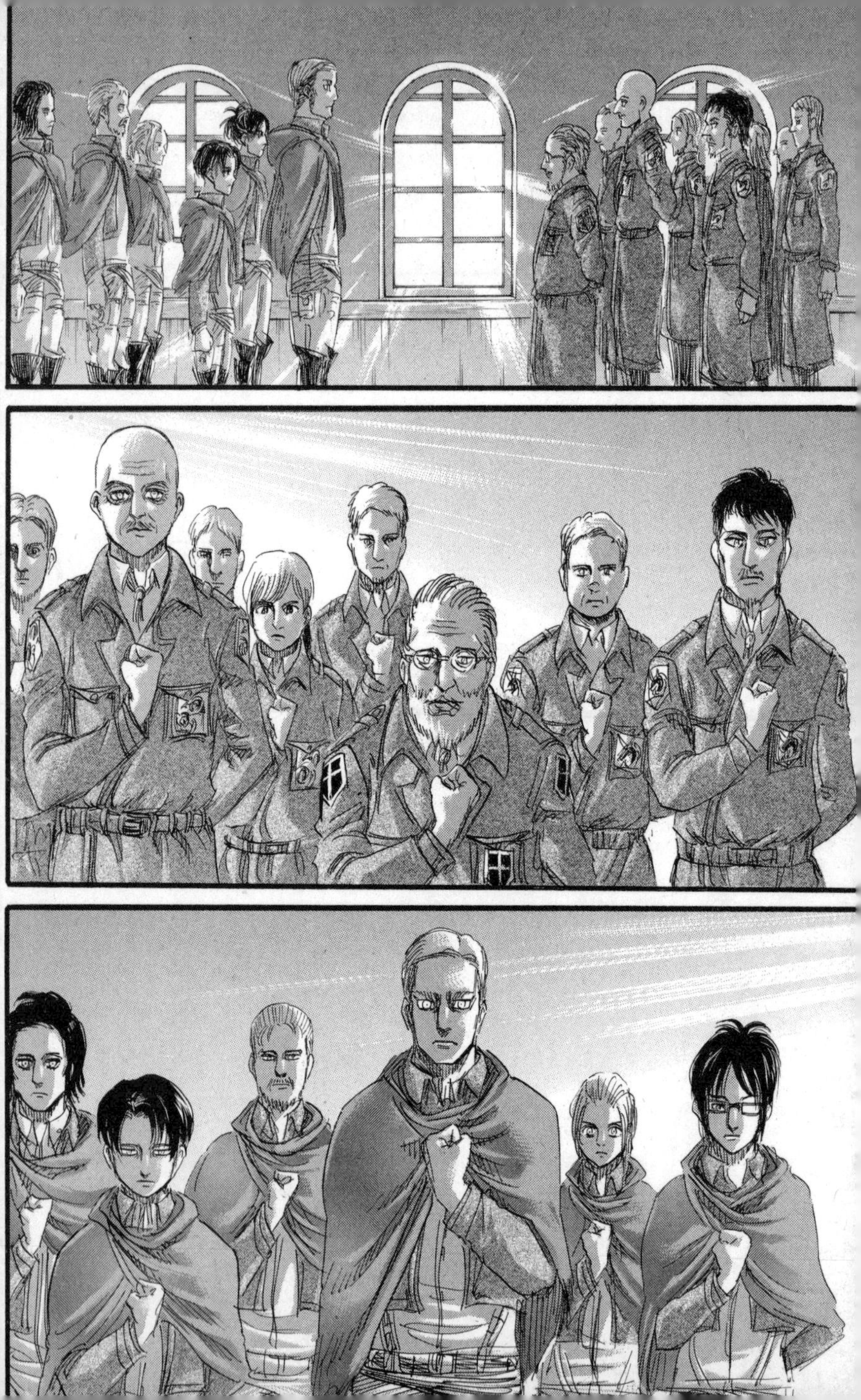

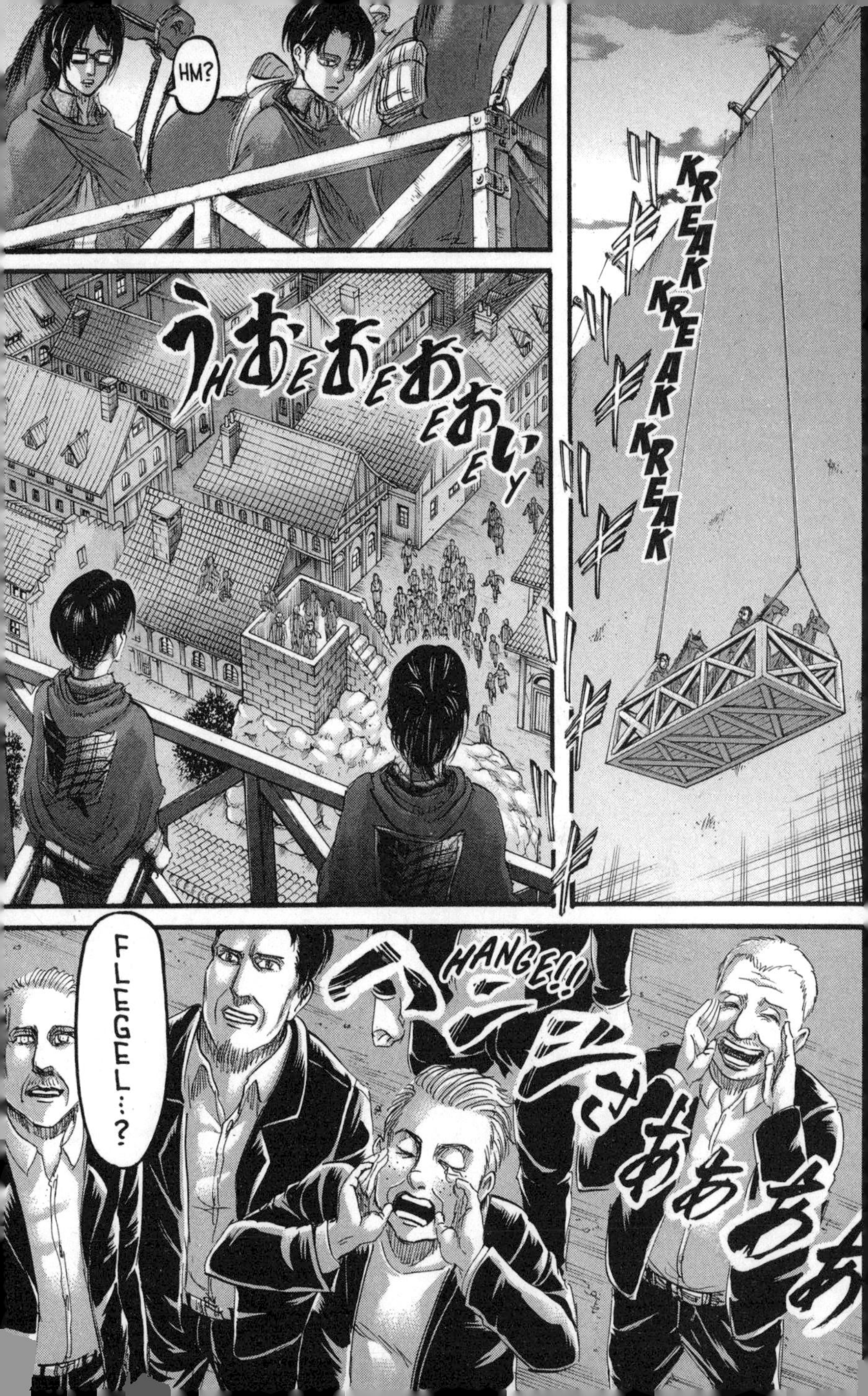
KREAK KREAK KREAK KREAK
HM?
HEEEEY
HANGE!!!
FLEGEL...?

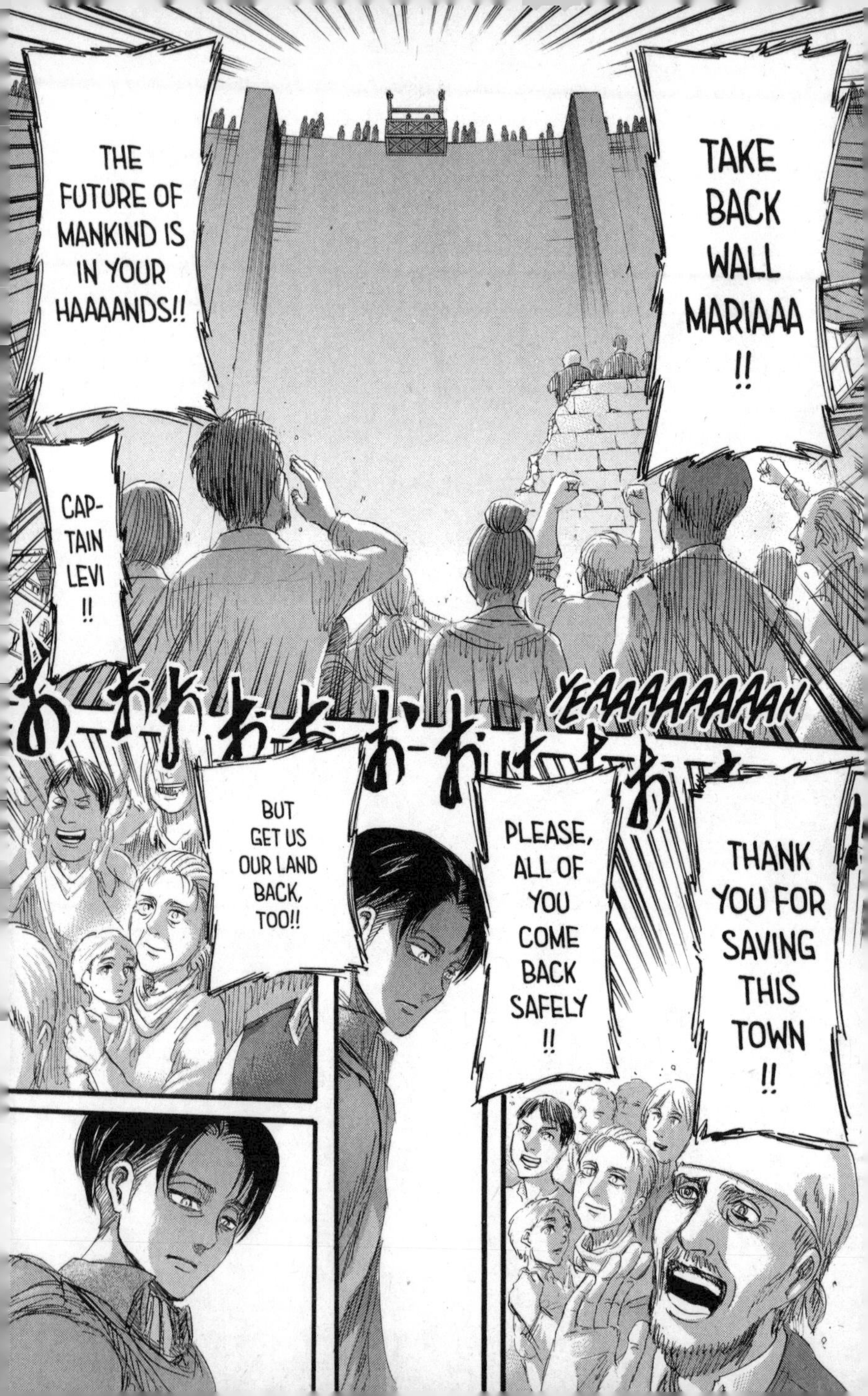
TAKE BACK WALL MARIAAA!!
THE FUTURE OF MANKIND IS IN YOUR HAAAANDS!!
CAP-TAIN LEVI!!
YEAAAAAAAH
THANK YOU FOR SAVING THIS TOWN!!
PLEASE, ALL OF YOU COME BACK SAFELY!!
BUT GET US OUR LAND BACK, TOO!!

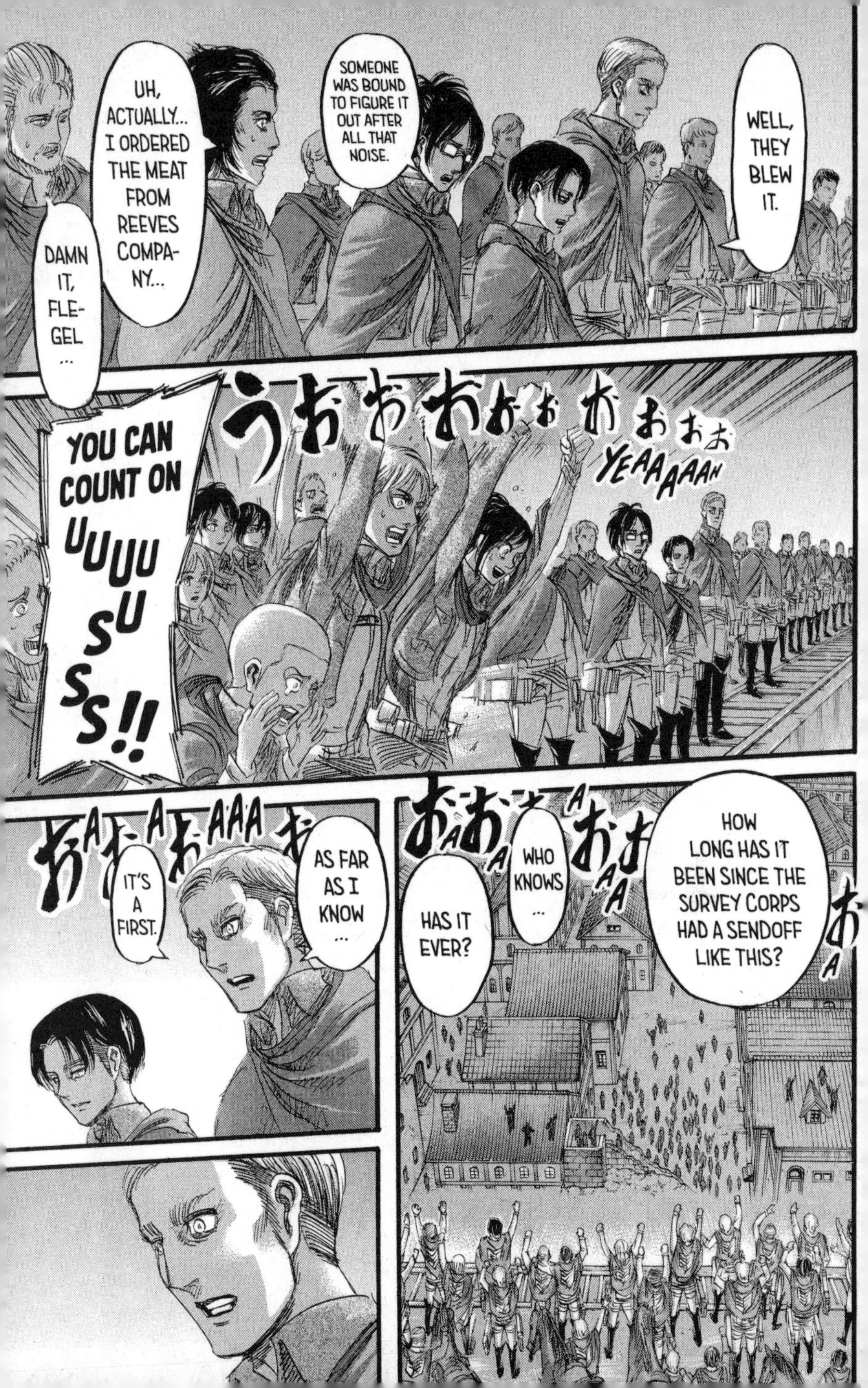
WELL, THEY BLEW IT.
SOMEONE WAS BOUND TO FIGURE IT OUT AFTER ALL THAT NOISE.
UH, ACTUALLY... I ORDERED THE MEAT FROM REEVES COMPANY...
DAMN IT, FLEGEL...
うおおおおお おおおお
YEAAAAAAH
YOU CAN COUNT ON UUUUUSSSS!!
HOW LONG HAS IT BEEN SINCE THE SURVEY CORPS HAD A SENDOFF LIKE THIS?
WHO KNOWS...
HAS IT EVER?
AS FAR AS I KNOW...
IT'S A FIRST.

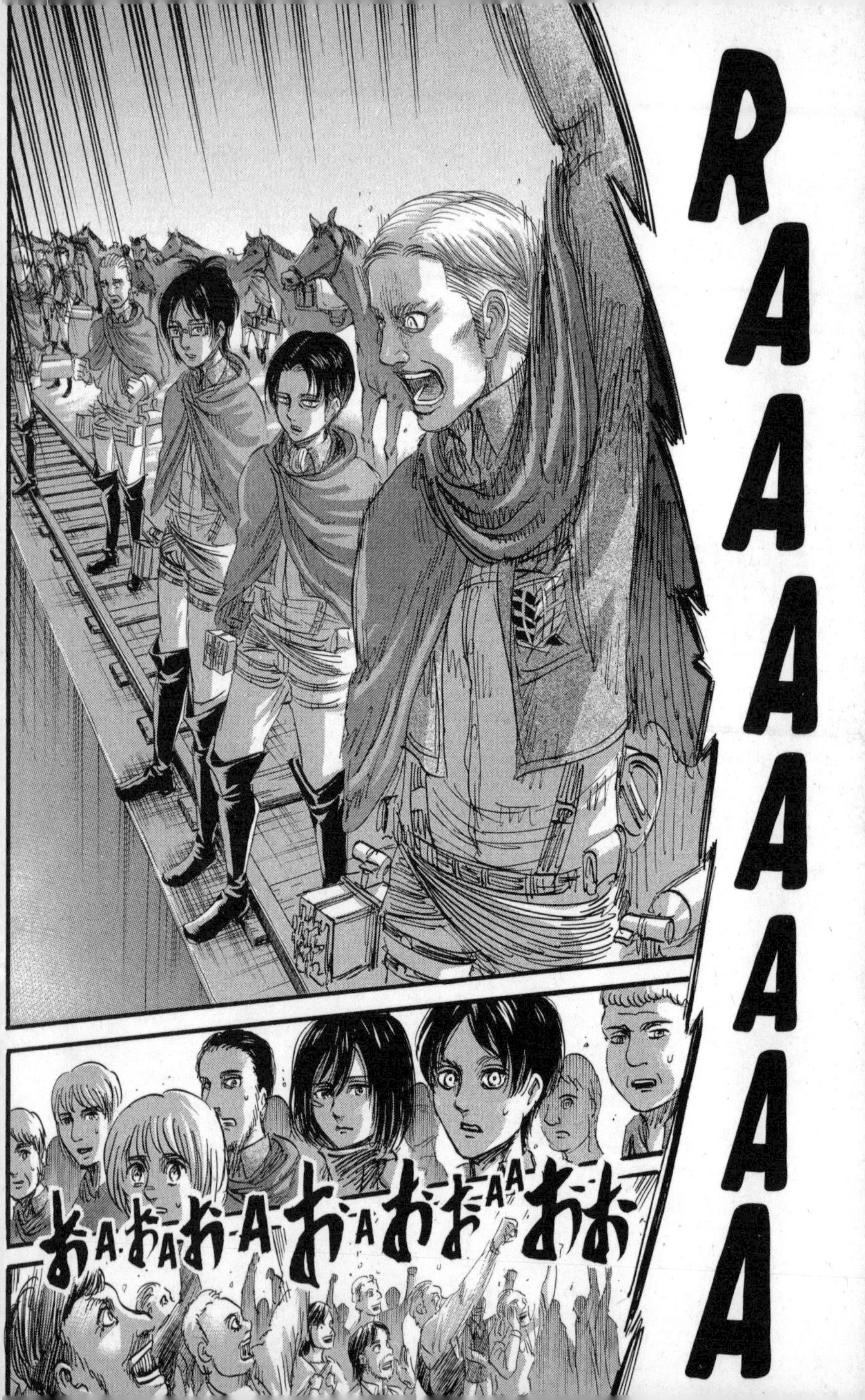
RAAAAAAAAAAA
おAおAおAおAおおAAおお

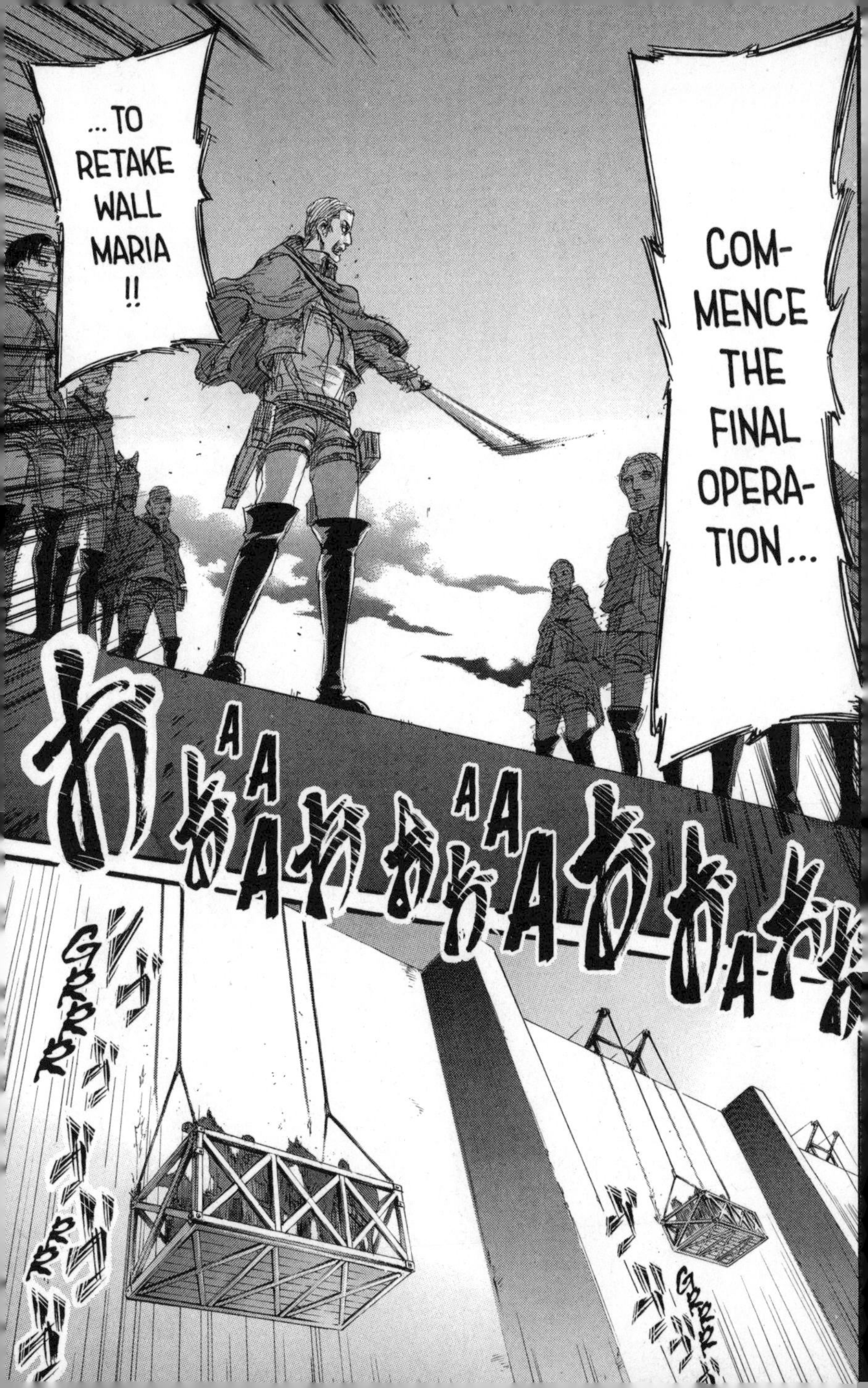
COM-MENCE THE FINAL OPERA-TION...
...TO RETAKE WALL MARIA!!
AAAAAAA
GRRRR
RRRR
GRRRR

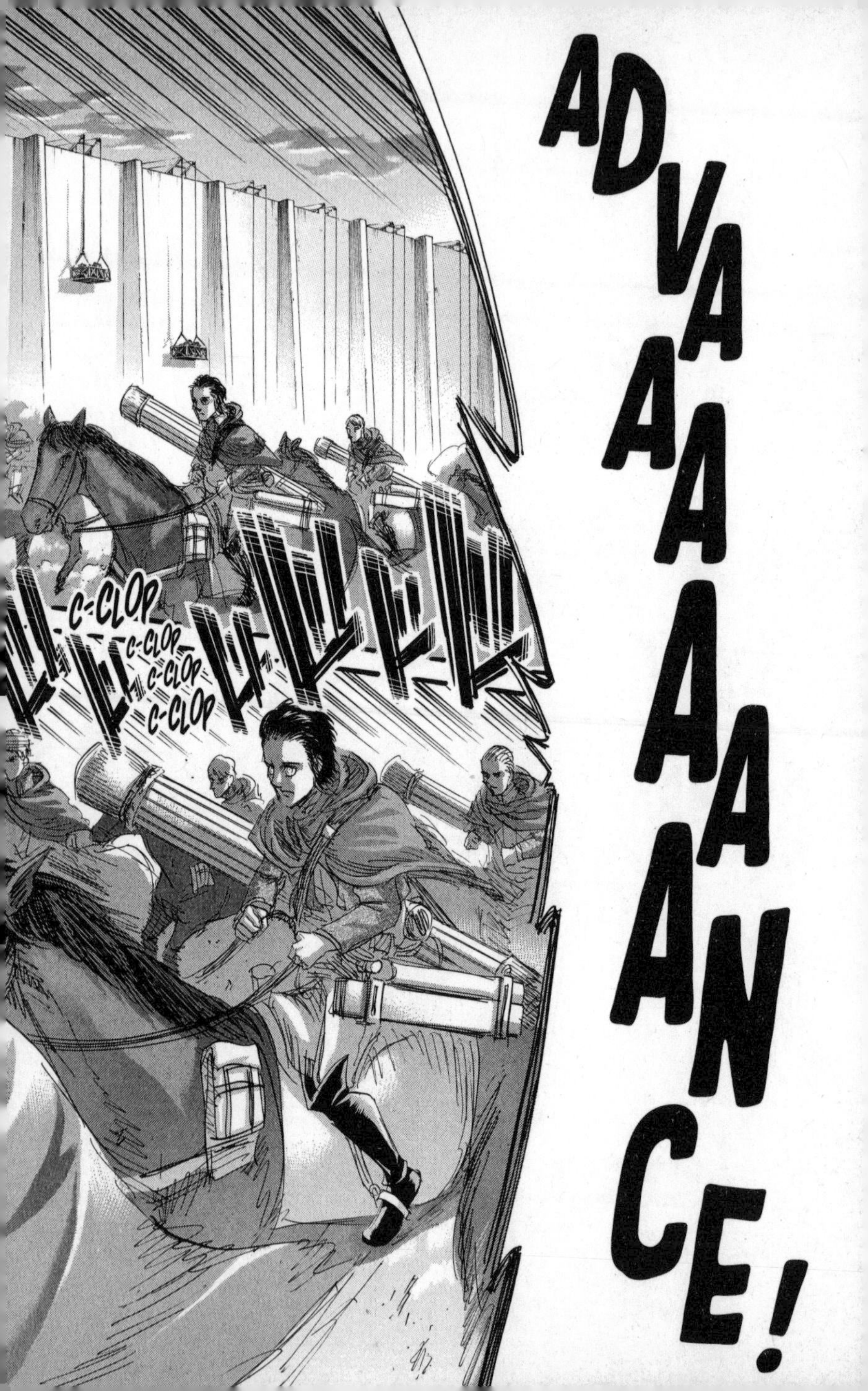
ADVAAAAAAAANCE!
C-CLOP
C-CLOP
C-CLOP
C-CLOP

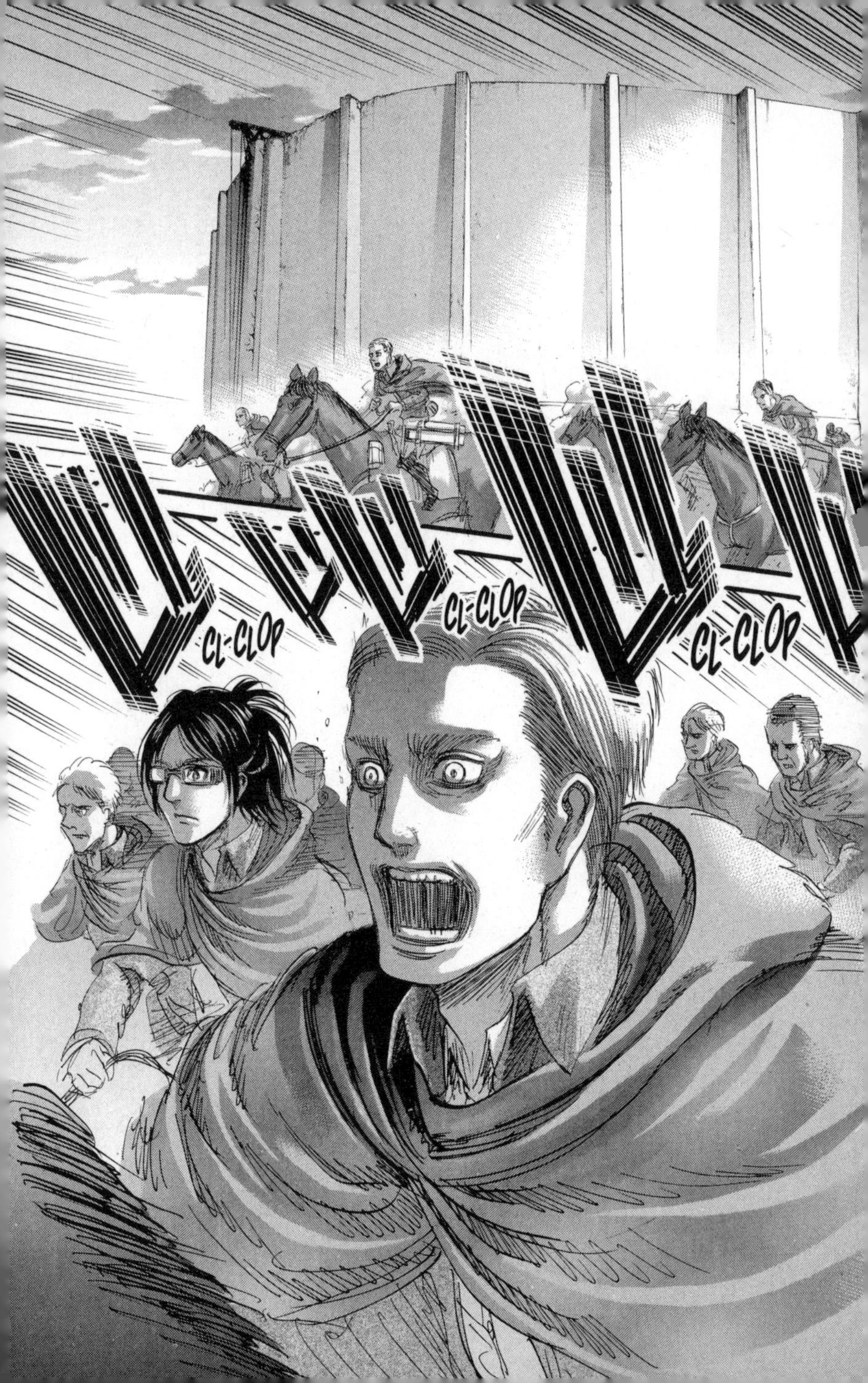
CL-CLOP
CL-CLOP
CL-CLOP

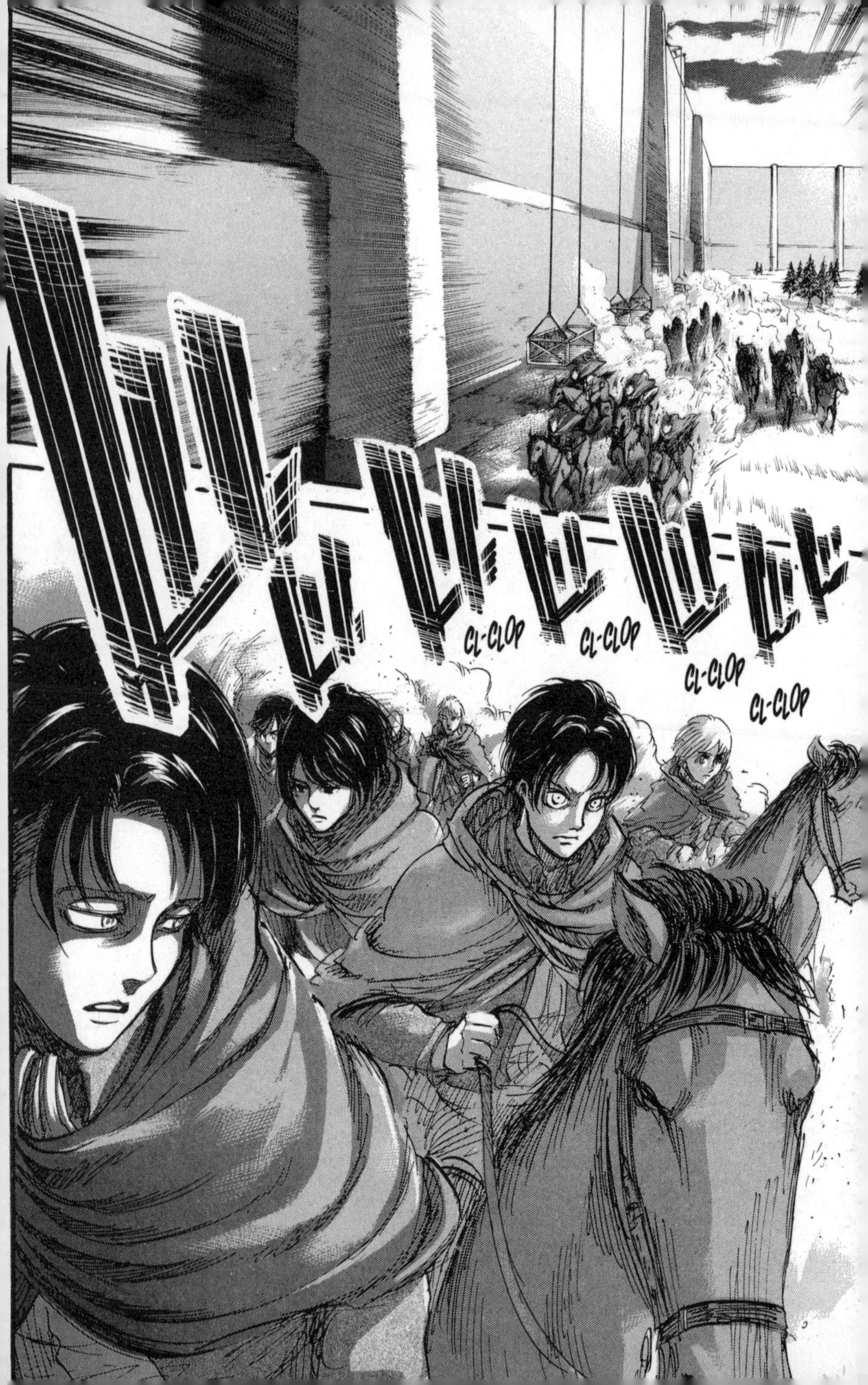
CL-CLOP
CL-CLOP
CL-CLOP
CL-CLOP

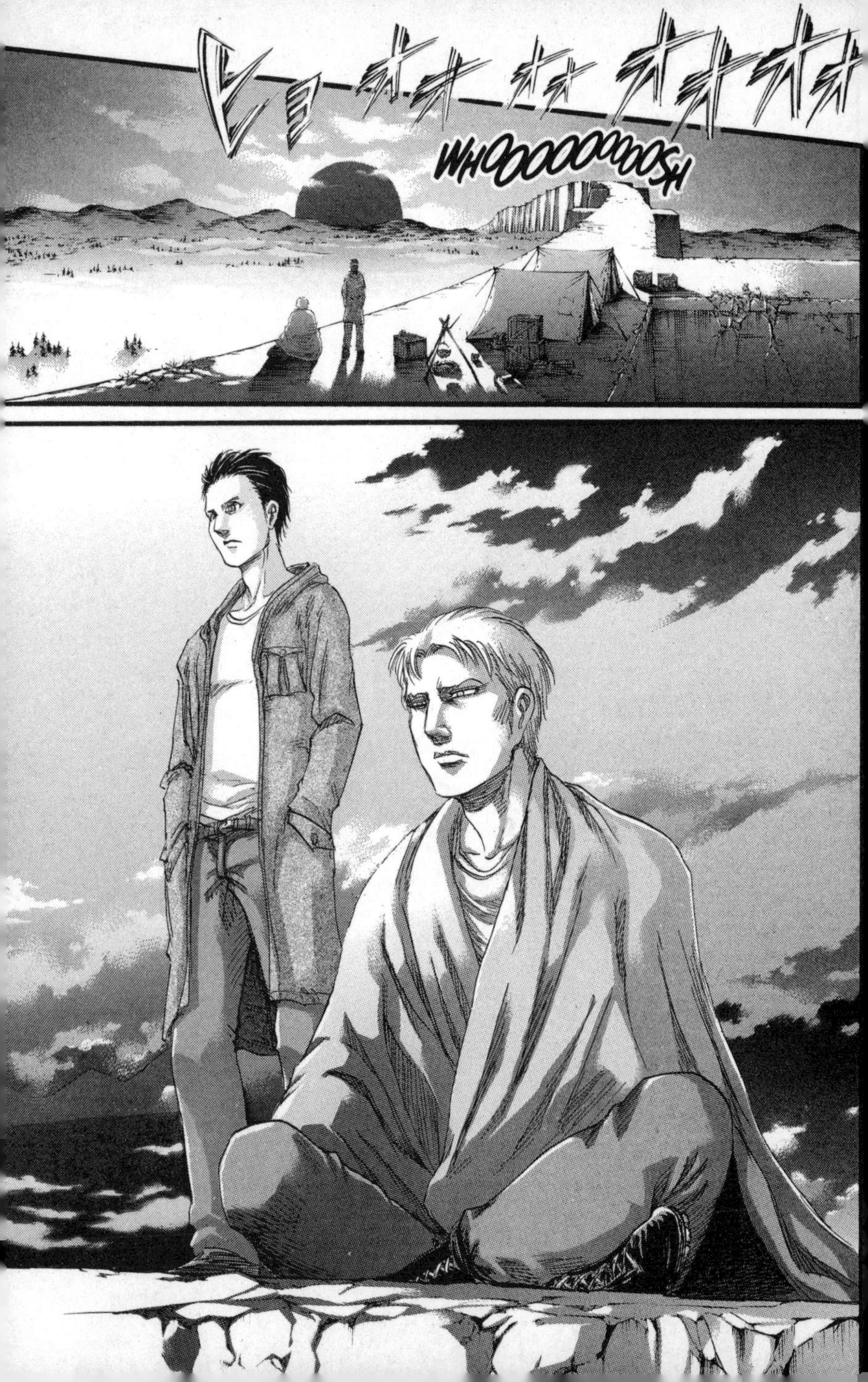
ヒョオオォォオオオオ
WHOOOOOOOOOSH

ATTACK on TITAN

Episode 73: The Town Where Everything Began

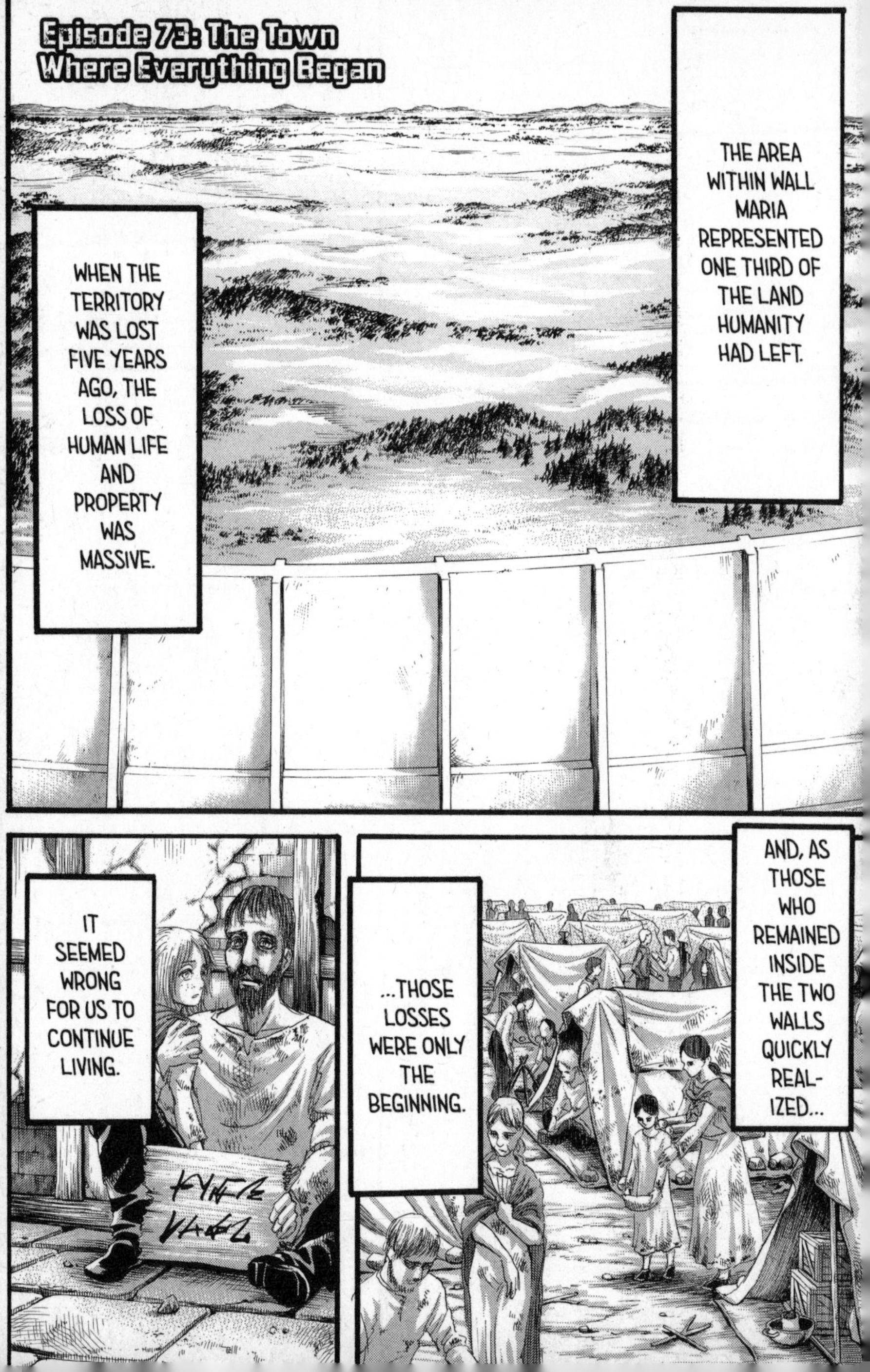
THE AREA WITHIN WALL MARIA REPRESENTED ONE THIRD OF THE LAND HUMANITY HAD LEFT.
WHEN THE TERRITORY WAS LOST FIVE YEARS AGO, THE LOSS OF HUMAN LIFE AND PROPERTY WAS MASSIVE.
AND, AS THOSE WHO REMAINED INSIDE THE TWO WALLS QUICKLY REAL-IZED...
...THOSE LOSSES WERE ONLY THE BEGINNING.
IT SEEMED WRONG FOR US TO CONTINUE LIVING.

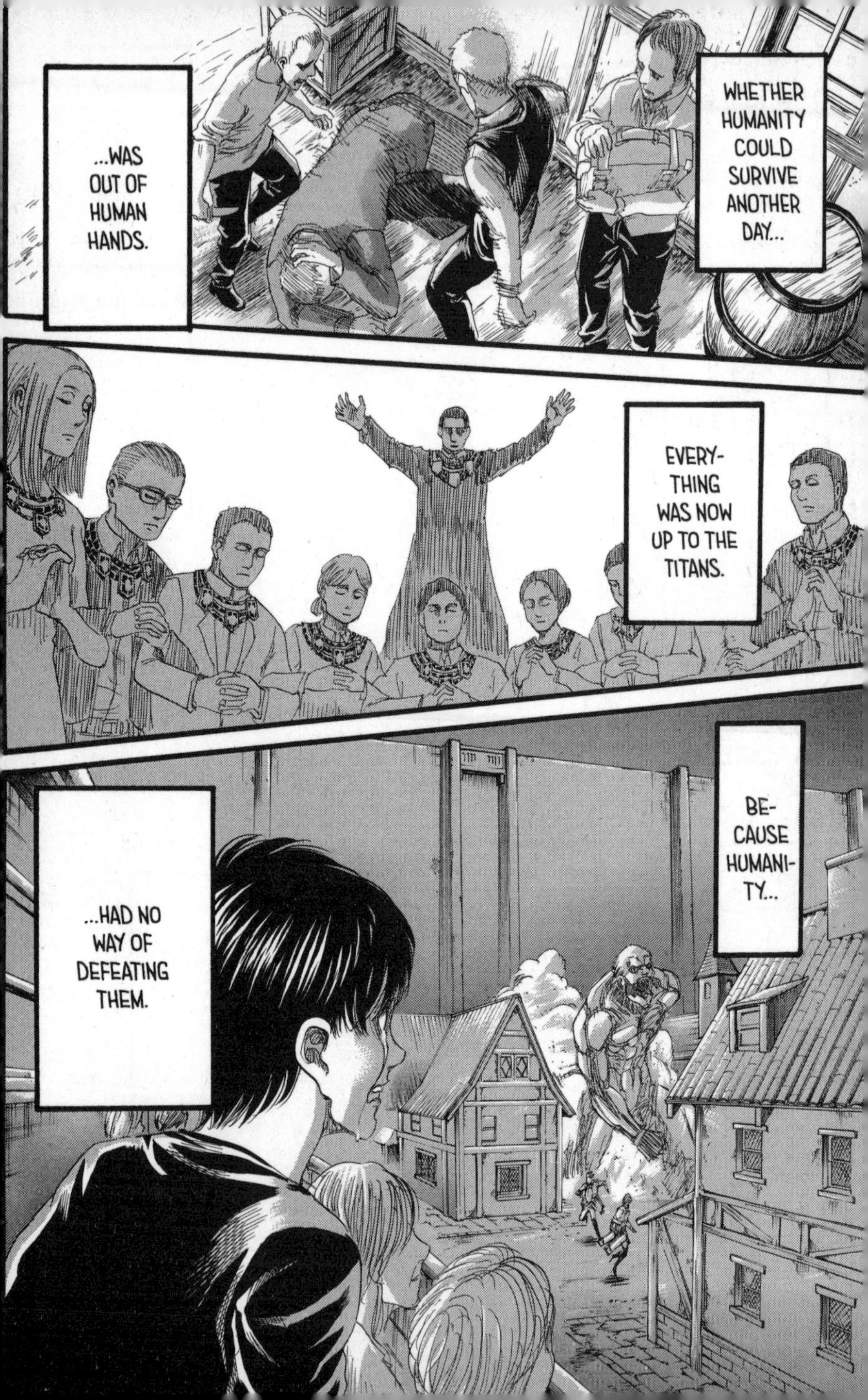
WHETHER HUMANITY COULD SURVIVE ANOTHER DAY...
...WAS OUT OF HUMAN HANDS.
EVERY-THING WAS NOW UP TO THE TITANS.
BE-CAUSE HUMANI-TY...
...HAD NO WAY OF DEFEATING THEM.

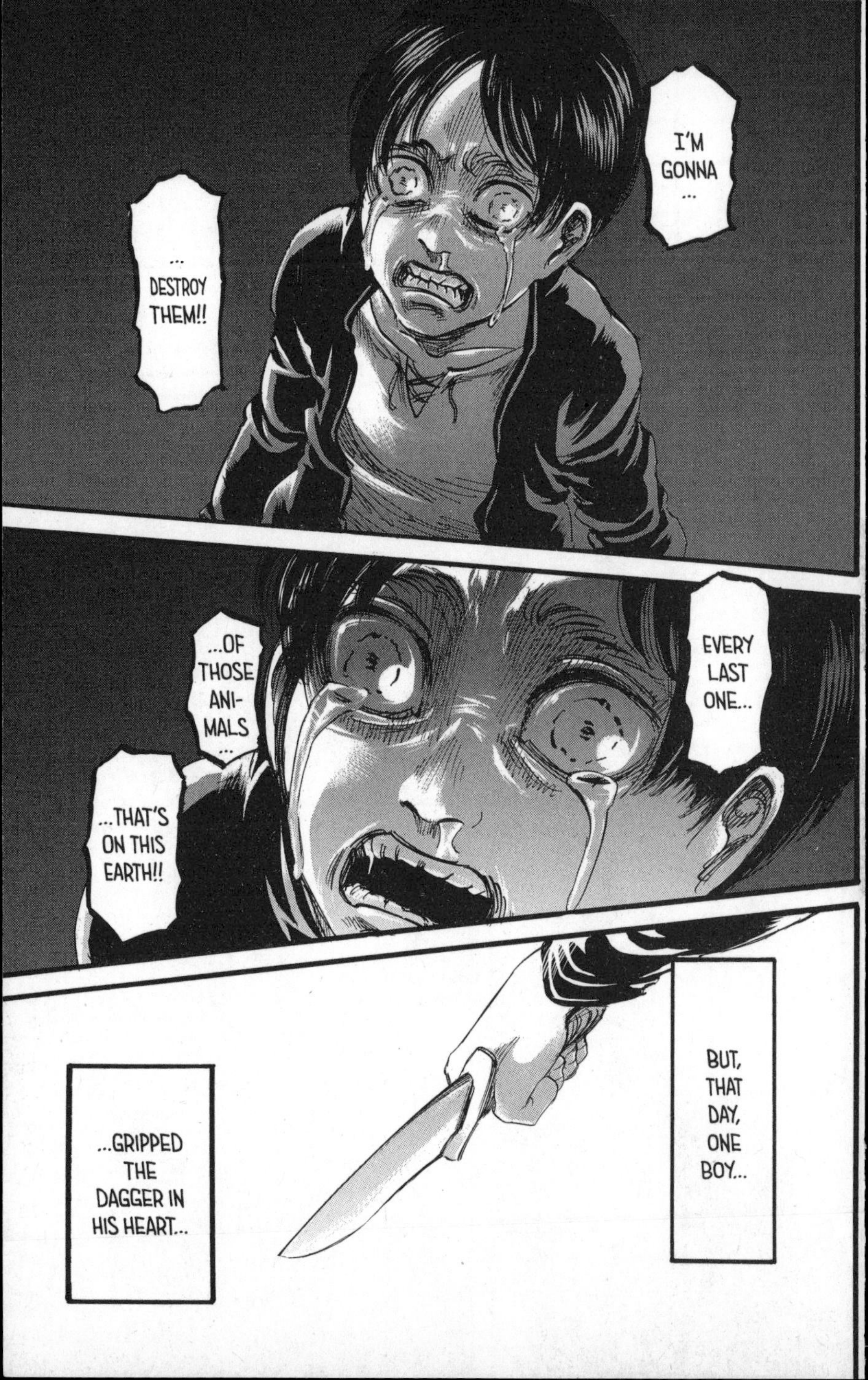
I'M GONNA ...
... DESTROY THEM!!
EVERY LAST ONE...
...OF THOSE ANI-MALS ...
...THAT'S ON THIS EARTH!!
BUT, THAT DAY, ONE BOY...
...GRIPPED THE DAGGER IN HIS HEART...

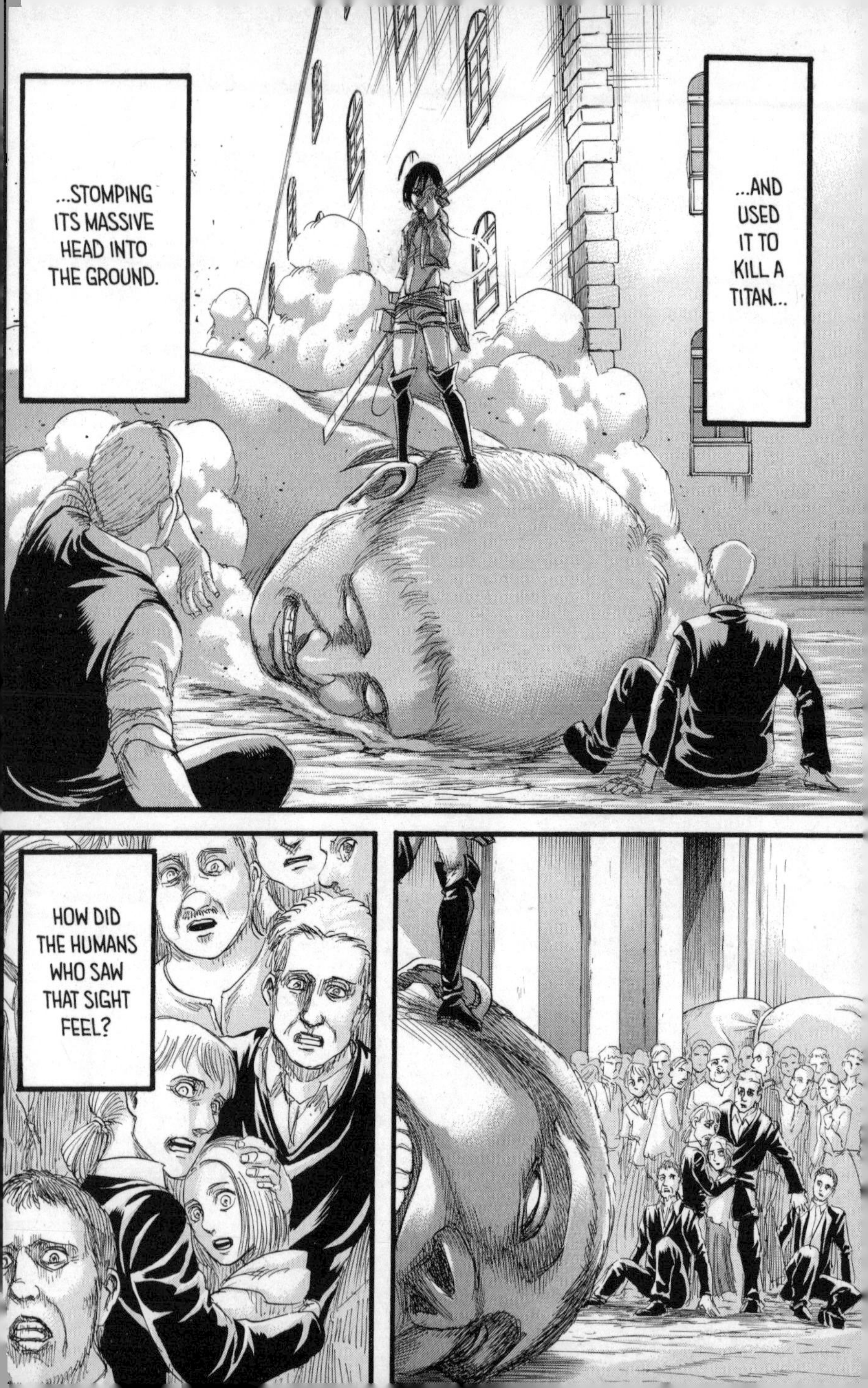
...AND USED IT TO KILL A TITAN...
...STOMPING ITS MASSIVE HEAD INTO THE GROUND.
HOW DID THE HUMANS WHO SAW THAT SIGHT FEEL?

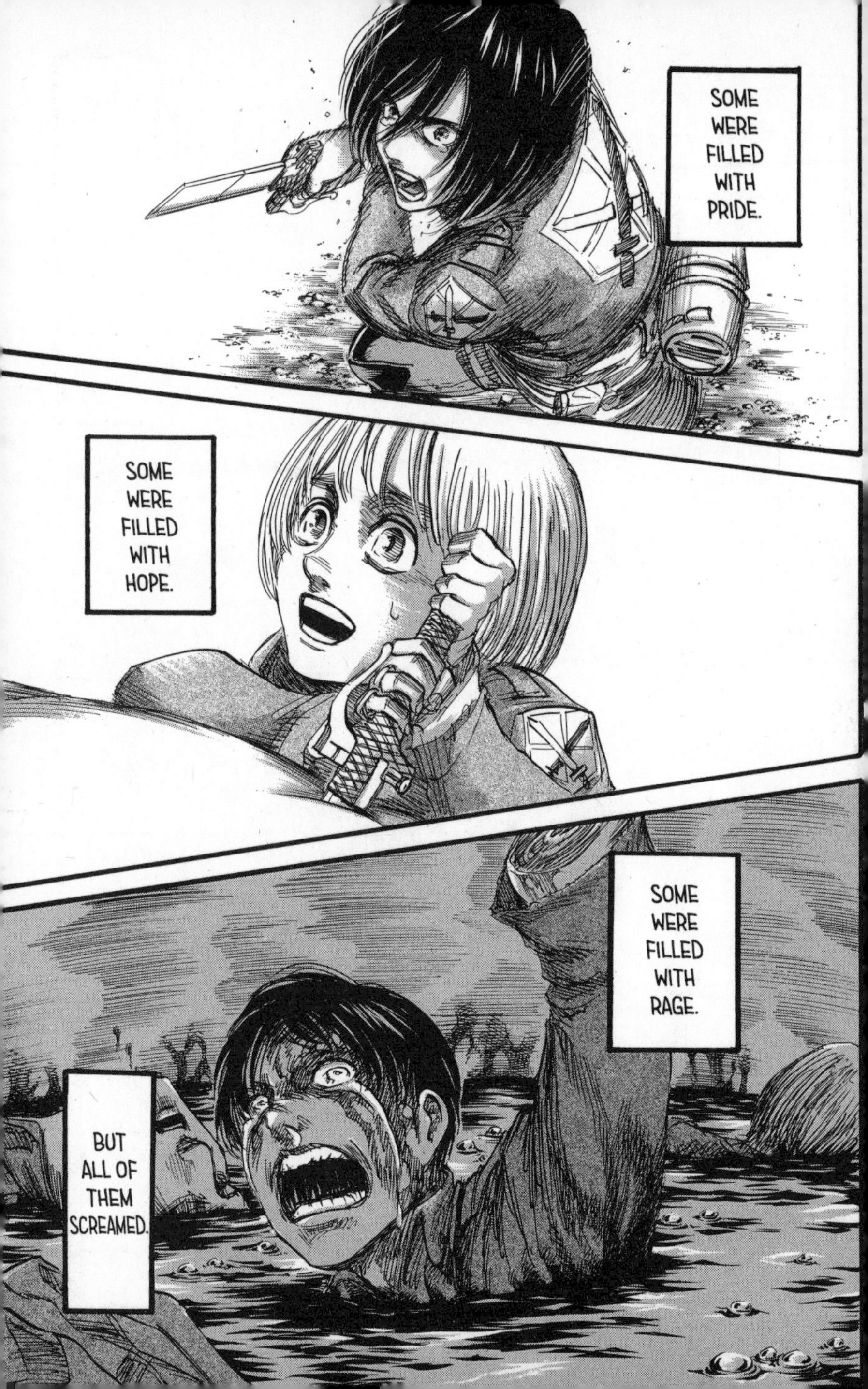
SOME WERE FILLED WITH PRIDE.
SOME WERE FILLED WITH HOPE.
SOME WERE FILLED WITH RAGE.
BUT ALL OF THEM SCREAMED.

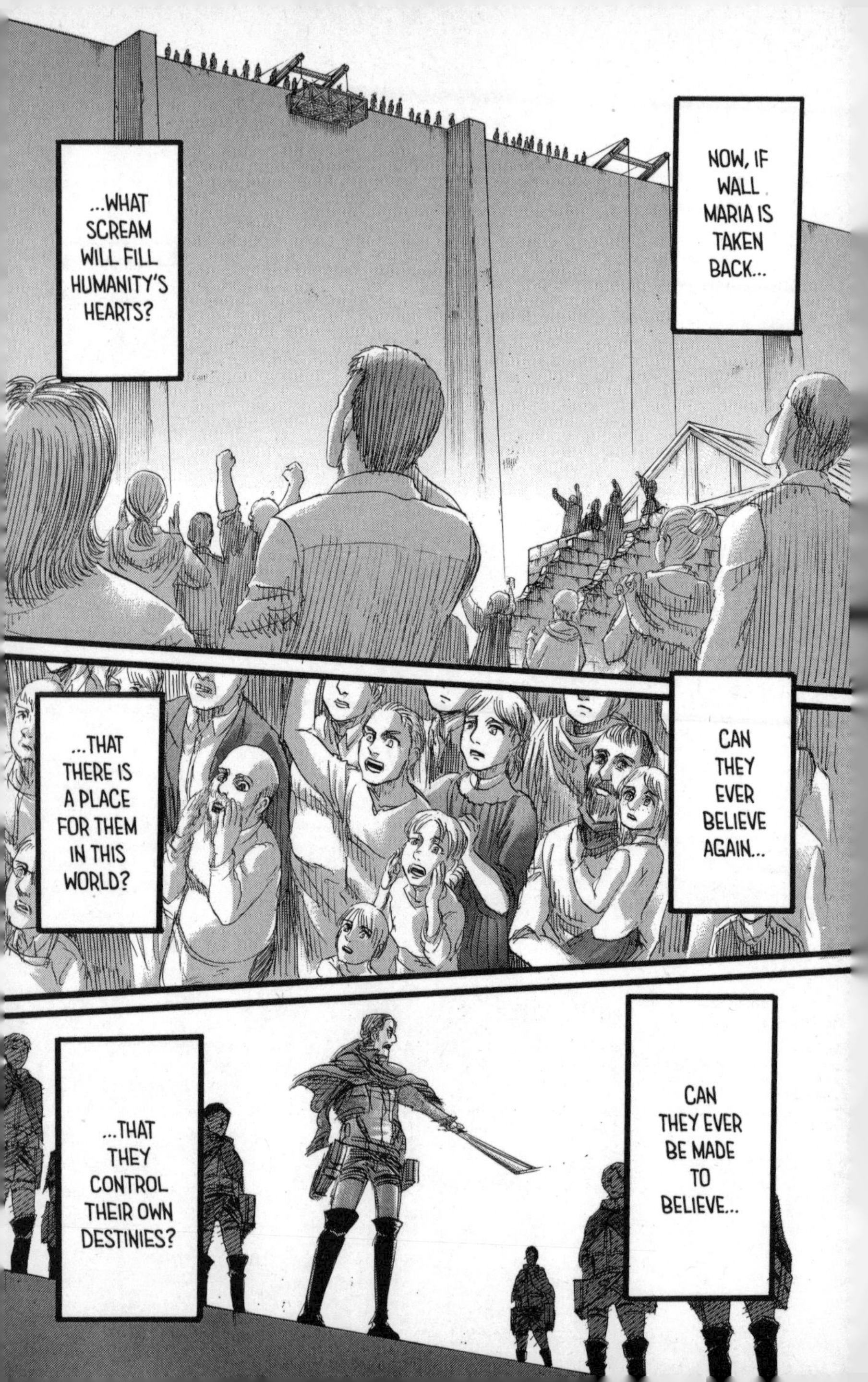
NOW, IF WALL MARIA IS TAKEN BACK...
...WHAT SCREAM WILL FILL HUMANITY'S HEARTS?
CAN THEY EVER BELIEVE AGAIN...
...THAT THERE IS A PLACE FOR THEM IN THIS WORLD?
CAN THEY EVER BE MADE TO BELIEVE...
...THAT THEY CONTROL THEIR OWN DESTINIES?

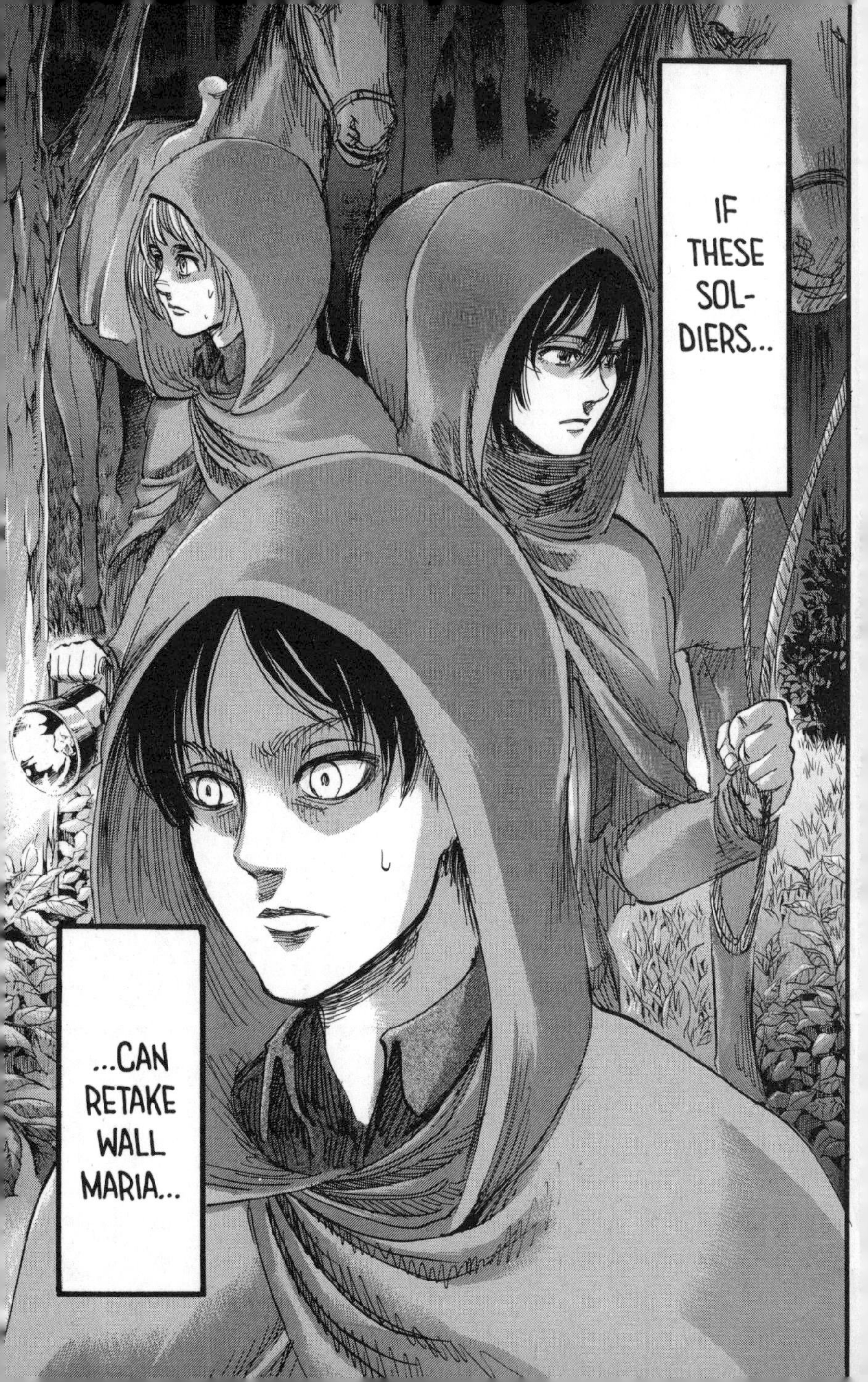
IF THESE SOL- DIERS...
...CAN RETAKE WALL MARIA...

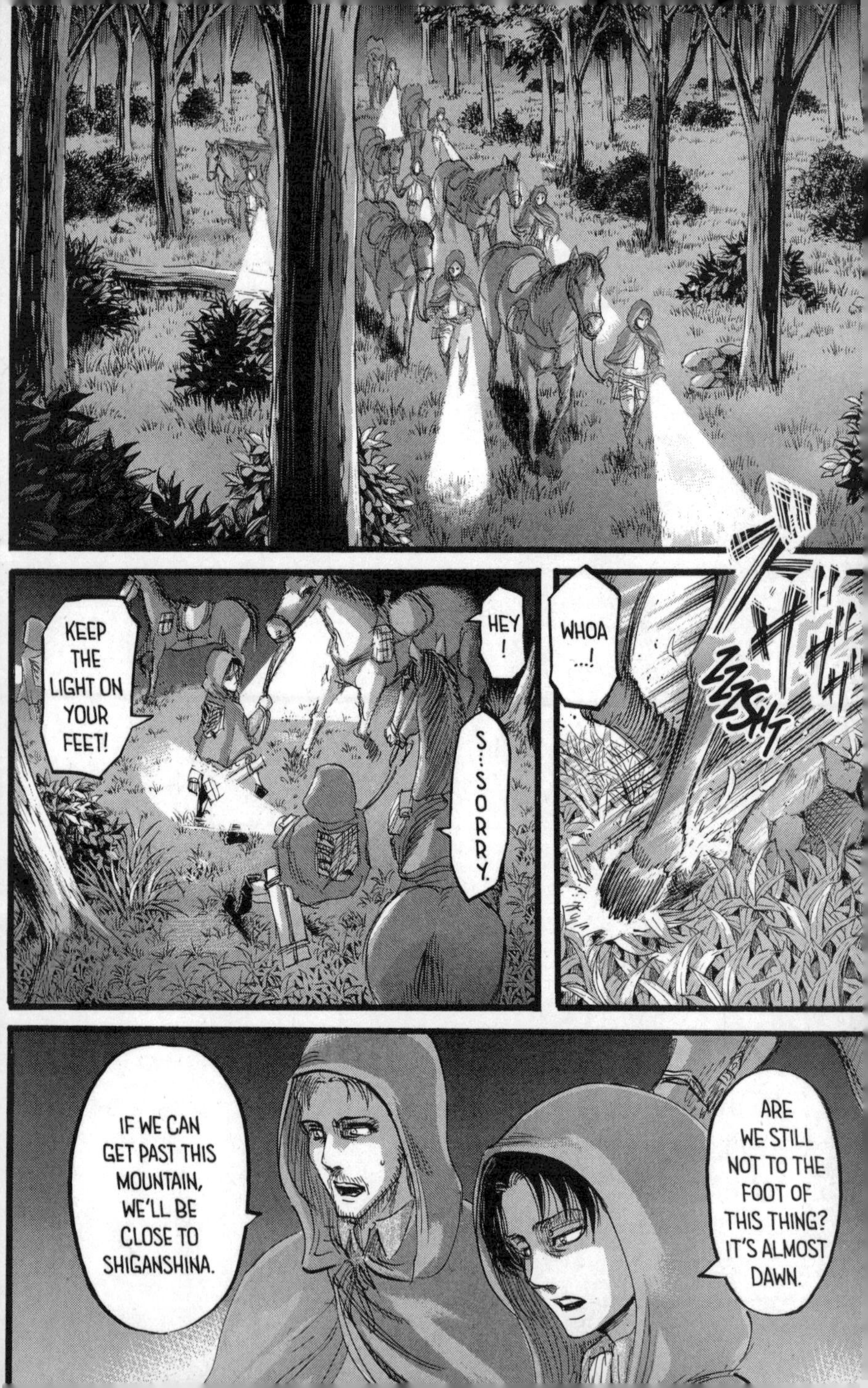

WHOA ...!
ZZZSHT
HEY!
KEEP THE LIGHT ON YOUR FEET!
S...SORRY.
ARE WE STILL NOT TO THE FOOT OF THIS THING? IT'S ALMOST DAWN.
IF WE CAN GET PAST THIS MOUNTAIN, WE'LL BE CLOSE TO SHIGANSHINA.

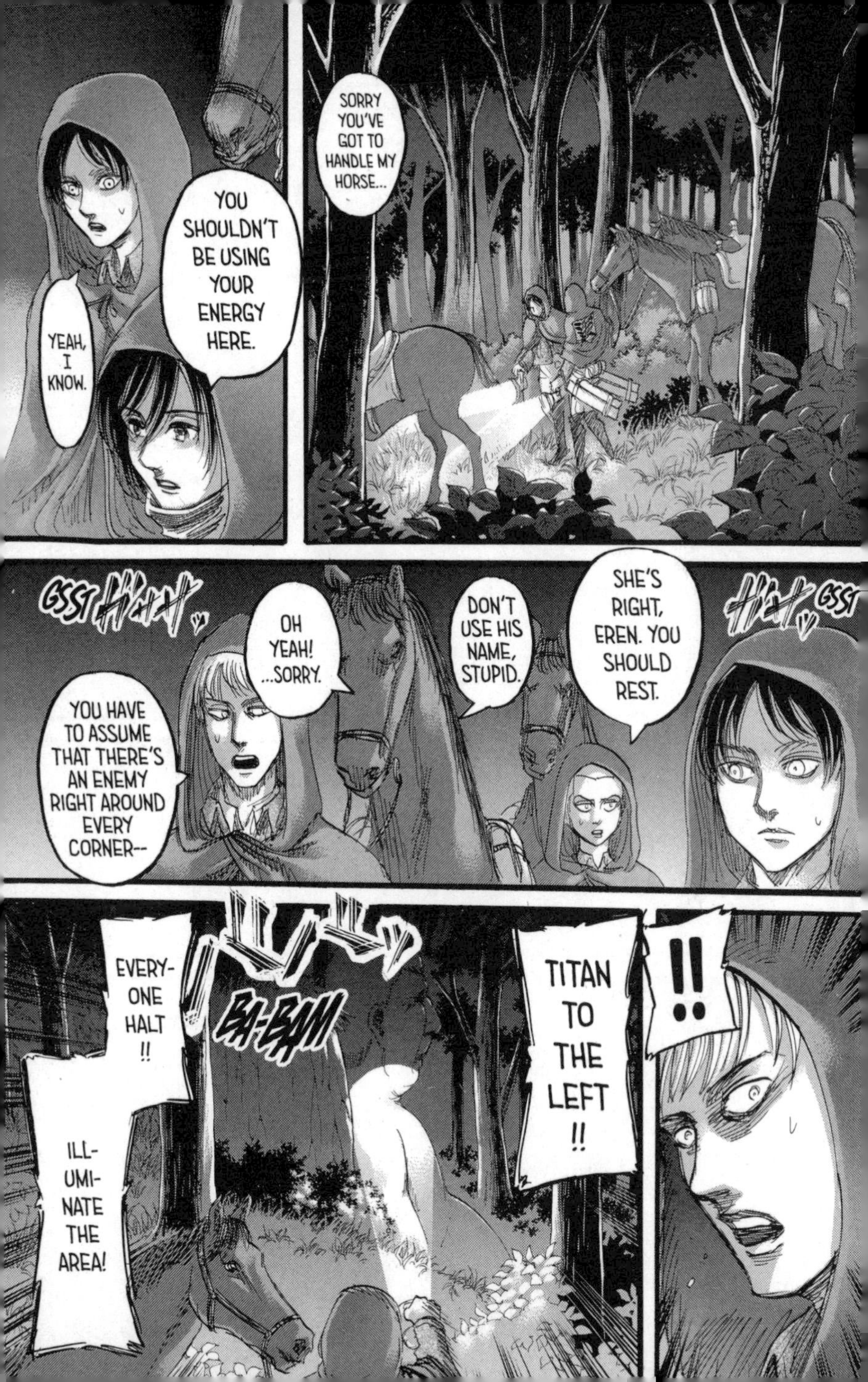
SORRY YOU'VE GOT TO HANDLE MY HORSE...
YOU SHOULDN'T BE USING YOUR ENERGY HERE.
YEAH, I KNOW.
GSST
SHE'S RIGHT, EREN. YOU SHOULD REST.
DON'T USE HIS NAME, STUPID.
OH YEAH! ...SORRY.
YOU HAVE TO ASSUME THAT THERE'S AN ENEMY RIGHT AROUND EVERY CORNER--
GSST
!!
TITAN TO THE LEFT !!
BA-BAM
EVERY-ONE HALT !!
ILL-UMI-NATE THE AREA!

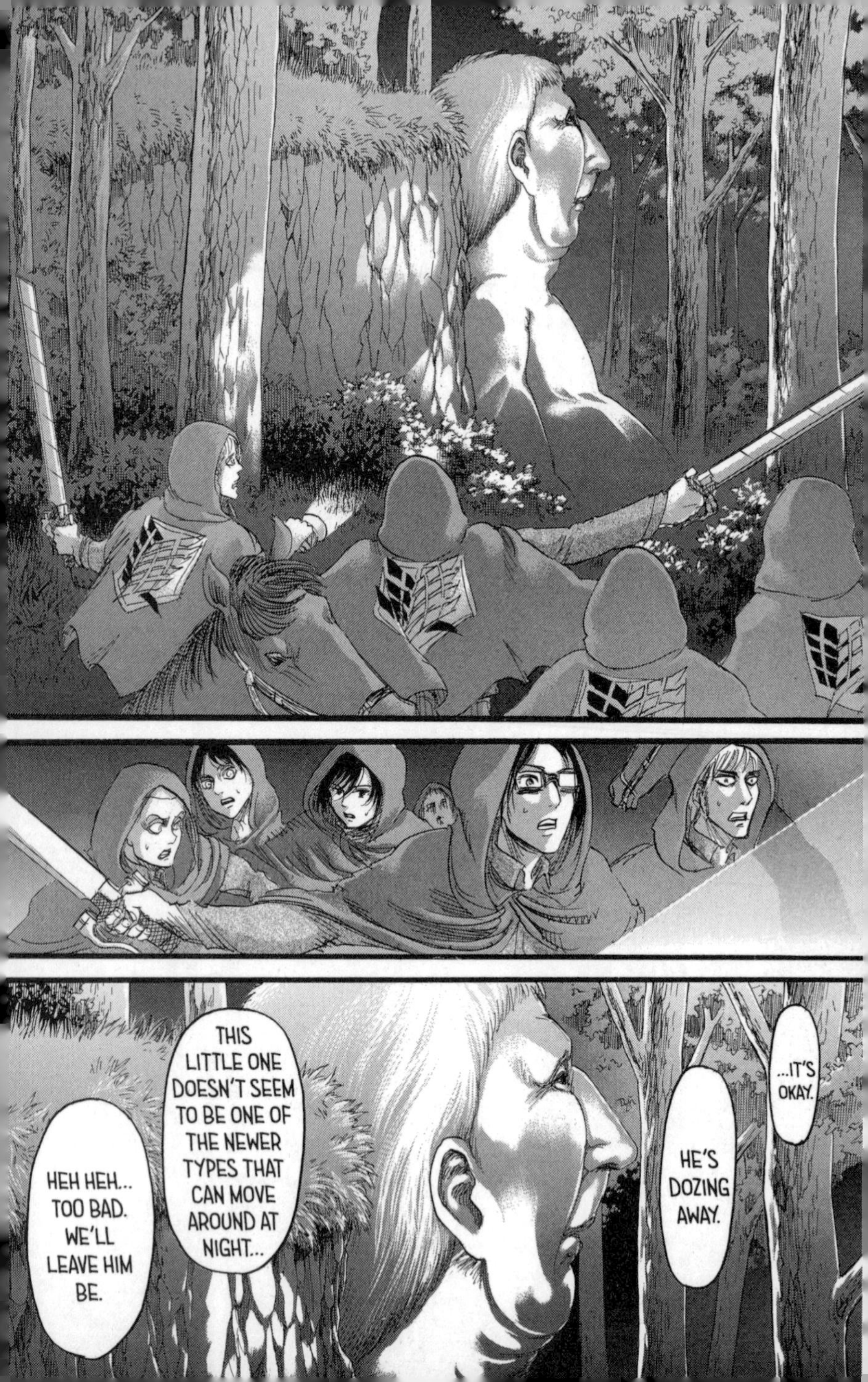
...IT'S OKAY.
HE'S DOZING AWAY.
THIS LITTLE ONE DOESN'T SEEM TO BE ONE OF THE NEWER TYPES THAT CAN MOVE AROUND AT NIGHT...
HEH HEH... TOO BAD. WE'LL LEAVE HIM BE.

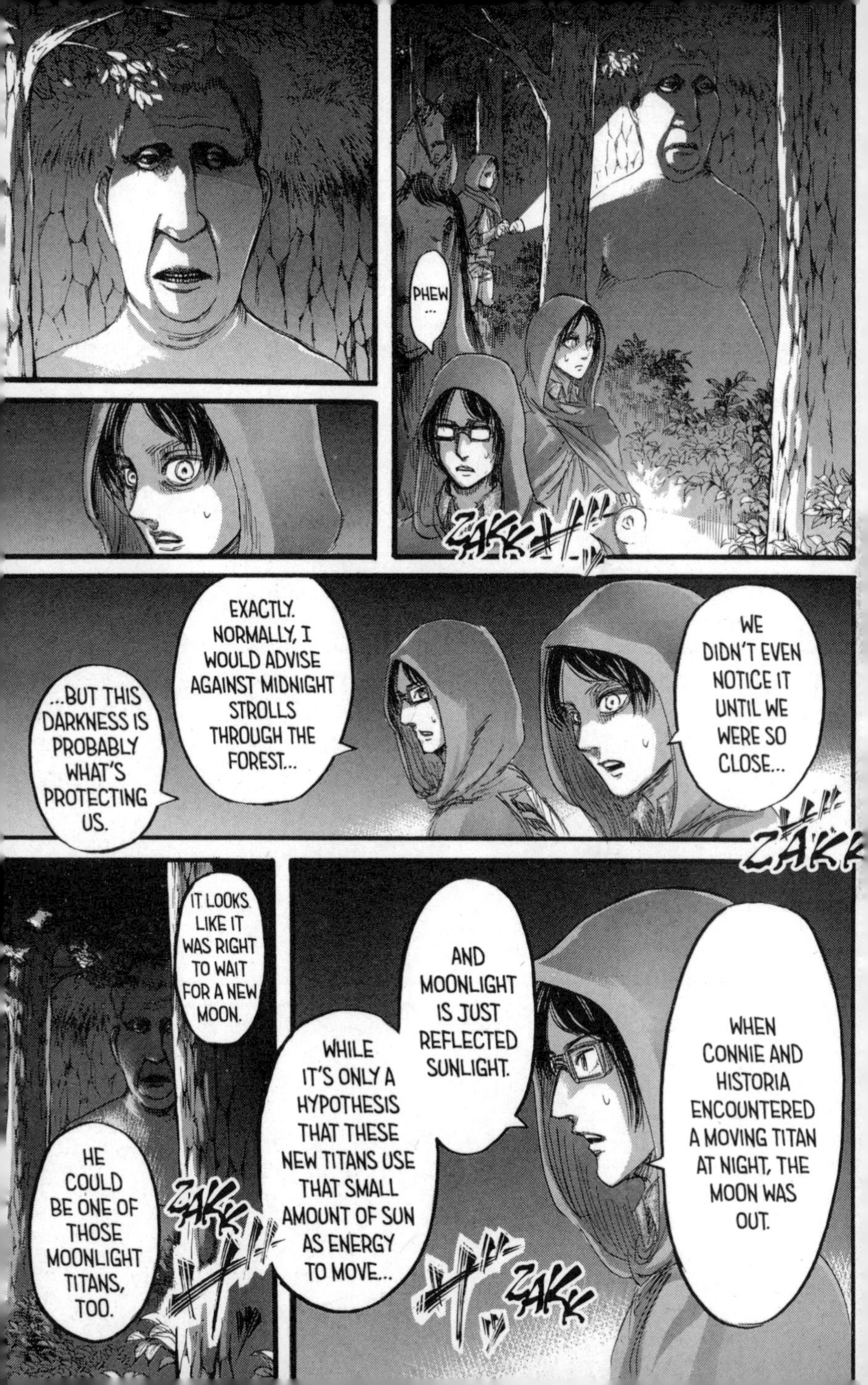
PHEW ...
ZAKK
WE DIDN'T EVEN NOTICE IT UNTIL WE WERE SO CLOSE...
ZAKK
EXACTLY. NORMALLY, I WOULD ADVISE AGAINST MIDNIGHT STROLLS THROUGH THE FOREST...
...BUT THIS DARKNESS IS PROBABLY WHAT'S PROTECTING US.
WHEN CONNIE AND HISTORIA ENCOUNTERED A MOVING TITAN AT NIGHT, THE MOON WAS OUT.
AND MOONLIGHT IS JUST REFLECTED SUNLIGHT.
WHILE IT'S ONLY A HYPOTHESIS THAT THESE NEW TITANS USE THAT SMALL AMOUNT OF SUN AS ENERGY TO MOVE...
ZAKK
IT LOOKS LIKE IT WAS RIGHT TO WAIT FOR A NEW MOON.
ZAKK
HE COULD BE ONE OF THOSE MOONLIGHT TITANS, TOO.

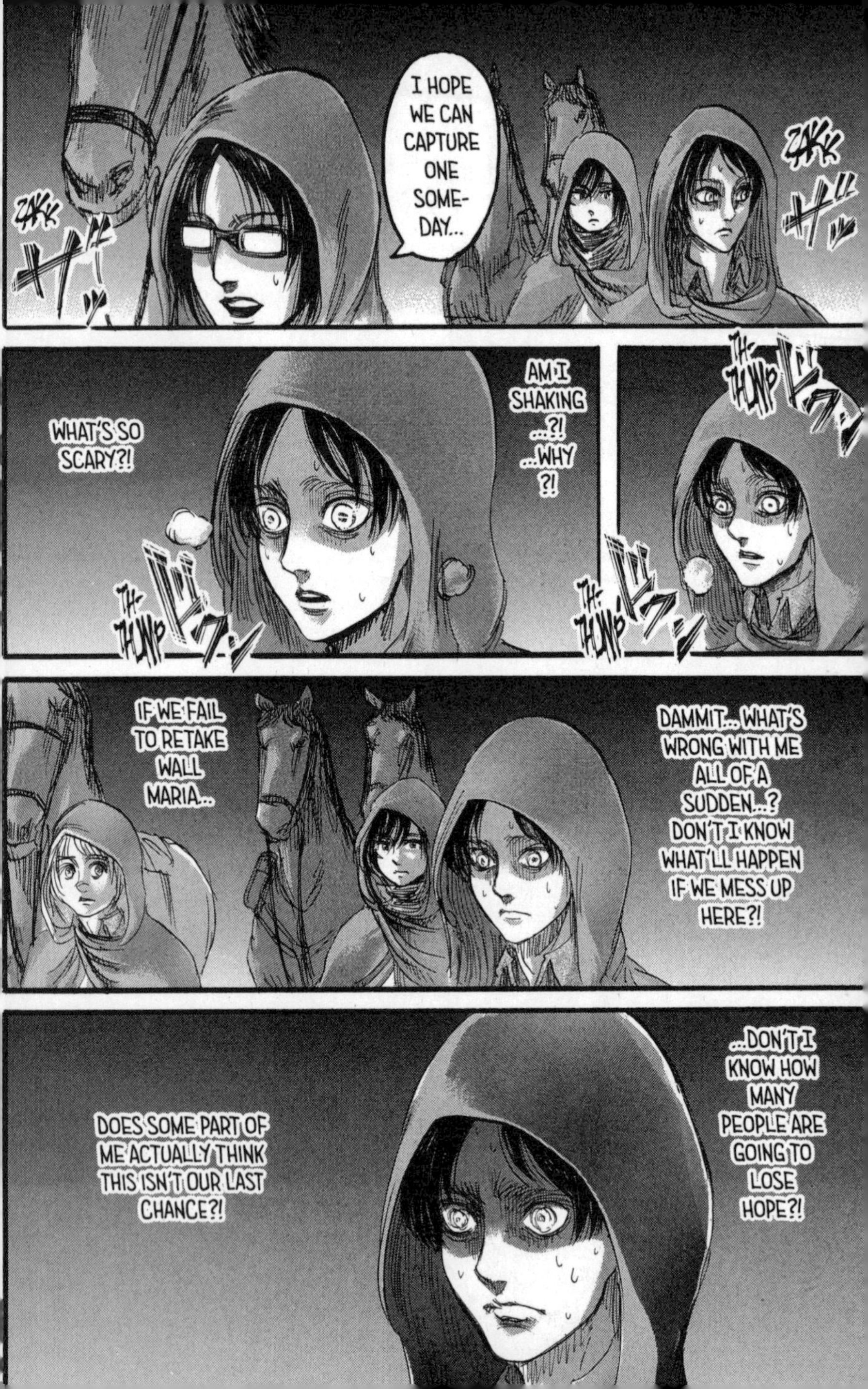
ZAK
I HOPE WE CAN CAPTURE ONE SOME-DAY...
ZAK
TH-THUMP
TH-THUMP
AM I SHAKING ...?! ...WHY ?!
WHAT'S SO SCARY?!
TH-THUMP
DAMMIT... WHAT'S WRONG WITH ME ALL OF A SUDDEN...? DON'T I KNOW WHAT'LL HAPPEN IF WE MESS UP HERE?!
IF WE FAIL TO RETAKE WALL MARIA...
...DON'T I KNOW HOW MANY PEOPLE ARE GOING TO LOSE HOPE?!
DOES SOME PART OF ME ACTUALLY THINK THIS ISN'T OUR LAST CHANCE?!

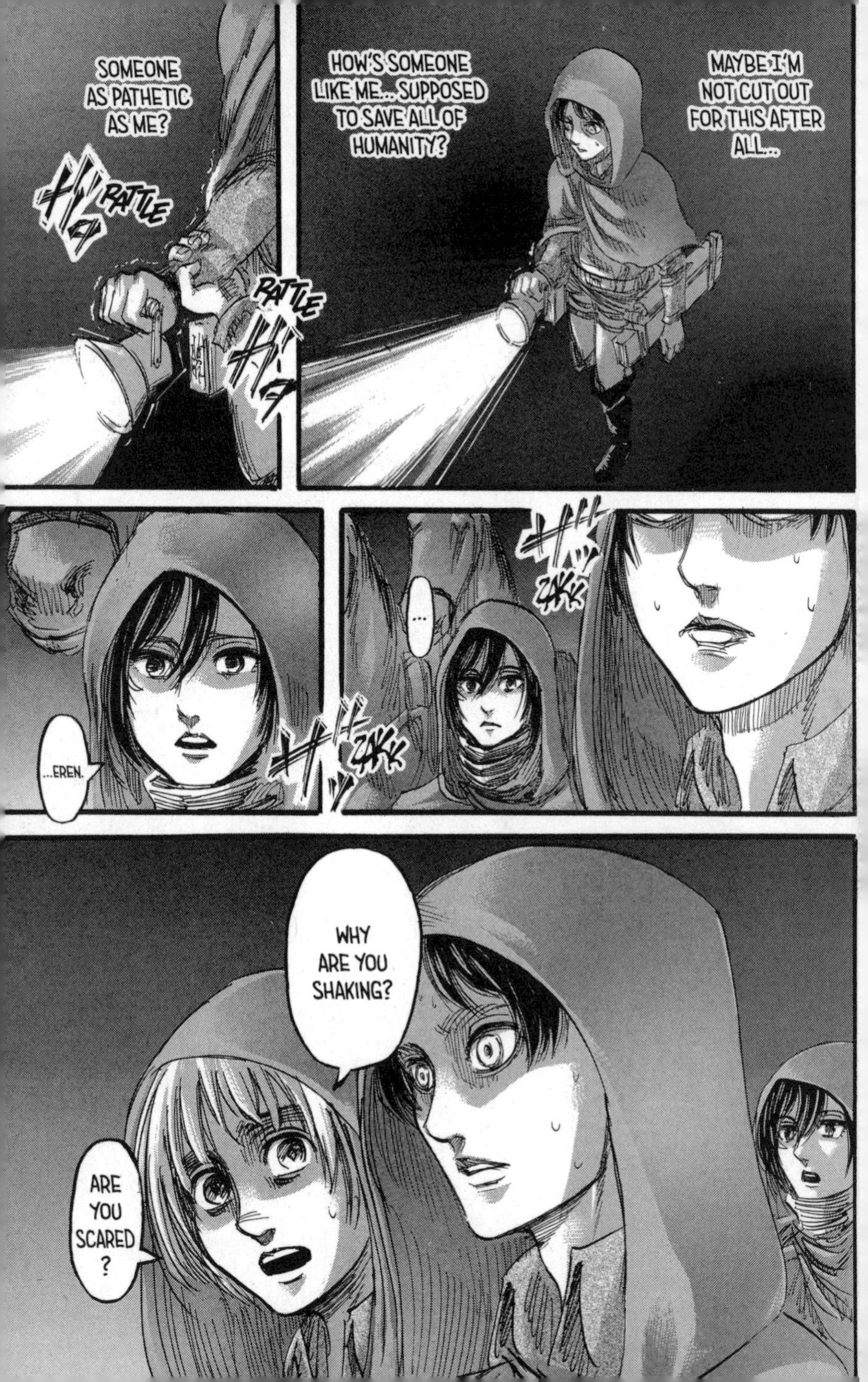
MAYBE I'M NOT CUT OUT FOR THIS AFTER ALL...
HOW'S SOMEONE LIKE ME... SUPPOSED TO SAVE ALL OF HUMANITY?
RATTLE
SOMEONE AS PATHETIC AS ME?
RATTLE
ZAK
...
ZAK
...EREN.
WHY ARE YOU SHAKING?
ARE YOU SCARED ?

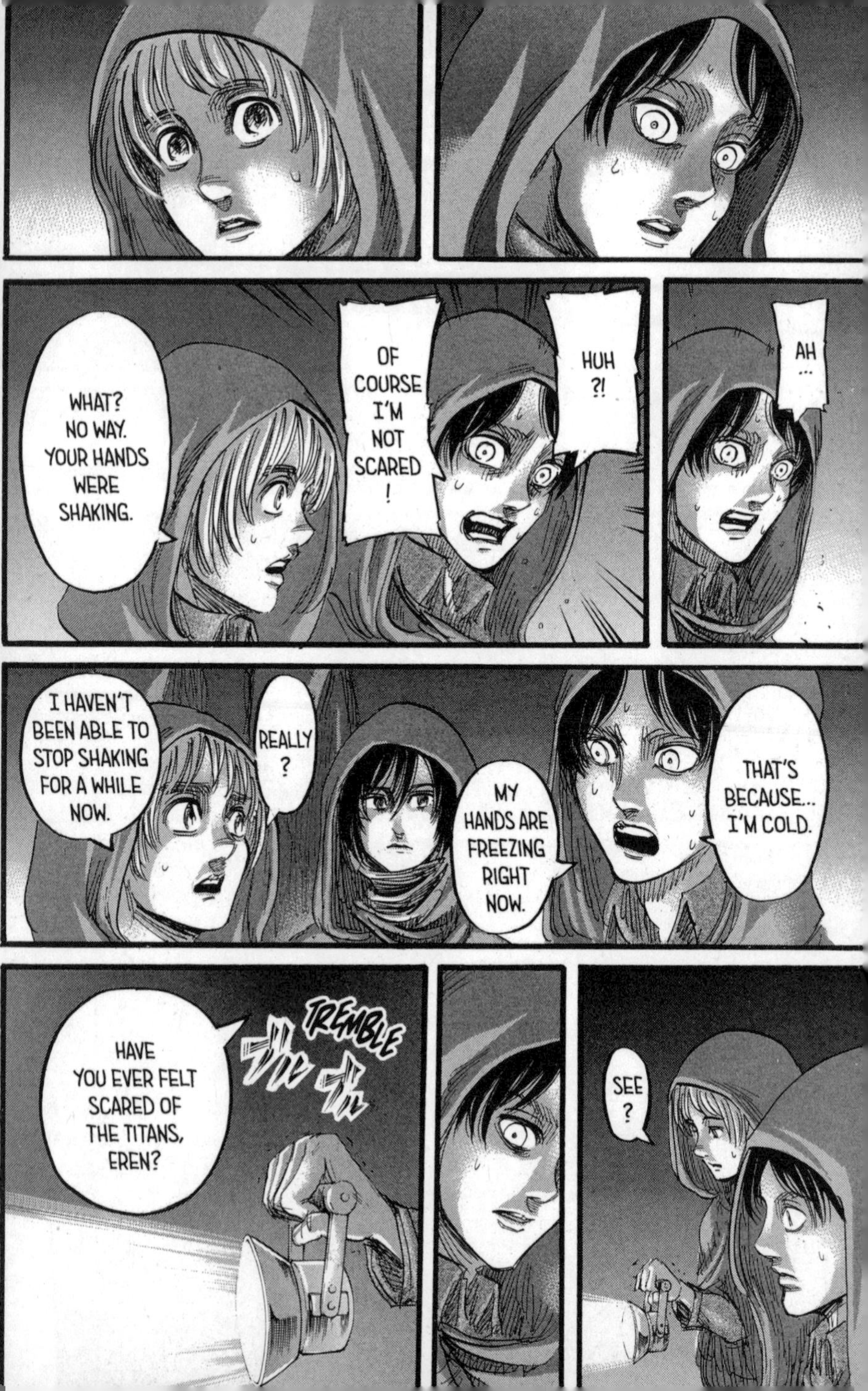
WHAT? NO WAY. YOUR HANDS WERE SHAKING.
HUH?!
OF COURSE I'M NOT SCARED!
AH ...
I HAVEN'T BEEN ABLE TO STOP SHAKING FOR A WHILE NOW.
REALLY?
THAT'S BECAUSE... I'M COLD.
MY HANDS ARE FREEZING RIGHT NOW.
HAVE YOU EVER FELT SCARED OF THE TITANS, EREN?
TREMBLE
SEE?

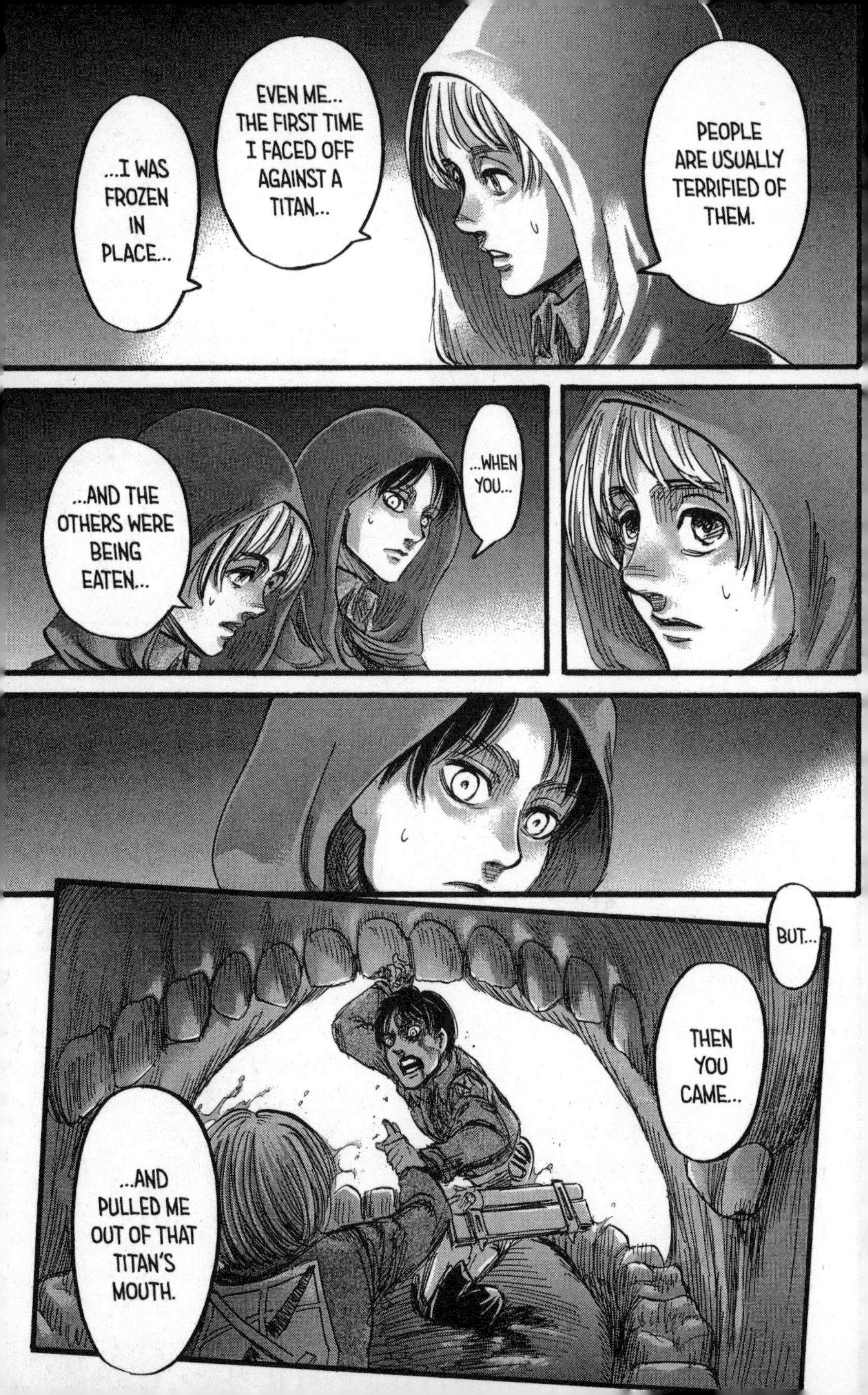
PEOPLE ARE USUALLY TERRIFIED OF THEM.
EVEN ME... THE FIRST TIME I FACED OFF AGAINST A TITAN...
...I WAS FROZEN IN PLACE...
...WHEN YOU...
...AND THE OTHERS WERE BEING EATEN...
BUT...
THEN YOU CAME...
...AND PULLED ME OUT OF THAT TITAN'S MOUTH.

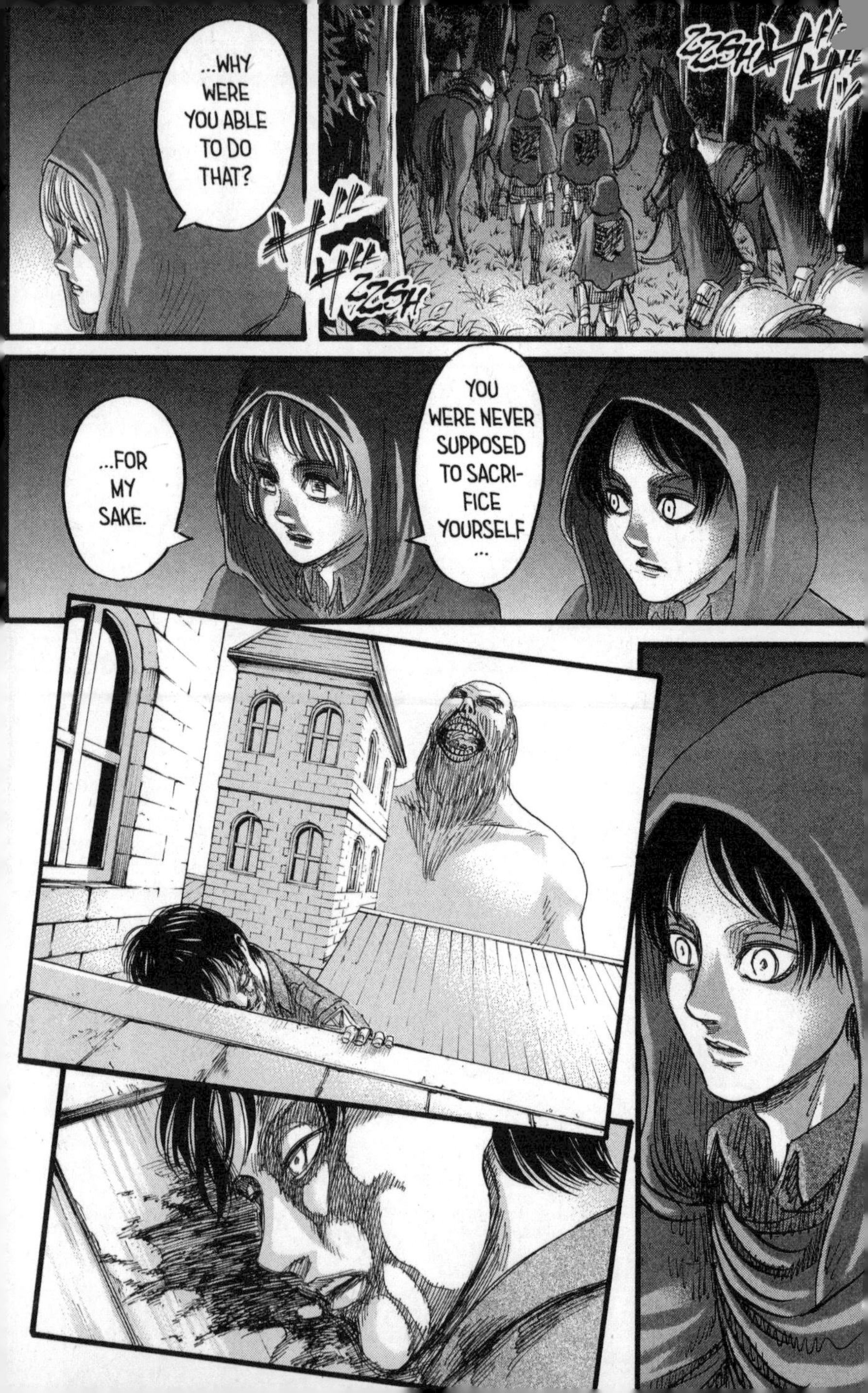
ZZSH
ZZSH
...WHY WERE YOU ABLE TO DO THAT?
YOU WERE NEVER SUPPOSED TO SACRI-FICE YOURSELF ...
...FOR MY SAKE.

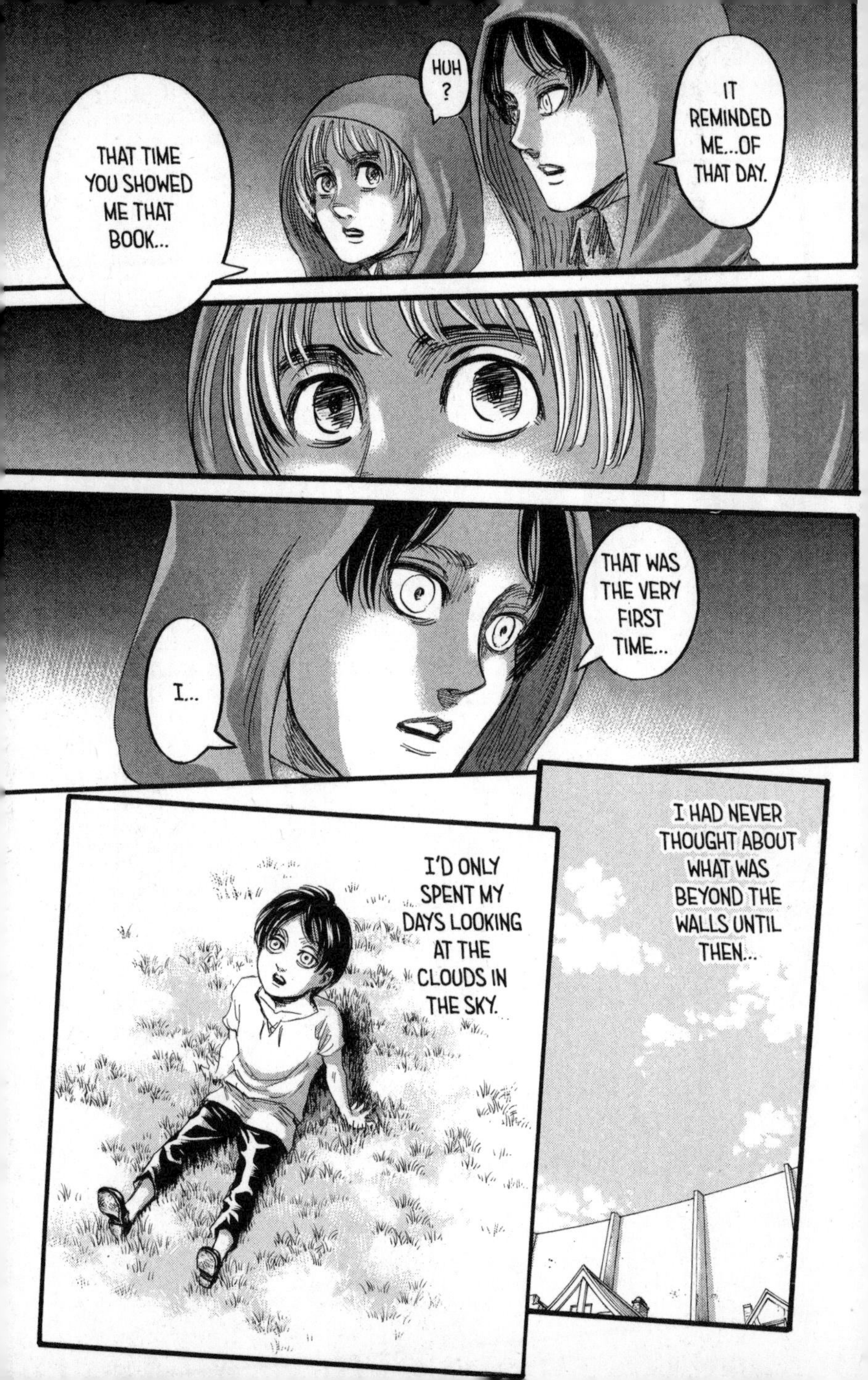
IT REMINDED ME...OF THAT DAY.
HUH?
THAT TIME YOU SHOWED ME THAT BOOK...
THAT WAS THE VERY FIRST TIME...
I...
I HAD NEVER THOUGHT ABOUT WHAT WAS BEYOND THE WALLS UNTIL THEN...
I'D ONLY SPENT MY DAYS LOOKING AT THE CLOUDS IN THE SKY...

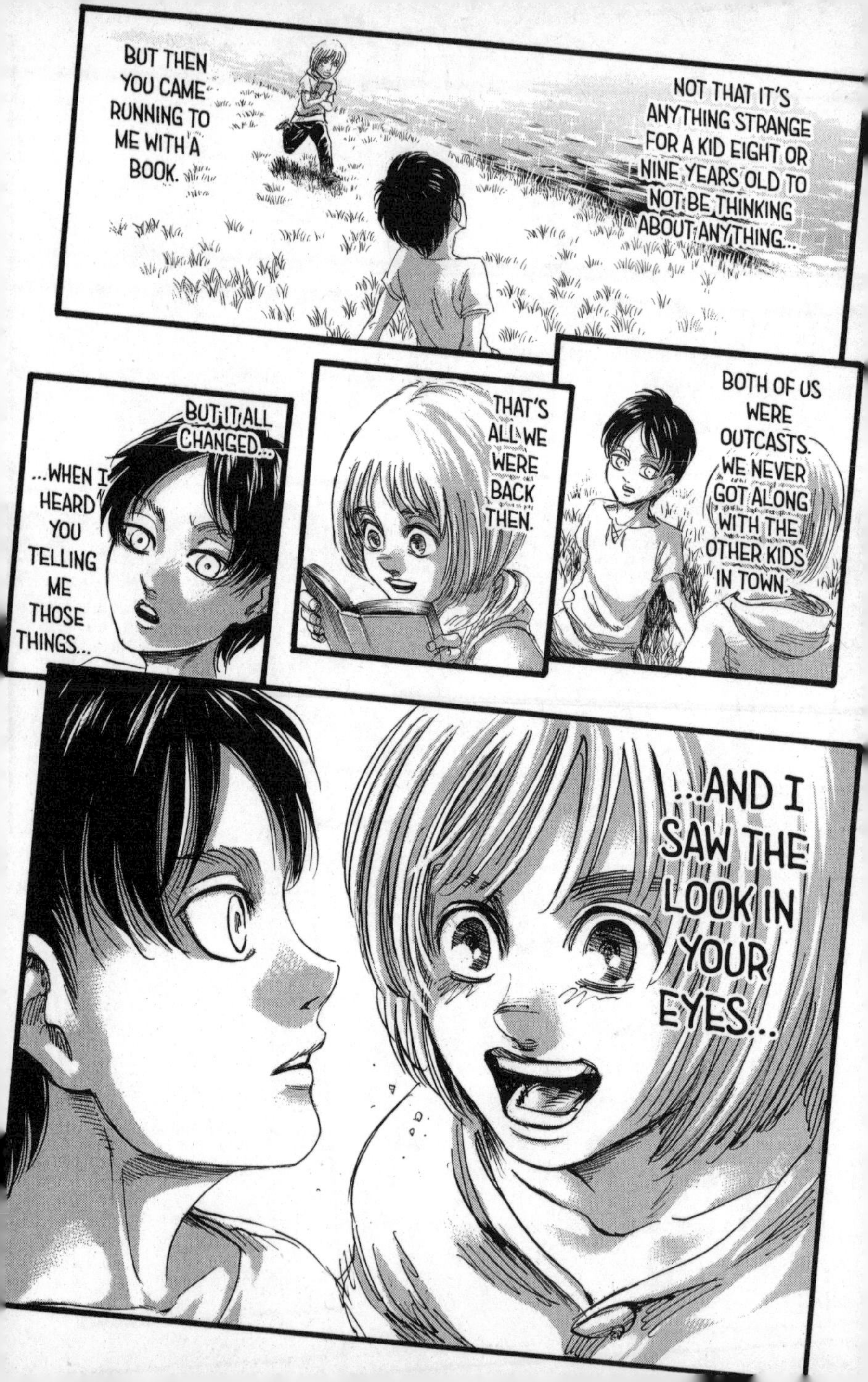
NOT THAT IT'S ANYTHING STRANGE FOR A KID EIGHT OR NINE YEARS OLD TO NOT BE THINKING ABOUT ANYTHING...
BUT THEN YOU CAME RUNNING TO ME WITH A BOOK.
BOTH OF US WERE OUTCASTS. WE NEVER GOT ALONG WITH THE OTHER KIDS IN TOWN.
THAT'S ALL WE WERE BACK THEN.
BUT IT ALL CHANGED...
...WHEN I HEARD YOU TELLING ME THOSE THINGS...
...AND I SAW THE LOOK IN YOUR EYES...

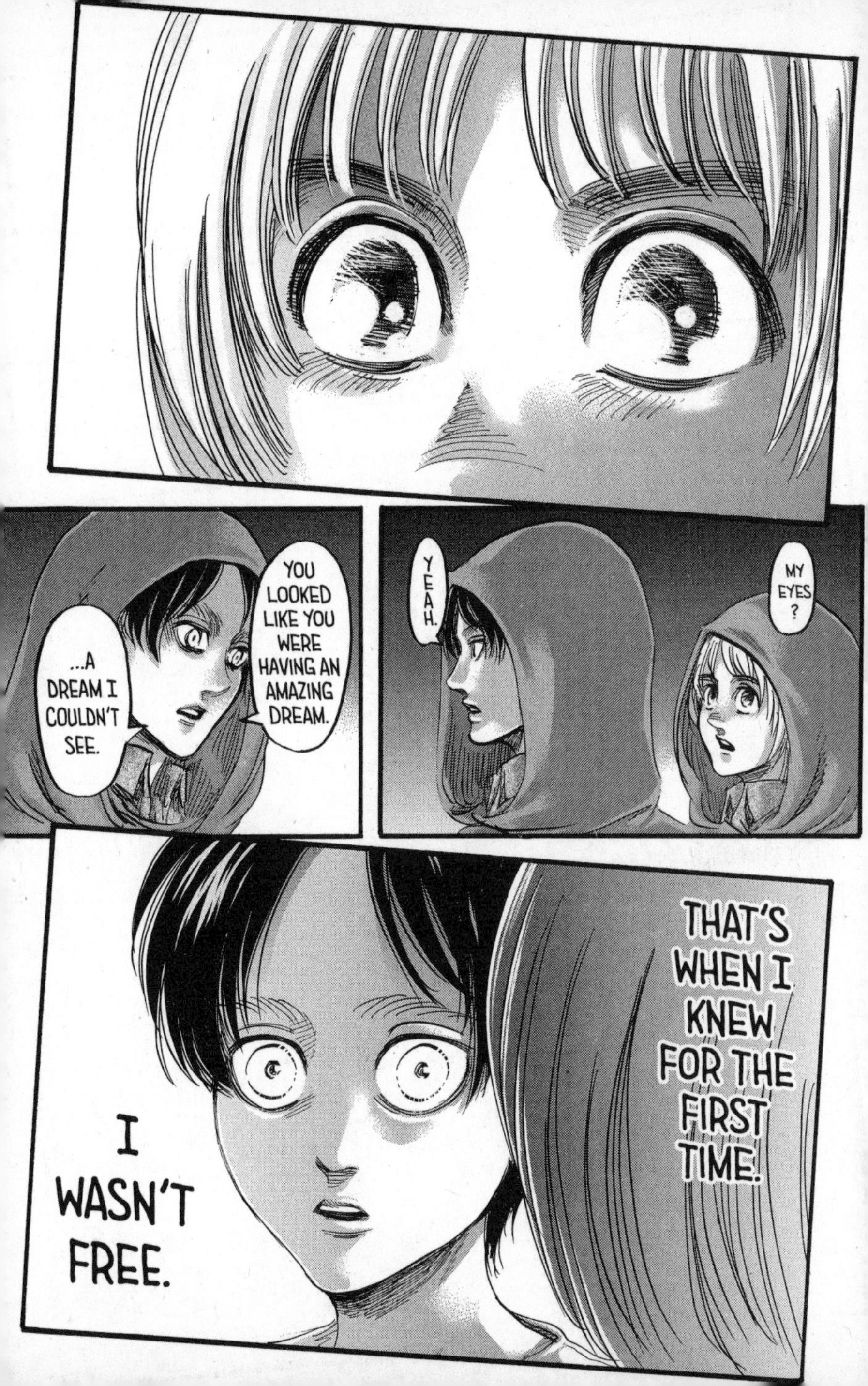
MY EYES?
YEAH.
YOU LOOKED LIKE YOU WERE HAVING AN AMAZING DREAM.
...A DREAM I COULDN'T SEE.
THAT'S WHEN I KNEW FOR THE FIRST TIME.
I WASN'T FREE.

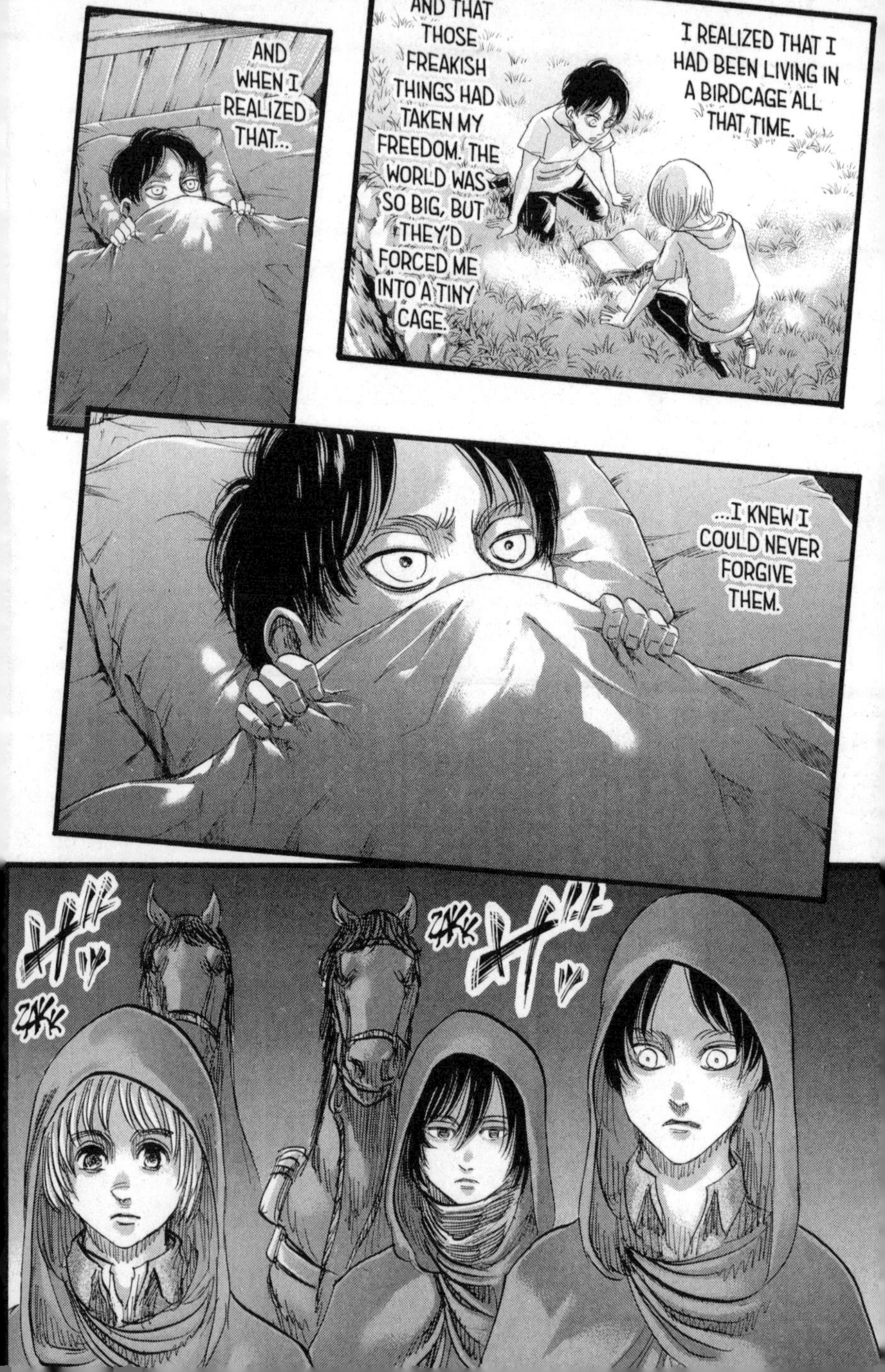
I REALIZED THAT I HAD BEEN LIVING IN A BIRDCAGE ALL THAT TIME.
AND THAT THOSE FREAKISH THINGS HAD TAKEN MY FREEDOM. THE WORLD WAS SO BIG, BUT THEY'D FORCED ME INTO A TINY CAGE.
AND WHEN I REALIZED THAT...
...I KNEW I COULD NEVER FORGIVE THEM.
ZAK
ZAK

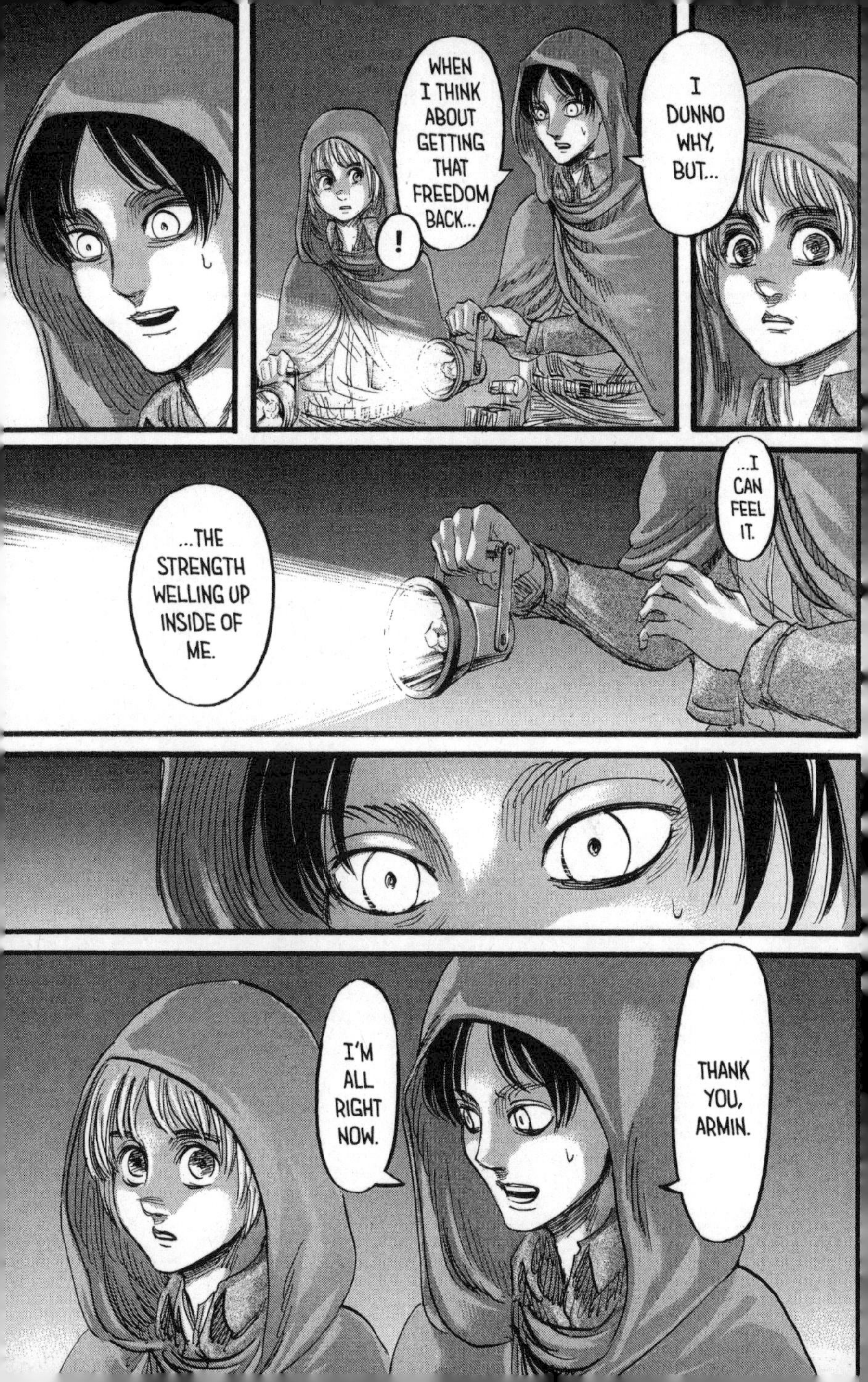
I DUNNO WHY, BUT...
WHEN I THINK ABOUT GETTING THAT FREEDOM BACK...
!
...I CAN FEEL IT.
...THE STRENGTH WELLING UP INSIDE OF ME.
THANK YOU, ARMIN.
I'M ALL RIGHT NOW.

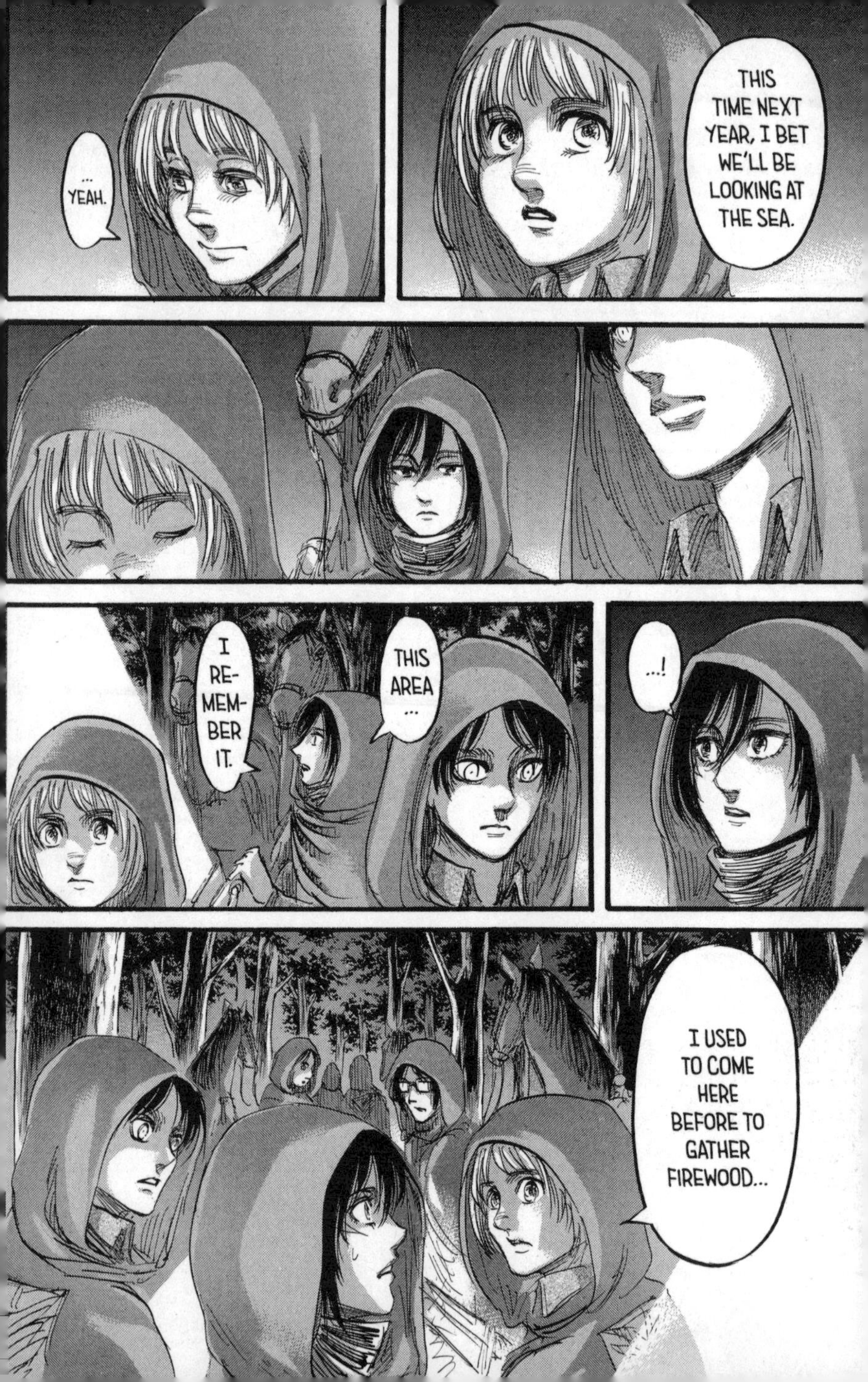
THIS TIME NEXT YEAR, I BET WE'LL BE LOOKING AT THE SEA.
... YEAH.
...!
THIS AREA ...
I RE-MEM-BER IT.
I USED TO COME HERE BEFORE TO GATHER FIREWOOD...

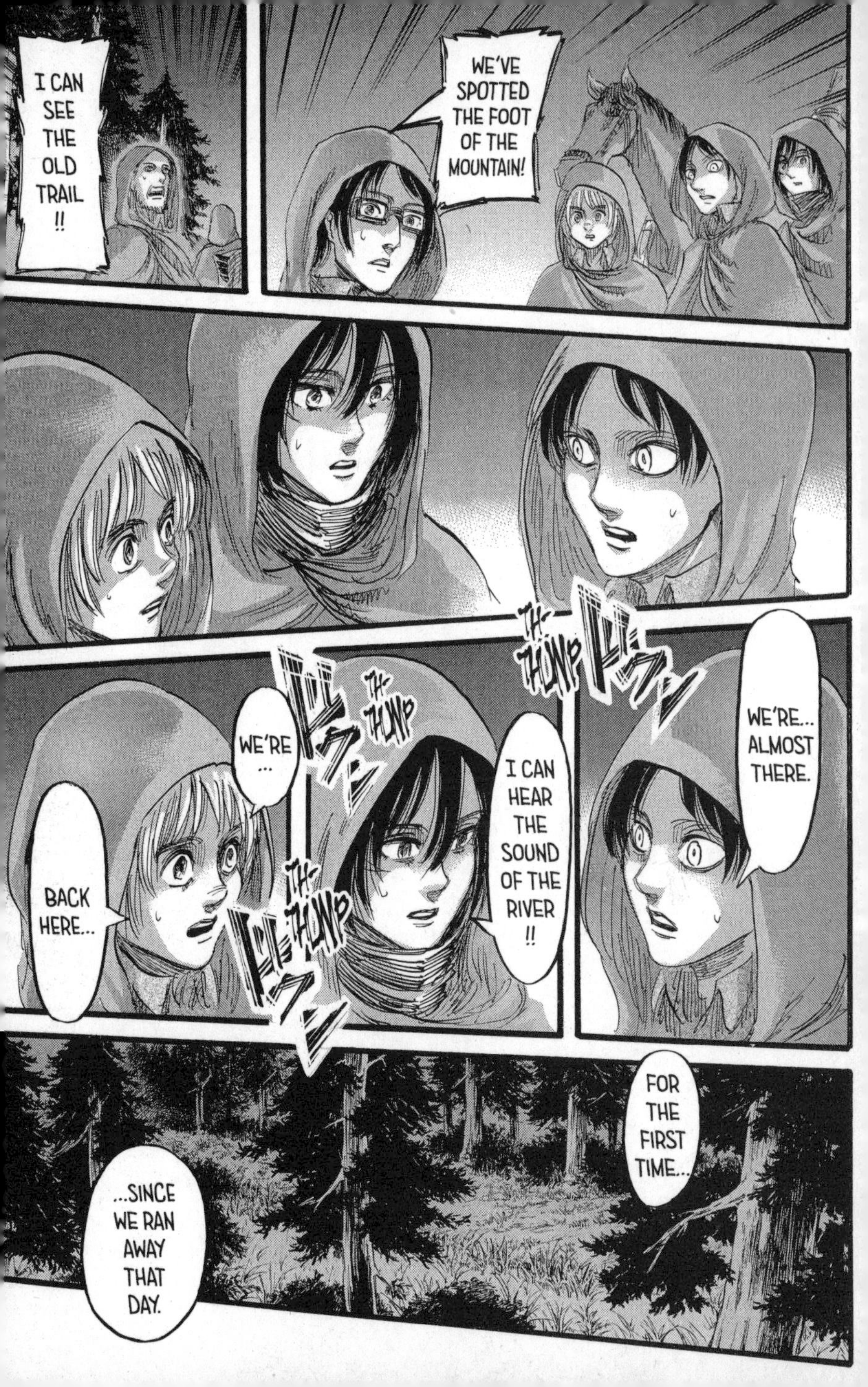
WE'VE SPOTTED THE FOOT OF THE MOUNTAIN!
I CAN SEE THE OLD TRAIL !!
TH-THUMP
WE'RE... ALMOST THERE.
TH-THUMP
I CAN HEAR THE SOUND OF THE RIVER !!
TH-THUMP
WE'RE ...
BACK HERE...
FOR THE FIRST TIME...
...SINCE WE RAN AWAY THAT DAY.

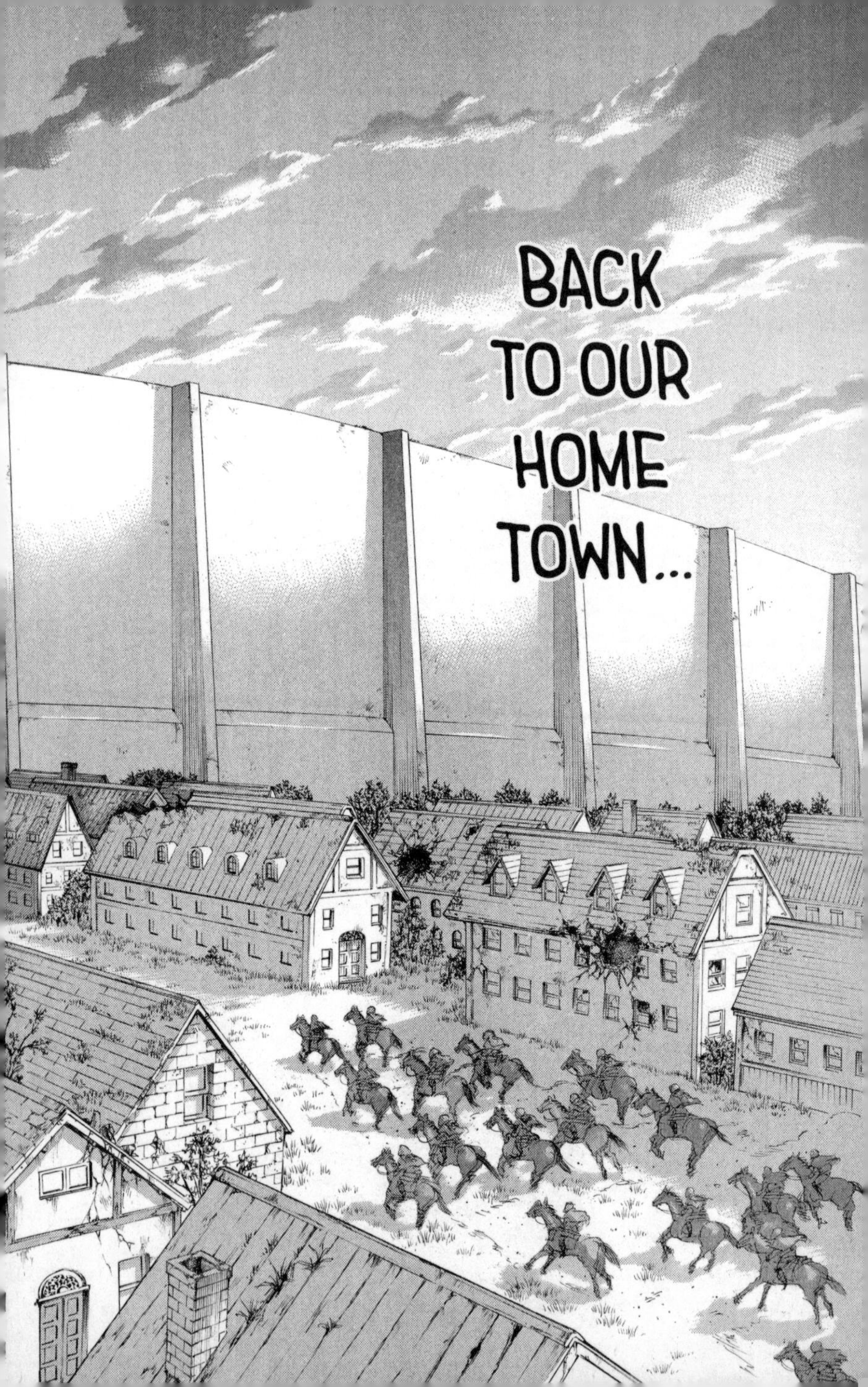
BACK TO OUR HOME TOWN...

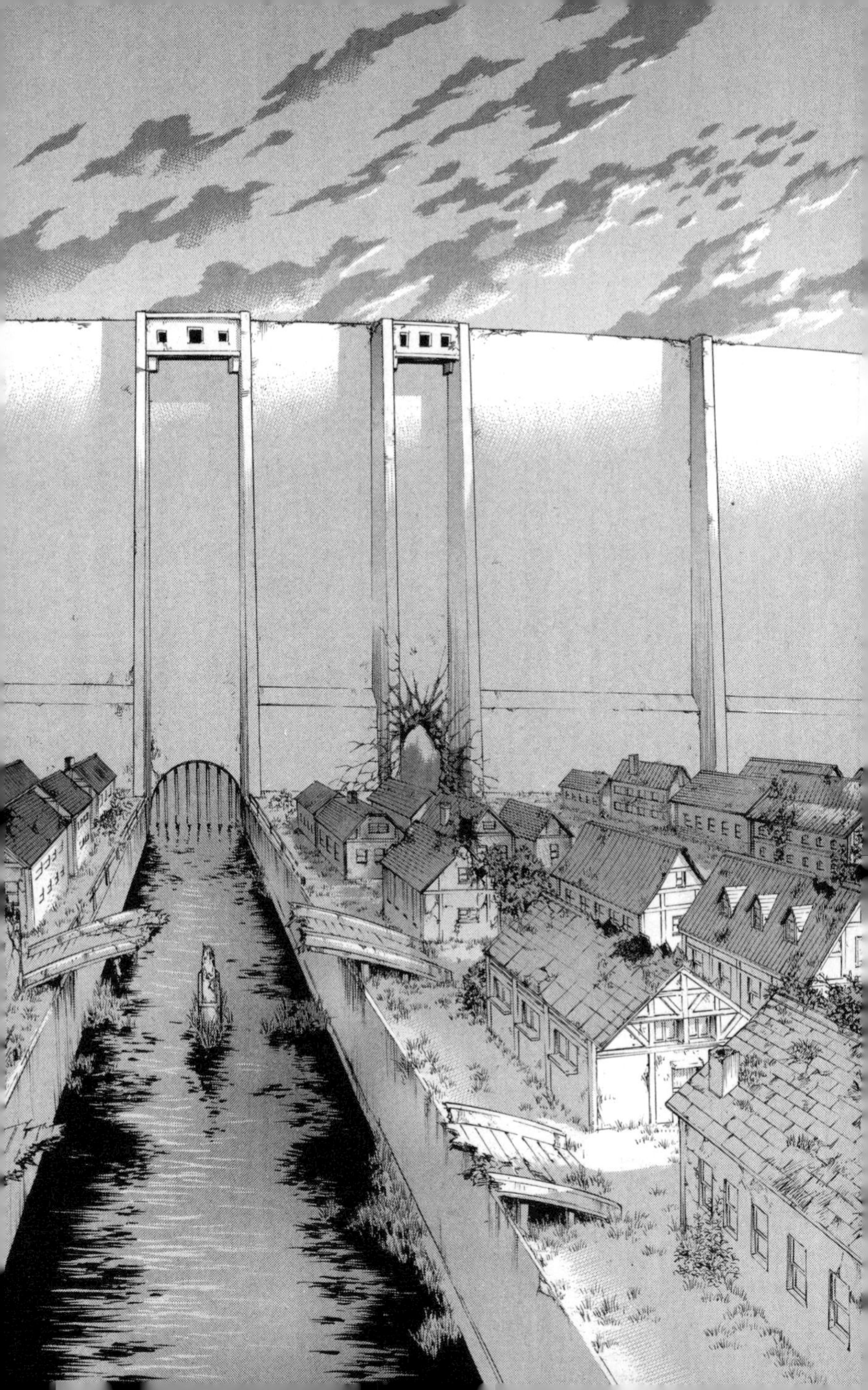

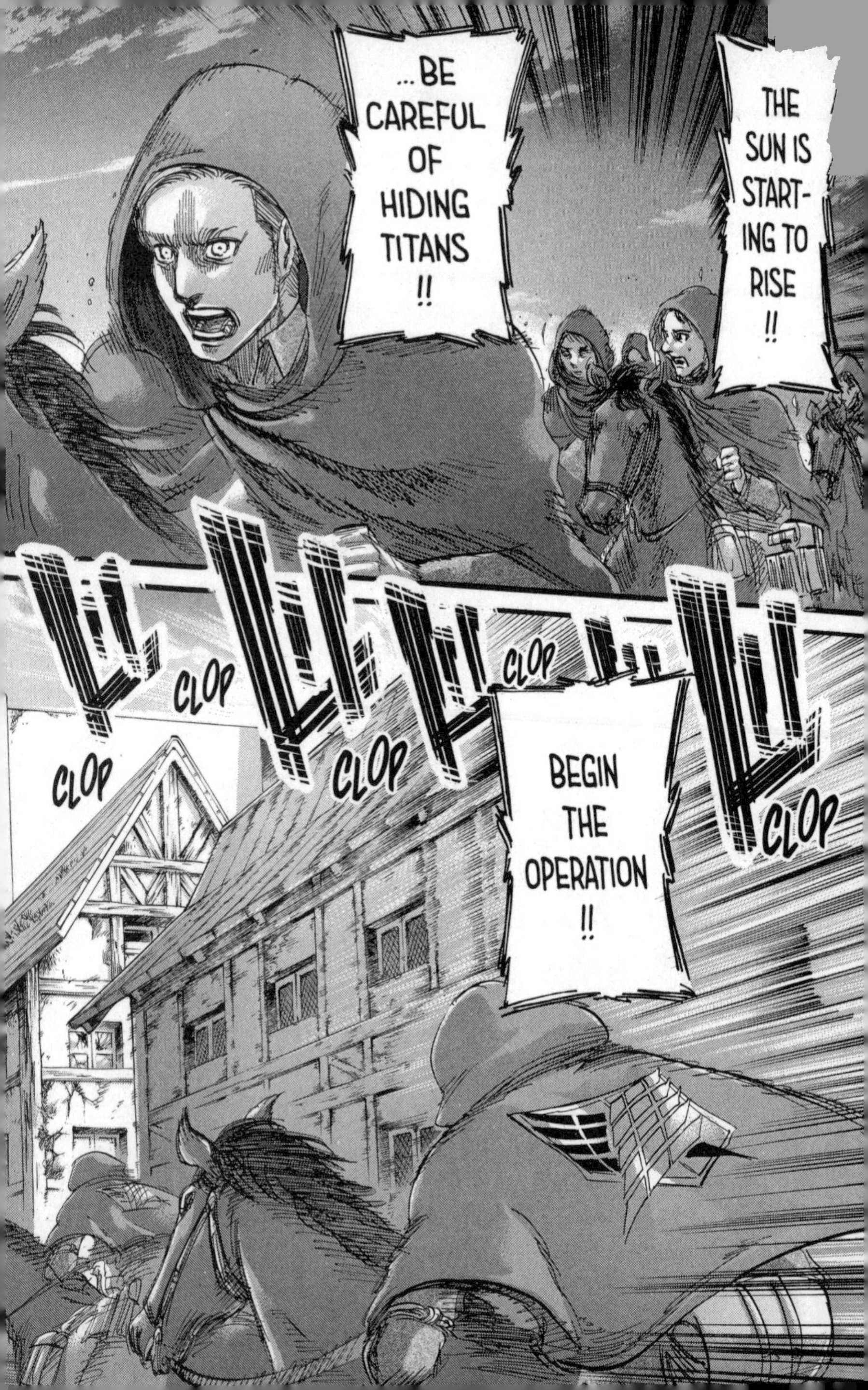
THE SUN IS START-ING TO RISE!!
...BE CAREFUL OF HIDING TITANS!!
CLOP
CLOP
BEGIN THE OPERATION!!
CLOP
CLOP
CLOP

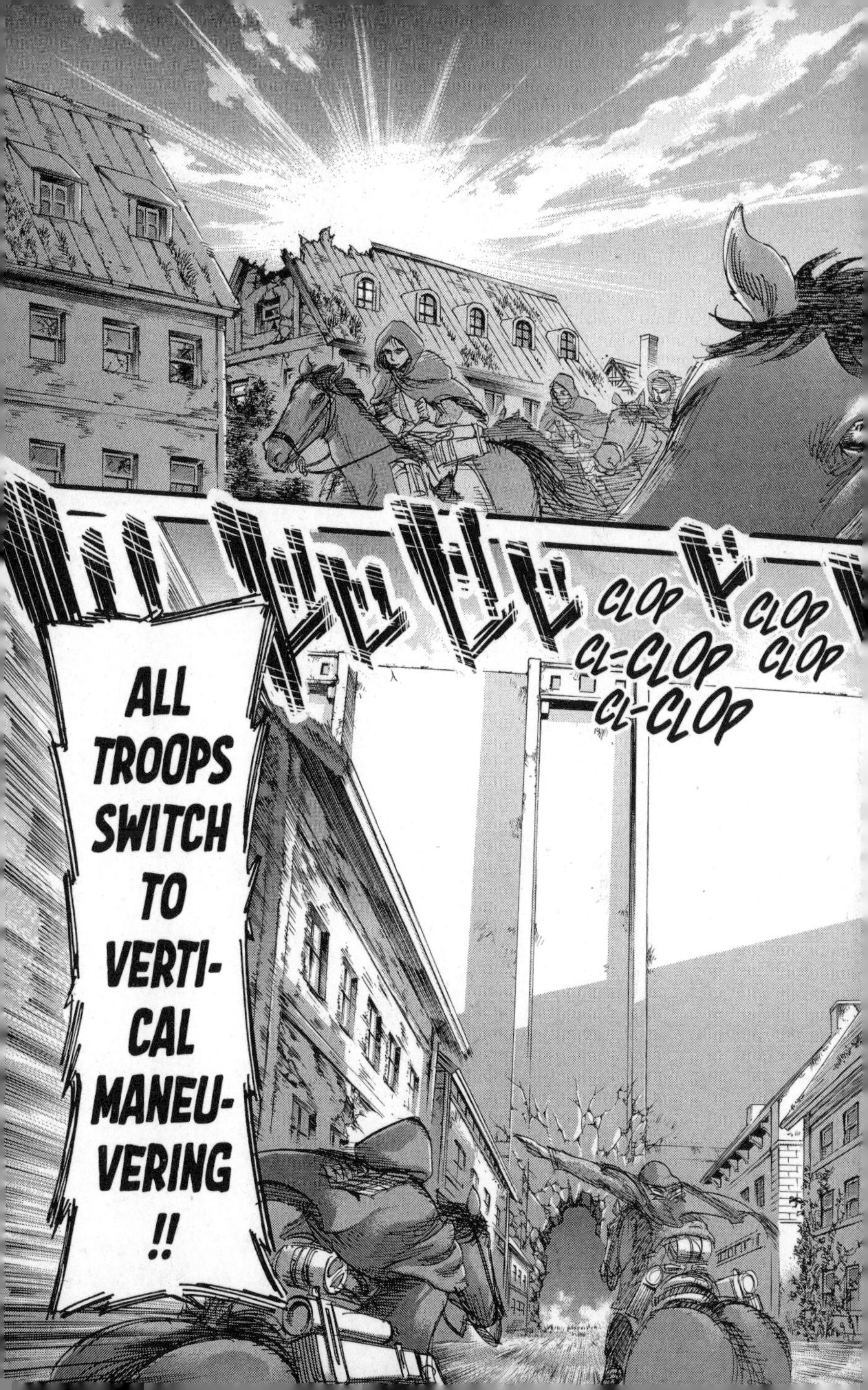
CLOP
CLOP
CL-CLOP
CLOP
CL-CLOP
ALL TROOPS SWITCH TO VERTI-CAL MANEU-VERING!!

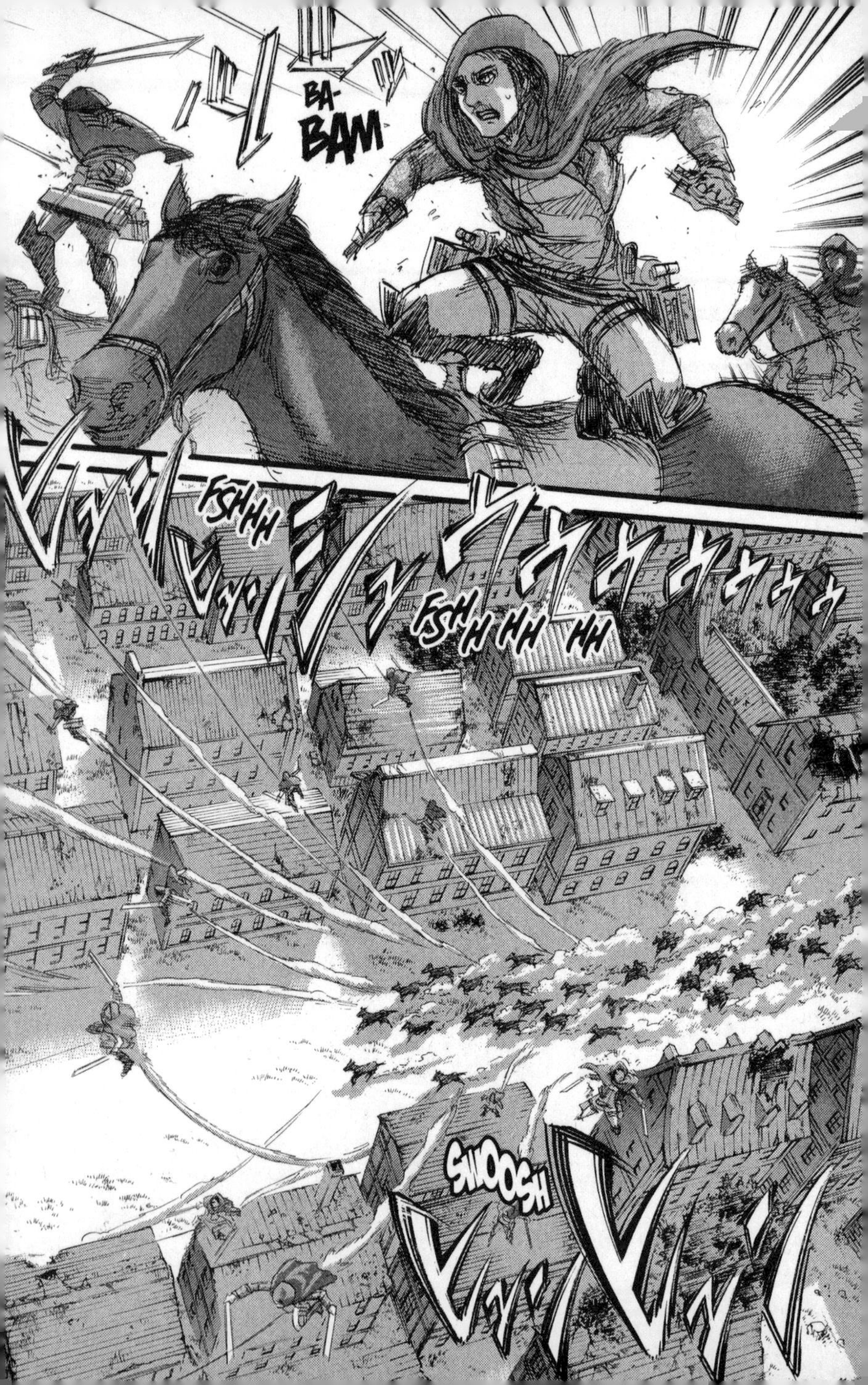
BA-
BAM
FSHHH
FSHHH HH HH
SWOOSH

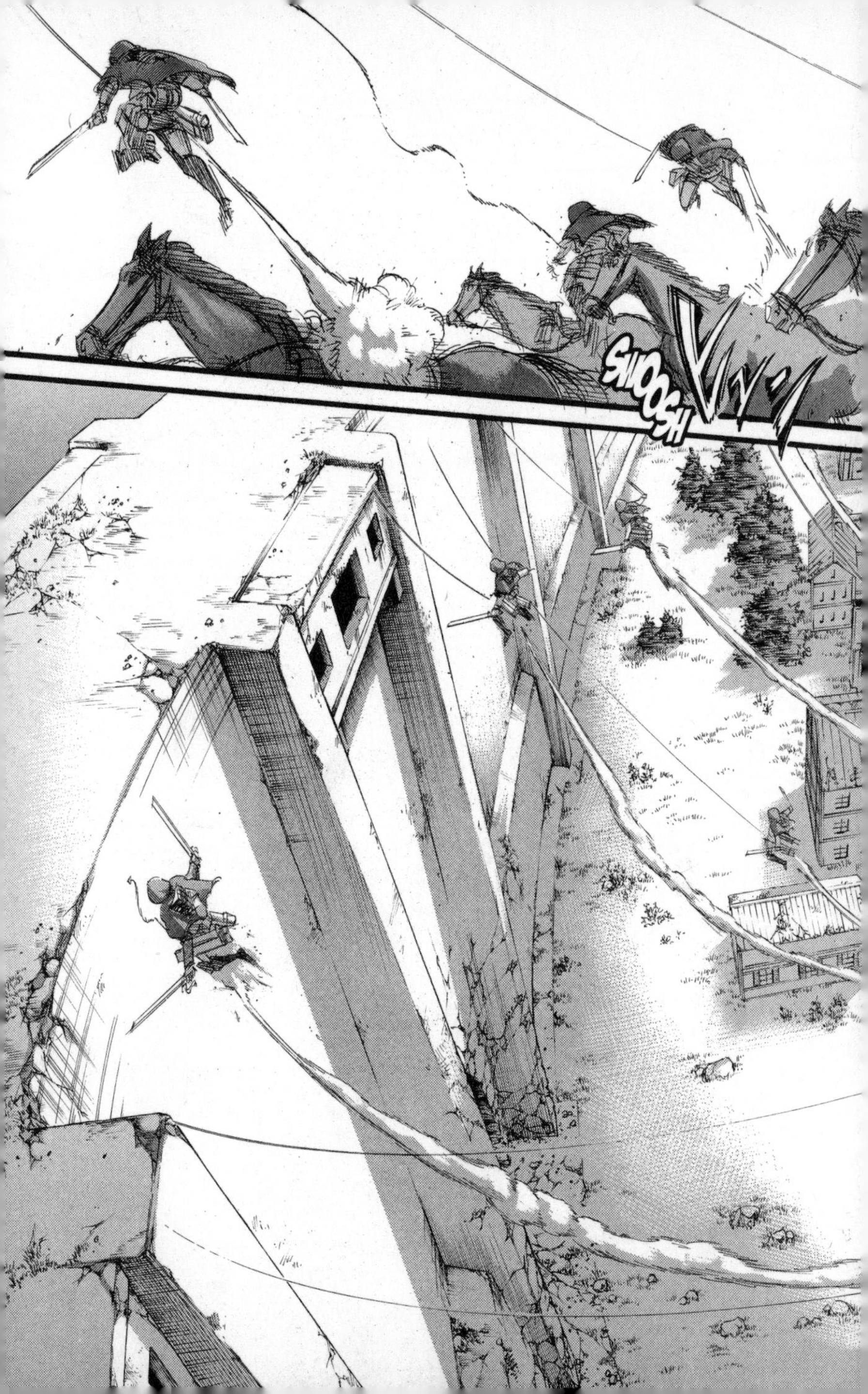
SWOOSH

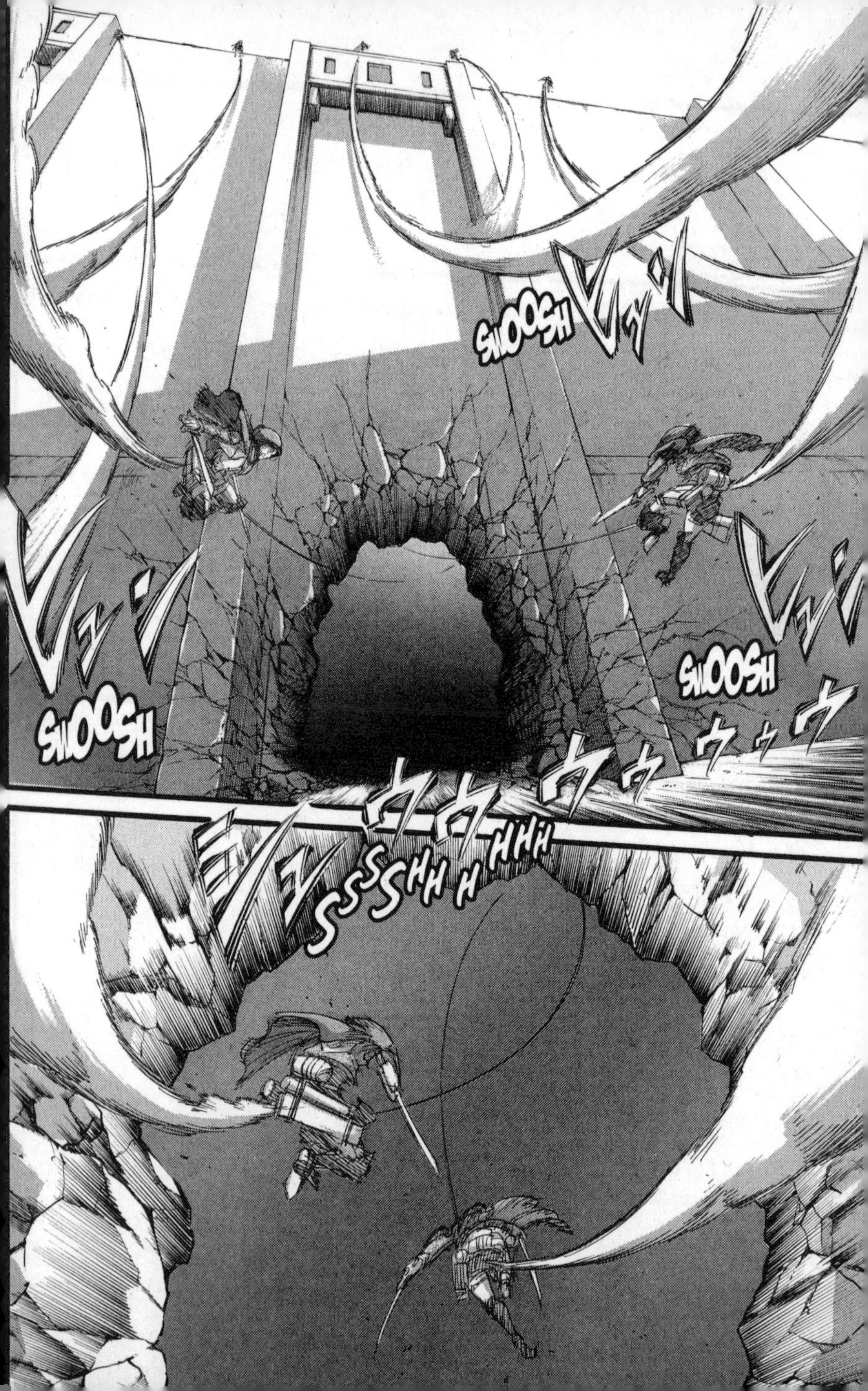
SWOOSH
SWOOSH
SWOOSH
SSSSHHHHHHH

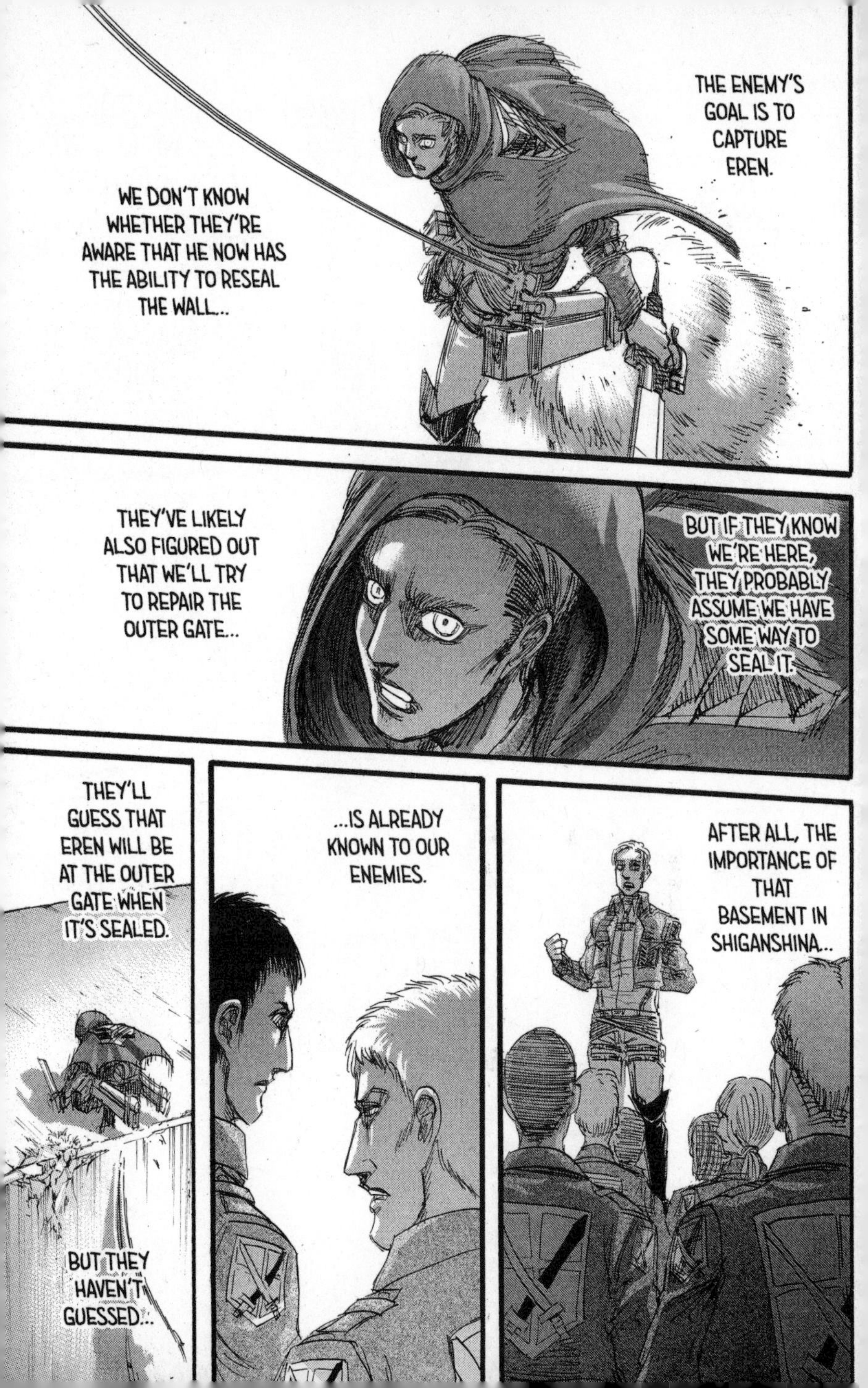
THE ENEMY'S GOAL IS TO CAPTURE EREN.
WE DON'T KNOW WHETHER THEY'RE AWARE THAT HE NOW HAS THE ABILITY TO RESEAL THE WALL...
THEY'VE LIKELY ALSO FIGURED OUT THAT WE'LL TRY TO REPAIR THE OUTER GATE...
BUT IF THEY KNOW WE'RE HERE, THEY PROBABLY ASSUME WE HAVE SOME WAY TO SEAL IT.
AFTER ALL, THE IMPORTANCE OF THAT BASEMENT IN SHIGANSHINA...
...IS ALREADY KNOWN TO OUR ENEMIES.
THEY'LL GUESS THAT EREN WILL BE AT THE OUTER GATE WHEN IT'S SEALED.
BUT THEY HAVEN'T GUESSED...

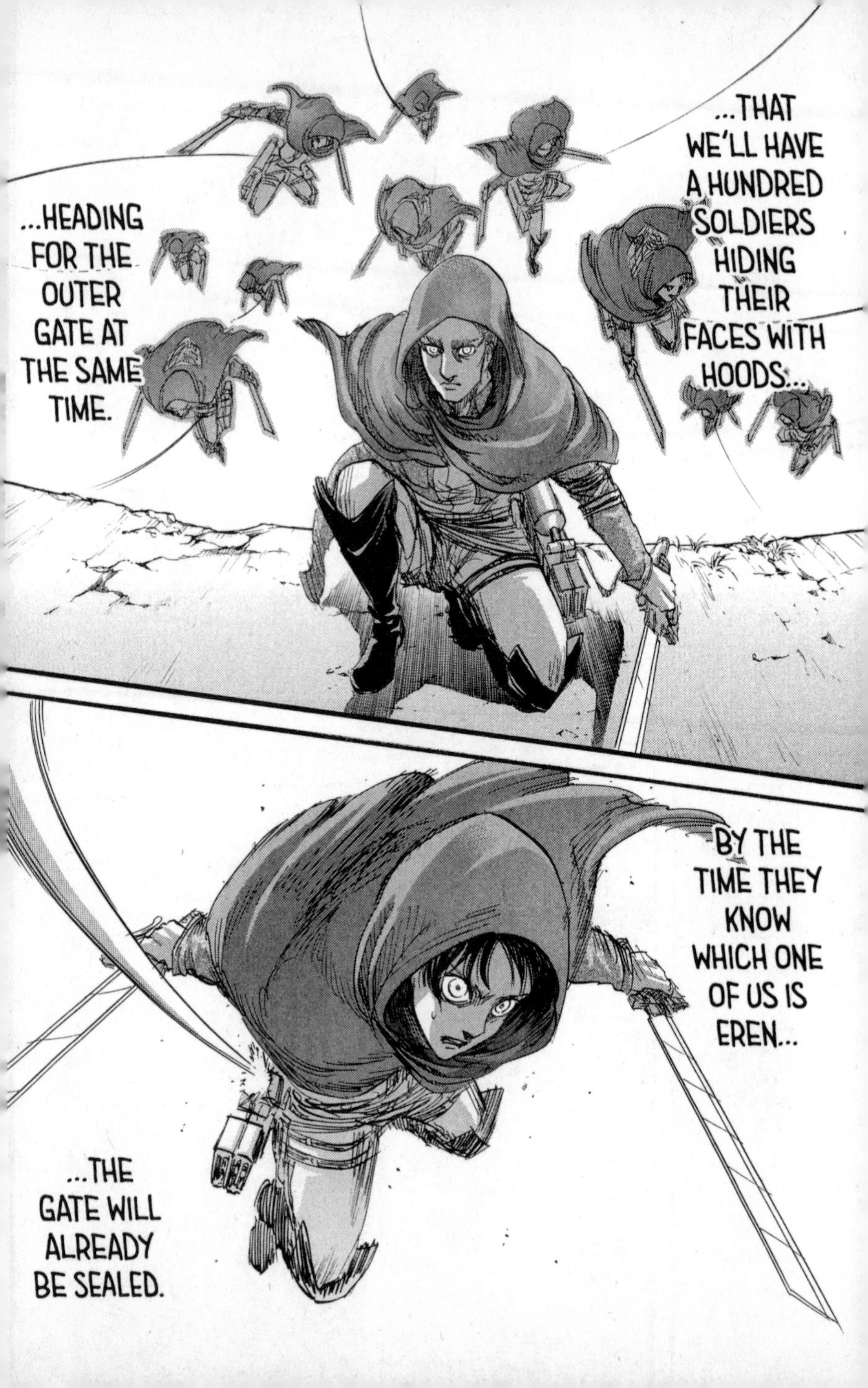
...THAT WE'LL HAVE A HUNDRED SOLDIERS HIDING THEIR FACES WITH HOODS...
...HEADING FOR THE OUTER GATE AT THE SAME TIME.
BY THE TIME THEY KNOW WHICH ONE OF US IS EREN...
...THE GATE WILL ALREADY BE SEALED.

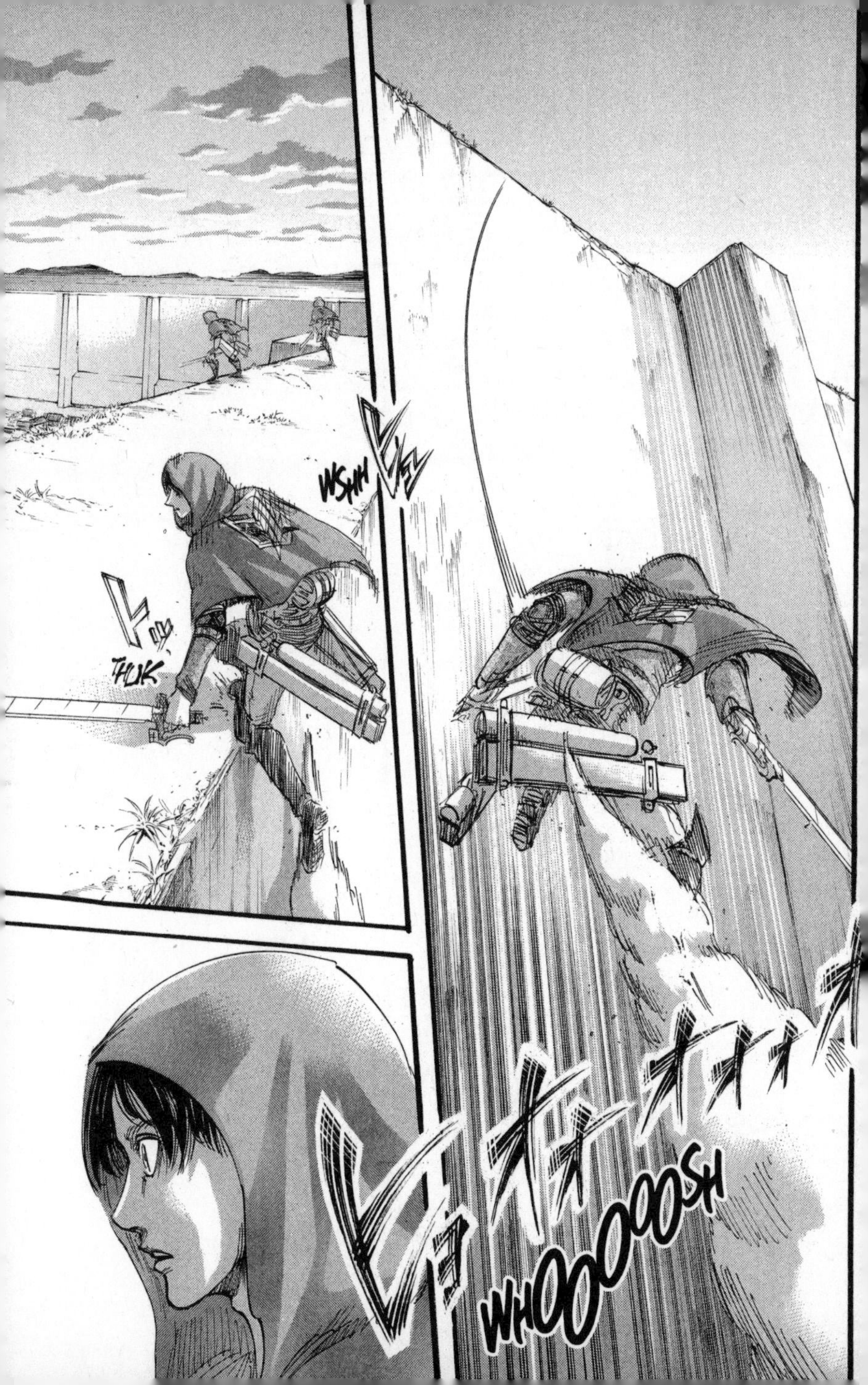
WHOOOOOSH
WSHH
THUK

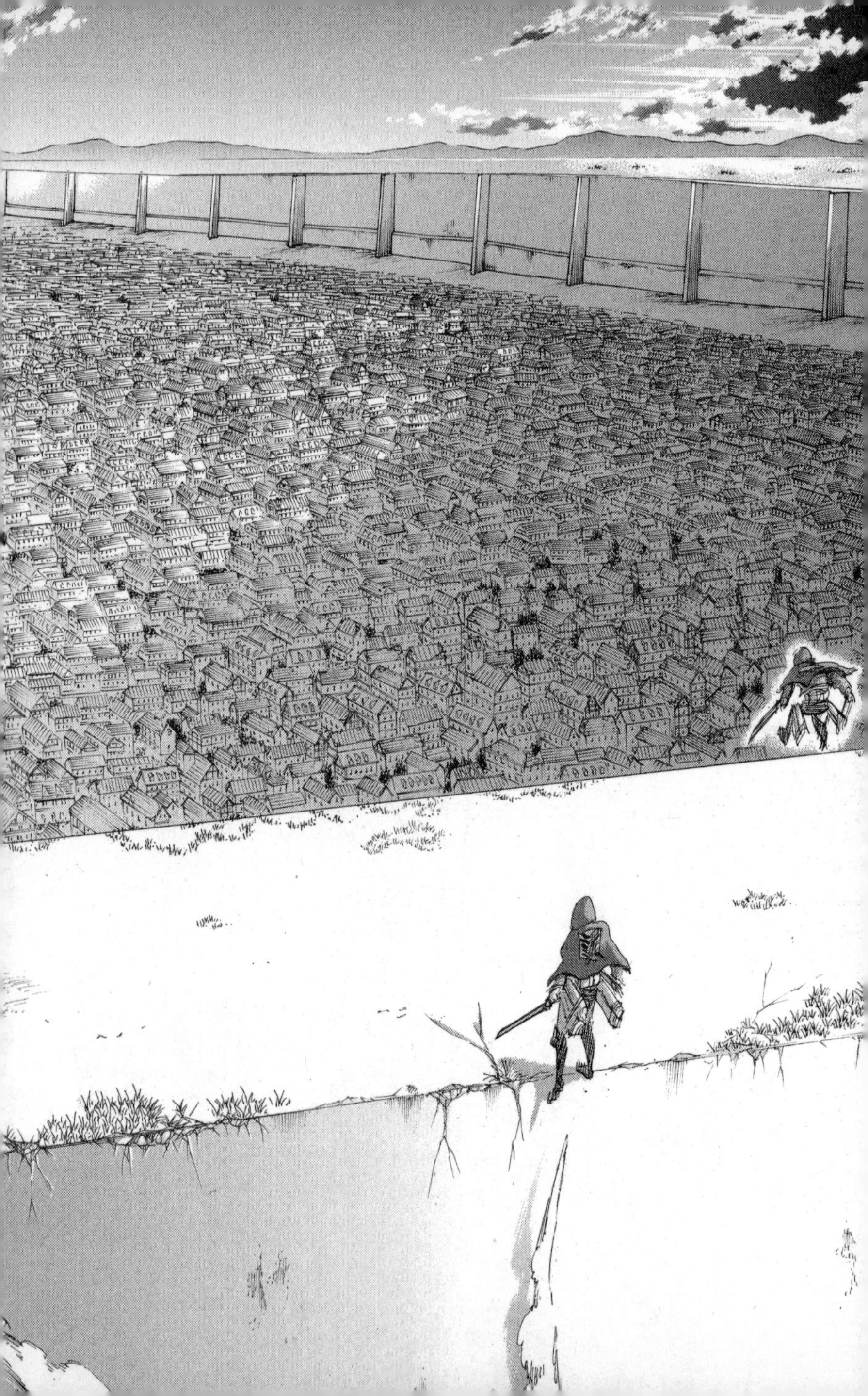

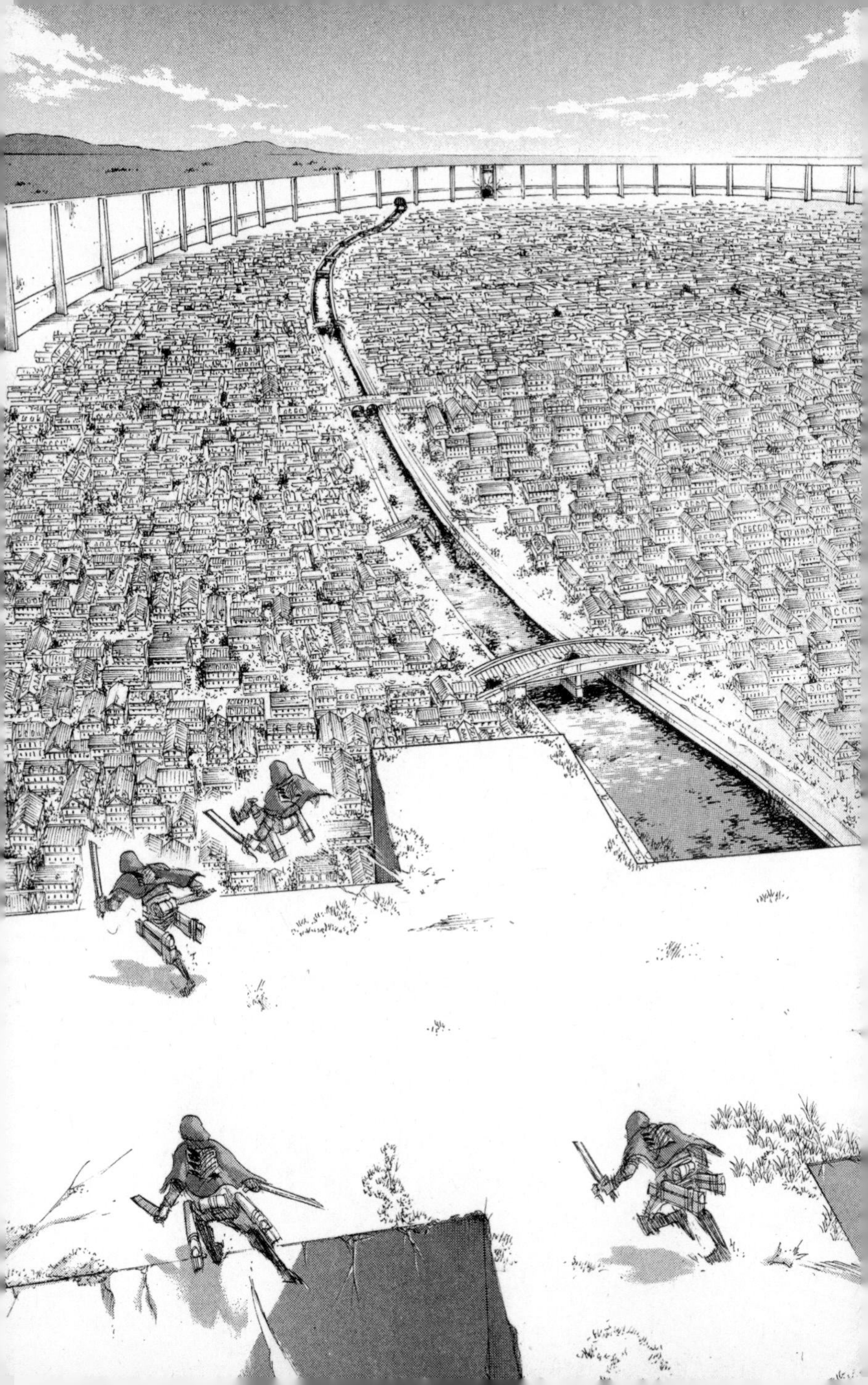

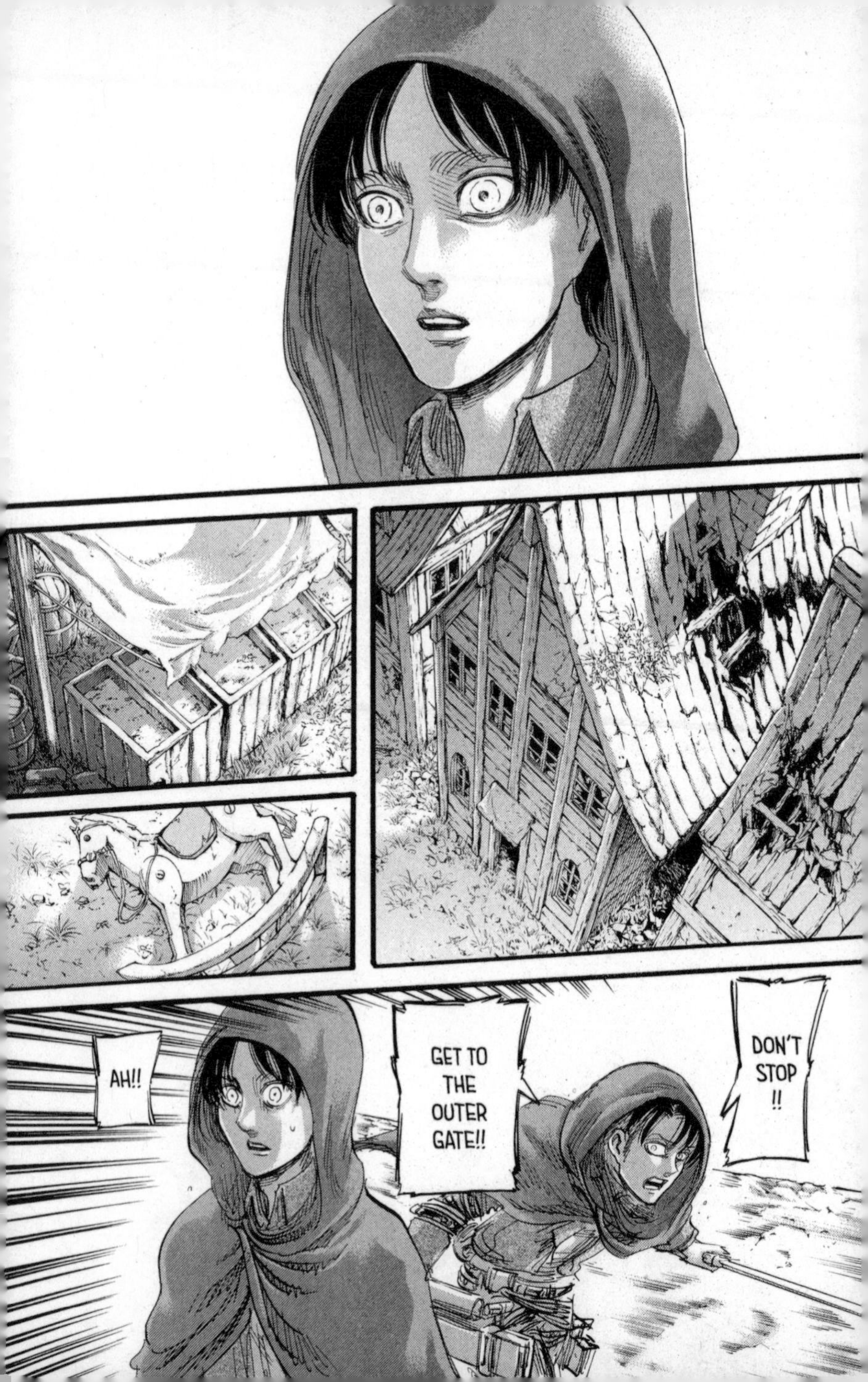
DON'T STOP!!
GET TO THE OUTER GATE!!
AH!!

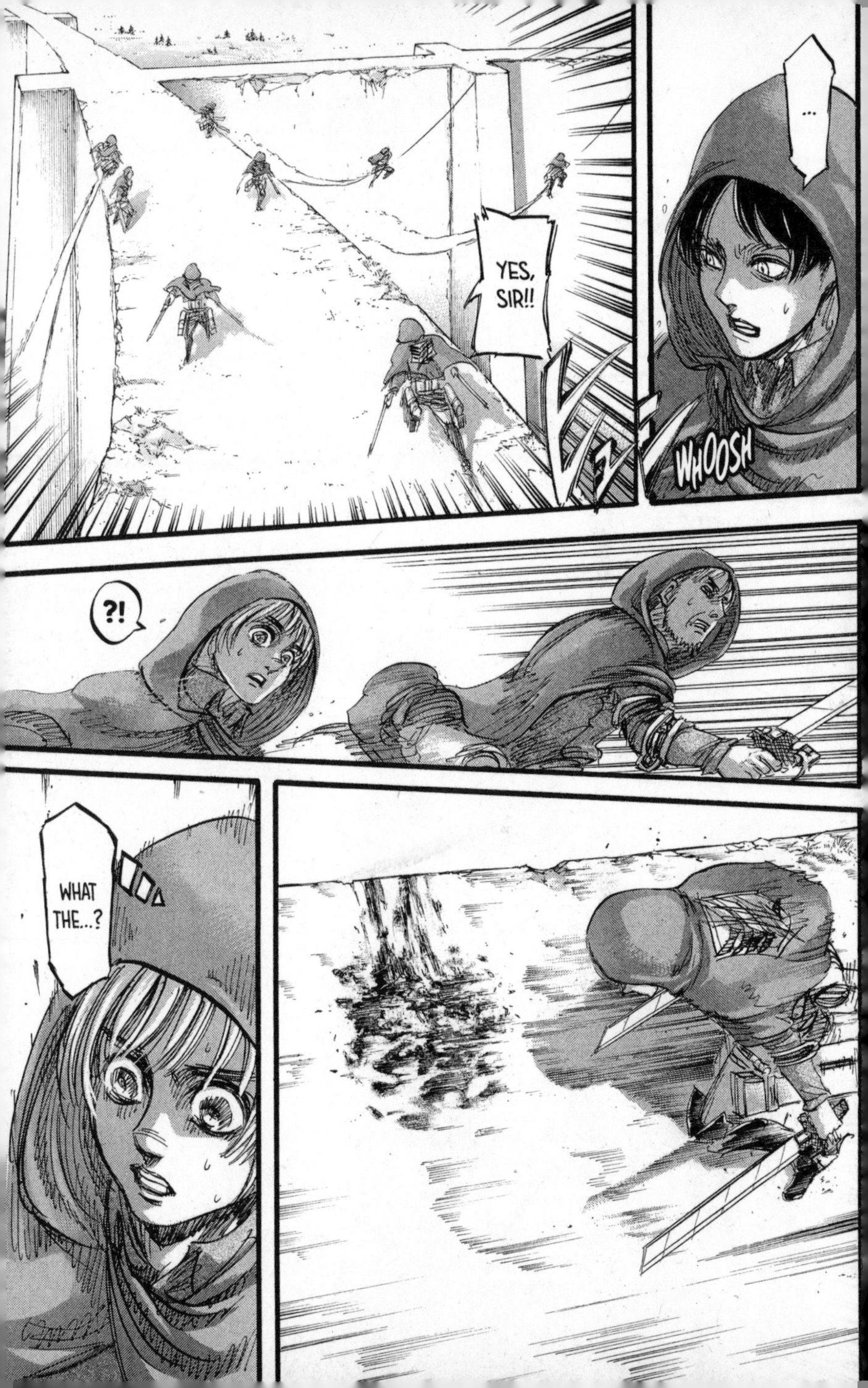
...
WHOOSH
YES, SIR!!
?!
WHAT THE...?

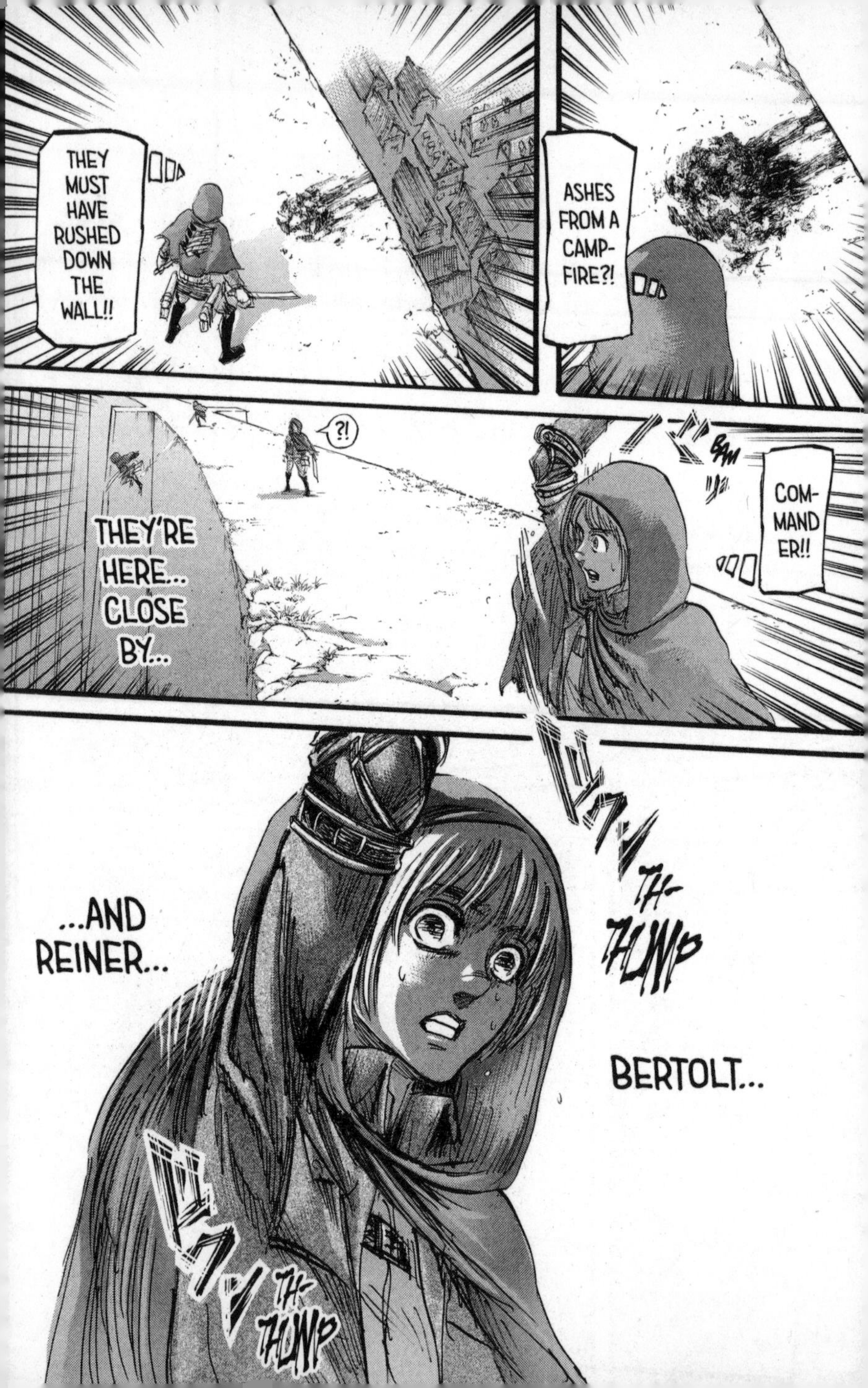
ASHES FROM A CAMP-FIRE?!
THEY MUST HAVE RUSHED DOWN THE WALL!!
COM-MAND ER!!
BAM
?!
THEY'RE HERE... CLOSE BY...
TH-THUMP
BERTOLT...
...AND REINER...
TH-THUMP

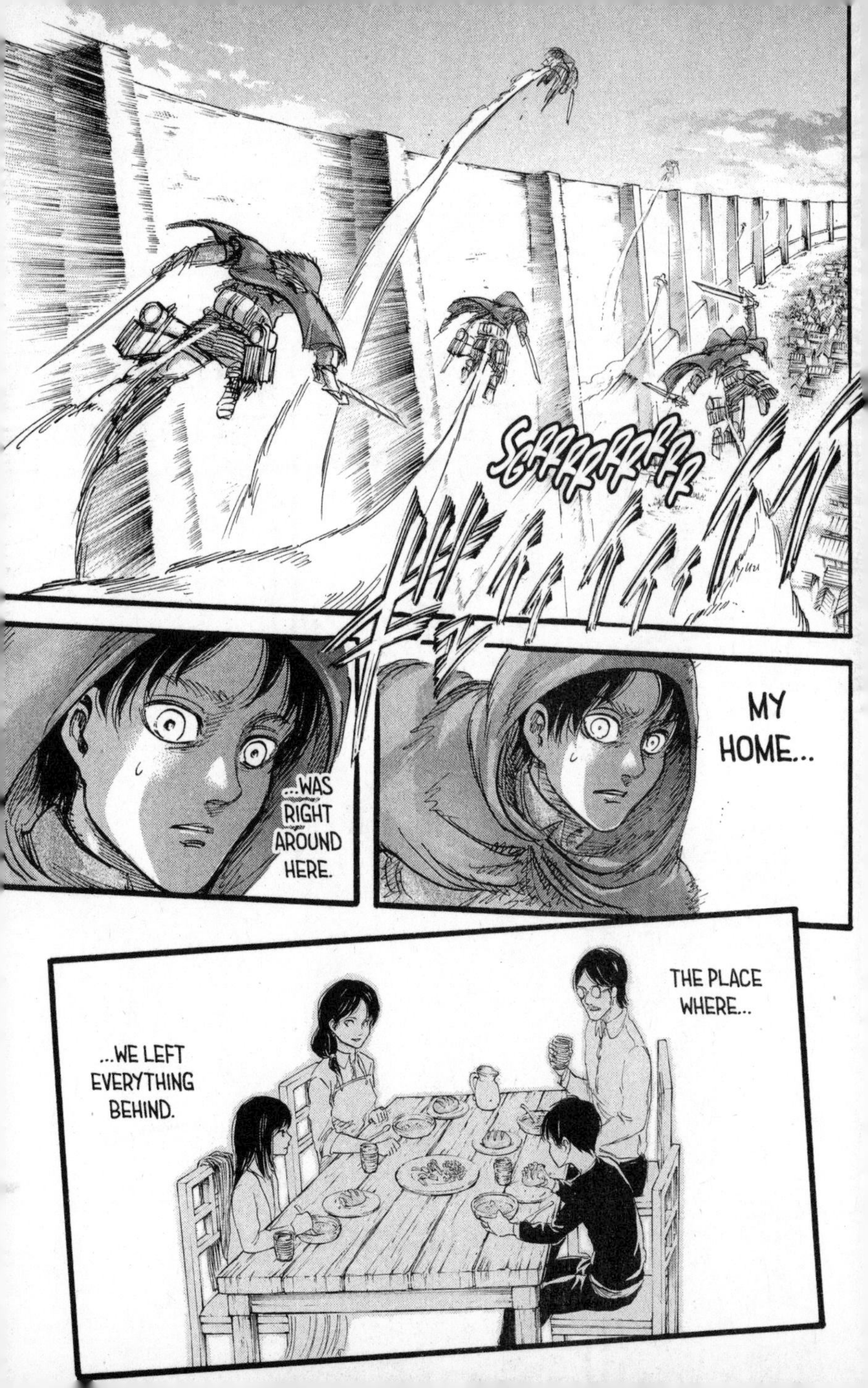
MY HOME...
...WAS RIGHT AROUND HERE.
THE PLACE WHERE...
...WE LEFT EVERYTHING BEHIND.

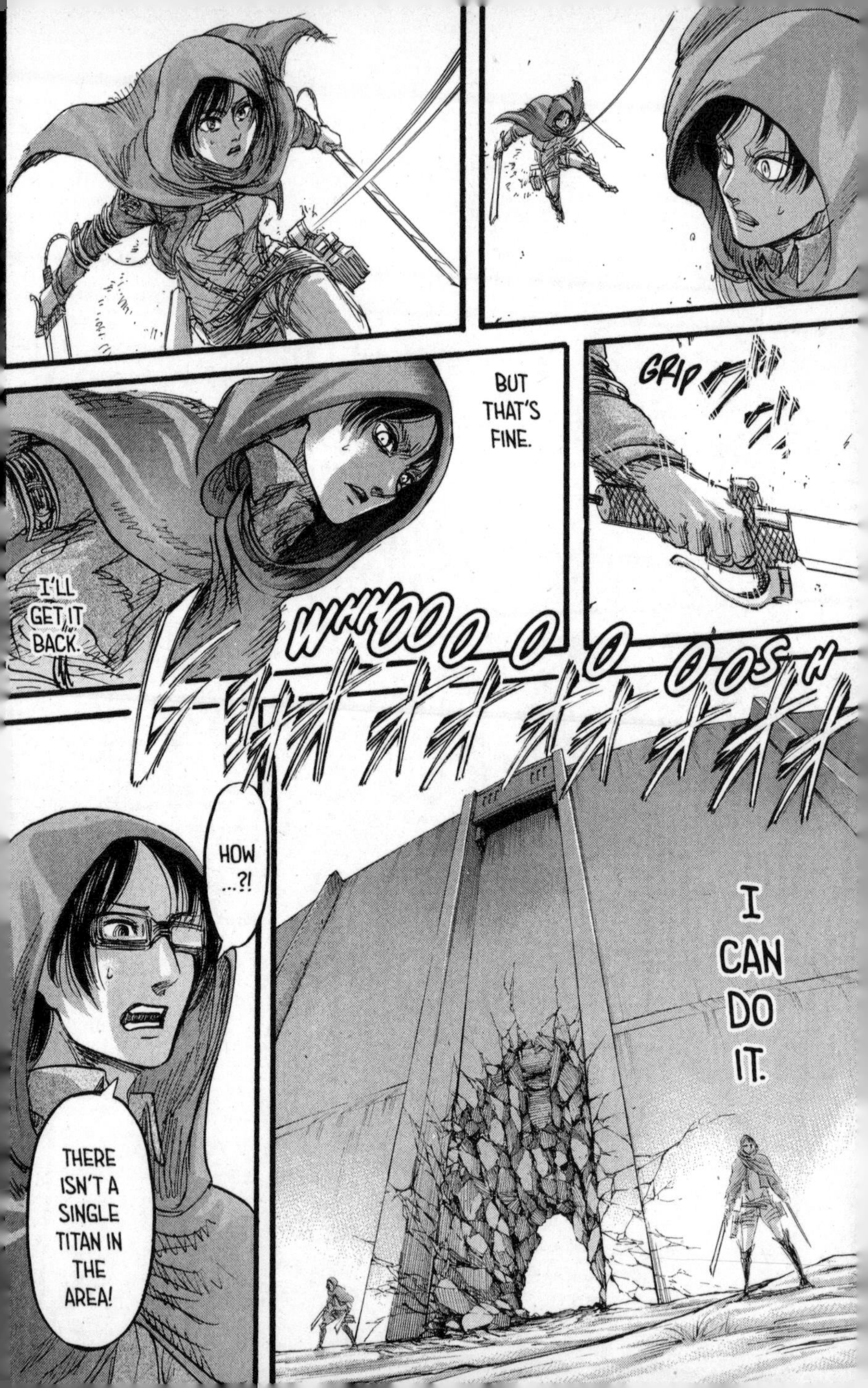
GRIP
BUT THAT'S FINE.
I'LL GET IT BACK.
WHHOOOO O O O OOSH
I CAN DO IT.
HOW ...?!
THERE ISN'T A SINGLE TITAN IN THE AREA!

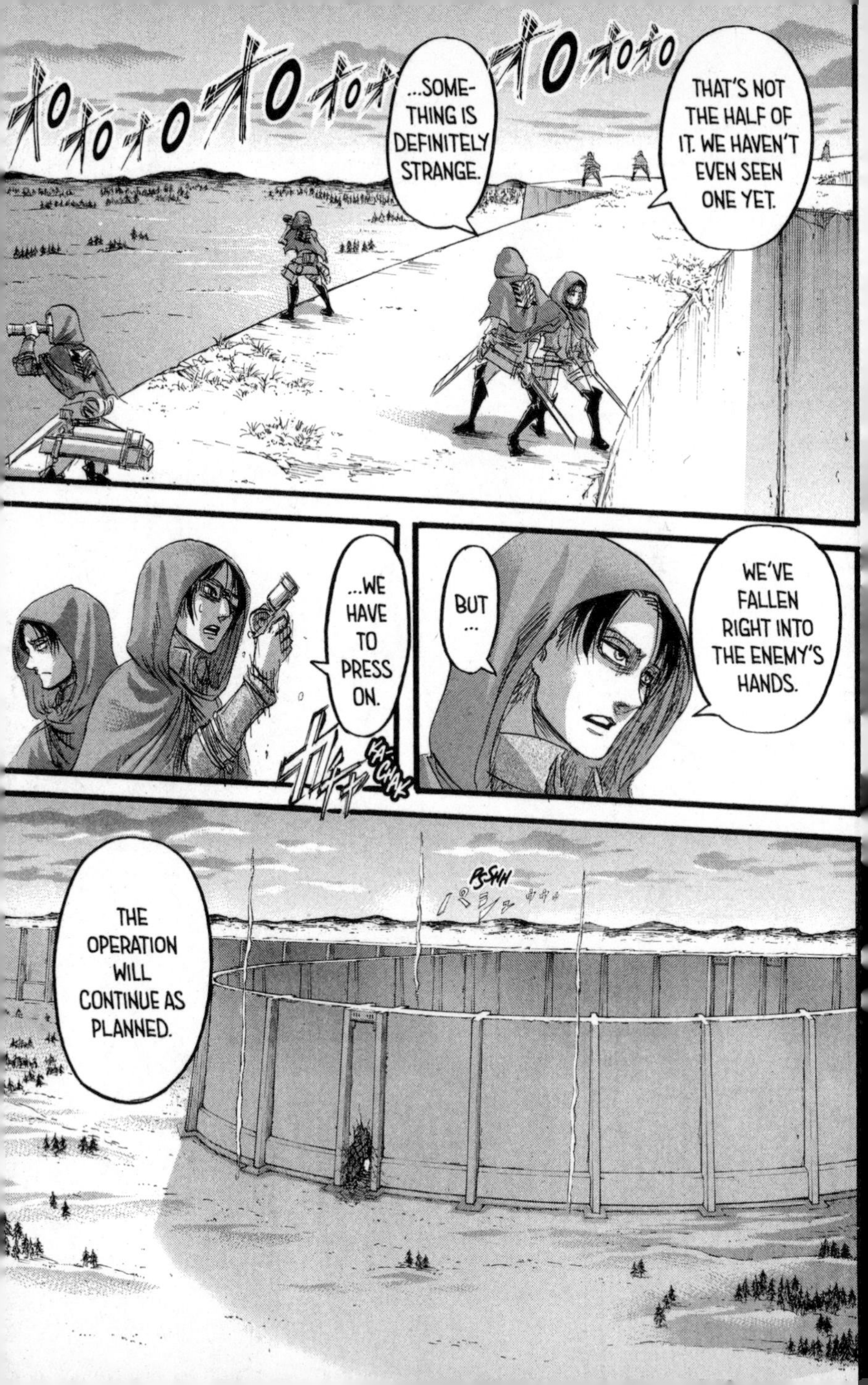

THAT'S NOT THE HALF OF IT. WE HAVEN'T EVEN SEEN ONE YET.
...SOME-THING IS DEFINITELY STRANGE.
WE'VE FALLEN RIGHT INTO THE ENEMY'S HANDS.
BUT ...
...WE HAVE TO PRESS ON.
KA-CHAK
PSSHH
THE OPERATION WILL CONTINUE AS PLANNED.

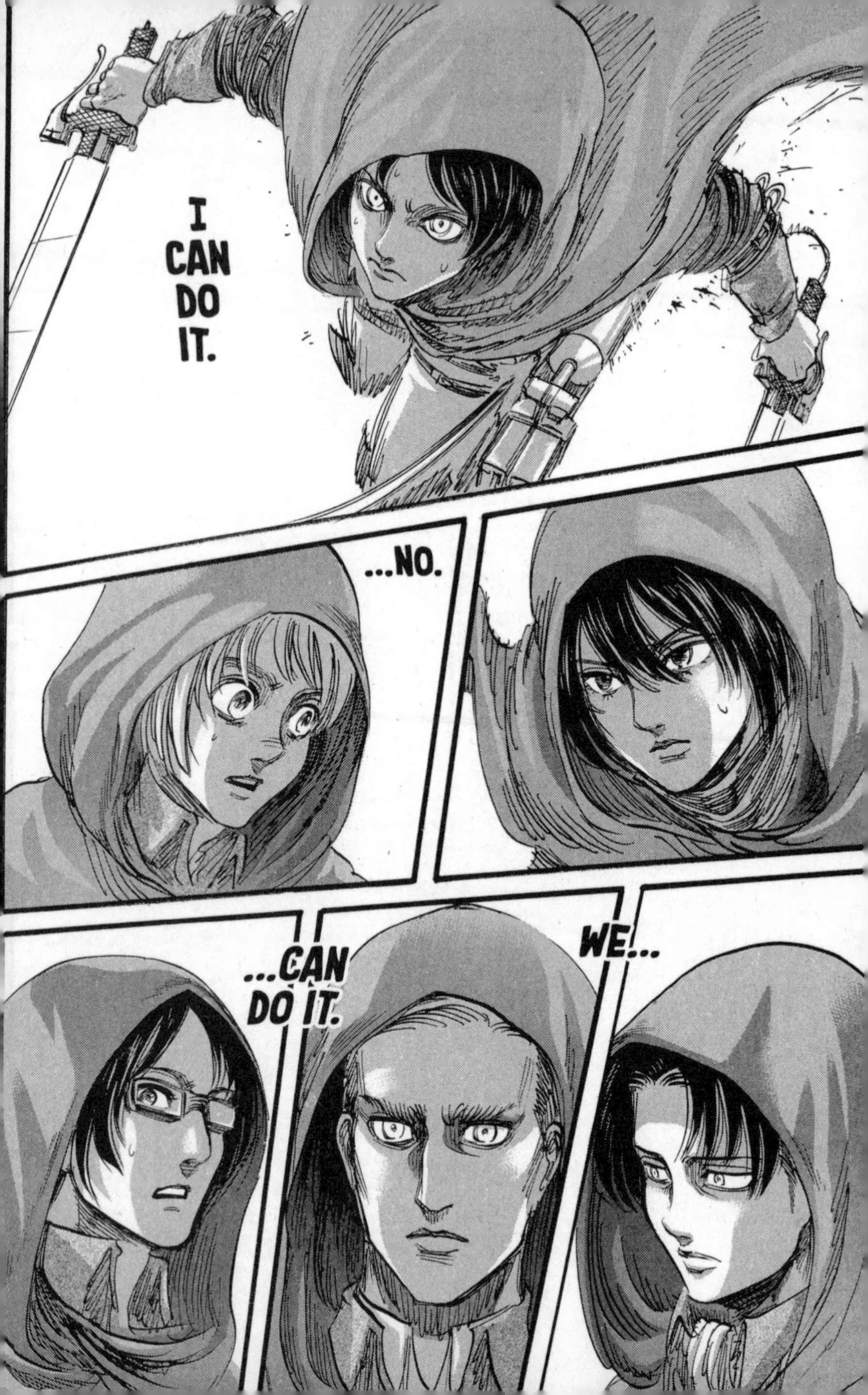
I CAN DO IT.
...NO.
WE...
...CAN DO IT.

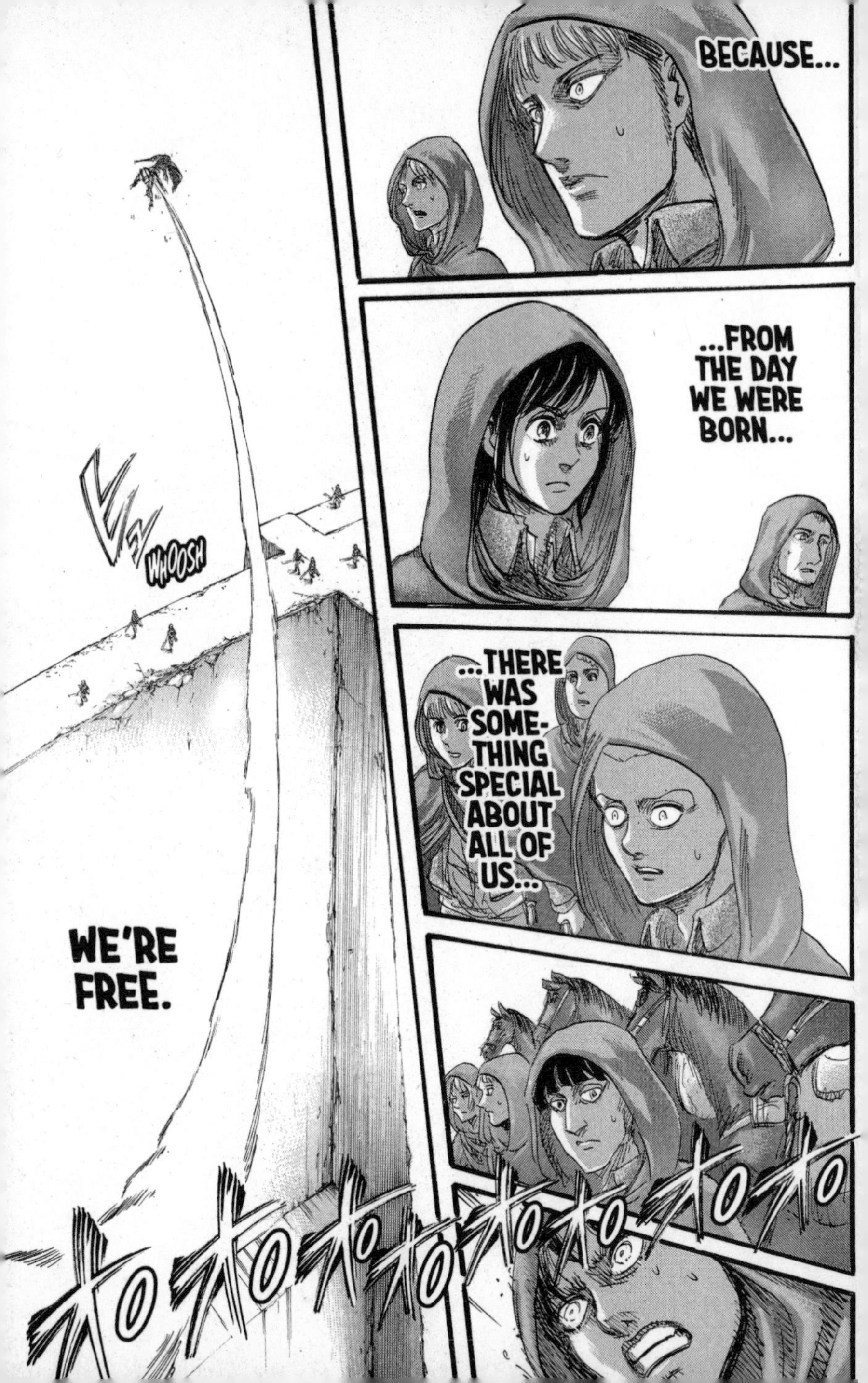
BECAUSE...
...FROM THE DAY WE WERE BORN...
...THERE WAS SOME-THING SPECIAL ABOUT ALL OF US...
WHOOSH
WE'RE FREE.

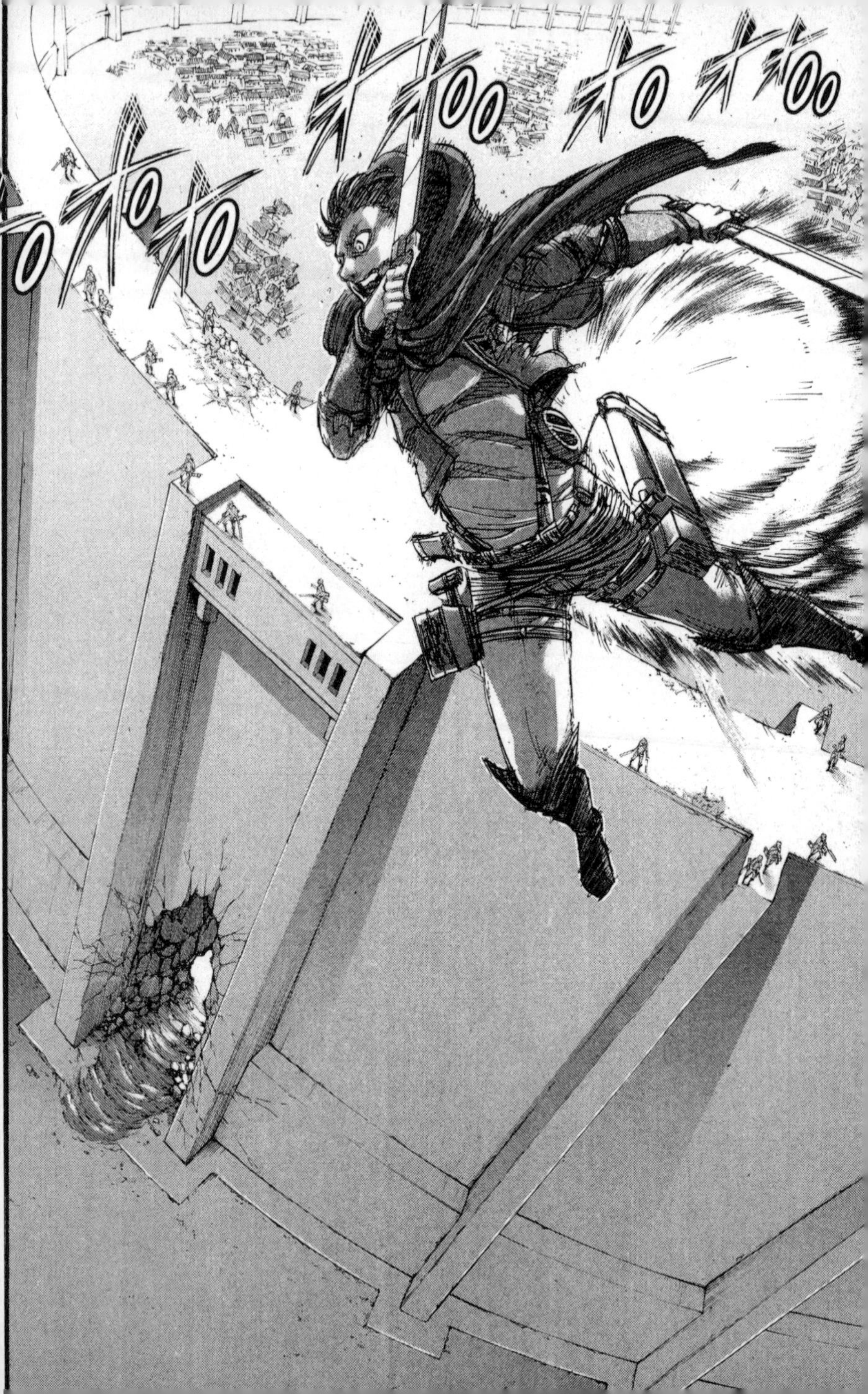

オオォォ
オォ オォォ
ォ オォ オォ

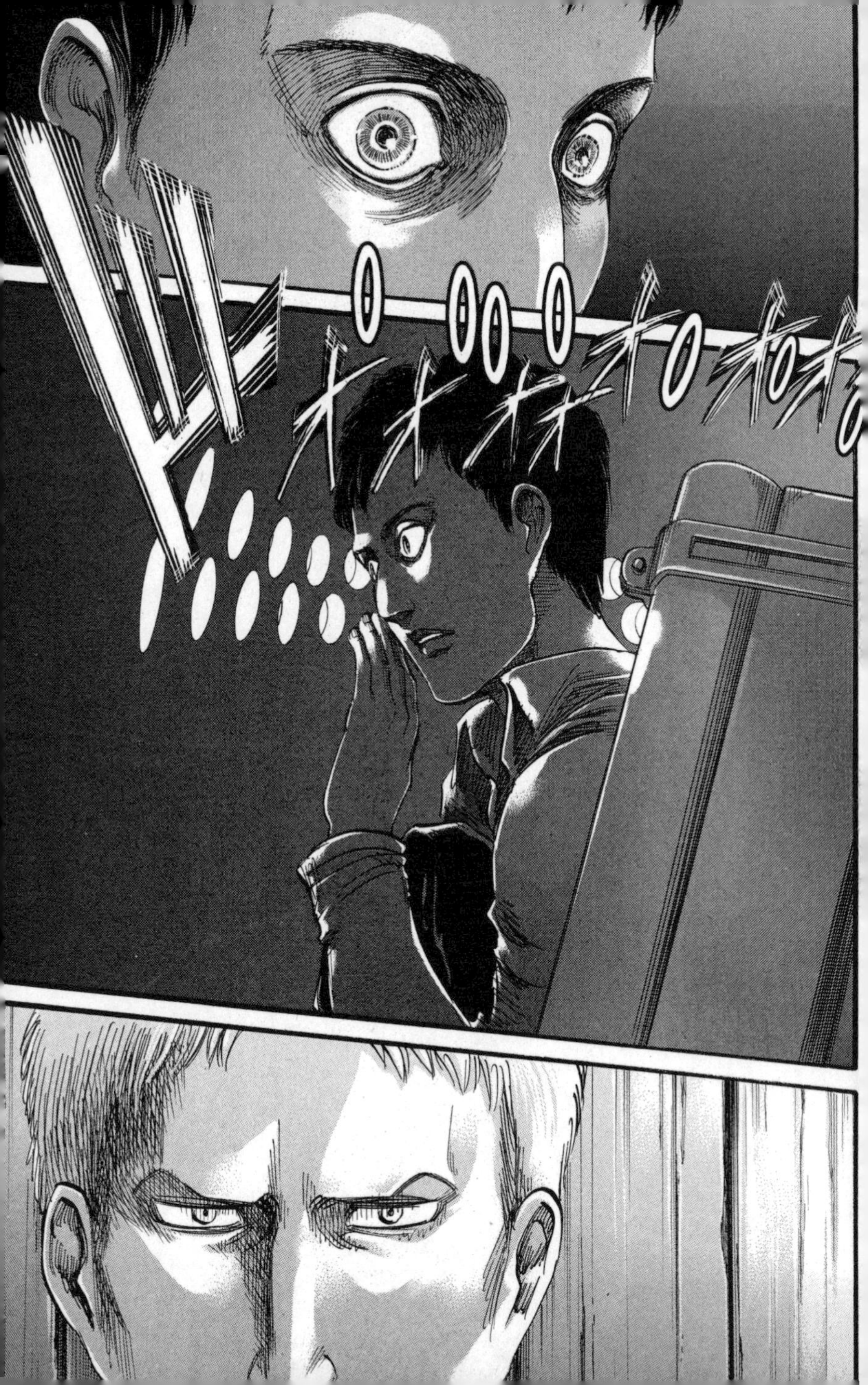

ATTACK on TITAN

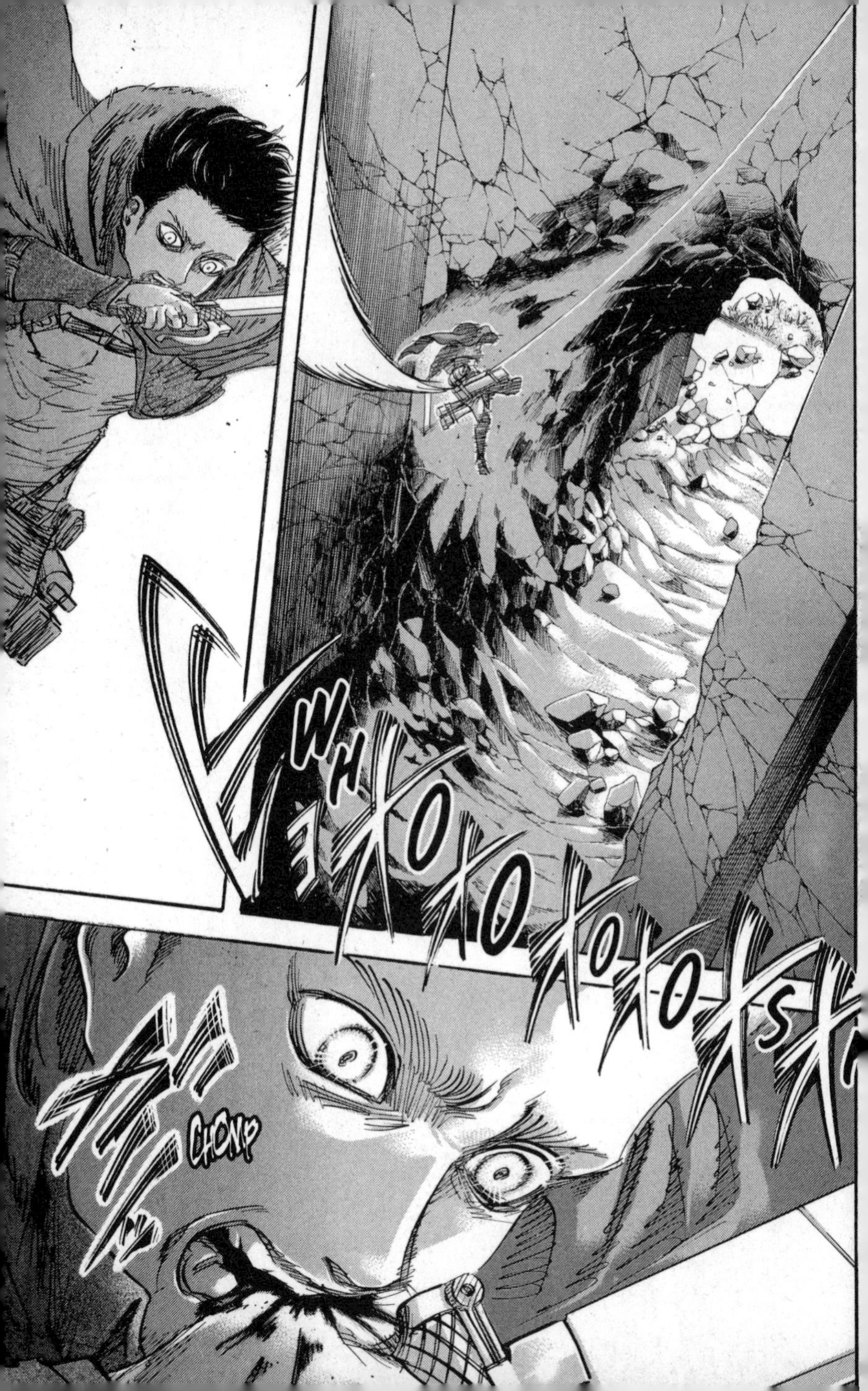
WHOOOOS
CHOMP

Episode 74:
Mission Objectives

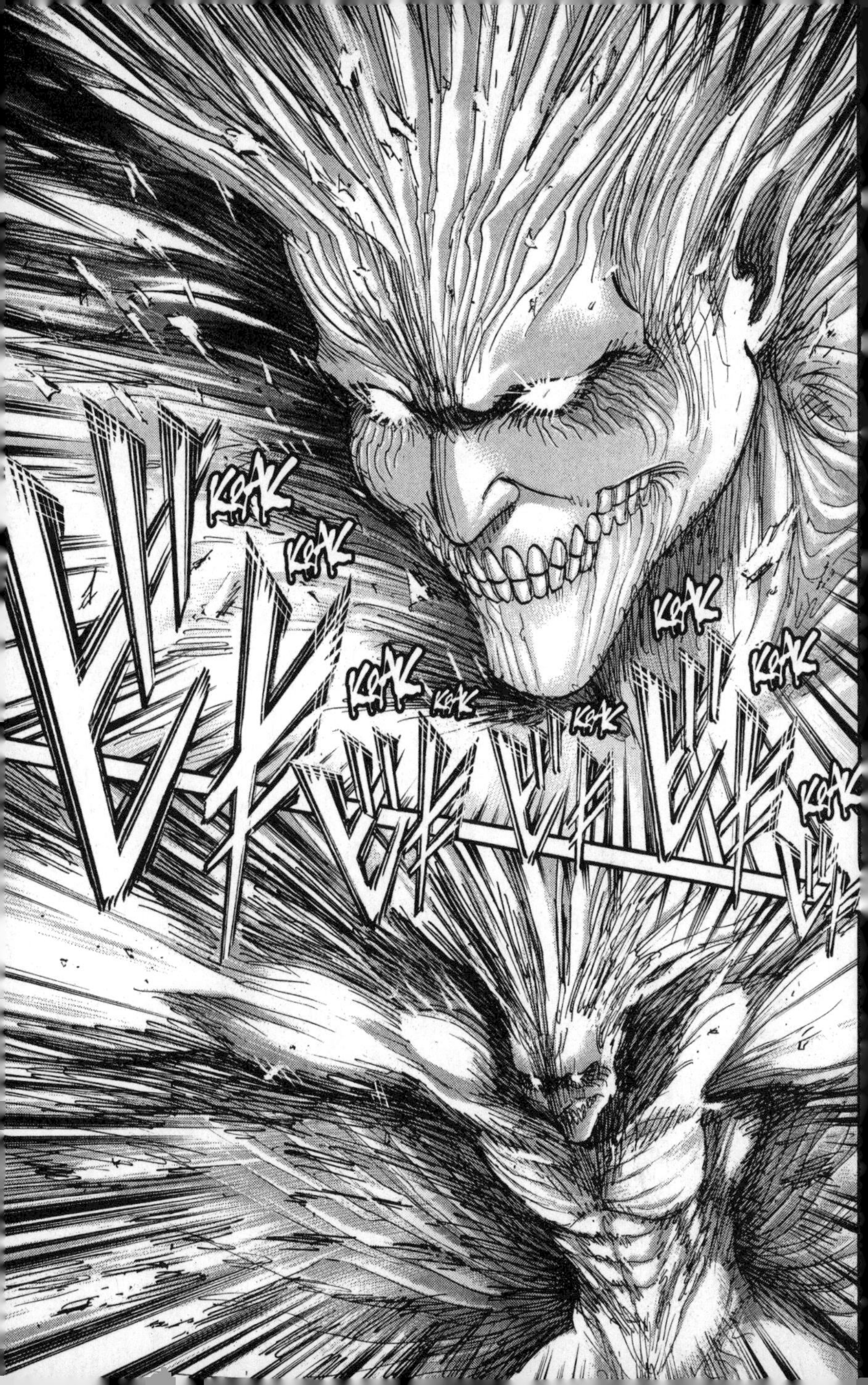
KRAK
KRAK
KRAK
KRAK
KRAK
KRAK
KRAK
KRAK

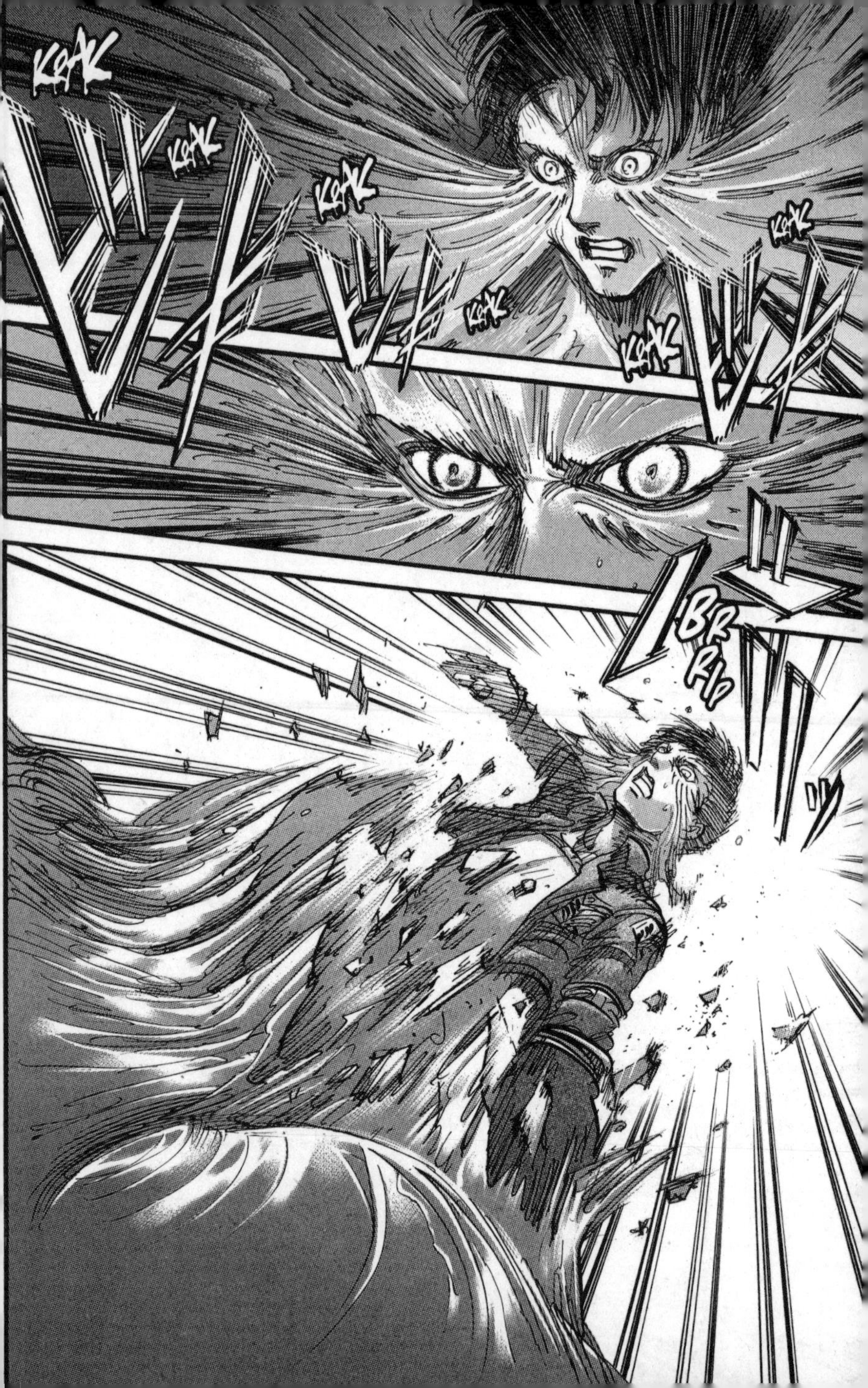
KRAK
KRAK
KRAK
KRAK
KRAK
KRAK
BRRRIP

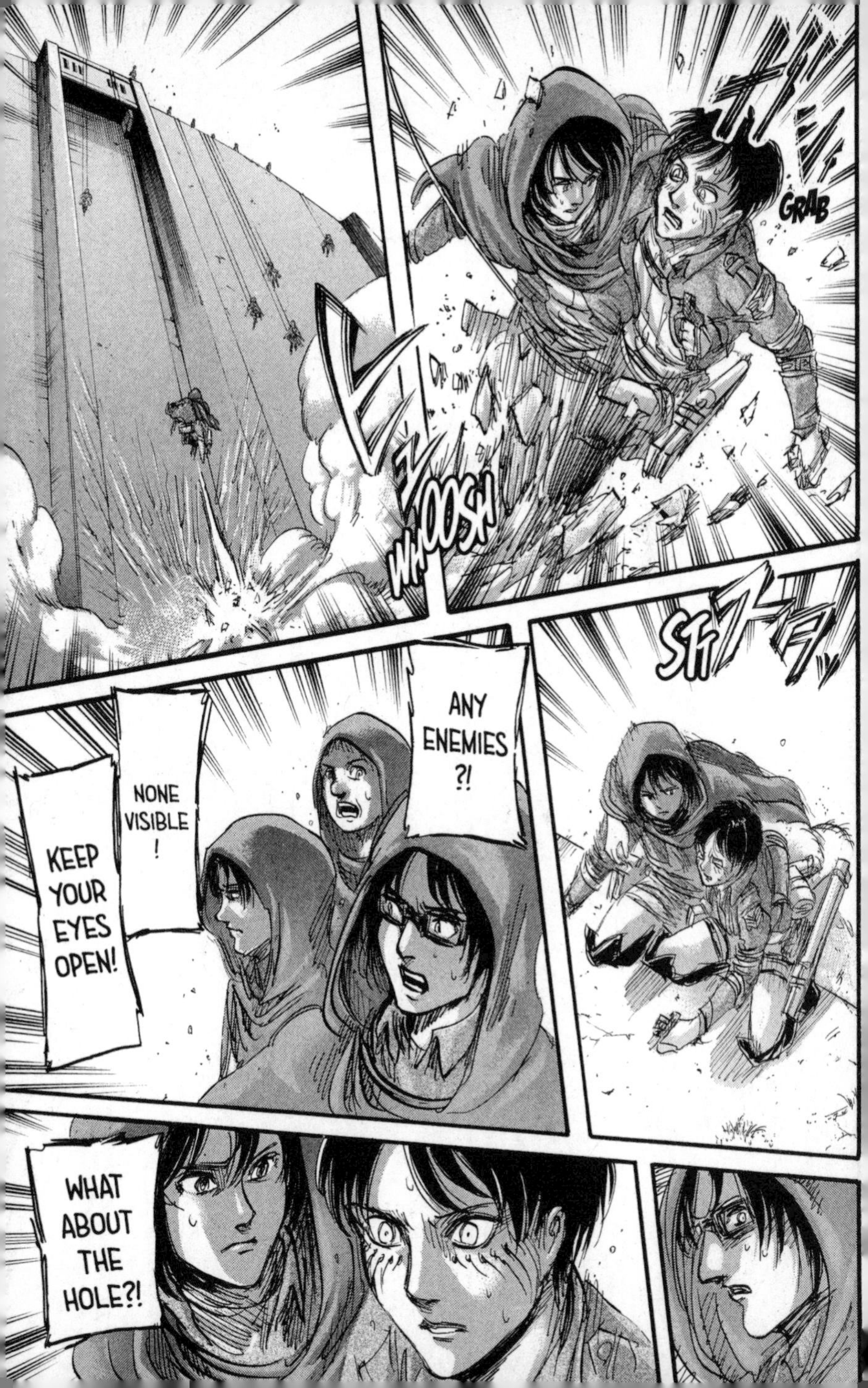
GRAB
WHOOSH
STT
ANY ENEMIES ?!
NONE VISIBLE !
KEEP YOUR EYES OPEN!
WHAT ABOUT THE HOLE?!

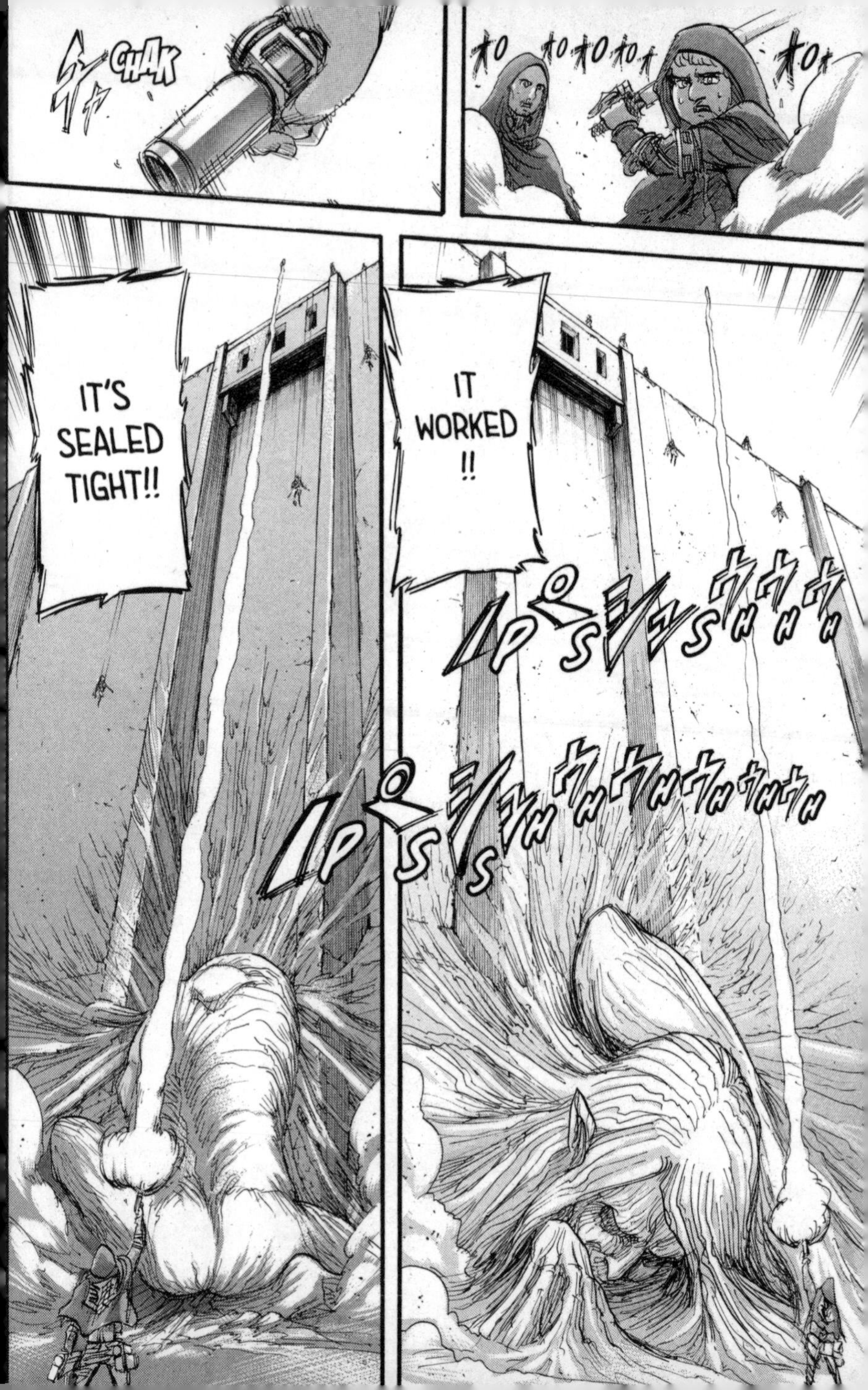
CHAK
IT WORKED!!
IT'S SEALED TIGHT!!

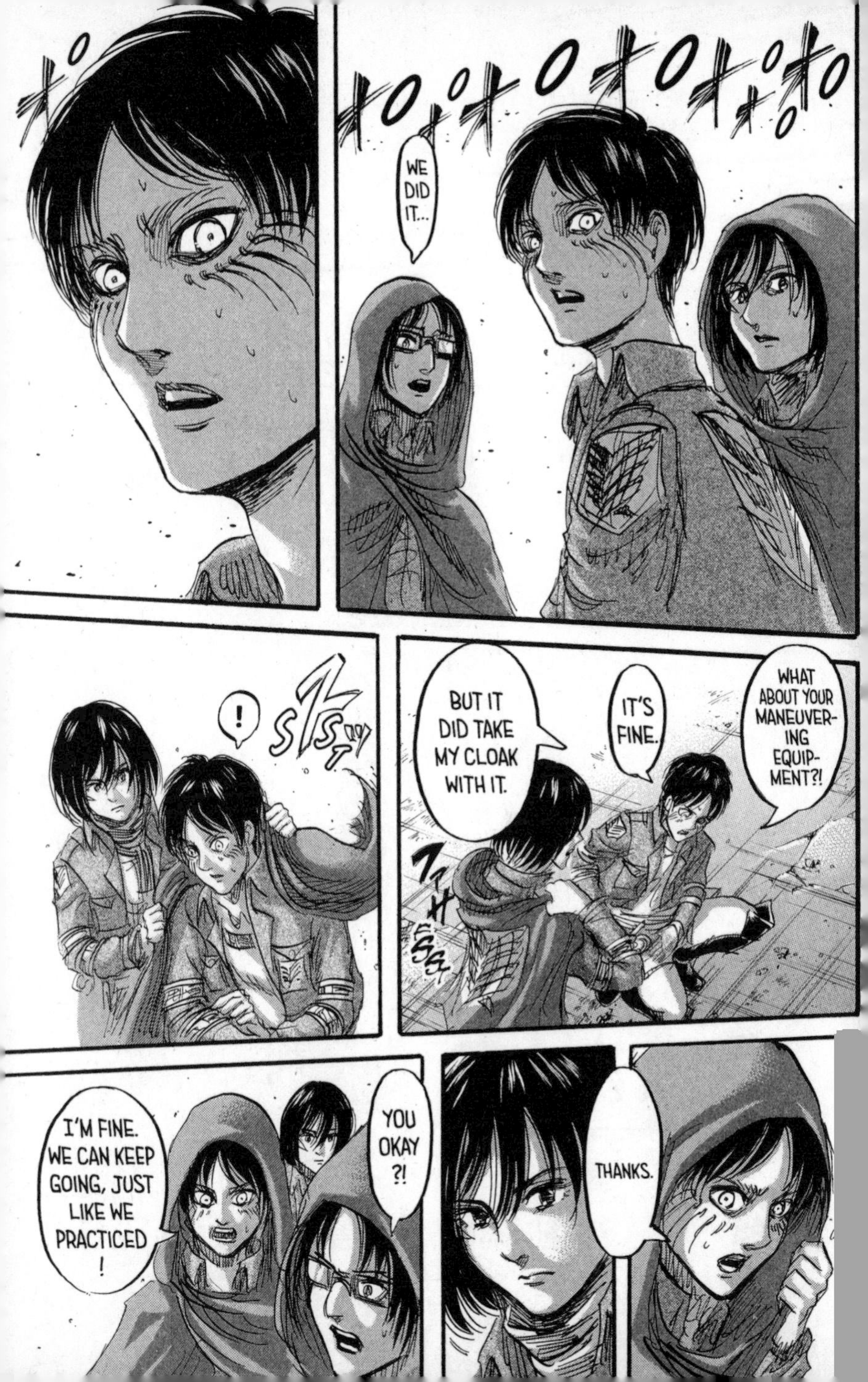
WE DID IT...
WHAT ABOUT YOUR MANEUVERING EQUIPMENT?!
IT'S FINE.
BUT IT DID TAKE MY CLOAK WITH IT.
!
THANKS.
YOU OKAY?!
I'M FINE. WE CAN KEEP GOING, JUST LIKE WE PRACTICED!

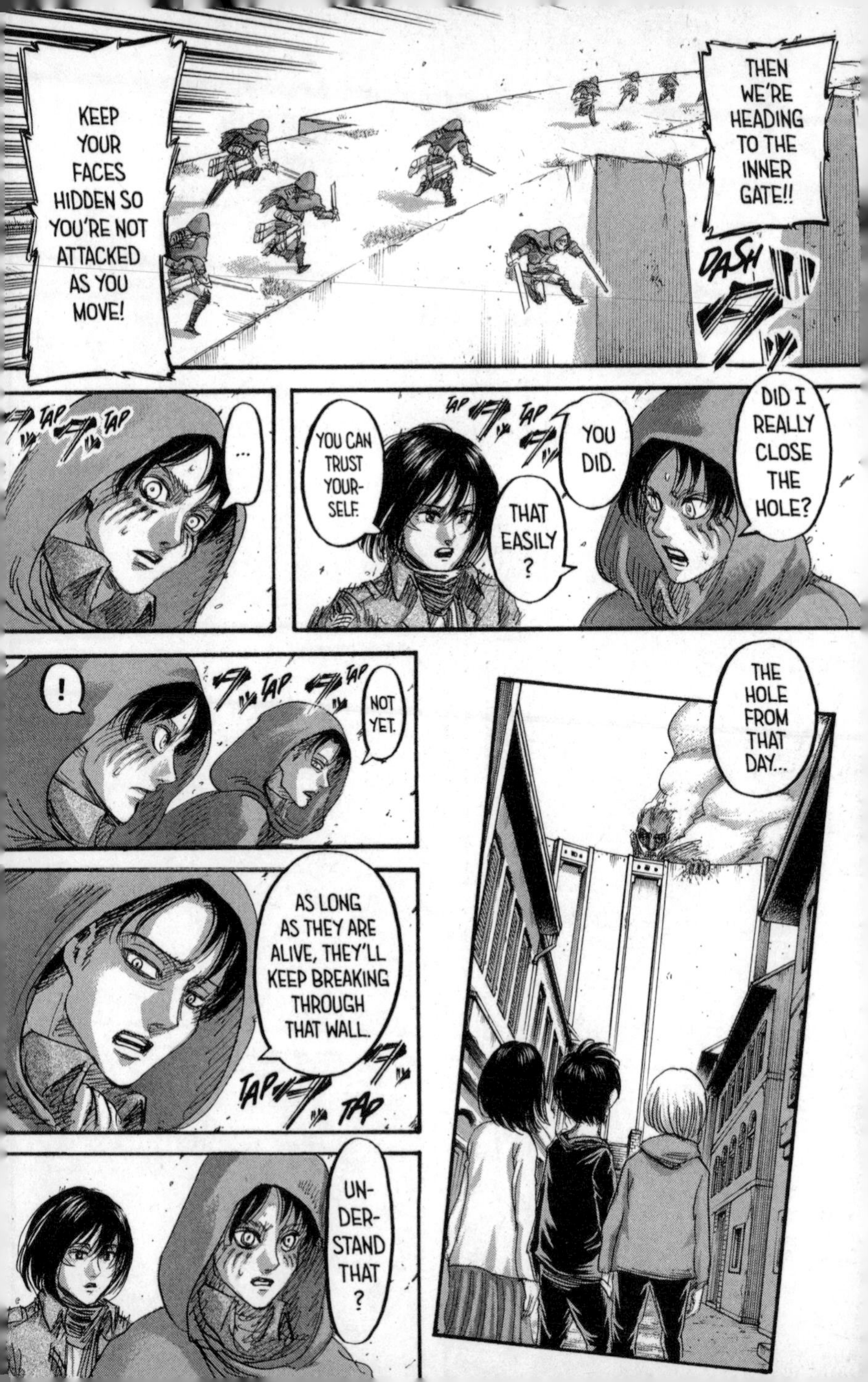
THEN WE'RE HEADING TO THE INNER GATE!!
DASH
KEEP YOUR FACES HIDDEN SO YOU'RE NOT ATTACKED AS YOU MOVE!
DID I REALLY CLOSE THE HOLE?
TAP TAP
YOU DID.
THAT EASILY?
YOU CAN TRUST YOURSELF.
TAP TAP
...
THE HOLE FROM THAT DAY...
NOT YET.
TAP TAP
!
AS LONG AS THEY ARE ALIVE, THEY'LL KEEP BREAKING THROUGH THAT WALL.
TAP TAP
UNDERSTAND THAT?

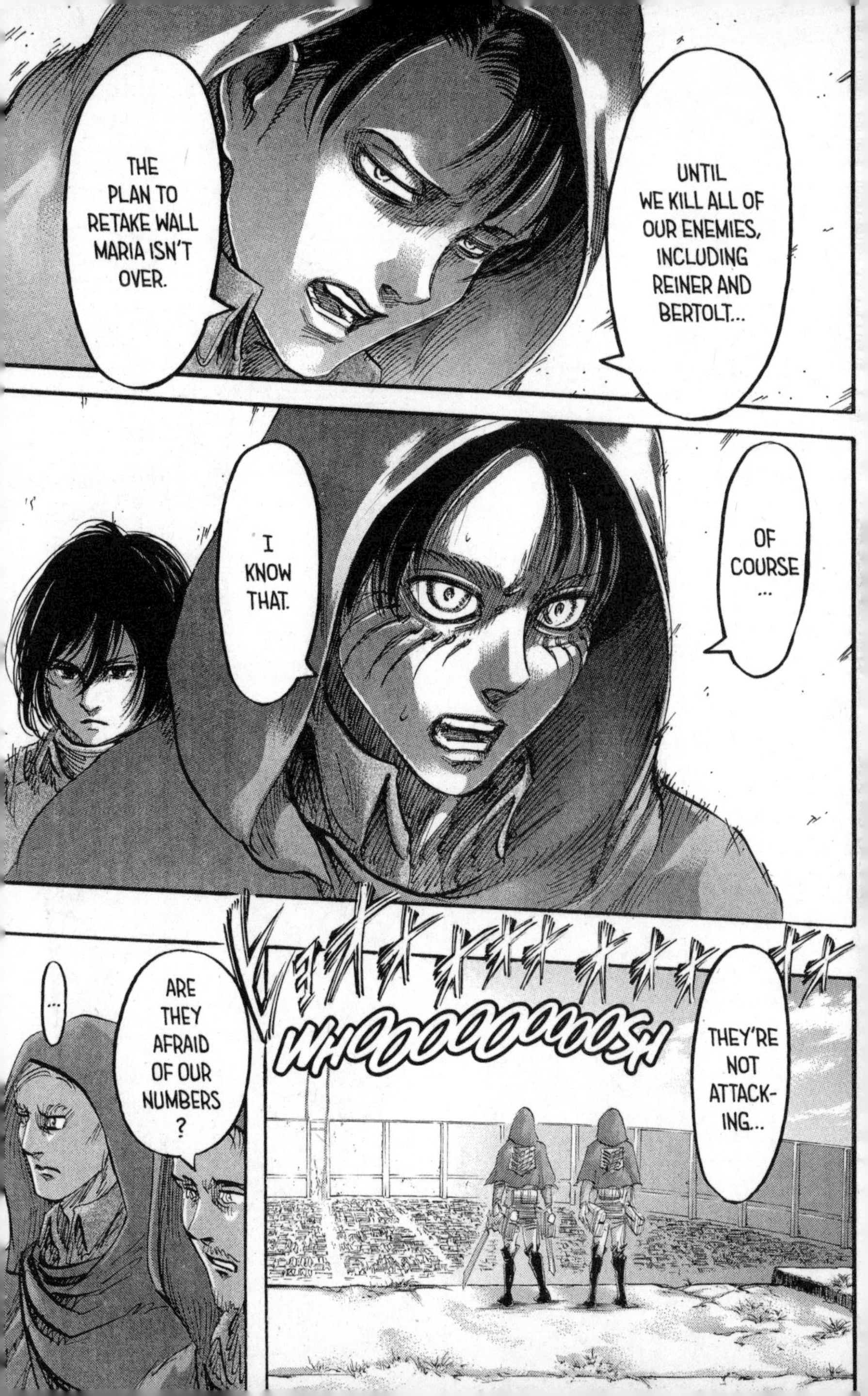
UNTIL WE KILL ALL OF OUR ENEMIES, INCLUDING REINER AND BERTOLT...
THE PLAN TO RETAKE WALL MARIA ISN'T OVER.
OF COURSE...
I KNOW THAT.
THEY'RE NOT ATTACK-ING...
WHOOOOOOOOOOSH
ARE THEY AFRAID OF OUR NUMBERS?
...

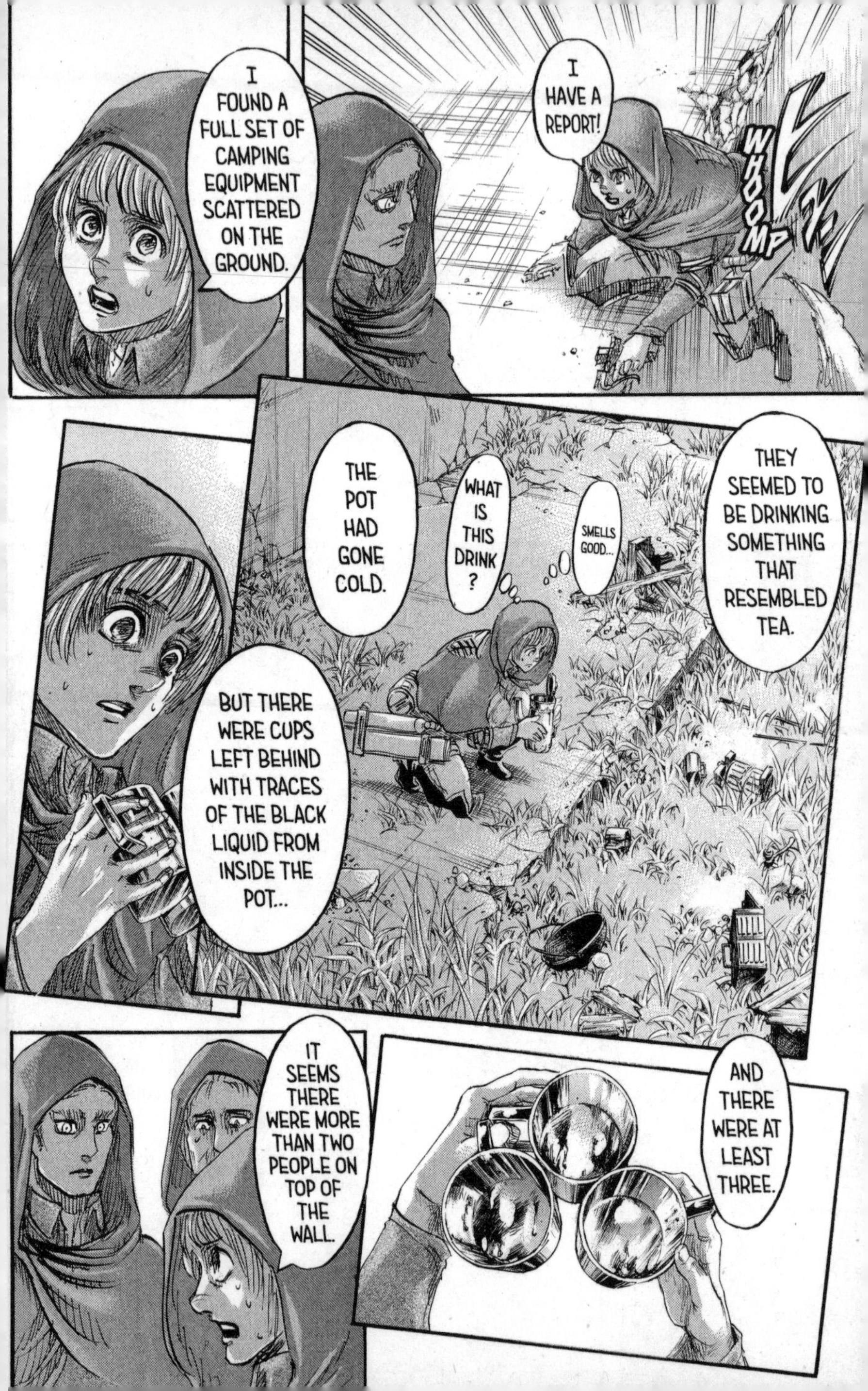
WHOOMP
I HAVE A REPORT!
I FOUND A FULL SET OF CAMPING EQUIPMENT SCATTERED ON THE GROUND.
THEY SEEMED TO BE DRINKING SOMETHING THAT RESEMBLED TEA.
SMELLS GOOD...
WHAT IS THIS DRINK?
THE POT HAD GONE COLD.
BUT THERE WERE CUPS LEFT BEHIND WITH TRACES OF THE BLACK LIQUID FROM INSIDE THE POT...
AND THERE WERE AT LEAST THREE.
IT SEEMS THERE WERE MORE THAN TWO PEOPLE ON TOP OF THE WALL.

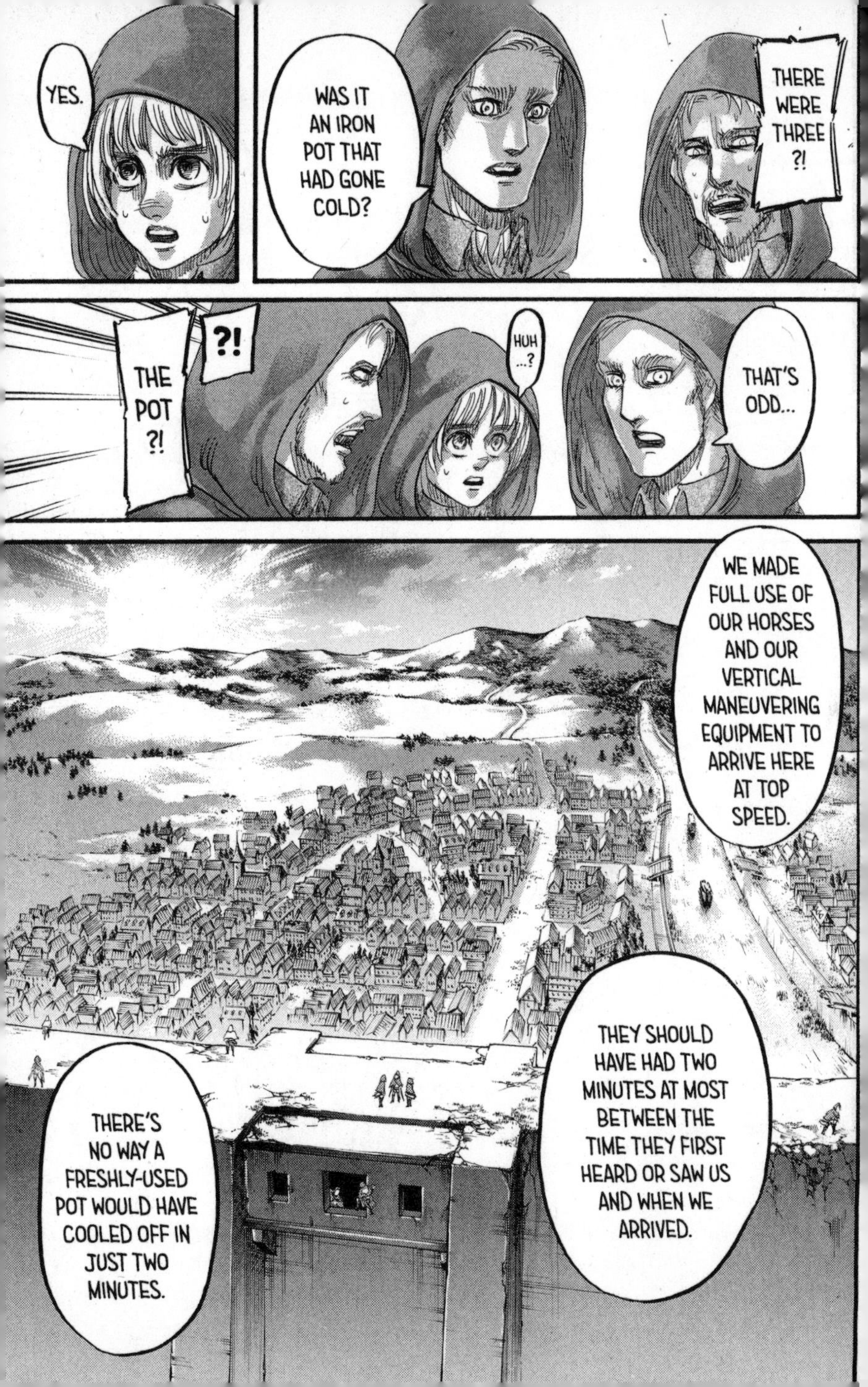
THERE WERE THREE ?!
WAS IT AN IRON POT THAT HAD GONE COLD?
YES.
THAT'S ODD...
HUH ...?
?!
THE POT ?!
WE MADE FULL USE OF OUR HORSES AND OUR VERTICAL MANEUVERING EQUIPMENT TO ARRIVE HERE AT TOP SPEED.
THEY SHOULD HAVE HAD TWO MINUTES AT MOST BETWEEN THE TIME THEY FIRST HEARD OR SAW US AND WHEN WE ARRIVED.
THERE'S NO WAY A FRESHLY-USED POT WOULD HAVE COOLED OFF IN JUST TWO MINUTES.

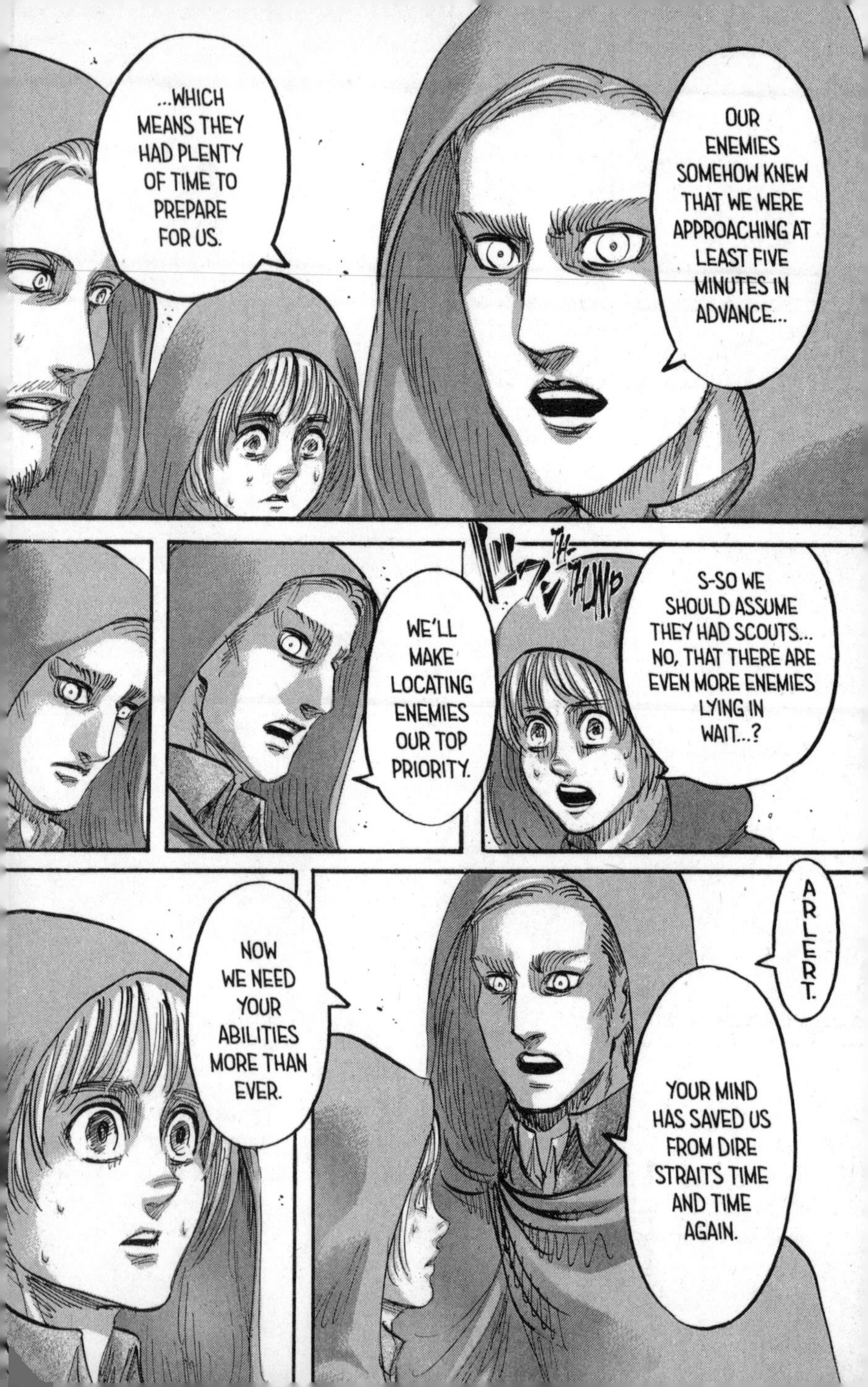
OUR ENEMIES SOMEHOW KNEW THAT WE WERE APPROACHING AT LEAST FIVE MINUTES IN ADVANCE...
...WHICH MEANS THEY HAD PLENTY OF TIME TO PREPARE FOR US.
TH-THUMP
S-SO WE SHOULD ASSUME THEY HAD SCOUTS... NO, THAT THERE ARE EVEN MORE ENEMIES LYING IN WAIT...?
WE'LL MAKE LOCATING ENEMIES OUR TOP PRIORITY.
ARLERT.
YOUR MIND HAS SAVED US FROM DIRE STRAITS TIME AND TIME AGAIN.
NOW WE NEED YOUR ABILITIES MORE THAN EVER.

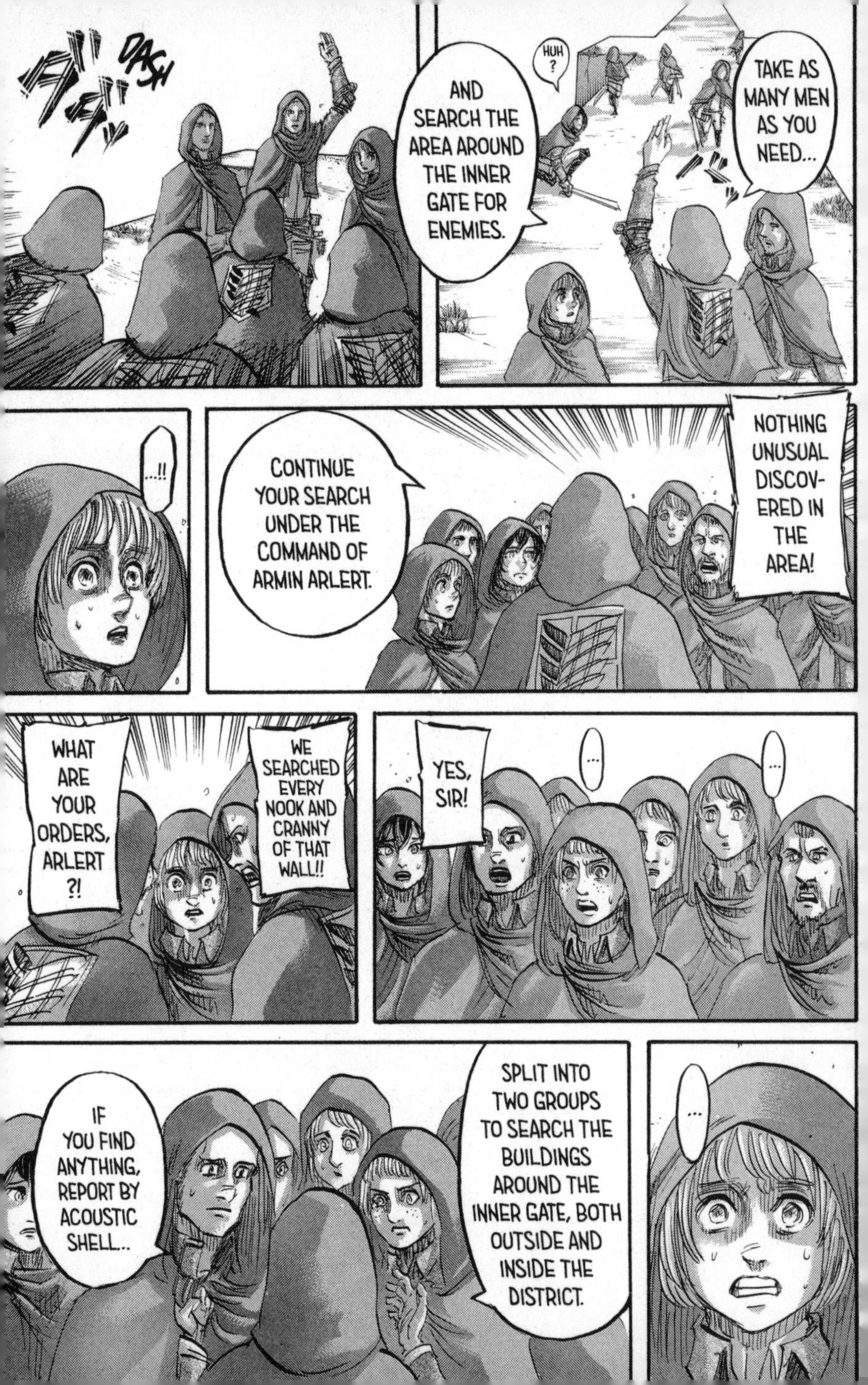
TAKE AS MANY MEN AS YOU NEED...
HUH ?
AND SEARCH THE AREA AROUND THE INNER GATE FOR ENEMIES.
DASH
NOTHING UNUSUAL DISCOV-ERED IN THE AREA!
CONTINUE YOUR SEARCH UNDER THE COMMAND OF ARMIN ARLERT.
...!!
...
...
YES, SIR!
WE SEARCHED EVERY NOOK AND CRANNY OF THAT WALL!!
WHAT ARE YOUR ORDERS, ARLERT ?!
...
SPLIT INTO TWO GROUPS TO SEARCH THE BUILDINGS AROUND THE INNER GATE, BOTH OUTSIDE AND INSIDE THE DISTRICT.
IF YOU FIND ANYTHING, REPORT BY ACOUSTIC SHELL...

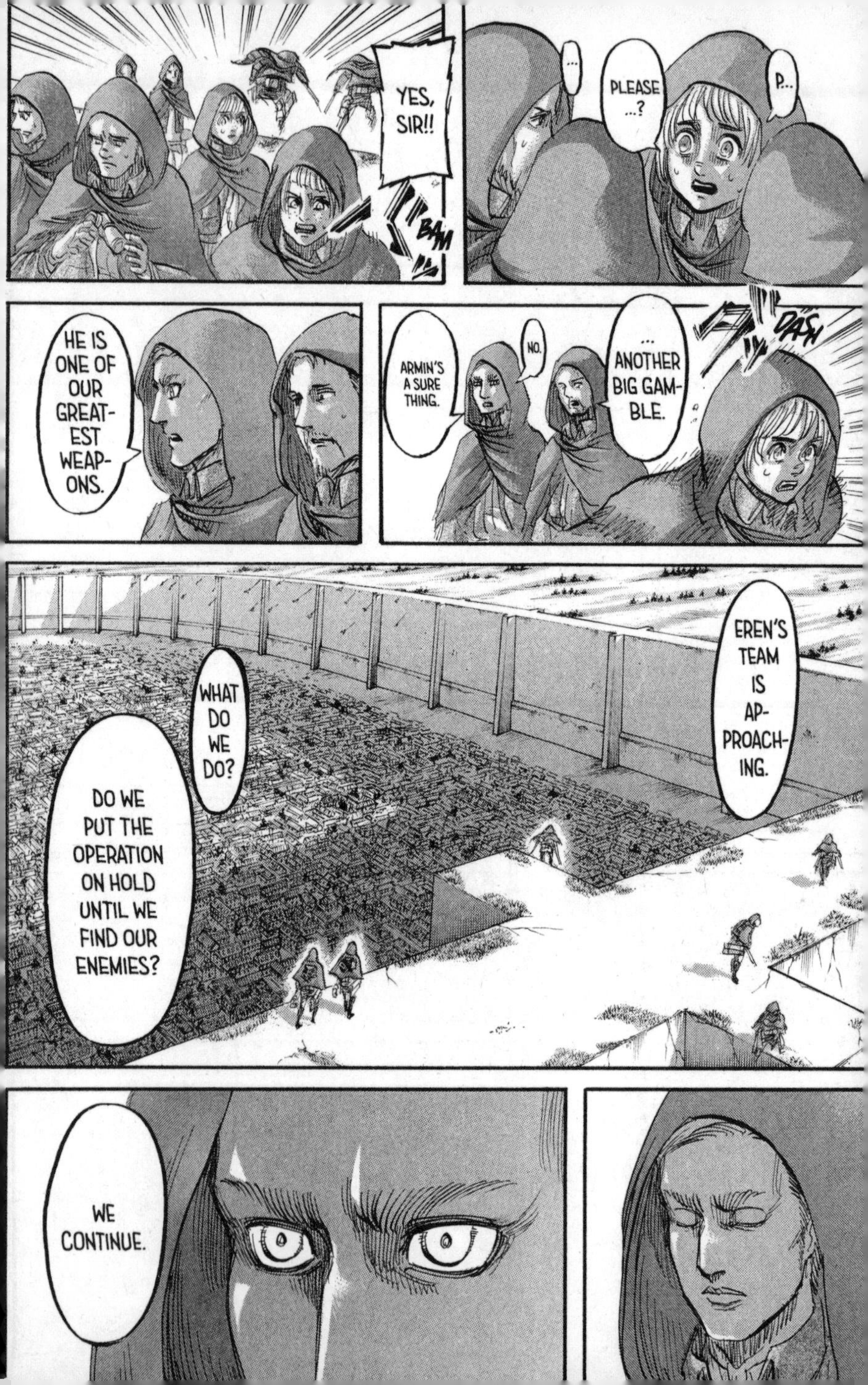

P...
PLEASE ...?
...
YES, SIR!!
BAM
DASH
... ANOTHER BIG GAMBLE.
NO.
ARMIN'S A SURE THING.
HE IS ONE OF OUR GREATEST WEAPONS.
EREN'S TEAM IS APPROACHING.
WHAT DO WE DO?
DO WE PUT THE OPERATION ON HOLD UNTIL WE FIND OUR ENEMIES?
WE CONTINUE.

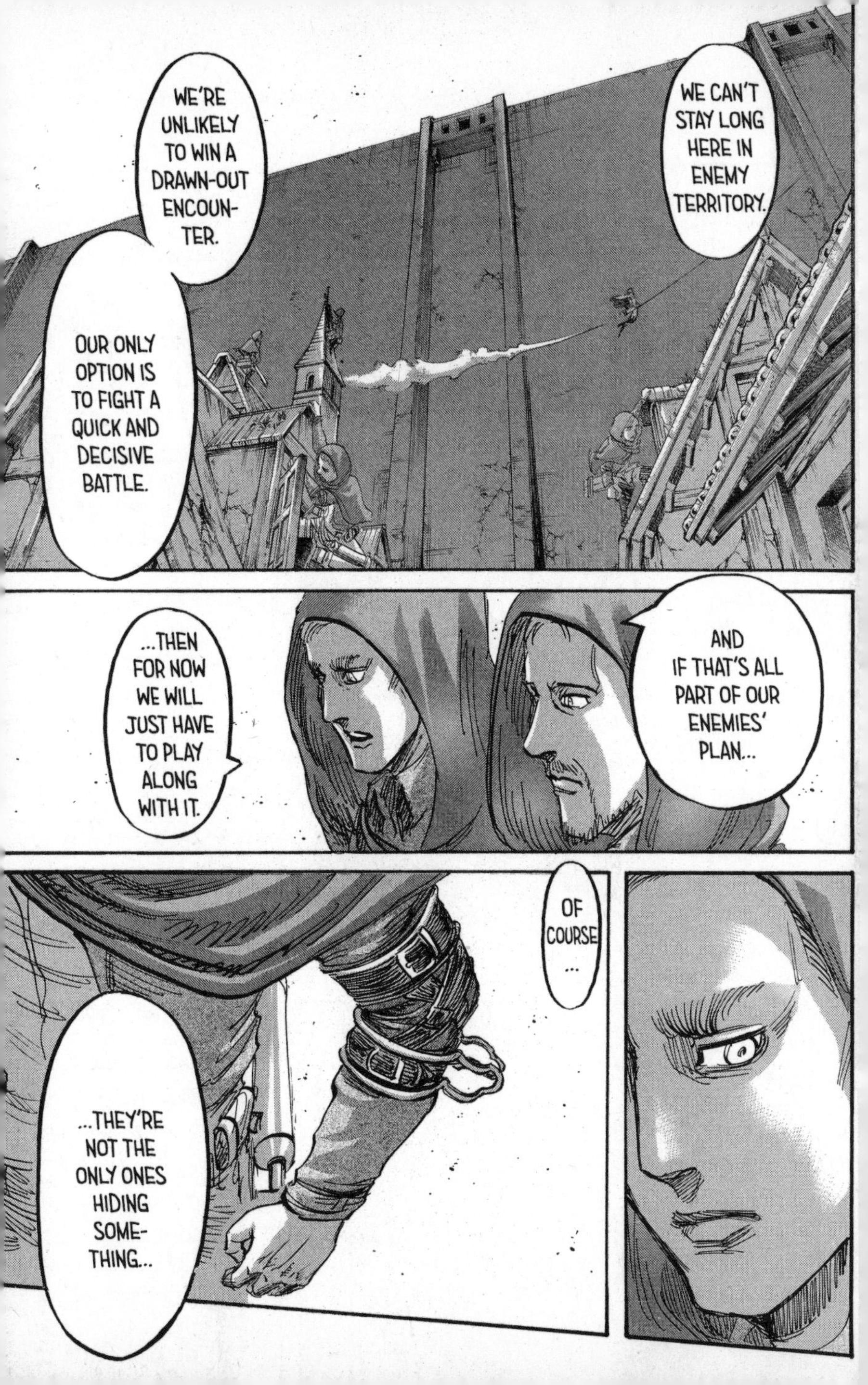
WE CAN'T STAY LONG HERE IN ENEMY TERRITORY.
WE'RE UNLIKELY TO WIN A DRAWN-OUT ENCOUN-TER.
OUR ONLY OPTION IS TO FIGHT A QUICK AND DECISIVE BATTLE.
AND IF THAT'S ALL PART OF OUR ENEMIES' PLAN...
...THEN FOR NOW WE WILL JUST HAVE TO PLAY ALONG WITH IT.
OF COURSE ...
...THEY'RE NOT THE ONLY ONES HIDING SOME-THING...

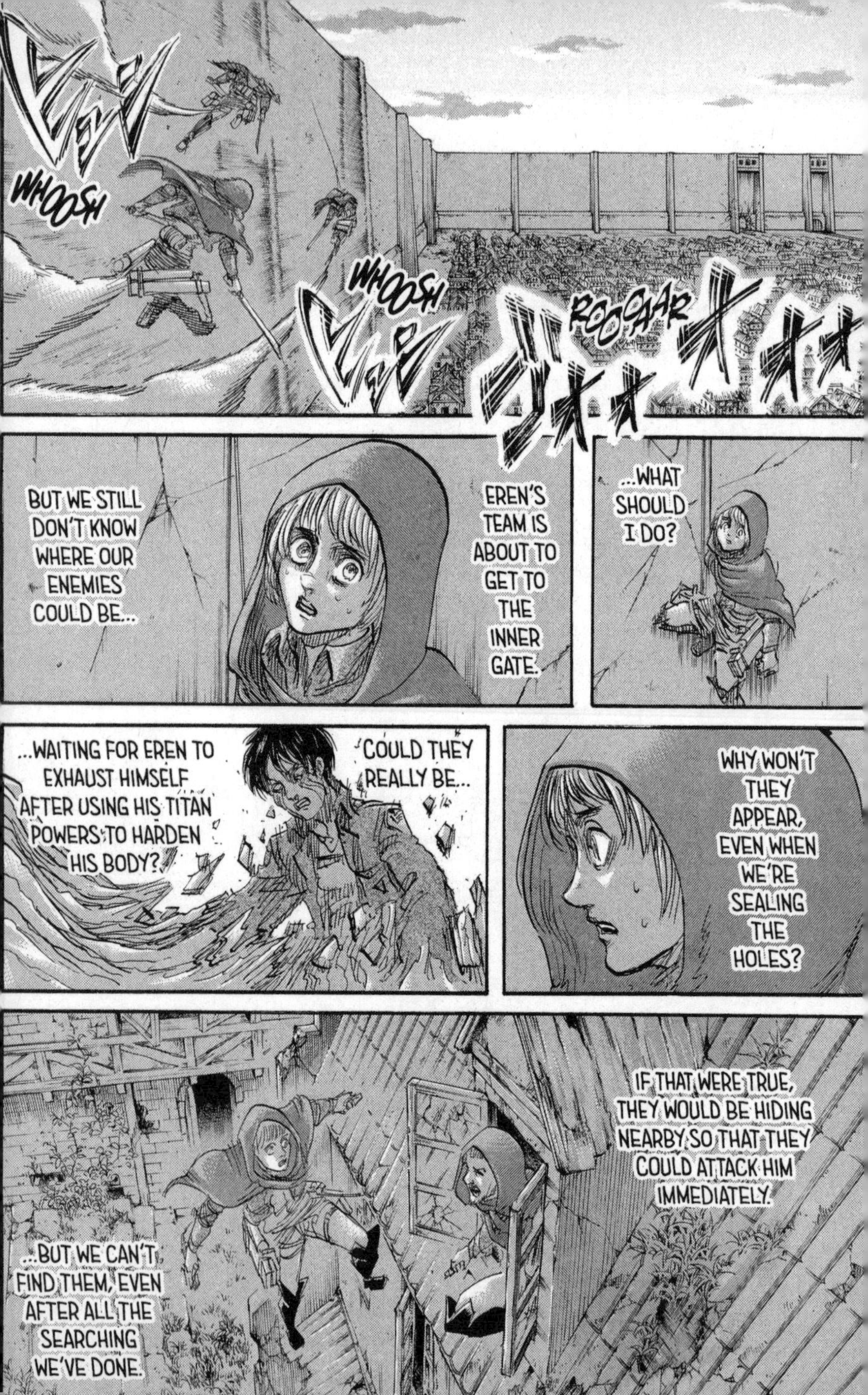
ROOOAAR
WHOOSH
WHOOSH
...WHAT SHOULD I DO?
EREN'S TEAM IS ABOUT TO GET TO THE INNER GATE.
BUT WE STILL DON'T KNOW WHERE OUR ENEMIES COULD BE...
WHY WON'T THEY APPEAR, EVEN WHEN WE'RE SEALING THE HOLES?
COULD THEY REALLY BE...
...WAITING FOR EREN TO EXHAUST HIMSELF AFTER USING HIS TITAN POWERS TO HARDEN HIS BODY?
IF THAT WERE TRUE, THEY WOULD BE HIDING NEARBY SO THAT THEY COULD ATTACK HIM IMMEDIATELY.
...BUT WE CAN'T FIND THEM, EVEN AFTER ALL THE SEARCHING WE'VE DONE.

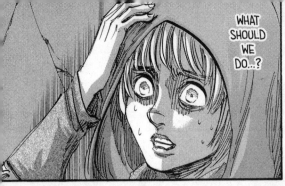

THIS IS BAD...
WHAT SHOULD WE DO...?
IF THIS FAILS...IT REALLY IS THE END.
IT'LL ALL BE OVER. EVERYTHING.
THE COMMANDER WON'T STOP THE OPERATION.
EVEN IF WE END UP GIVING OUR ENEMY THE PERFECT OPENING, OUR ONLY OPTION WILL BE TO MEET THEM AND STRIKE BACK.
THE MORE TIME WE GIVE THEM, THE WORSE OUR POSITION GETS...
I DON'T KNOW...THEY ALWAYS ATTACK US IN WAYS WE COULD NEVER IMAGINE, USING WHAT SEEM LIKE IMPOSSIBLE TACTICS.
WE'RE ALWAYS AT A DISADVANTAGE...
BECAUSE WE KNOW SO LITTLE...
...ABOUT THE TITANS.

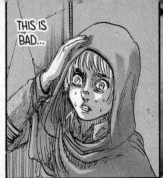

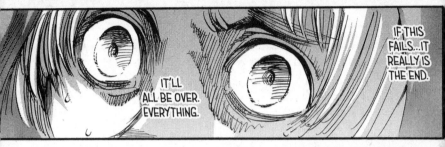

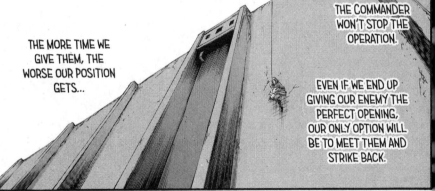

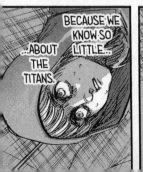

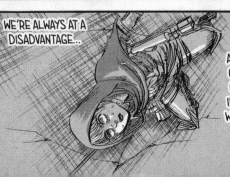

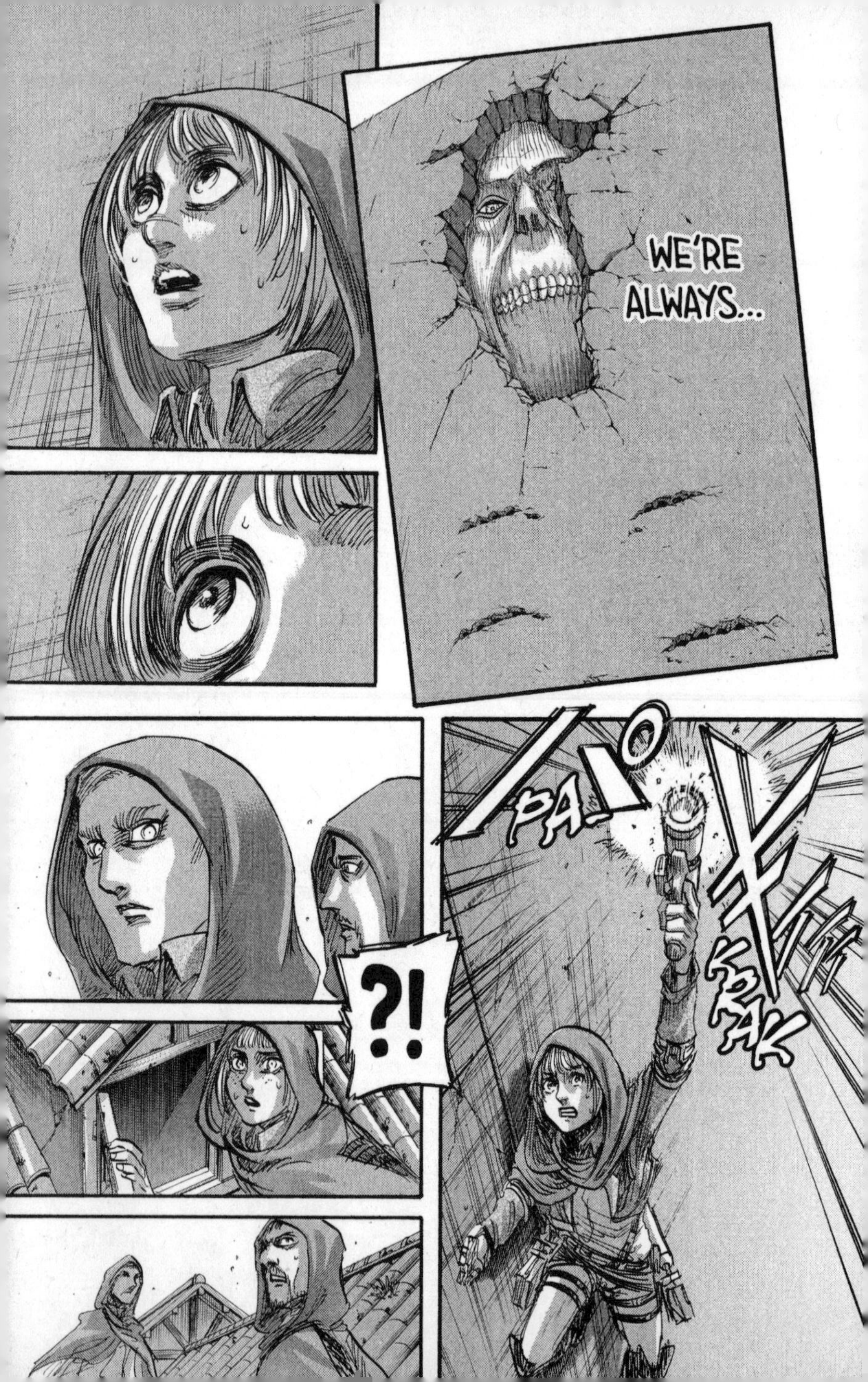
WE'RE ALWAYS...
PA-
KRAK
?!

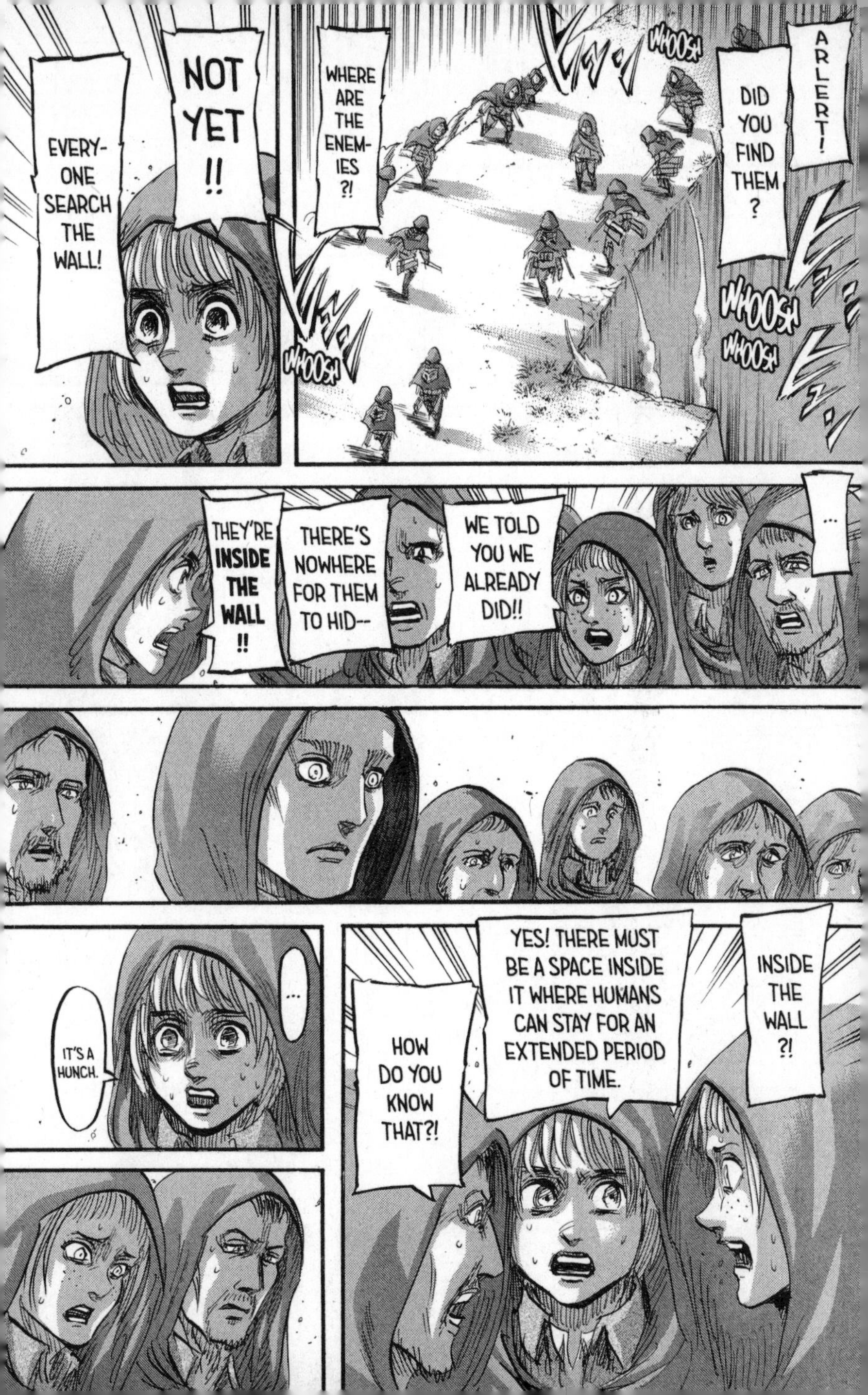
ARLERT!
DID YOU FIND THEM?
WHOOSH
WHOOSH
WHOOSH
WHERE ARE THE ENEMIES?!
WHOOSH
NOT YET!!
EVERYONE SEARCH THE WALL!
...
WE TOLD YOU WE ALREADY DID!!
THERE'S NOWHERE FOR THEM TO HID--
THEY'RE **INSIDE THE WALL**!!
INSIDE THE WALL?!
YES! THERE MUST BE A SPACE INSIDE IT WHERE HUMANS CAN STAY FOR AN EXTENDED PERIOD OF TIME.
HOW DO YOU KNOW THAT?!
...
IT'S A HUNCH.

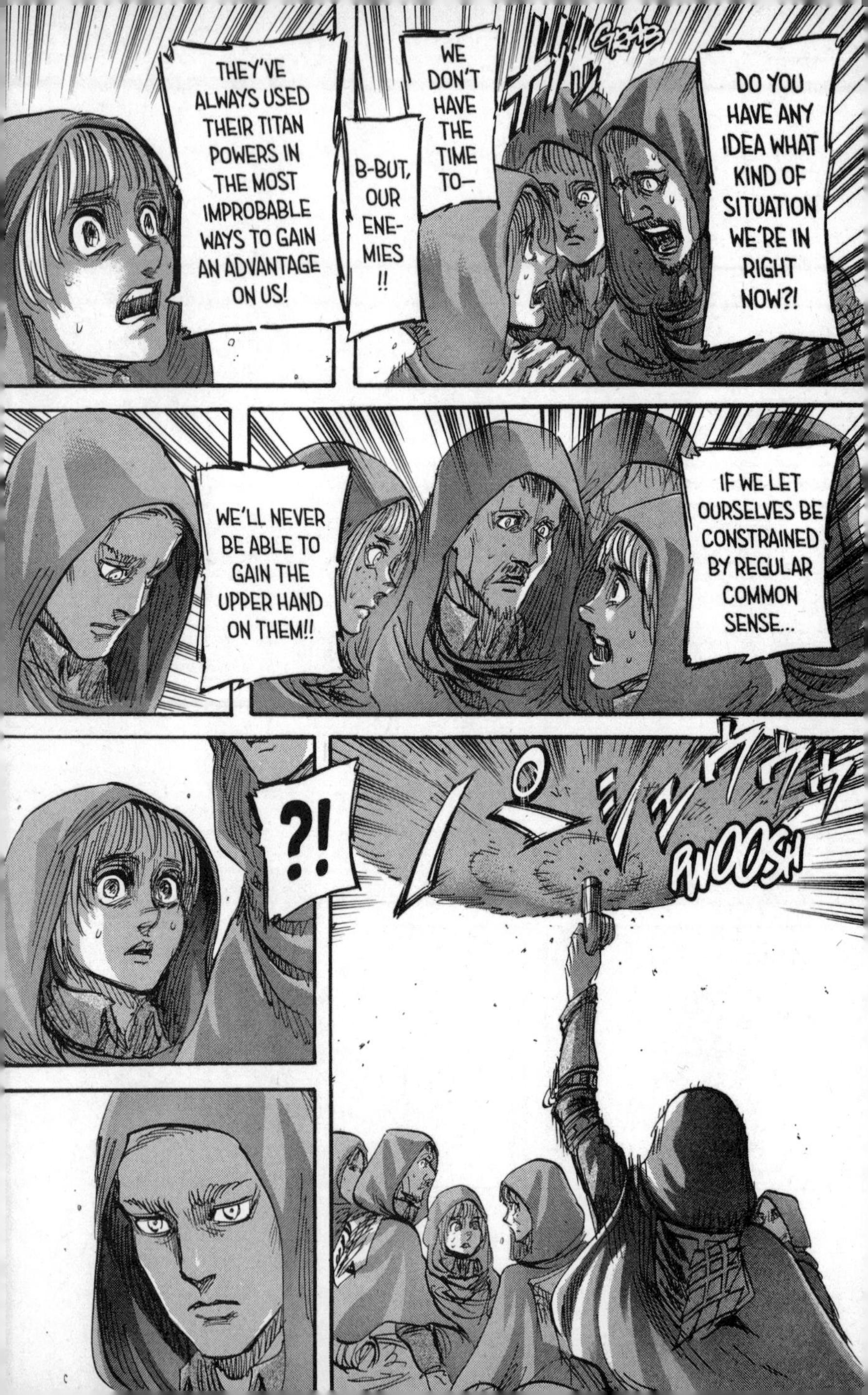
GRAB
DO YOU HAVE ANY IDEA WHAT KIND OF SITUATION WE'RE IN RIGHT NOW?!
WE DON'T HAVE THE TIME TO—
B-BUT, OUR ENE-MIES!!
THEY'VE ALWAYS USED THEIR TITAN POWERS IN THE MOST IMPROBABLE WAYS TO GAIN AN ADVANTAGE ON US!
IF WE LET OURSELVES BE CONSTRAINED BY REGULAR COMMON SENSE...
WE'LL NEVER BE ABLE TO GAIN THE UPPER HAND ON THEM!!
PWOOSH
?!

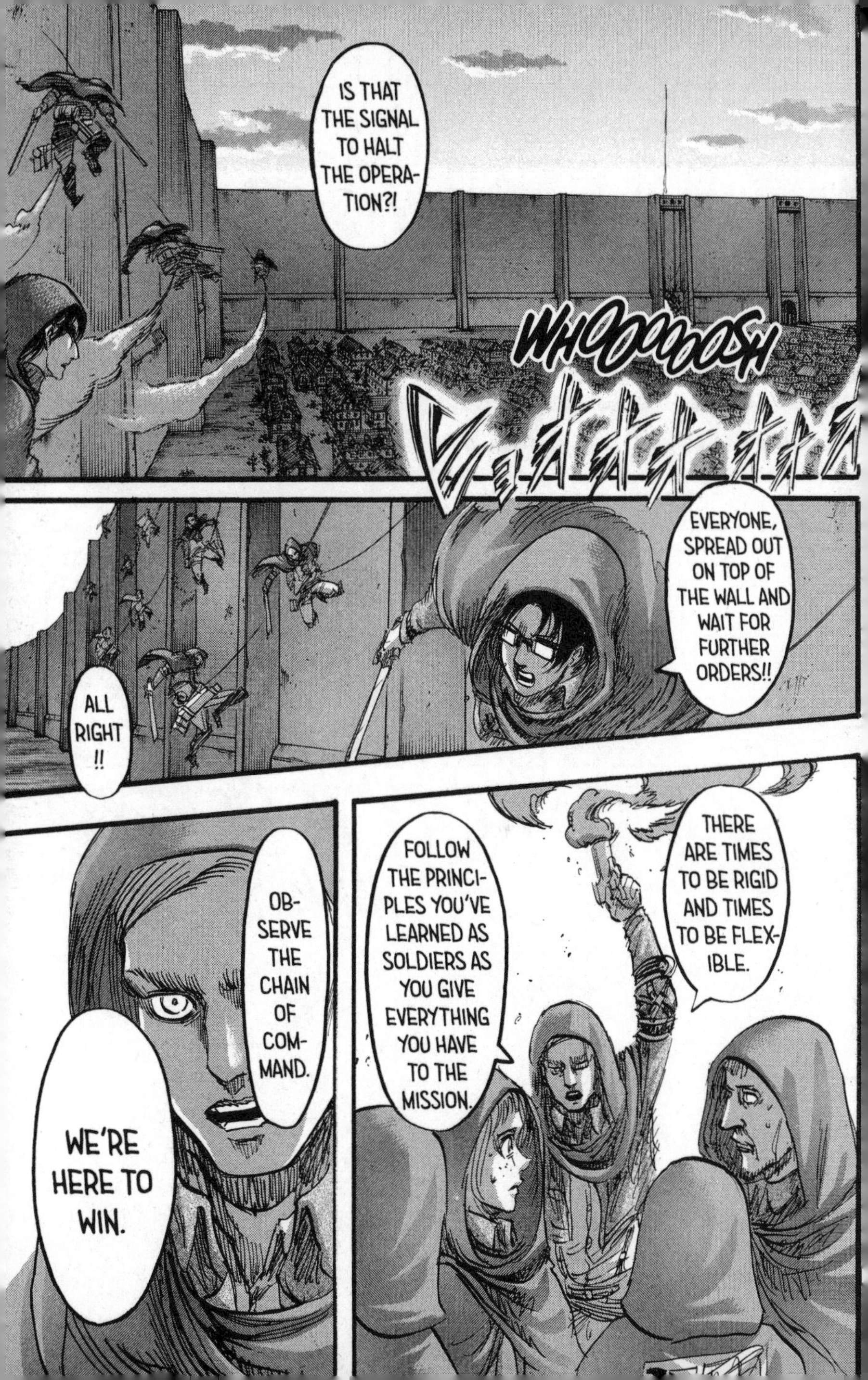
IS THAT THE SIGNAL TO HALT THE OPERATION?!
WHOOOOOOOSH
EVERYONE, SPREAD OUT ON TOP OF THE WALL AND WAIT FOR FURTHER ORDERS!!
ALL RIGHT!!
THERE ARE TIMES TO BE RIGID AND TIMES TO BE FLEX-IBLE.
FOLLOW THE PRINCI-PLES YOU'VE LEARNED AS SOLDIERS AS YOU GIVE EVERYTHING YOU HAVE TO THE MISSION.
OB-SERVE THE CHAIN OF COM-MAND.
WE'RE HERE TO WIN.

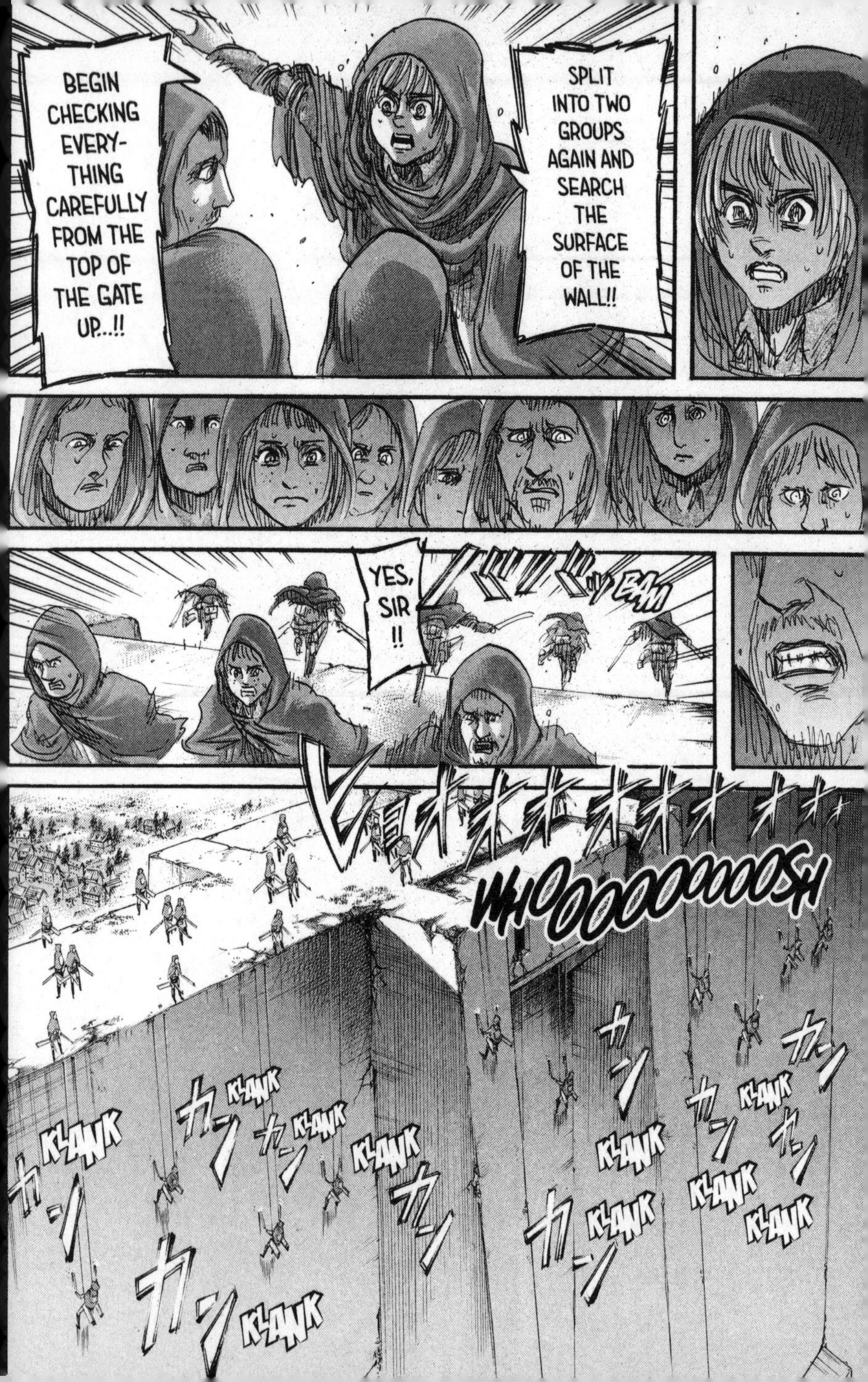
SPLIT INTO TWO GROUPS AGAIN AND SEARCH THE SURFACE OF THE WALL!!
BEGIN CHECKING EVERYTHING CAREFULLY FROM THE TOP OF THE GATE UP...!!
BAM
YES, SIR!!
WHOOOOOOOOOSH
KLANK
KLANK
KLANK
KLANK
KLANK
KLANK
KLANK
KLANK
KLANK
KLANK

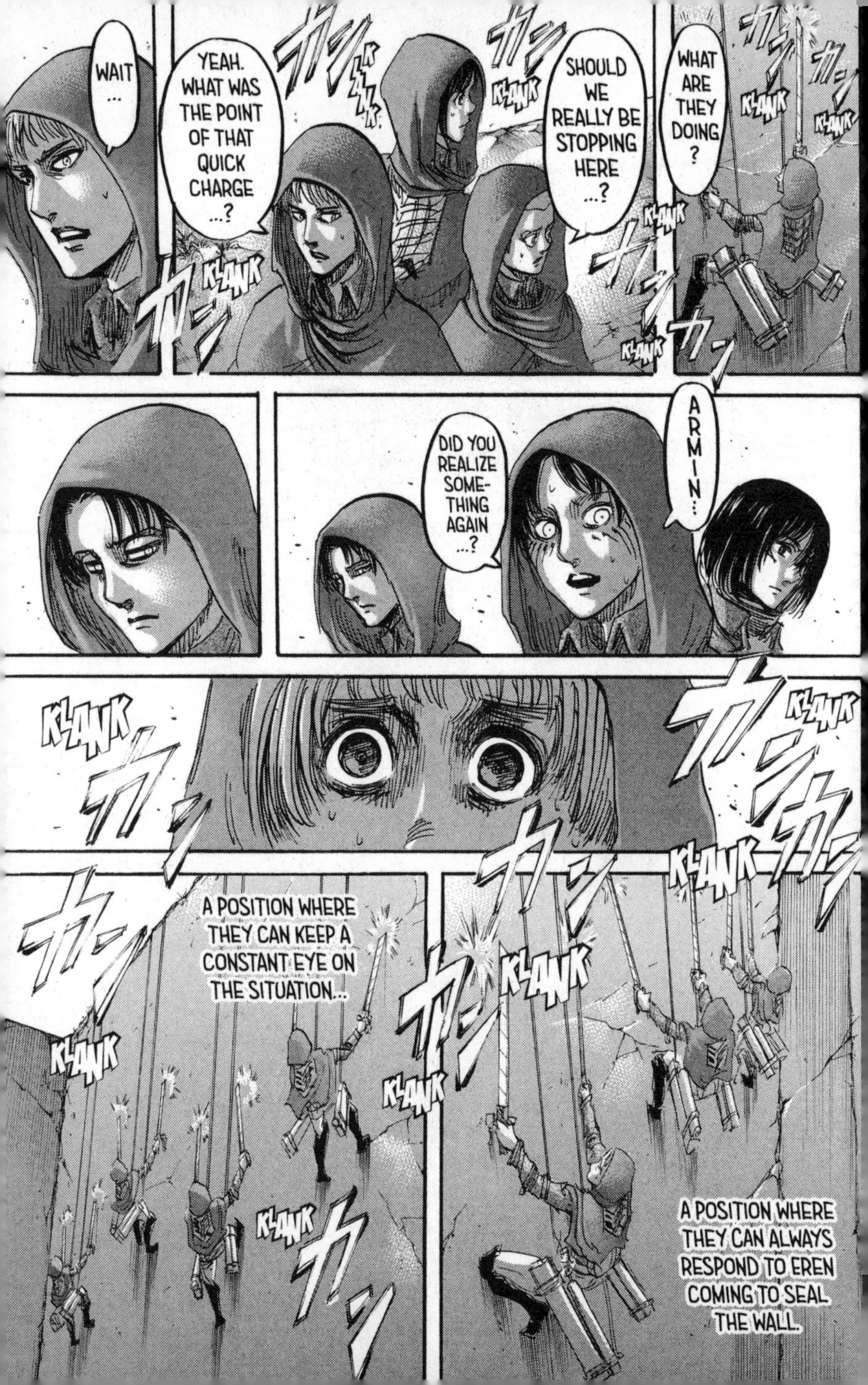
KLANK
KLANK
WHAT ARE THEY DOING?
KLANK
KLANK
SHOULD WE REALLY BE STOPPING HERE...?
KLANK
KLANK
YEAH. WHAT WAS THE POINT OF THAT QUICK CHARGE...?
KLANK
WAIT...
ARMIN...
DID YOU REALIZE SOMETHING AGAIN...?
KLANK
KLANK
KLANK
A POSITION WHERE THEY CAN ALWAYS RESPOND TO EREN COMING TO SEAL THE WALL.
KLANK
A POSITION WHERE THEY CAN KEEP A CONSTANT EYE ON THE SITUATION...
KLANK
KLANK
KLANK

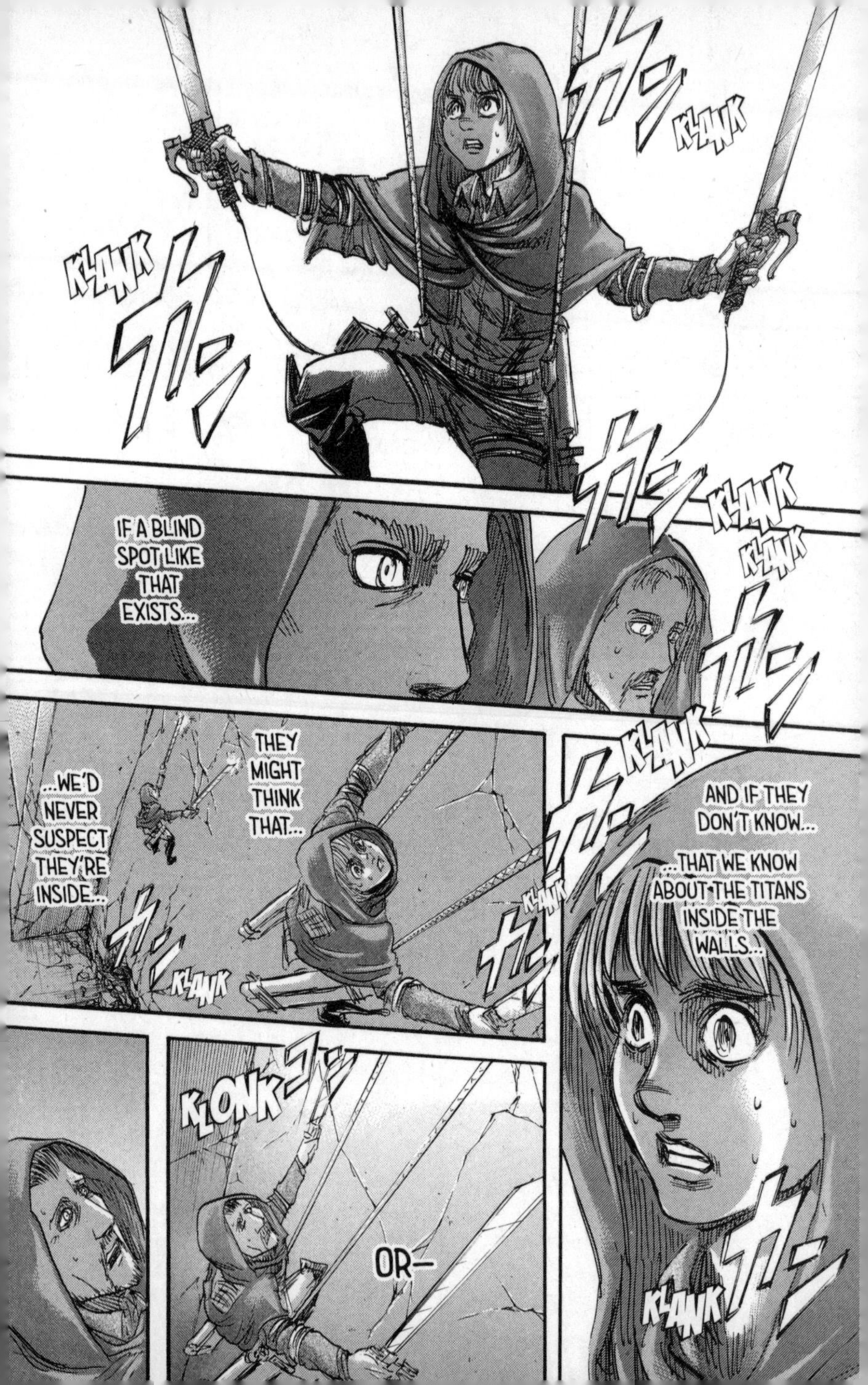
KLANK
KLANK
KLANK
KLANK
KLANK
IF A BLIND SPOT LIKE THAT EXISTS...
KLANK
AND IF THEY DON'T KNOW...
...THAT WE KNOW ABOUT THE TITANS INSIDE THE WALLS...
KLANK
THEY MIGHT THINK THAT...
...WE'D NEVER SUSPECT THEY'RE INSIDE...
KLANK
KLANK
KLONK
OR-

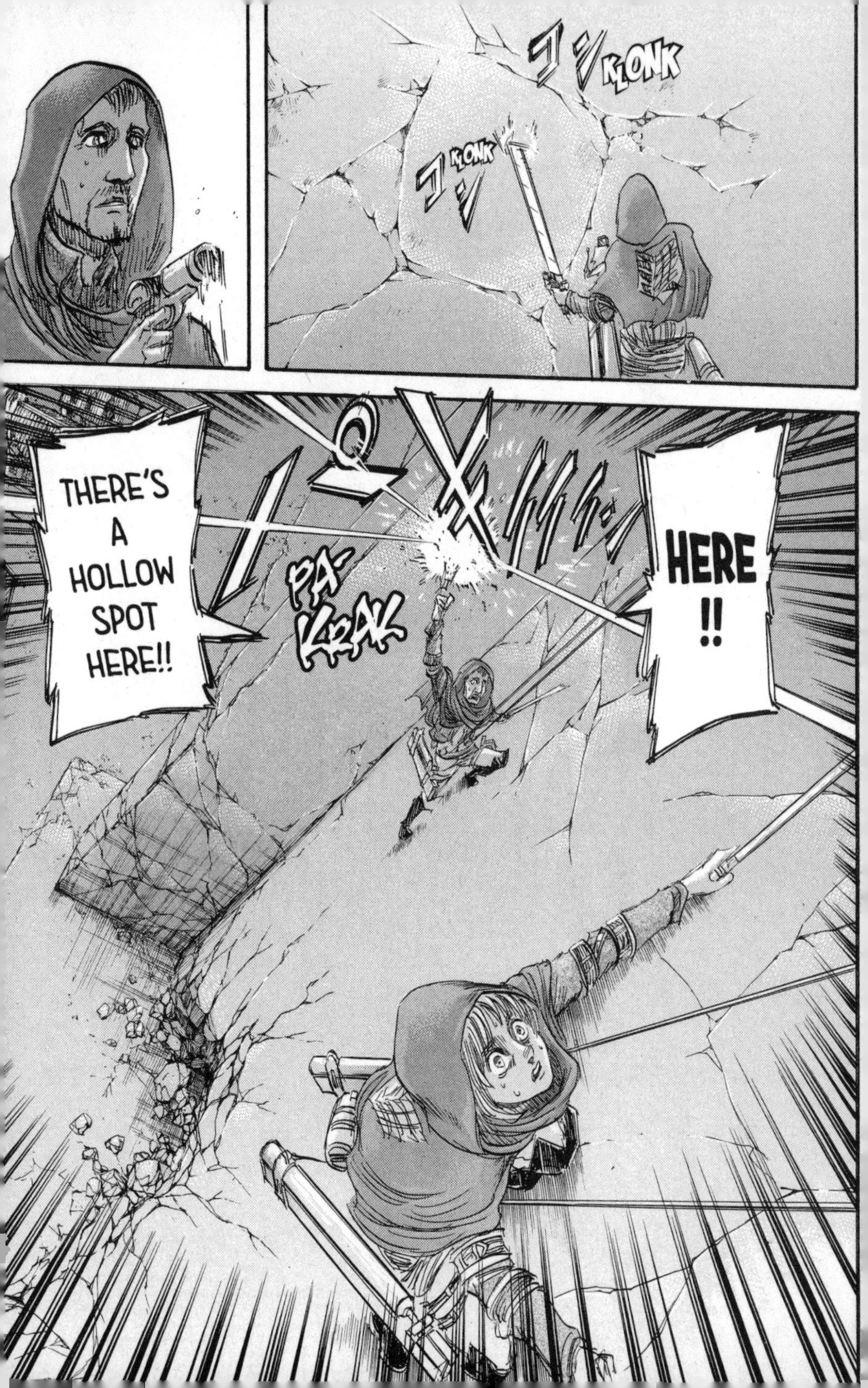
KLONK
KLONK
HERE!!
PA-KRAK
THERE'S A HOLLOW SPOT HERE!!

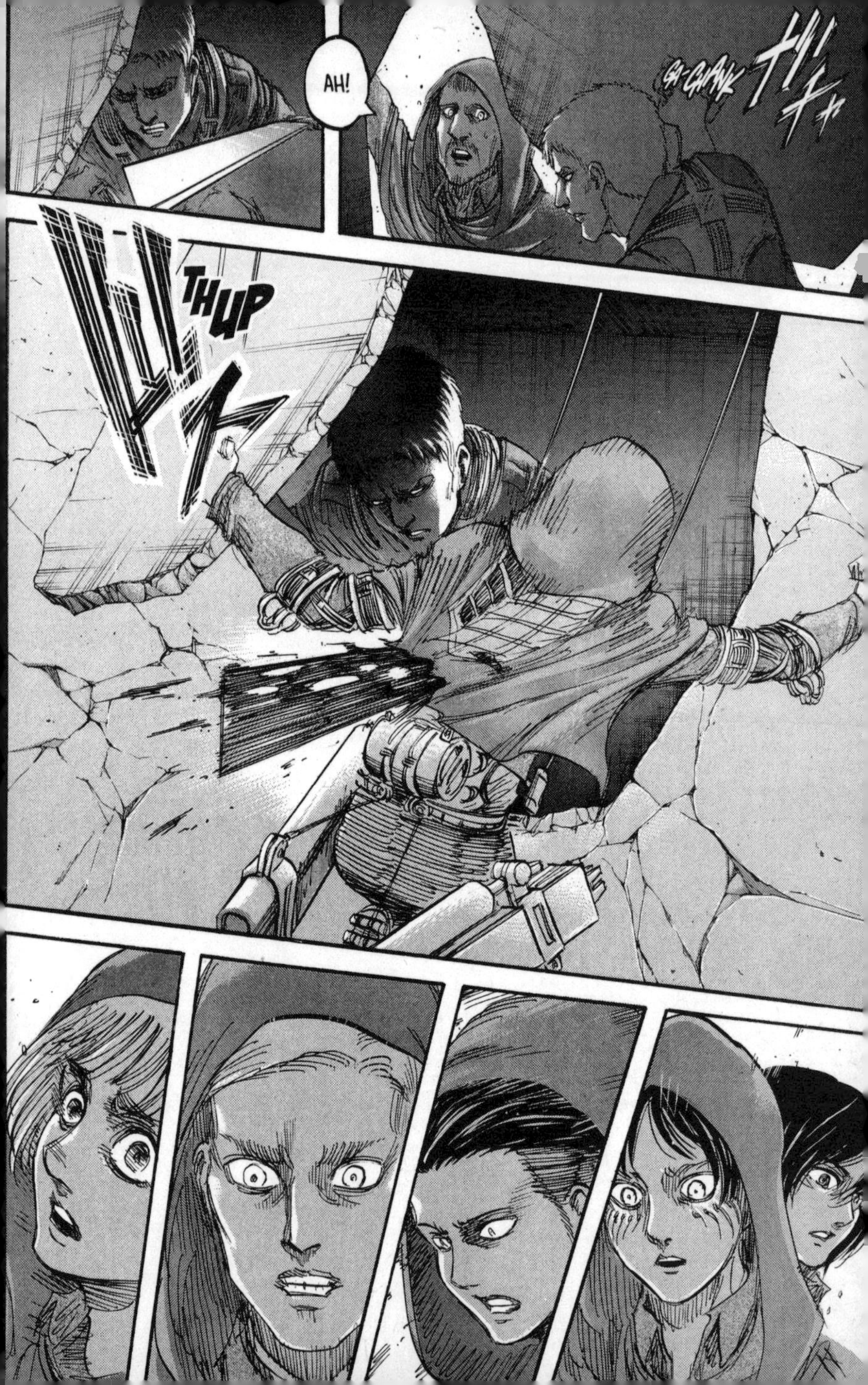
GA-CHANK
AH!
THUP

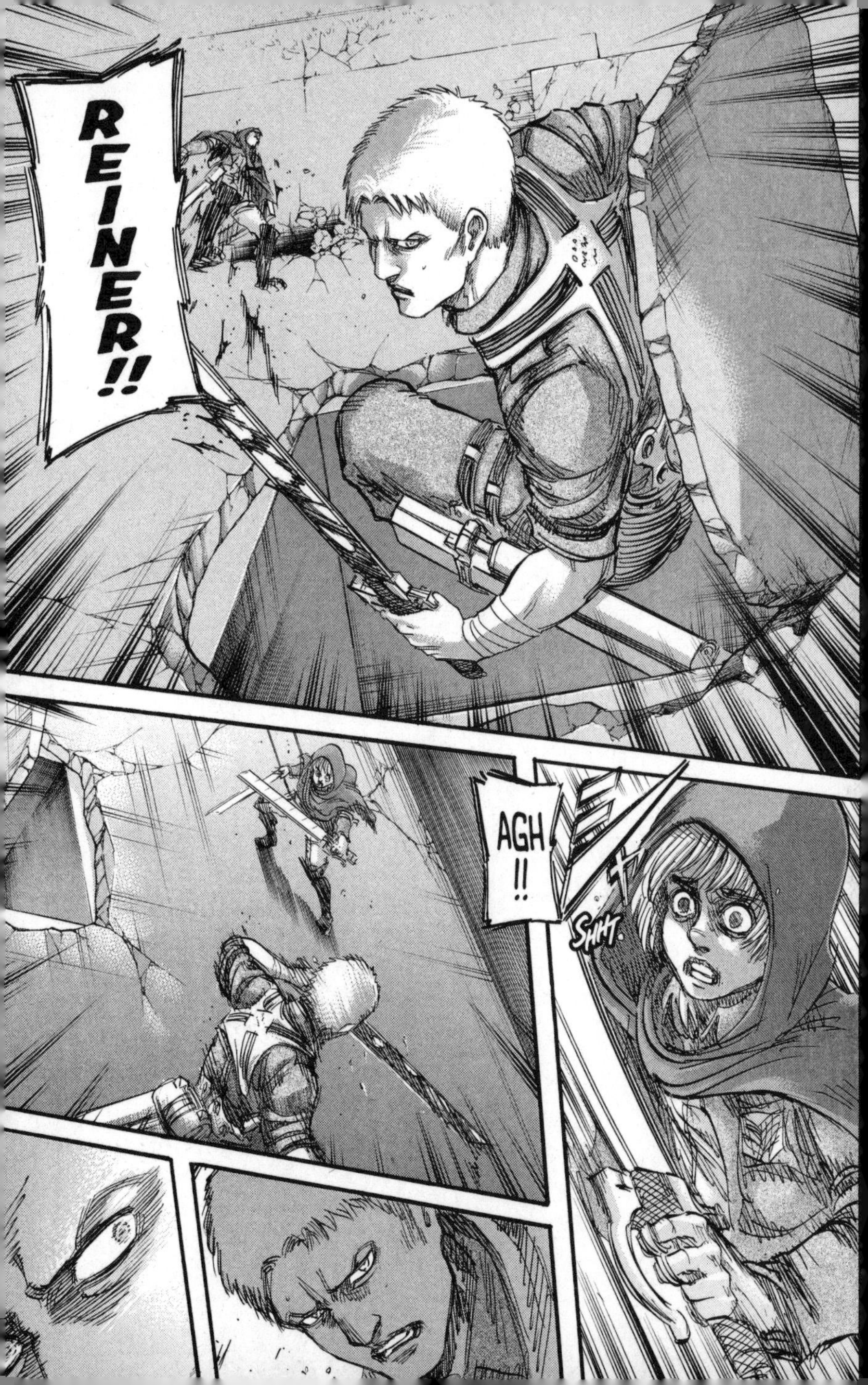
REINER!!
AGH !!
SHHT

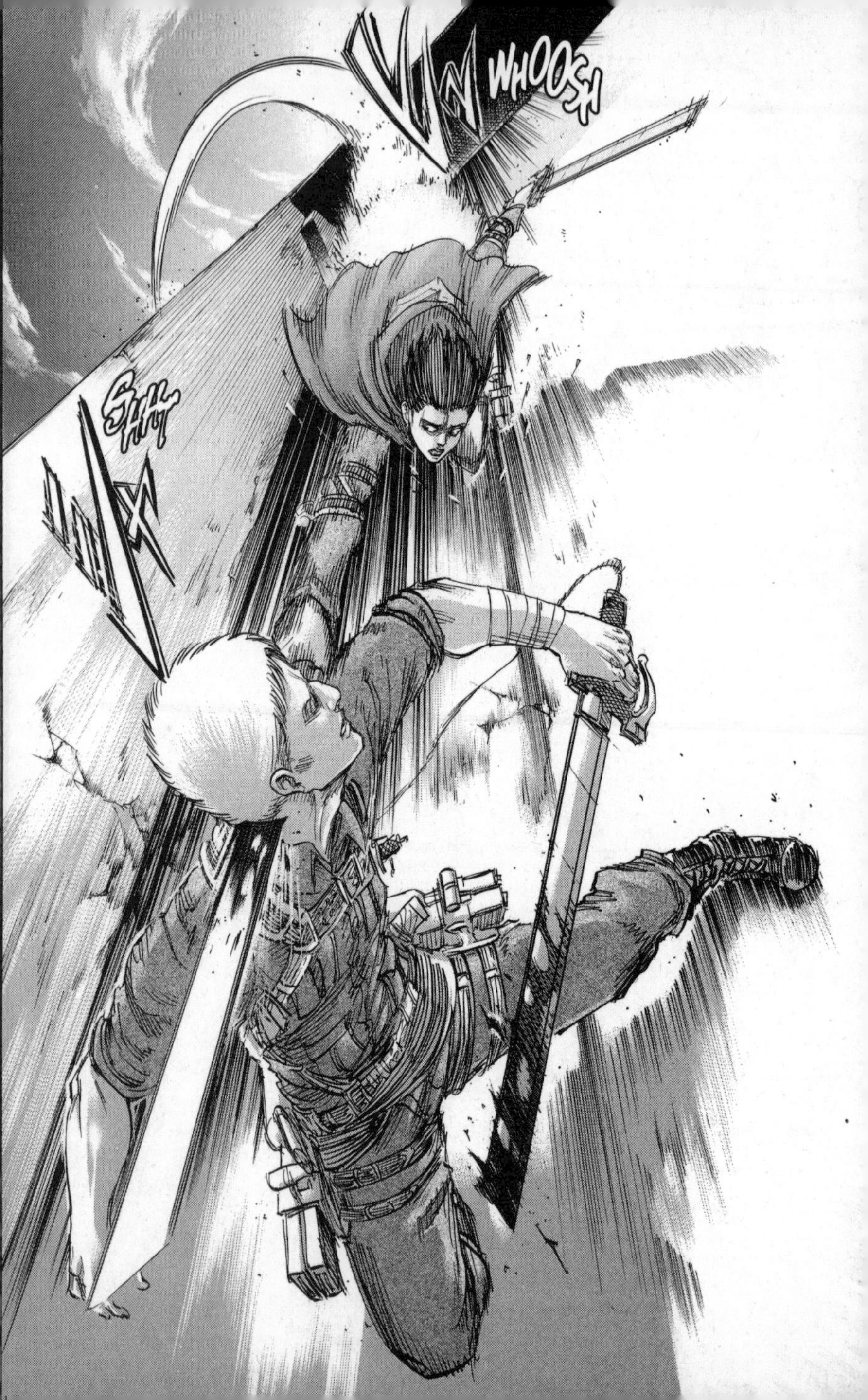
WHOOSH
SHH

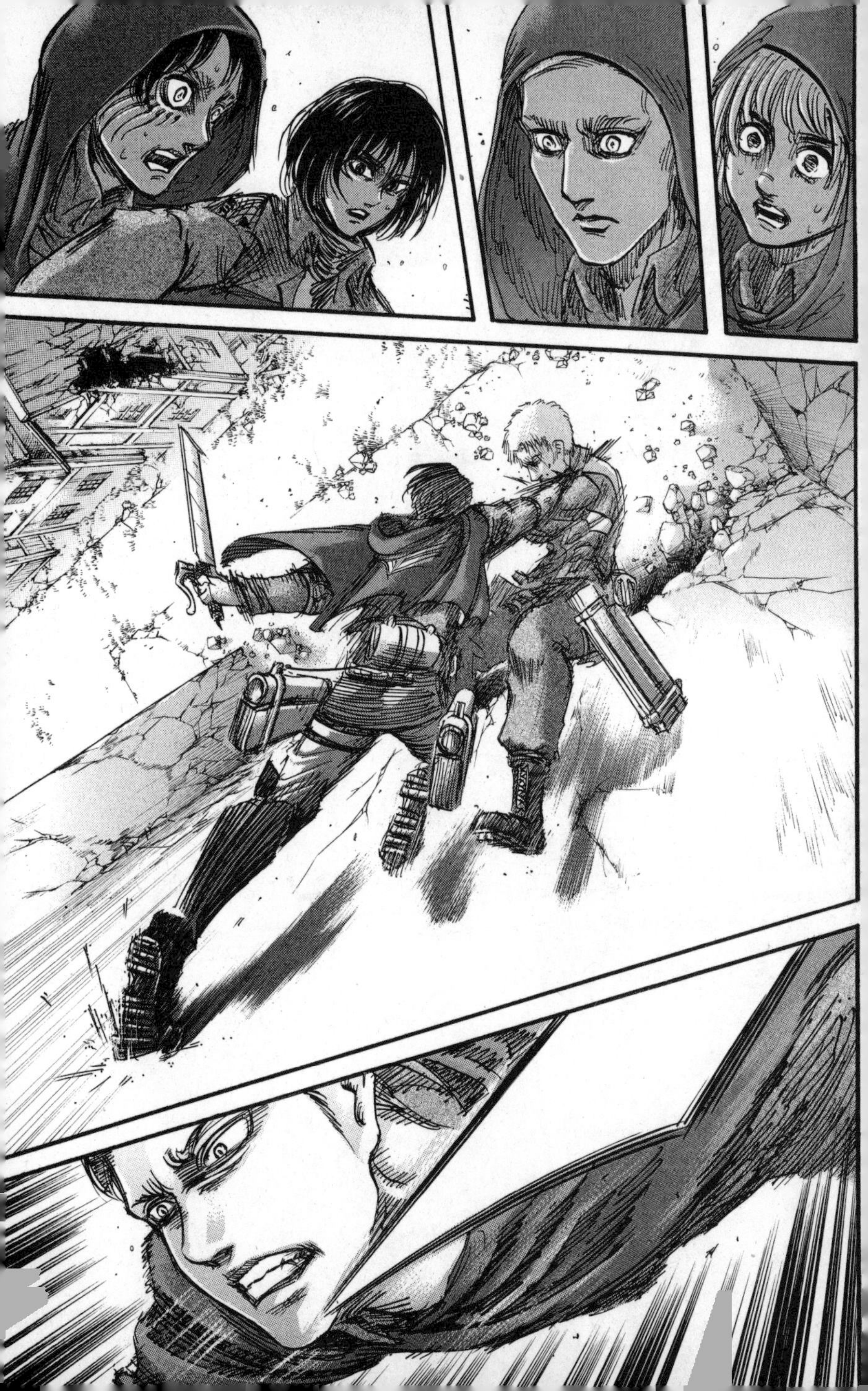

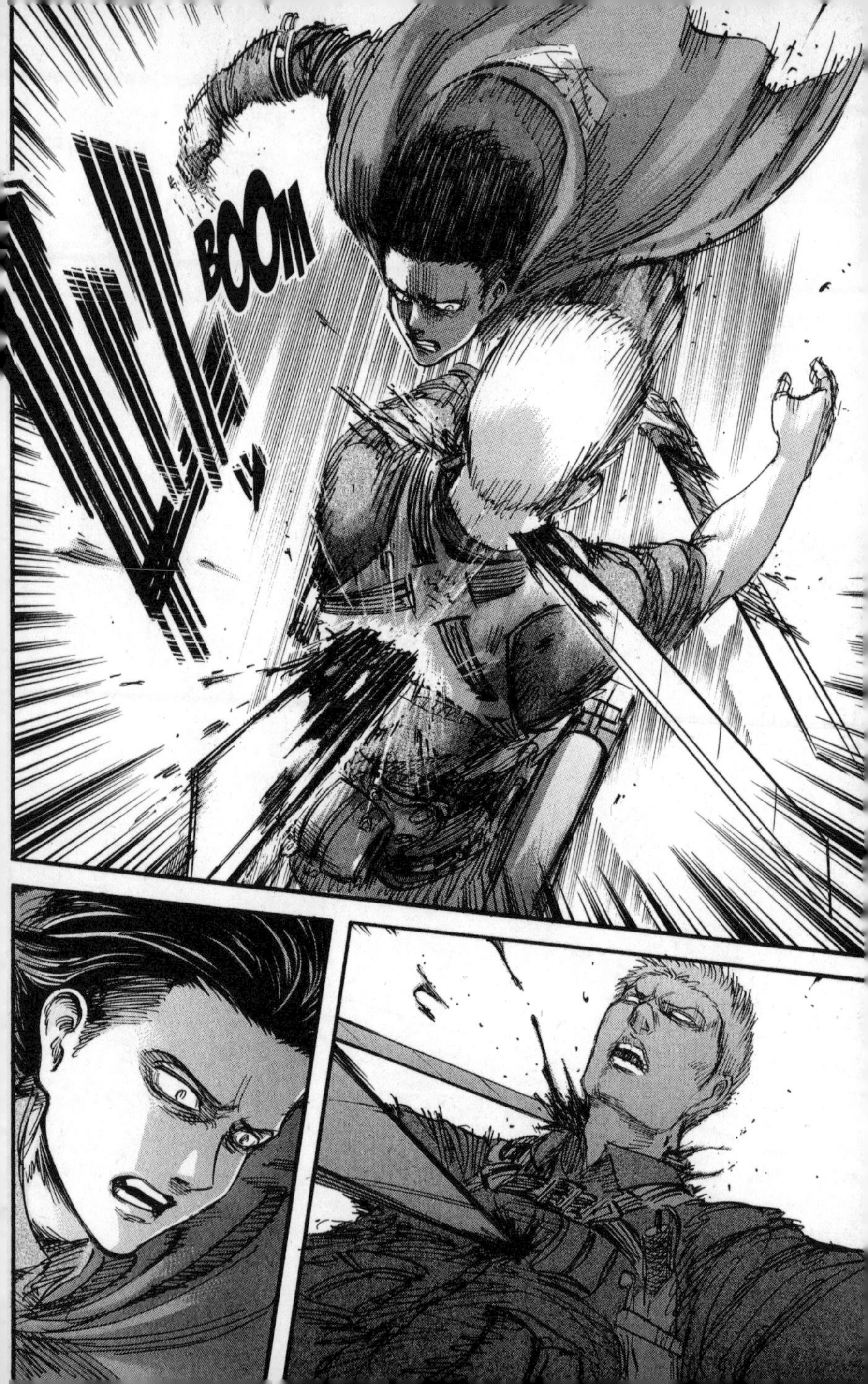
BOOM

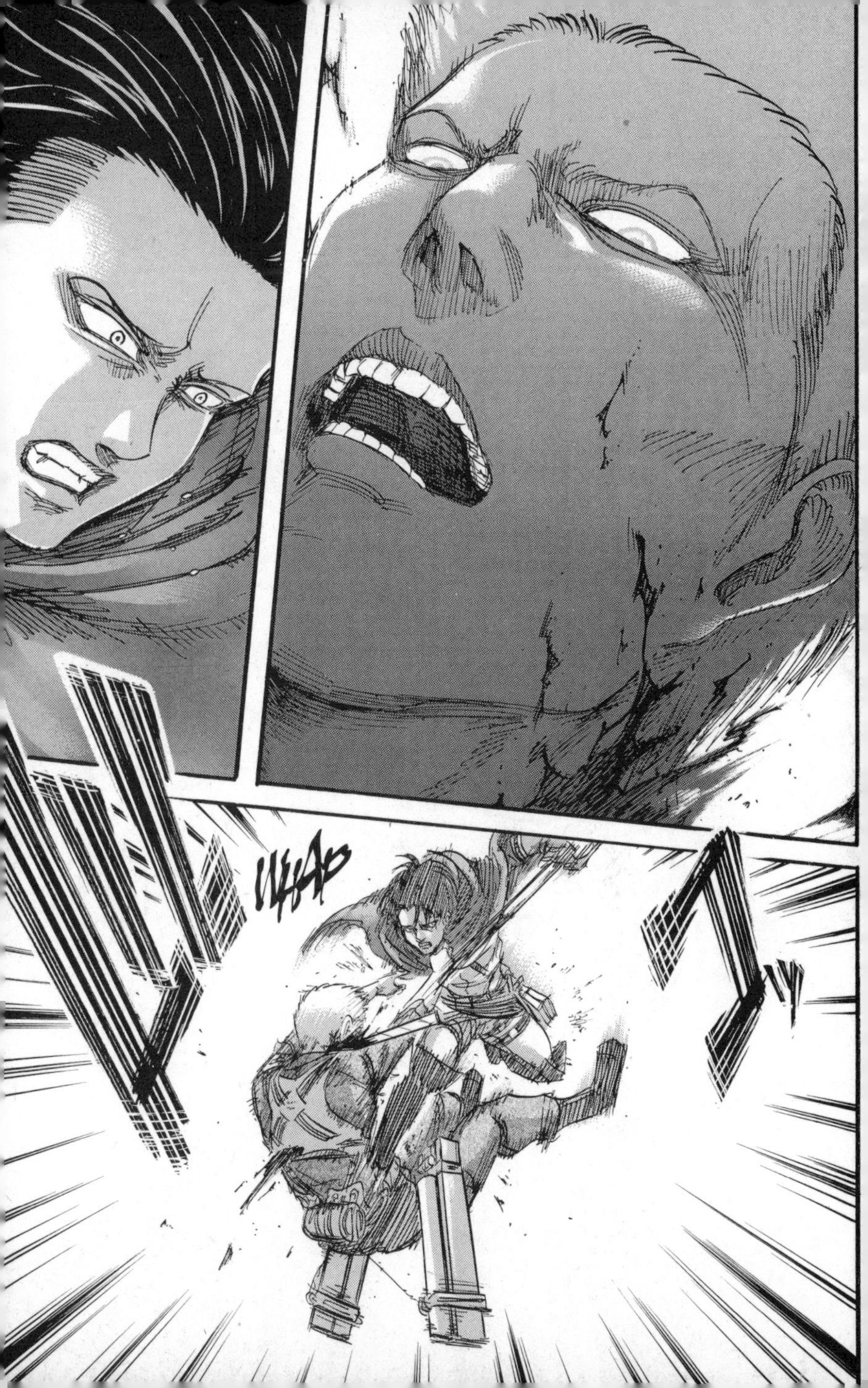
WHAP

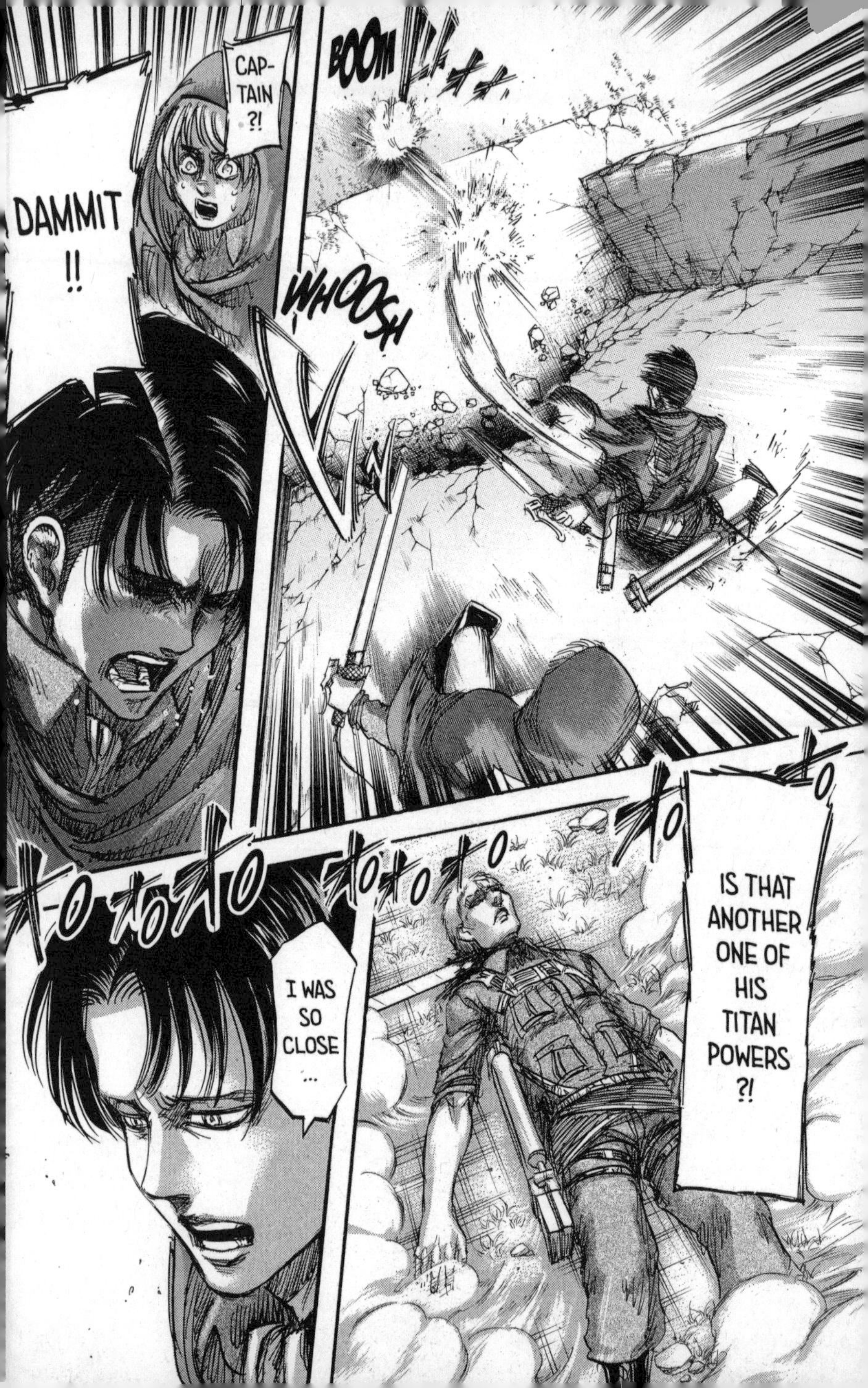
BOOM
WHOOSH
CAP-TAIN ?!
DAMMIT !!
IS THAT ANOTHER ONE OF HIS TITAN POWERS ?!
I WAS SO CLOSE ...

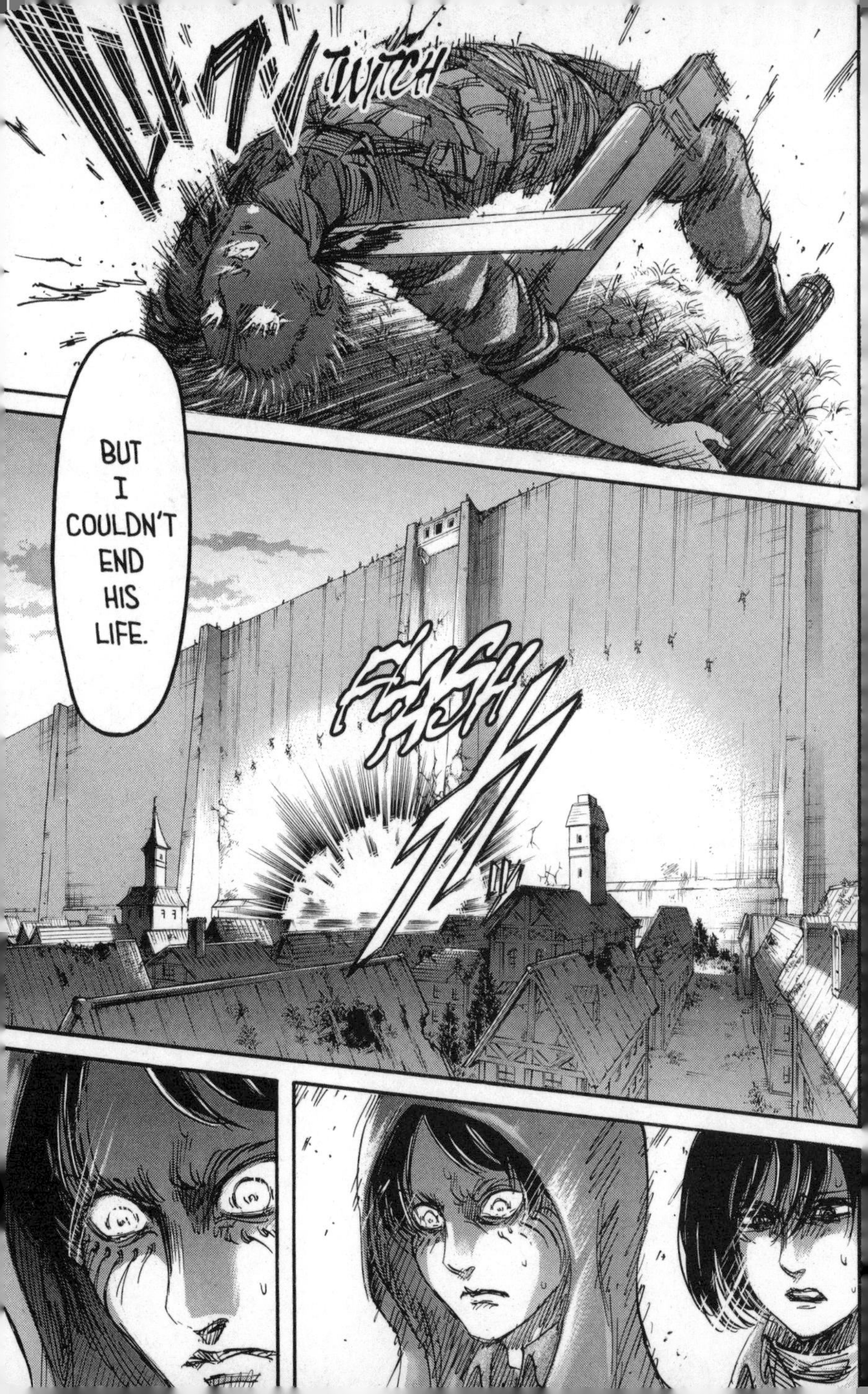
TWITCH
BUT I COULDN'T END HIS LIFE.
FLASH

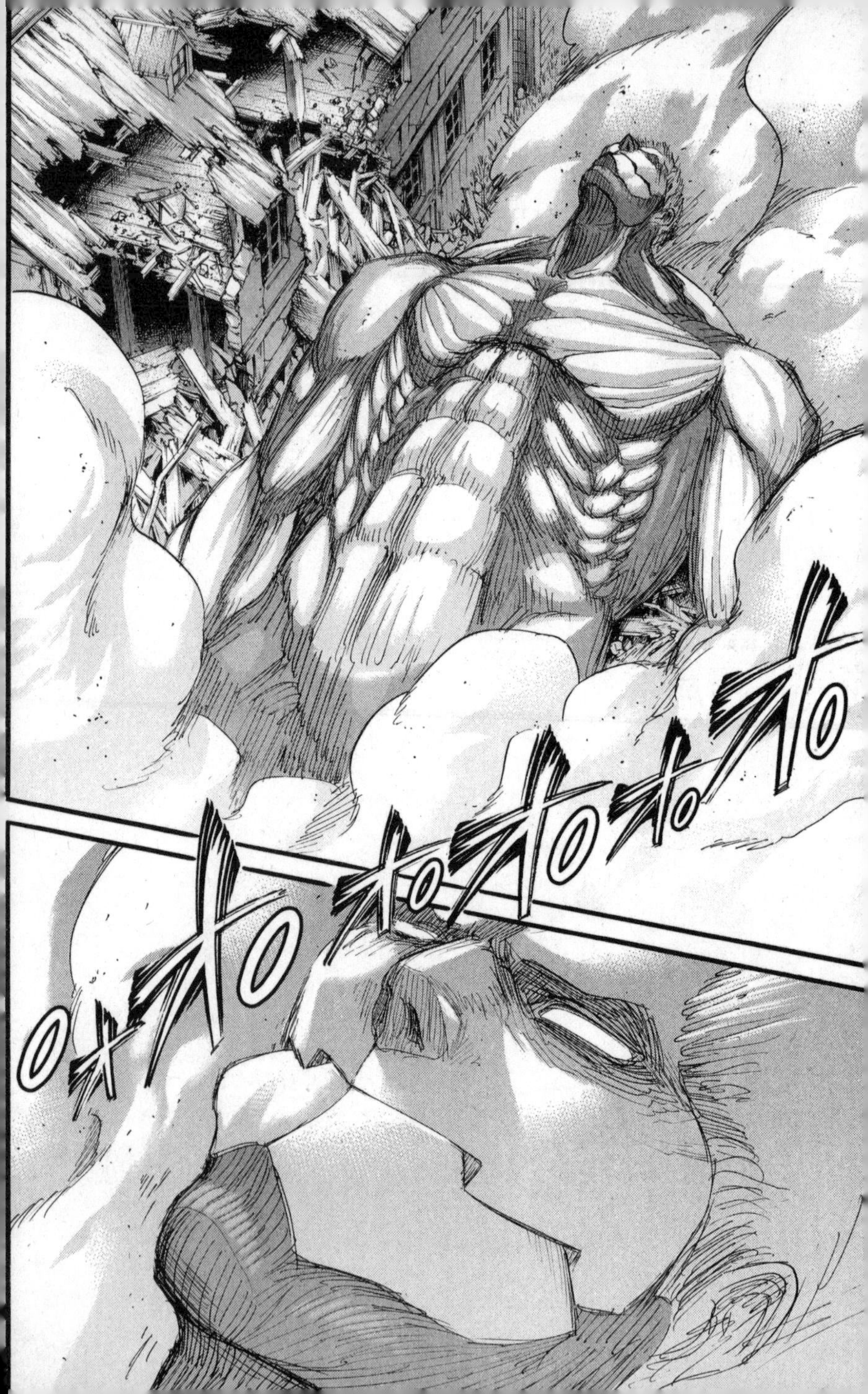

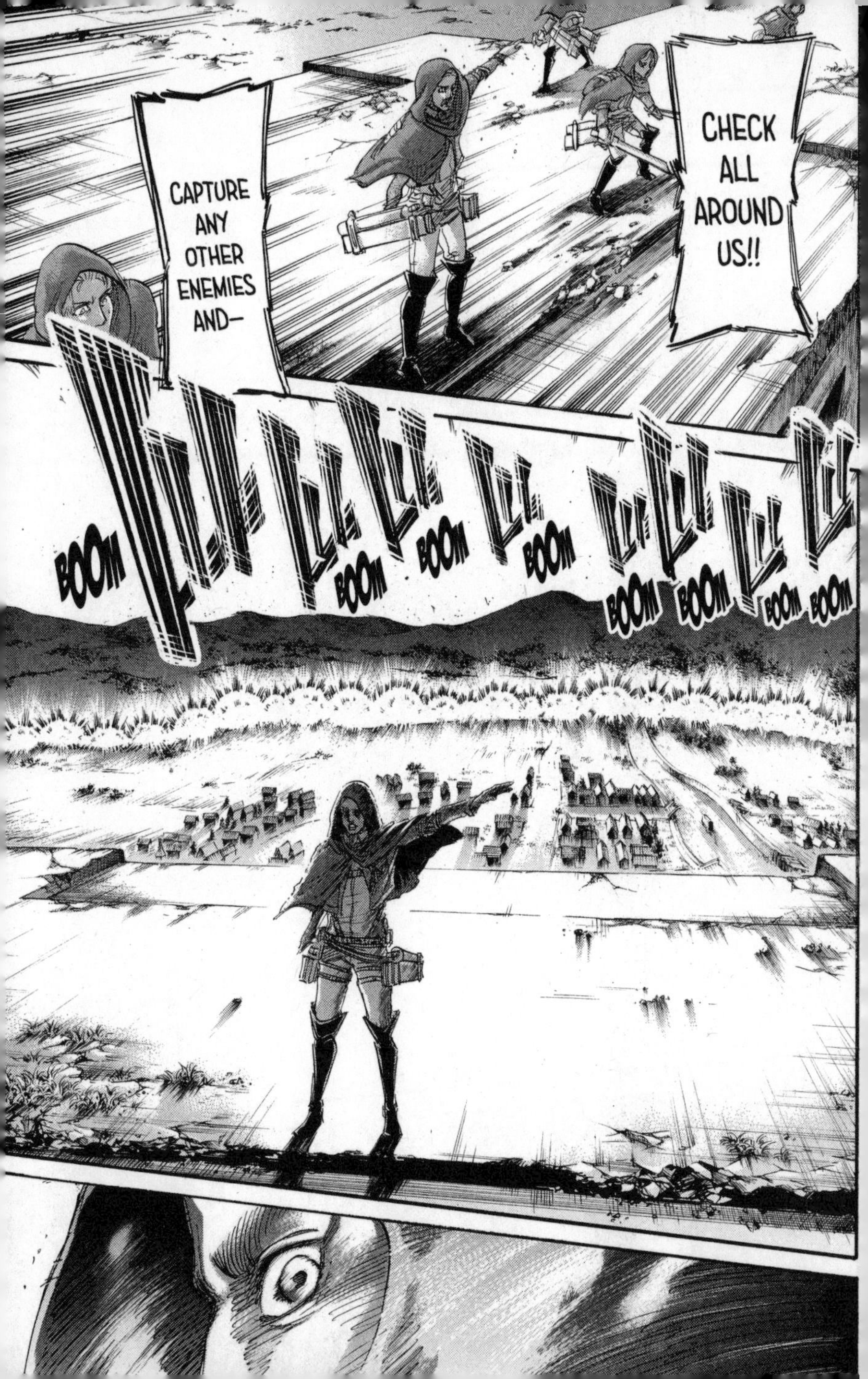
CHECK ALL AROUND US!!
CAPTURE ANY OTHER ENEMIES AND—
BOOM BOOM BOOM BOOM
BOOM BOOM BOOM BOOM

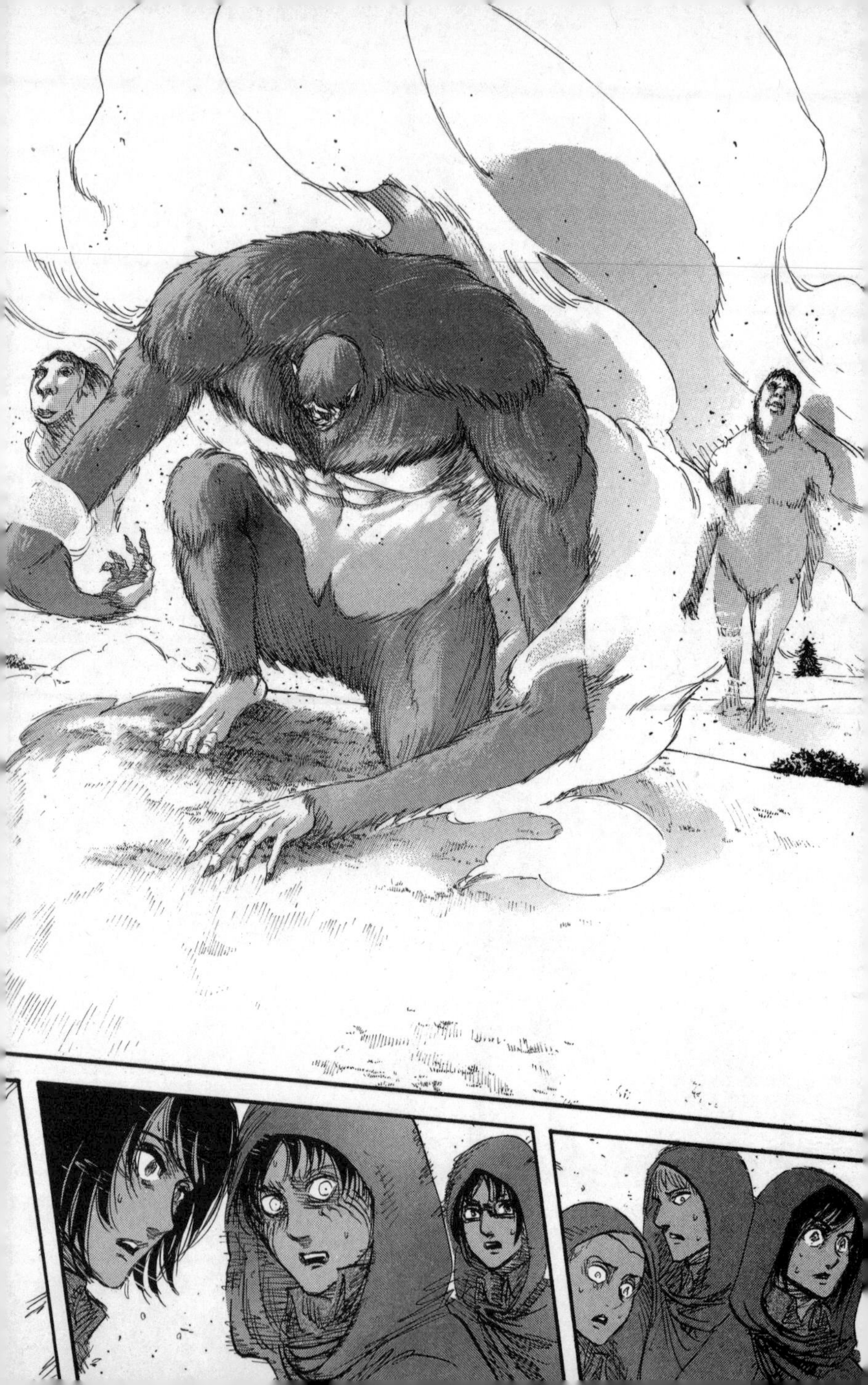

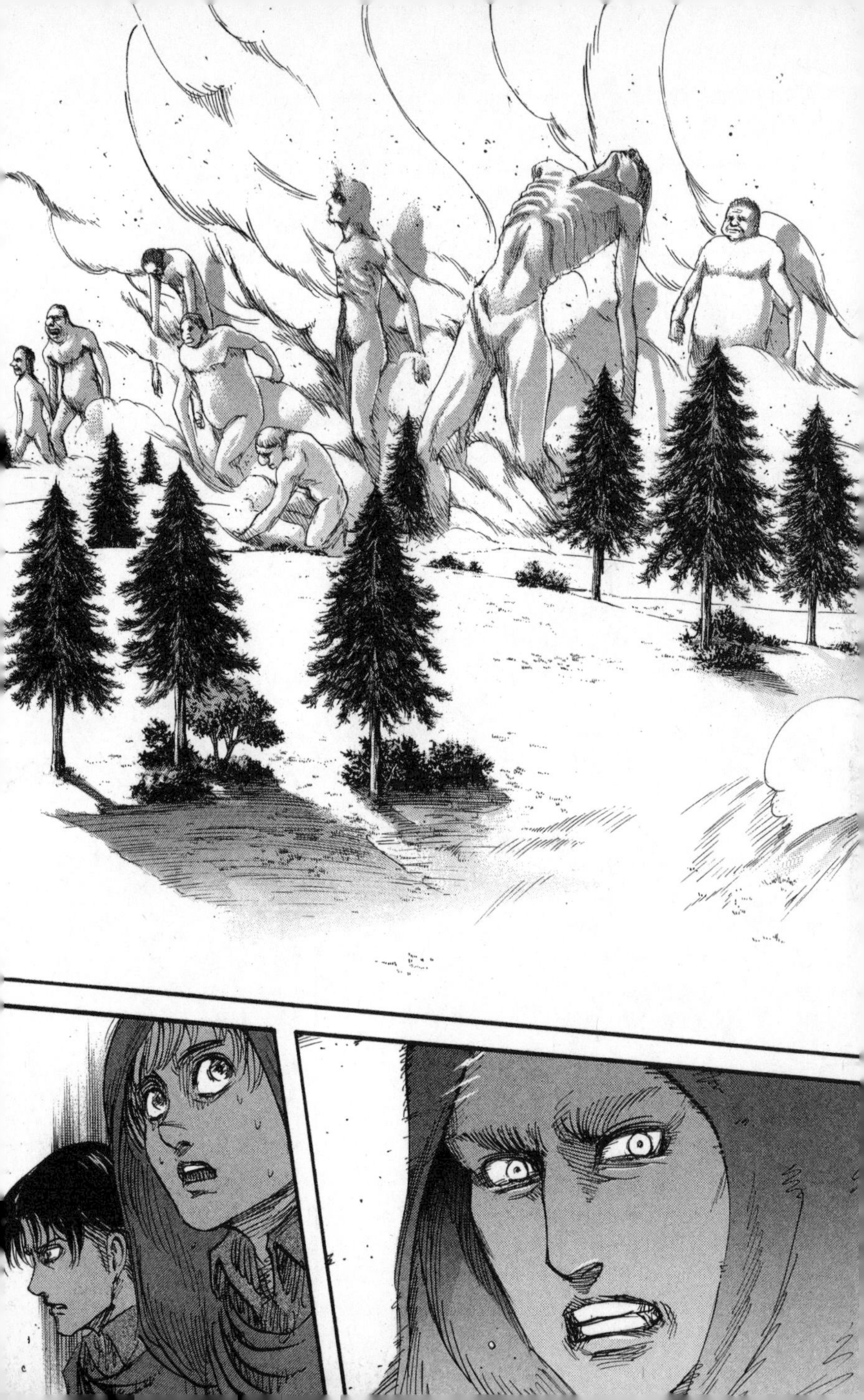

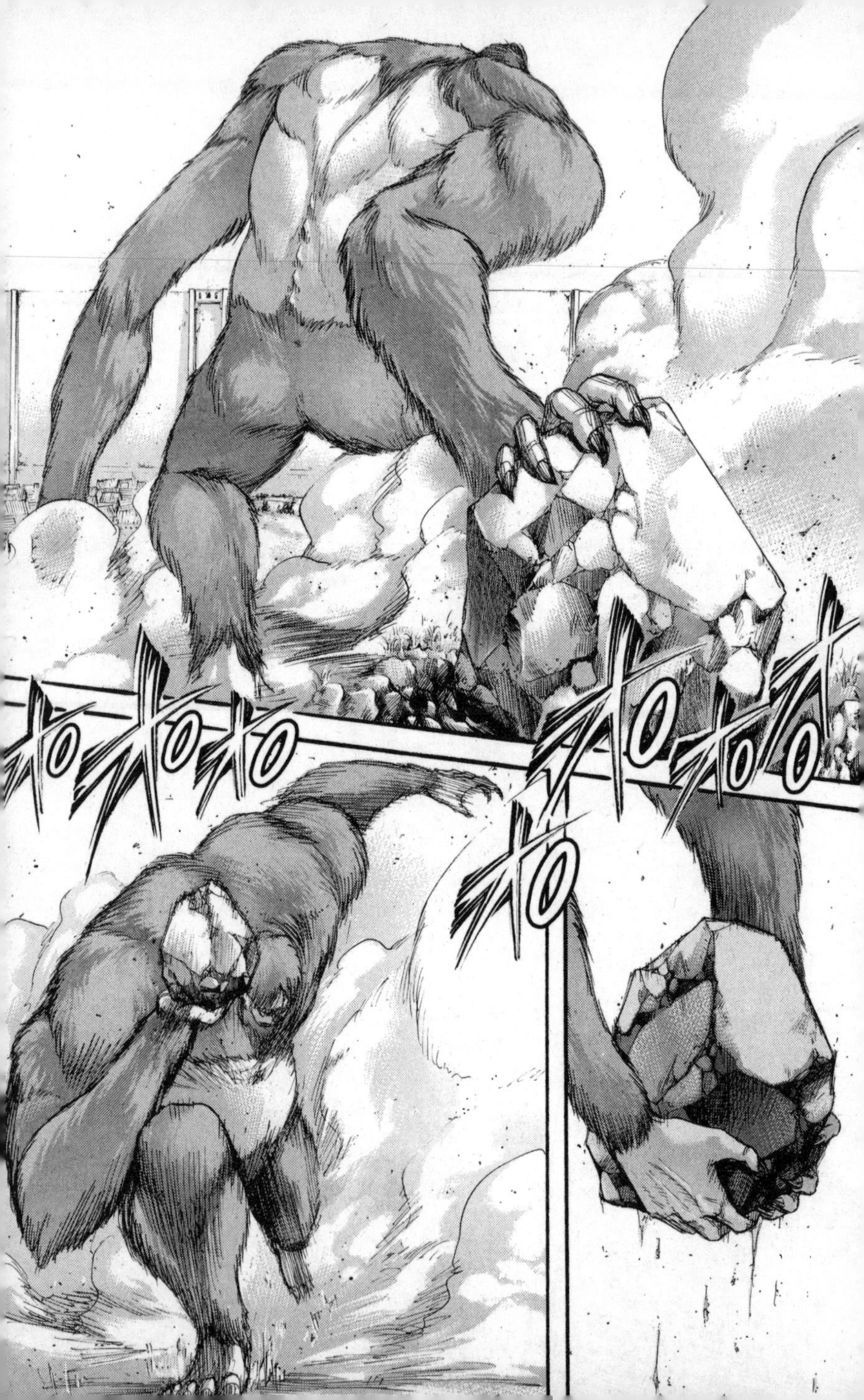

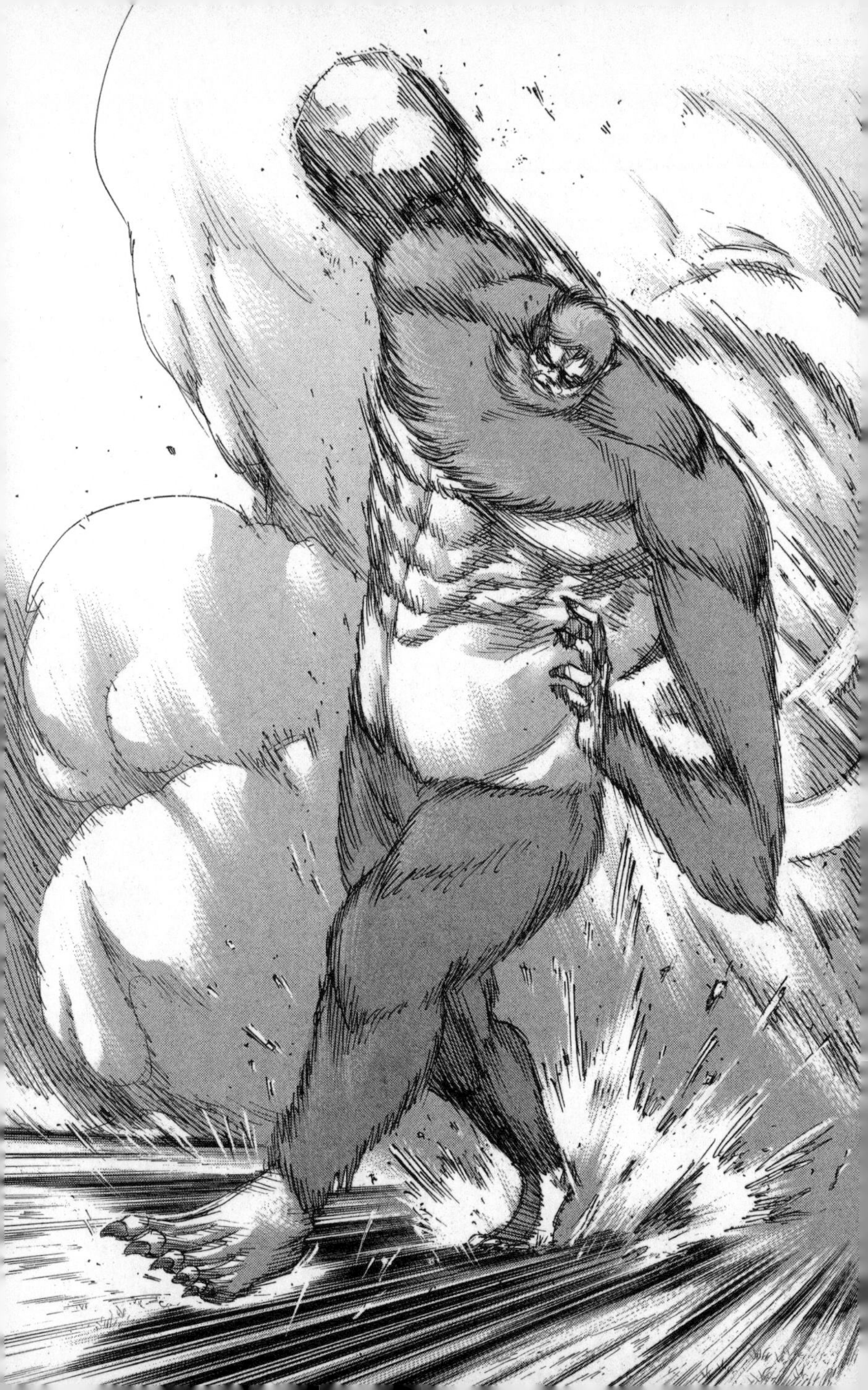

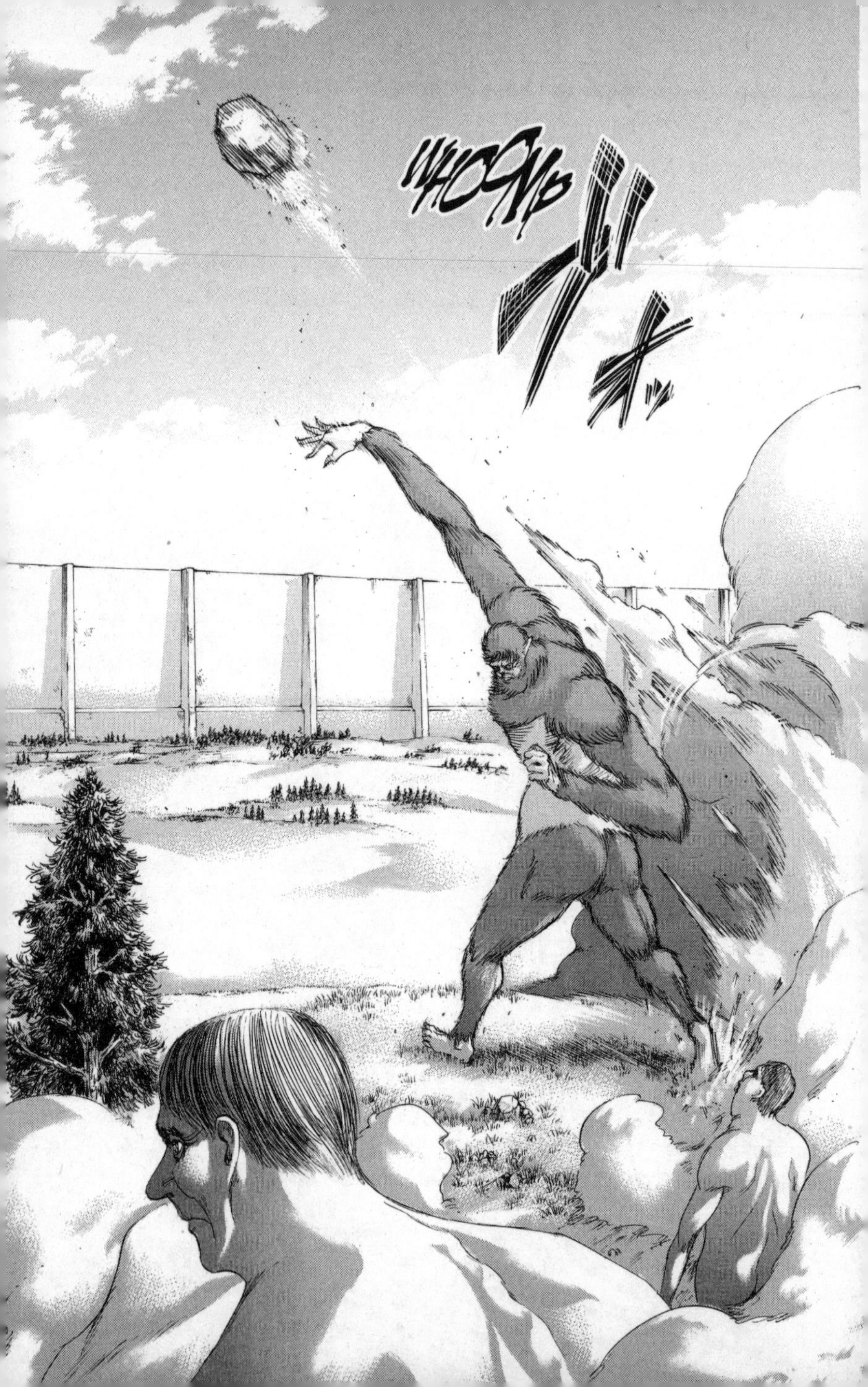

WHOOMP
ズオッ

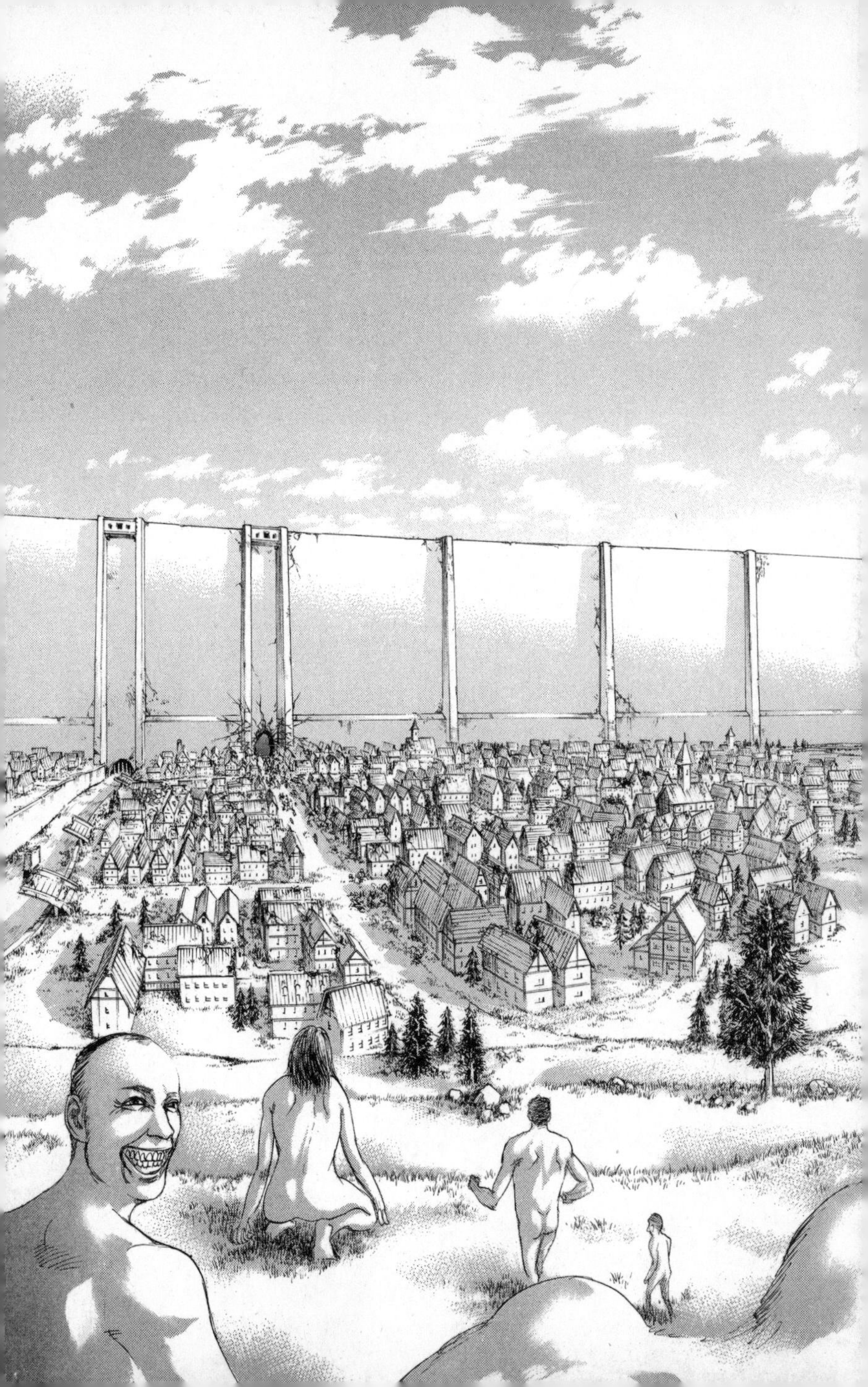

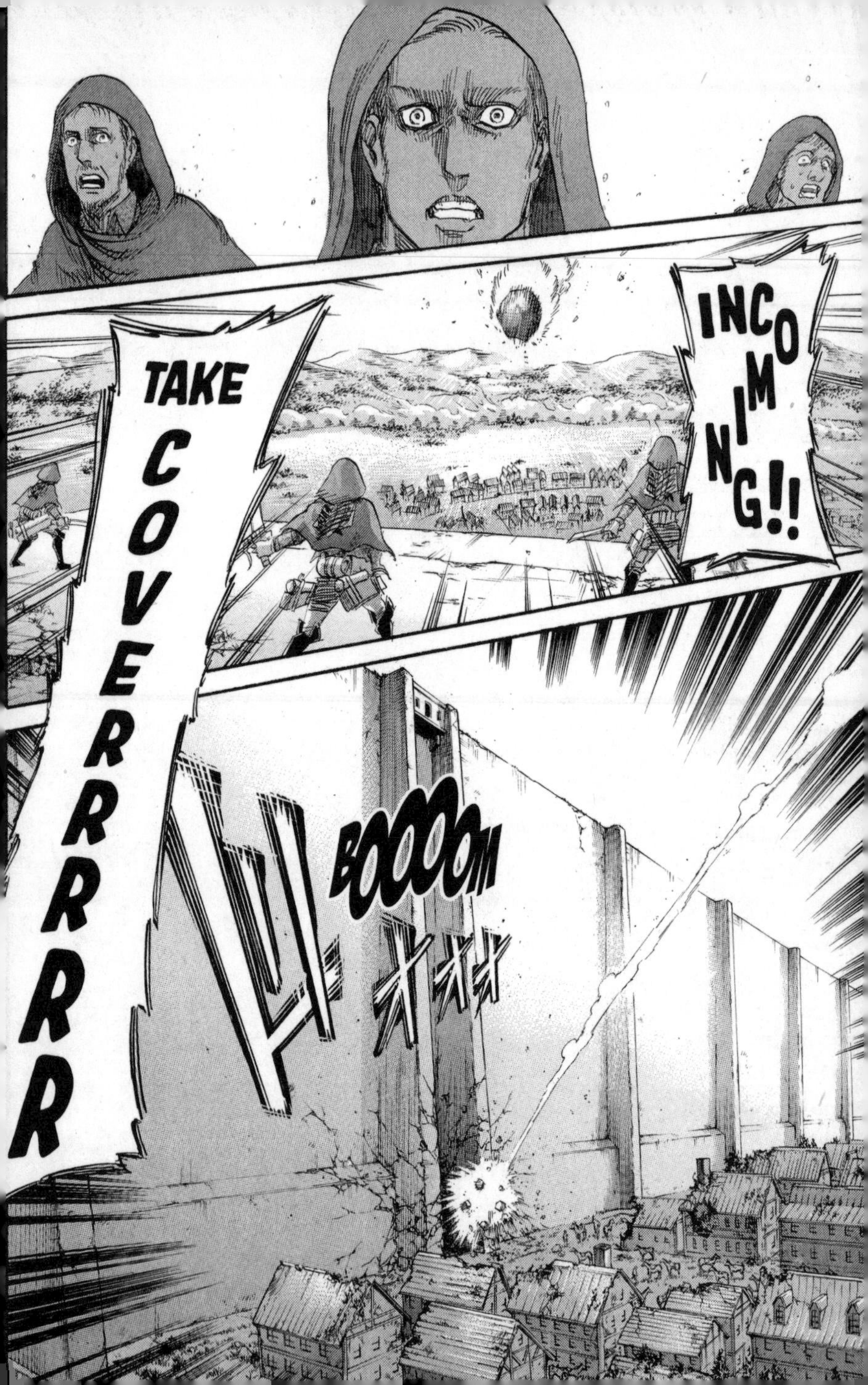
INCOMING!!
TAKE COVERRRRR
BOOOOM

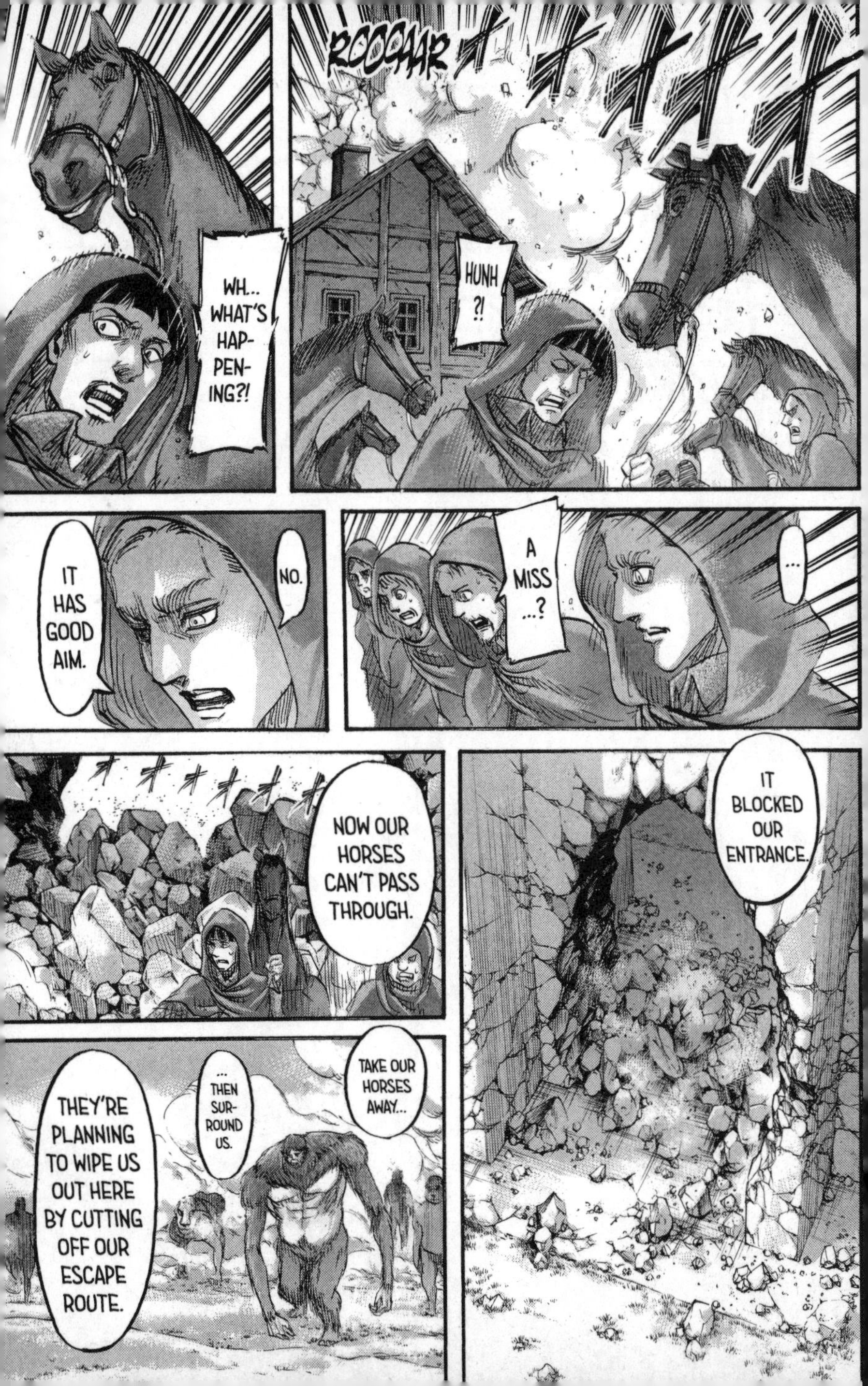
ROOOAAR
HUNH?!
WH... WHAT'S HAP-PEN-ING?!
...
A MISS ...?
NO.
IT HAS GOOD AIM.
IT BLOCKED OUR ENTRANCE.
NOW OUR HORSES CAN'T PASS THROUGH.
TAKE OUR HORSES AWAY...
...THEN SUR-ROUND US.
THEY'RE PLANNING TO WIPE US OUT HERE BY CUTTING OFF OUR ESCAPE ROUTE.

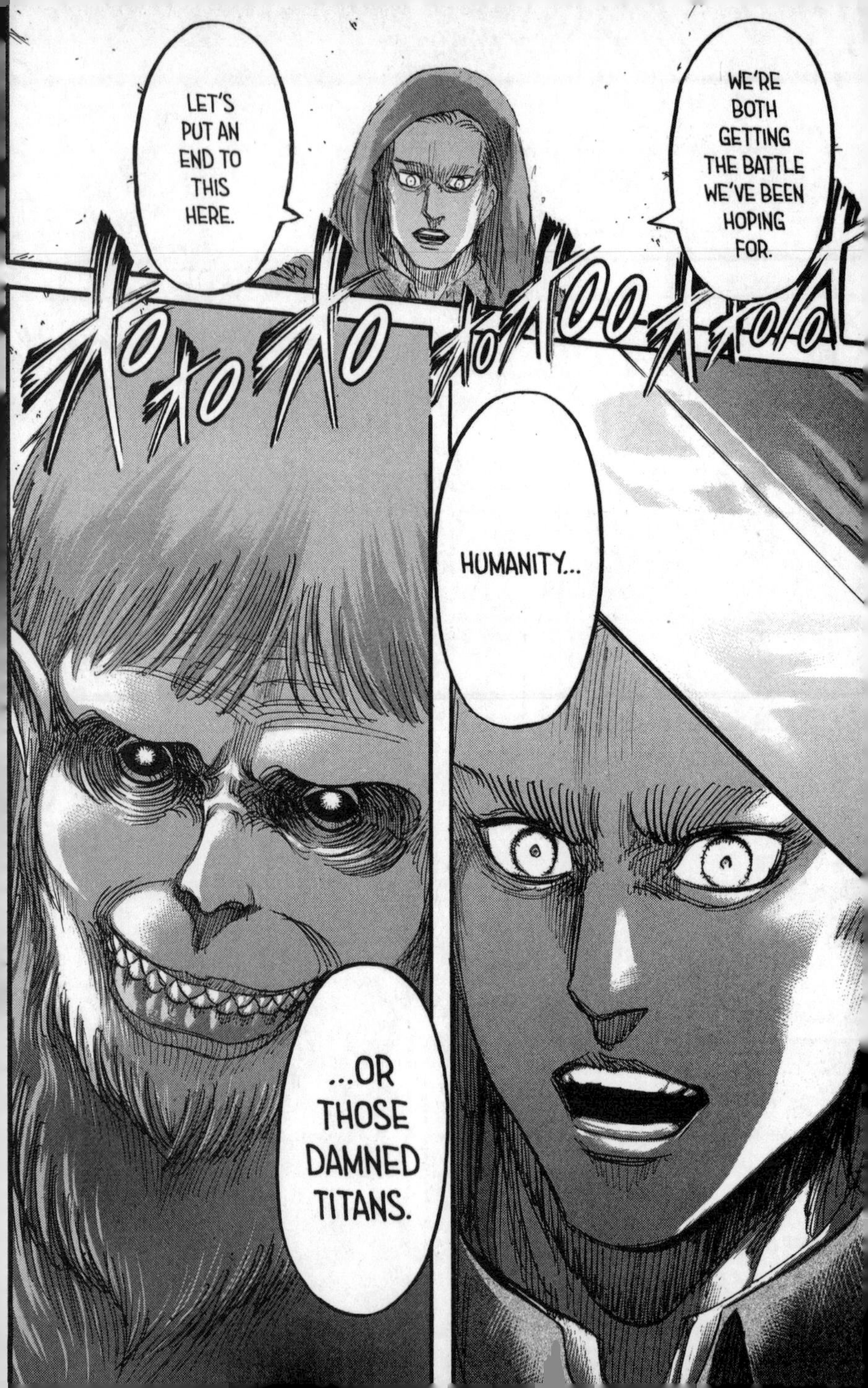
WE'RE BOTH GETTING THE BATTLE WE'VE BEEN HOPING FOR.
LET'S PUT AN END TO THIS HERE.
HUMANITY...
...OR THOSE DAMNED TITANS.

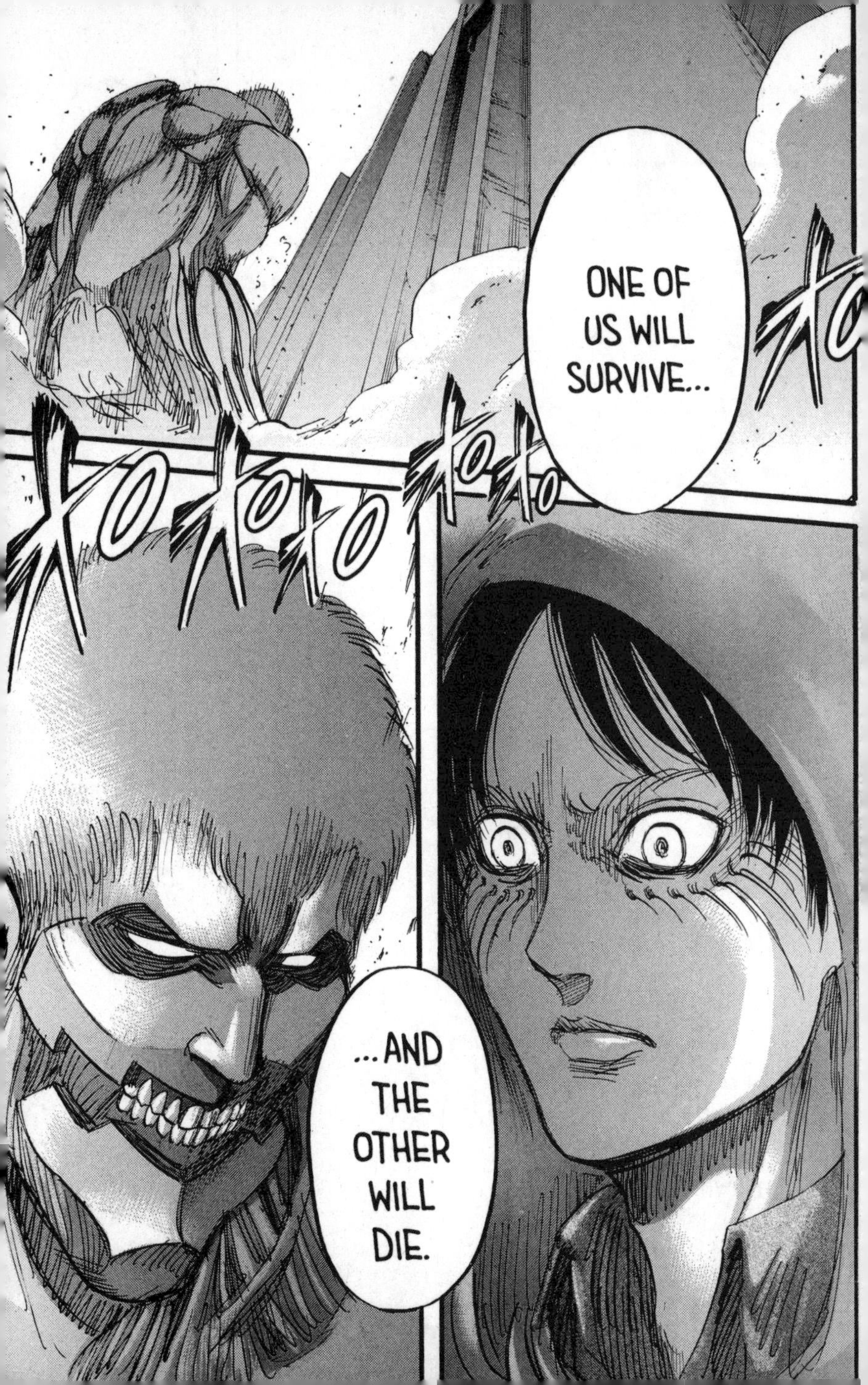
ONE OF US WILL SURVIVE...
...AND THE OTHER WILL DIE.

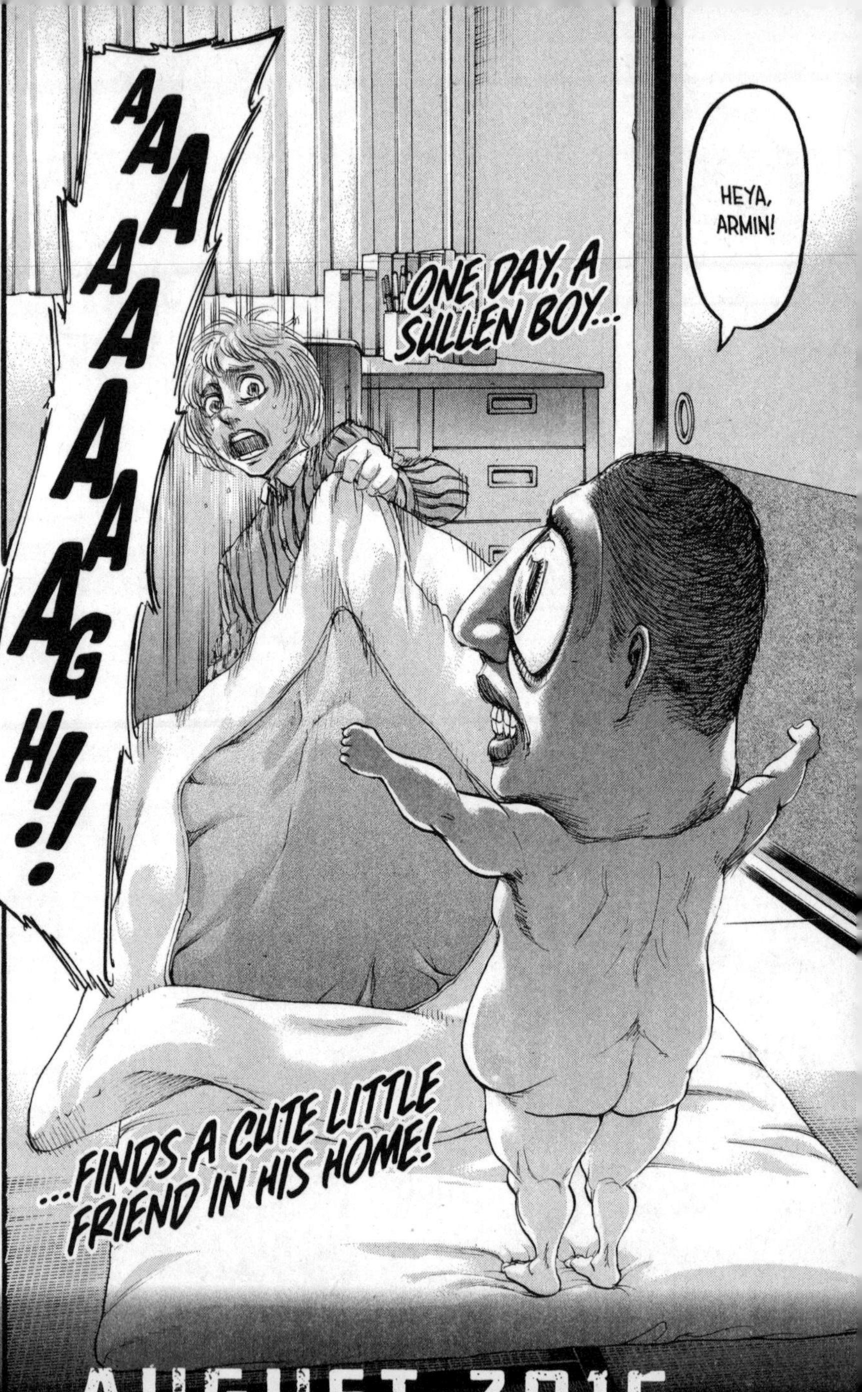
HEYA, ARMIN!
ONE DAY, A SULLEN BOY...
AAAAAAAAAGH!!
...FINDS A CUTE LITTLE FRIEND IN HIS HOME!

AUGUST 2016

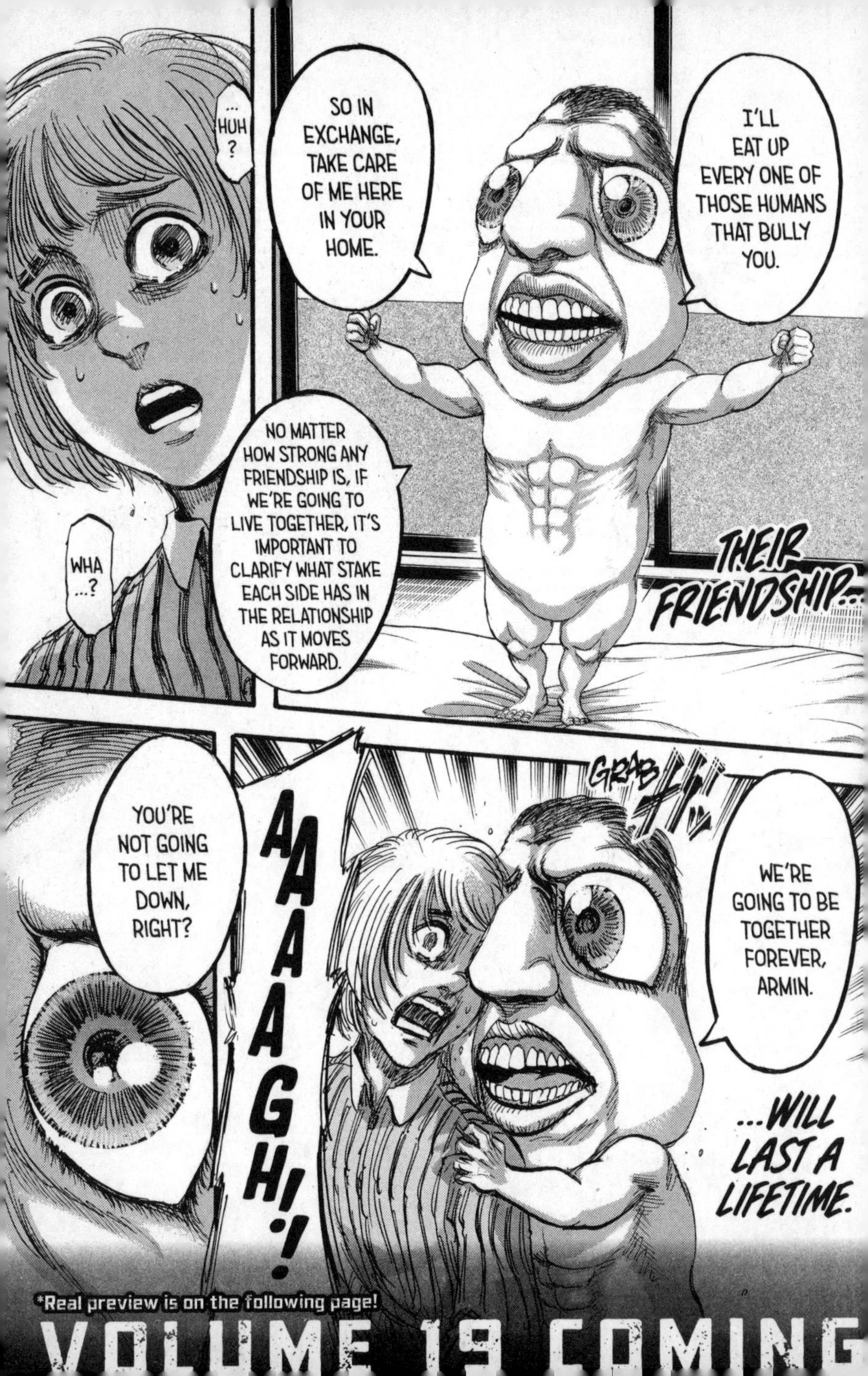
I'LL EAT UP EVERY ONE OF THOSE HUMANS THAT BULLY YOU.
SO IN EXCHANGE, TAKE CARE OF ME HERE IN YOUR HOME.
NO MATTER HOW STRONG ANY FRIENDSHIP IS, IF WE'RE GOING TO LIVE TOGETHER, IT'S IMPORTANT TO CLARIFY WHAT STAKE EACH SIDE HAS IN THE RELATIONSHIP AS IT MOVES FORWARD.
THEIR FRIENDSHIP...
...HUH?
WHA...?
GRAB
WE'RE GOING TO BE TOGETHER FOREVER, ARMIN.
AAAAGH!!
...WILL LAST A LIFETIME.
YOU'RE NOT GOING TO LET ME DOWN, RIGHT?
*Real preview is on the following page!
VOLUME 19 COMING

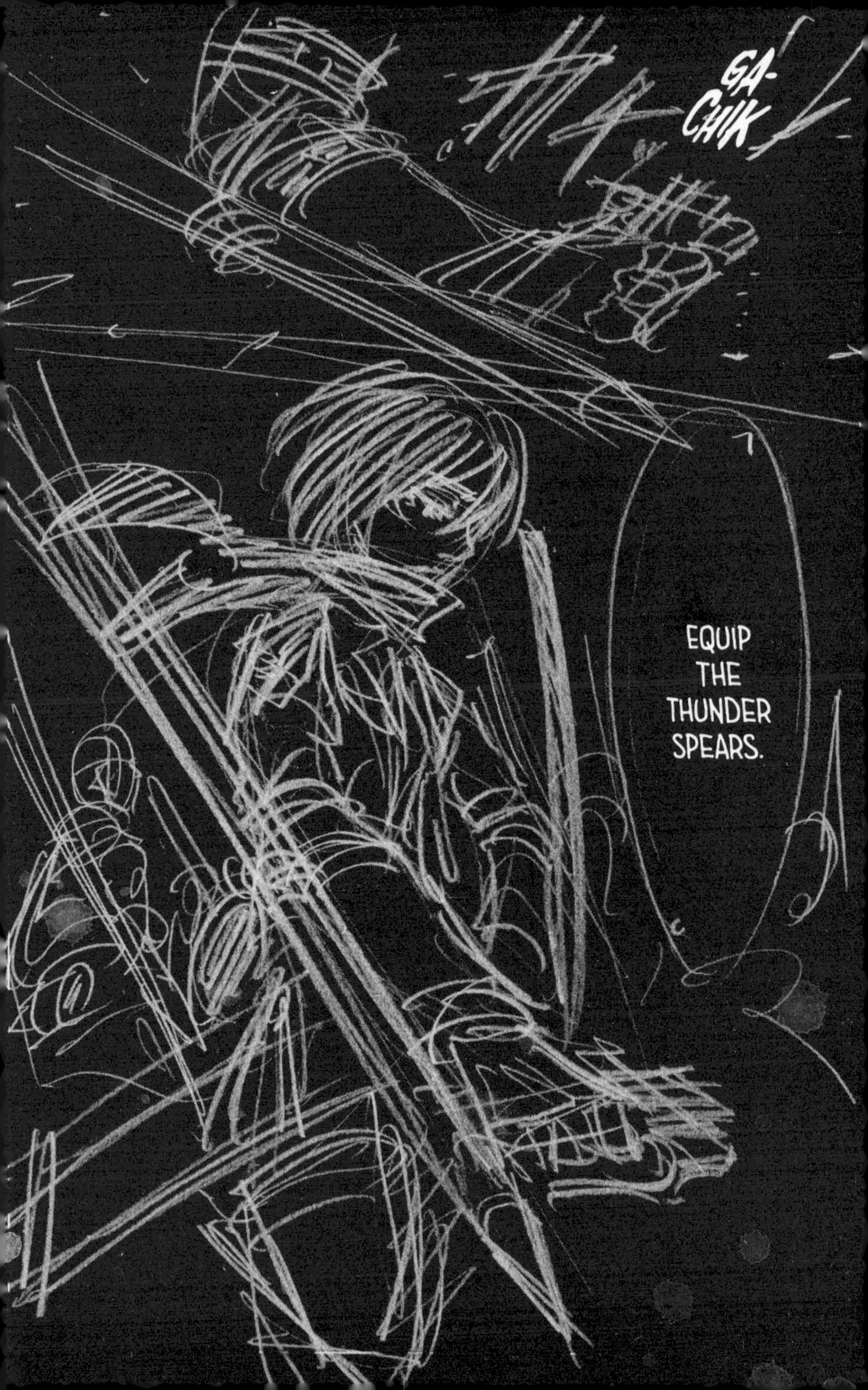
GA-CHIK
EQUIP THE THUNDER SPEARS.

TAKE BACK WHAT WAS ONCE HELD IN ORDER TO MOVE FORWARD. USE YOUR NEW WEAPONS TO ANNIHILATE YOUR ENEMIES.

VOLUME 19 COMING AUG. 2016!

Attack on Titan volume 18 is a work of fiction. Names, characters, places, and incidents are the products of the author's imagination or are used fictitiously. Any resemblance to actual events, locales, or persons, living or dead, is entirely coincidental.

A Kodansha Comics Trade Paperback Original
Attack on Titan volume 18 copyright © 2015 Hajime Isayama
English translation copyright © 2016 Hajime Isayama

All rights reserved.

Published in the United States by Kodansha Comics, an imprint of Kodansha USA Publishing, LLC, New York.

Publication rights for this English edition arranged through Kodansha Ltd, Tokyo.

First published in Japan in 2015 by Kodansha Ltd., Tokyo as *Shingeki no Kyojin*, volume 18.

ISBN 978-1-63236-211-7

Original cover design by Takashi Shimoyama (Red Rooster)

Printed in the United States of America.

www.kodanshacomics.com

9 8 7 6 5 4 3 2 1
Translation: Ko Ransom
Lettering: Steve Wands
Editing: Ben Applegate
Kodansha Comics edition cover design by Phil Balsman